IN THE COMPANY OF WOLVES

Frontispiece. Gustave Doré, *Little Red Riding Hood in Bed with the Wolf*

IN THE COMPANY OF WOLVES

Werewolves, wolves and wild children

Edited by
Sam George and Bill Hughes

Manchester University Press

Copyright © Manchester University Press 2020

While copyright in the volume as a whole is vested in Manchester University Press, copyright in individual chapters belongs to their respective authors, and no chapter may be reproduced wholly or in part without the express permission in writing of both author and publisher.

Published by Manchester University Press
Oxford Road, Manchester M13 9PL
www.manchesteruniversitypress.co.uk

British Library Cataloguing-in-Publication Data is available

ISBN 978 1 5261 2903 1 hardback
ISBN 978 1 5261 7197 9 paperback

First published by Manchester University Press in hardback 2020

This edition first published 2023

The publisher has no responsibility for the persistence or accuracy of URLs for any external or third-party internet websites referred to in this book, and does not guarantee that any content on such websites is, or will remain, accurate or appropriate.

Typeset by Toppan Best-set Premedia Limited

Contents

List of figures	*page* vii
Notes on contributors	ix
Preface – Sam George	xiv
Acknowledgements	xviii

	Introduction: from preternatural pastoral to paranormal romance Sam George and Bill Hughes	1

Part I: Cultural images of the wolf, the werewolf and the wolf-child

1	Wolves and lies: a writer's perspective Marcus Sedgwick	21
2	'Man is a wolf to man': wolf behaviour becoming wolfish nature Garry Marvin	34
3	When wolves cry: wolf-children, storytelling and the state of nature Sam George	48
4	'Children of the night. What music they make!': the sound of the cinematic werewolf Stacey Abbott	70

Part II: Innocence and experience: brute creation, wild beast or child of nature

5	Wild sanctuary: running into the forest in Russian fairy tales Shannon Scott	87
6	'No more than a brute or a wild beast': *Wagner the Wehr-wolf*, *Sweeney Todd* and the limits of human responsibility Joseph Crawford	101
7	The inner beast: scientific experimentation in George MacDonald's 'The History of Photogen and Nycteris' Rebecca Langworthy	113

8   Werewolves and white trash: brutishness, discrimination and
    the lower-class wolf-man from *The Wolf Man* to *True Blood*   129
    Victoria Amador

Part III: Reinventing the wolf: intertextual and metafictional manifestations

9   'The price of flesh is love': commodification, corporeality and
    paranormal romance in Angela Carter's beast tales   147
    Bill Hughes

10 Growing pains of the teenage werewolf: Young Adult literature
    and the metaphorical wolf   163
    Kaja Franck

11 'I am the Bad Wolf. I create myself': the metafictional meanings
    of lycanthropic transformations in *Doctor Who*   178
    Ivan Phillips

Part IV: Animal selves: becoming wolf

12 A running wolf and other grey animals: the various shapes of
    Marcus Coates   193
    Sarah Wade

13 'Stinking of me': transformations and animal selves in
    contemporary women's poetry   211
    Polly Atkin

14 Wearing the wolf: fur, fashion and species transvestism   227
    Catherine Spooner

Bibliography   243
Index   273

Figures

Frontispiece Gustave Doré, Scene from 'Little Red Riding Hood' by Charles Perrault: *Little Red Riding Hood in Bed with the Wolf* (1867) (Alamy Stock Photo).

2.1 Wolf predation on elk © Yellowstone National Park Press Service. *page* 37
2.2 Gustave Doré, *Wolf Turned Shepherd* (1885) (Wikimedia Commons). 40
2.3 *A Wolf in Sheep's Clothing*, after Francis Barlow (1687) (Wikimedia Commons). 42
3.1 'The Bear Boy of Lithuania' from *History of Poland* (1698), reproduced in Singh and Zingg, *Wolf-children*, p. 214. 50
3.2 Wolf Suckling Romulus and Remus, Siena Duomo, Tuscany, Italy (Getty Images). 51
3.3 Mother Wolf defends Mowgli and the wolf-cubs from Shere Khan by W.H. Drake, from Kipling, *The Two Jungle Books*, p. 13. 52
3.4 Mowgli receives news from Gray Brother by W.H. Drake, from Kipling, *The Two Jungle Books*, p. 125. 52
3.5 Amala and Kamala from Singh and Zingg, *Wolf-children* (1939); reproduced in Gesell, *Wolf Child*, facing p. 40. 54
3.6 Peter's collar, housed at Berkhamsted School. Reproduced by courtesy of Berkhamsted Collegiate School. 57
3.7 Peter's grave, St Mary's Church, Northchurch. 58
5.1 Viktor Vasnetsov, *Ivan Tsarevich Riding the Grey Wolf* (1889). 92
5.2 Ivan Bilibin, *Vasilisa the Beautiful* (1899). 98
12.1 Marcus Coates, *Stoat*, 1999. Digital video, 2:35 min. Courtesy of the artist, Kate MacGarry and Workplace Gallery. © Marcus Coates. 194
12.2 Marcus Coates, *Goshawk (Self-portrait)*, 1999. Silver gelatin print, dimensions variable. Photo: Jet. Courtesy of the artist, Kate MacGarry and Workplace Gallery. © Marcus Coates. 195

12.3 Marcus Coates, *Journey to the Lower World*, 2004. Performance, digital video, 28:13 min. Image: Journey to the Lower World, Coot, 2004. Photo: Nick David. Courtesy of the artist, Kate MacGarry and Workplace Gallery. © Marcus Coates. 198

12.4 Marcus Coates, *All the Grey Animals*, 2012. MDF, emulsion paint (colour: Mid Grey), dimensions variable. Installation view, Workplace Gallery, Gateshead, UK. Photo: Joe Clark. Courtesy of the artist, Kate MacGarry and Workplace Gallery. © Marcus Coates. 200

12.5 Robert Morris, *Two Columns*, 1961. Plywood, acrylic, two parts each 244 × 61 × 61 cm. © The artist, ARS, New York, 2017. Courtesy of the artist, Castelli Gallery and Sprüth Magers. 201

12.6 Marcus Coates, *Platonic Spirit: Running Grey Wolf*, 2012. MDF, emulsion paint (colour: Mid Grey), 204 × 98 × 33 cm. Installation view, Kate MacGarry, London, UK. Photo: Andy Keate. Courtesy of the artist, Kate MacGarry and Workplace Gallery. © Marcus Coates. 204

12.7 Mark Dion, *Mobile Wilderness Unit – Wolf*, 2006. Mixed media, 274 × 148 × 294 cm. Courtesy of the artist and Georg Kargl Fine Arts, Vienna. © Mark Dion. 206

14.1 Ralph Lauren Autumn/Winter 2015 campaign, Sanne Vloet with dogs. © Jimmy Nelson. 228

14.2 'The Race'. Illustration by Laurence Housman to Clemence Housman's *The Were-wolf*. 233

14.3 'Bad Gal Rihanna: The World's Wildest Style Icon'. Rihanna photographed by Mert and Marcus, styled by Edward Enninful, *W* magazine, September 2014. © Mert and Marcus. 239

Every effort has been made to obtain permission to reproduce copyright material, and the publisher will be pleased to be informed of any errors and omissions for correction in future editions.

Notes on contributors

Stacey Abbott is a Reader in Film and Television Studies at the University of Roehampton. Her main areas of research are Gothic and horror film and television, with a particular interest in screen monsters. She has written extensively on *Buffy the Vampire Slayer*, *Angel*, *Supernatural* and *True Blood*. She is the author of *Celluloid Vampires* (2007), *Angel: TV Milestone* (2009) and *Undead Apocalypse: Vampires and Zombies in the 21st Century* (2016) and is the co-author, with Lorna Jowett, of *TV Horror: Investigating the Dark Side of the Small Screen* (2013). She co-edited, with Lorna Jowett and Michael Starr, a special issue of *Horror Studies* examining the vampire on television and has written extensively about Dracula in film and television. She is currently co-editing, with Lorna Jowett, *Global TV Horror* (University of Wales Press, forthcoming) and is writing the BFI Classic on Kathryn Bigelow's *Near Dark*.

Victoria Amador earned her doctorate in creative writing and American literature from the University of Denver. Her research interests include feminist discourses in classical Hollywood cinema, vampire and Gothic representations in British and American film and literature, and fashion history. She has held two Fulbright Senior Lectureships in American literature, received three teaching awards and has worked as a professor as well as administrator in international higher education for over thirty years. Her book *Olivia de Havilland: Lady Triumphant* was published by the University of Kentucky Press in May 2019. Victoria is also one of the co-editors of *SXSE* Magazine, an online publication on photography of the American South, and a long-time member of the National Book Critics Circle.

Polly Atkin is a poet and researcher based in Cumbria. Her doctorate was on Dove Cottage and was conducted under the AHRC Landscape and Environment project, in collaboration with The Wordsworth Trust and the University of Lancaster, UK. She is working on a related monograph, exploring connections between Romantic legacies, ecopoetics and tourism. Her debut poetry collection *Basic Nest Architecture* (2017) was followed by *With Invisible Rain* (2018), which draws on Dorothy Wordsworth's late journals. She is collaborating on a non-fiction book reflecting on place, belonging and chronic illness.

Joseph Crawford is a Senior Lecturer in English Literature at the University of Exeter. He is the author of three academic monographs: *Raising Milton's Ghost* (2011), *Gothic Fiction and the Invention of Terrorism* (2013) and *The Twilight of the Gothic* (2014). He is currently working on a fourth monograph on the relationship between inspiration and insanity in post-Romantic British poetry. His research interests include Romantic poetry, Gothic fiction, romance novels, digital horror media and the interlinked cultural histories of terrorism, conspiracy theory, drug use, insanity, fringe religion, political radicalism and the occult.

Kaja Franck is a post-doctoral researcher with the Open Graves, Open Minds project. Her thesis explores the literary werewolf as an eco-Gothic monster, interrogating the relationship between wilderness, wolves and werewolves, and how language is used to demarcate animal alterity. Her publications include an essay on the lupine nature of Bram Stoker's Dracula, in *Werewolves, Wolves and the Gothic*, edited by Robert McKay and John Miller (2017), and 'Banishing the Beast: The Role of the Wolf in Walpurgis Night, or *Dracula's Guest*, and Its Omission from Dracula', *Journal of Supernatural Studies* (2016). She is the co-editor with Janine Hatter of the online journal *Revenant*'s special issue on werewolves (2016) She is currently working on a chapter on the eco-Gothic for Clive Bloom's *Gothic Handbook* and an article on werewolves in the Canadian wilderness and the Ginger Snaps trilogy for a folklore edition of *Gothic Studies* (forthcoming, 2019). She is writing her first novel, a tale of first love, the Fens and will-o'-the-wisps.

Sam George is Associate Professor in Research at the University of Hertfordshire, UK, and the Convenor of the Open Graves, Open Minds project. Her interviews have appeared in newspapers from the *Guardian* to the *Independent* and the *Wall Street Journal*. Her research straddles the boundaries between the life sciences, animal studies and the Gothic. She is the author of *Botany, Sexuality and Women's Writing* (2007) and the co-editor with Alison Martin of *Women and Botany* (2011). She has co-edited with Bill Hughes, *Open Graves, Open Minds* (2013), a special OGOM issue of *Gothic Studies* on vampires (2013), and a second on 'Wildness and Werewolves' (2019). Recent articles include but are not limited to: 'Spirited Away: Transylvania and the Pied Piper and Dracula Myths in Britain and Germany', in *Dracula: An International Perspective*, edited by Marius-Mircea Crişan (2017); 'Wolves in the Wolds: Late Capitalism, the English Eerie, and the Weird Case of "Old Stinker" the Hull Werewolf', *Gothic Studies*, Werewolves and Wildness 21.1 (May 2019) and, with Kaja Franck, 'Contemporary Werewolves', in *Twenty-First-Century Gothic: An Edinburgh Companion*, edited by Maisha Wester and Xavier Aldana Reyes (2019). She is completing a monograph on the cultural history of the shadow.

Bill Hughes is co-organiser, with Dr Sam George, of the Open Graves, Open Minds project at the University of Hertfordshire. He is co-editor (with Dr George) of *Open Graves, Open Minds: Vampires and the Undead from the Enlightenment to the Present Day* (2013). His most recent publications include 'But By Blood no Wolf Am I', an essay on language and agency in Maggie Stiefvater's Wolves of Mercy Falls series in *Werewolves, Wolves and the Gothic*, edited by Robert McKay and John Miller (2017). Bill has a doctorate in English Literature from the University of Sheffield, UK. He has publications out or forthcoming on communicative reason and the interrelation of the dialogue genre and English novels of the long eighteenth century. Bill has also published on Richard Hoggart, and intertextuality and the Semantic Web. He is currently researching contemporary paranormal romance and Young Adult Gothic from the perspectives of formalism, genre and critical theory. This apparently disparate research is not unfocused; it has at its core concerns with the Enlightenment as viewed through the Frankfurt School and the Marxist tradition.

Rebecca Langworthy has recently submitted her PhD to the University of Aberdeen; it focuses on the development of adult fantasy in the works of George MacDonald. Her research interests include Scottish literature, fantasy, the Gothic and Victorian literature. She has published on a range of authors including George MacDonald, C.S. Lewis, J.K. Rowling and Michel Faber.

Garry Marvin is Professor of Animal/Human relations at the University of Roehampton, UK. He is a social anthropologist whose work focuses on how animals figure, and are configured, in human cultures. One of his research interests is the contestations and conflicts, in terms of perspectives and practices, between different groups of people and different animal kinds. In this context he has written on the bullfight in modern Spain, trophy hunting and the experiences of hunters, and human–wildlife conflicts in regimes of conservation. He is the author of *Wolf* (2012) and, most recently, co-editor, with Susan McHugh of *Human–Animal Studies: Critical Concepts in the Social Sciences* (2018).

Ivan Phillips is Associate Dean (Learning and Teaching) in the School of Creative Arts at the University of Hertfordshire, UK. He has published on many aspects of literature and popular culture, including chapters in Sam George and Bill Hughes, *Open Graves, Open Minds* (2013); Paul Booth, *Fan Phenomena: Doctor Who* (2013); and Andrzej Gąsiorek and Nathan Waddell, *Wyndham Lewis: A Critical Guide* (2015). He also reviews and blogs for *Critical Studies in Television*. His book *Once Upon a Time Lord: The Myths and Stories of Doctor Who* will be published by Bloomsbury Academic in 2020.

Shannon Scott is an adjunct Professor of English at the University of St Thomas and Hamline University in St Paul, Minnesota, USA. She has published articles in a number of journals such as *Neo-Victorian Studies*, *Gothic Studies*, *Marvels & Tales*, *Senses of Cinema*, *Film & History* and the *Victorian Network*. In 2013, she co-edited with Alexis Easley the collection *Terrifying Transformations: An Anthology of Victorian Werewolf Fiction, 1838–1896*. In 2015, her essay 'Female Werewolf as Monstrous Other in Honoré Beaugrand's "The Werewolves"' was published in *She-wolf: A Cultural History of the Female Werewolf*, edited by Hannah Priest (2015). She continues to write both creatively and critically in the genres of Gothic and horror.

Marcus Sedgwick (1968–2022) was an internationally award-winning writer of over forty books for young people and adults, including both fiction and non-fiction. His work has been translated into over 30 languages. He was author-in-residence for three years at Bath Spa University, wrote for papers such as *The Guardian*, *The Independent*, and *The Sunday Times* and regularly taught creative writing at the Arvon Foundation and Tŷ Newydd. He judged numerous book awards, including the Guardian Children's Fiction Prize and the Costa Book Awards. His previous contribution to Open Graves, Open Minds was a chapter on the folkloric origins of the vampire in relation to his novel *My Swordhand is Singing* (2006). The chapter in this present work derived from his interest in feral children, having written the character of 'Mouse' in *The Dark Horse* (2002). He was born in East Kent and lived on a mountainside in the Haute-Savoie in the French Alps, where just once, at dusk, he heard the howl of a lone wolf.

Catherine Spooner is Professor of Literature and Culture at Lancaster University, UK. She has published widely on Gothic literature, film, fashion and popular culture, including the books *Fashioning Gothic Bodies*, *Contemporary Gothic* and *Post-Millennial Gothic: Comedy, Romance and the Rise of Happy Gothic*. She is the co-editor of *The Routledge Companion to Gothic* (with Emma McEvoy), *Monstrous Media / Spectral Subjects: Imaging the Gothic from the Nineteenth Century to the Present* (with Fred Botting) and *Return to Twin Peaks: New Approaches to Materiality, Theory and Genre on Television* (with Jeffrey A. Weinstock). She was co-president of the International Gothic Association 2013–2017. She is currently working on a cultural history of the white dress in Gothic fiction, film and fashion media.

Sarah Wade completed her PhD entitled 'Species of Wonder: Human–Animal Relations in Contemporary Art and Visual Culture' in the History of Art department at University College London in 2018. Her research interrogates human–animal relations and representations of animals in contemporary art and visual culture, particularly with regards to ecological concerns. Sarah was co-curator of the exhibition *Strange Creatures: The Art of Unknown Animals* (2015) at the Grant Museum of Zoology (University College London) and she organised the symposium *Transgressing Boundaries: On Wolves and Werewolves* (2015). She is currently editing her PhD research into a book.

Preface

Sam George

This volume of essays presents further research from the Open Graves, Open Minds Project (OGOM) at the University of Hertfordshire (soon to be an internationally recognised research centre).[1] The collection connects together innovative research on the cultural significance of wolves, wild children and werewolves from a variety of perspectives as portrayed in different media and genres ranging from folktales and Gothic literature through sound, fashion, film and television to contemporary poetry and visual art.

The book developed from the now legendary conference and series of events entitled 'The Company of Wolves: Sociality, Animality, and Subjectivity in Literary and Cultural Narratives – Werewolves, Shapeshifters, and Feral Humans' in August 2015.[2] OGOM hosted over fifty international speakers, together with invited keynotes from Sir Christopher Frayling, Prof. Garry Marvin, Dr Catherine Spooner, Dr Stacey Abbott, Dr Sam George and Dr Bill Hughes. There was a contribution on wolves from the field of fiction, from the prize-winning novelist Marcus Sedgwick. The idea for the conference came from discussions we were having with two of OGOM's funded PhD students, Kaja Franck and Matt Beresford. Kaja was writing a PhD on werewolves in literature and Matt, researching Byron and the Romantic vampire, had written a book on the European werewolf myth.[3] A number of the smaller, related events at the conference were also inspirational and important to the development of the research in this volume. For example, we visited the headstone inscribed 'Peter the Wild Boy', in the graveyard of St Mary's Church in Northchurch, the stone marking the Hertfordshire resting place of this famous feral child. We also viewed the plaque erected in the church in his honour. The strand in the book on wolf children developed directly out of the associations that had grown up between OGOM research and the local figure of Peter the Wild Boy. The conference also saw the beginning of our important collaboration with the UK Wolf Conservation Trust.[4] We invited delegates to directly interact with wolves and, following that, to hear an exclusive talk by members of the Trust on

'Re-wilding the wolf'. We closed our festival of events with the 'Lycanthropic Lantern of Fear' – a magic-lantern show on the theme of the werewolf in which David Annwn Jones took us on a journey to the edges of civilisation and sanity, in a spectacular show presented on a genuine Victorian magic lantern. The imaginative, Gothic element of our research was awakened again here, following our interactions earlier with the actual flesh-and-blood animal, the wolves behind the werewolf myth, via the UK Wolf Trust.

The Company of Wolves received unprecedented attention in the media and a large number of press articles were generated and published locally, internationally and globally. Two of our favourite stories were on BBC News: 'University to Host International Werewolf Conference' and 'Werewolf Conference: The People Seeking the Company of Wolves'.[5] We inspired articles as far afield and as diverse as the *Smithsonian Magazine* in the USA and the *South China Post*. The furore surrounding the research delivered at the conference was celebrated afterwards by Katherine Hughes in *The Guardian* and we received an acknowledgement from *Times Higher Education* that we had achieved a first for a UK Academy.[6]

Following the success of this strand of the OGOM project, we collaborated again with the UK Wolf Trust at the 'Being Human Festival' in November 2017 in an event entitled 'Redeeming the Wolf : A Story of Persecution, Loss and Rediscovery'.[7] We argued that wolves had been hunted to extinction in Britain but they still haunt the human imagination. Stories of the wolf had portrayed a vicious, snarling beast that emerged from the wilderness to attack humankind. The werewolves of popular culture had further fomented fear. But the lost wolf was making a comeback: conservation groups were working to reintroduce the animal to the British countryside. Our event brought together scholars, writers and conservationists to explore how literature, folklore, fairy tale, and film have shaped our perceptions of the wolf and could be impeding its return. Mike Collins, chief 'Wolf Keeper' at the UK Wolf Conservation Trust, contributed a piece to accompany a short film on the impact of wolves. This was preceded by a series of illustrated talks (Prof. Garry Marvin ('lupophobia'), Dr Sam George ('wolf-children'), Dr Kaja Franck ('monstrous werewolves') and Dr Bill Hughes ('beauties and beasts'). The audience was invited to debate the implications of redeeming and rewilding the much-maligned 'big bad wolf' and what the wolf can teach us about being human. I collaborated further with Mike Collins from the trust in an interview with the BBC on the impact of fairy tales on our perception and understanding of the wolf.[8] These projects and symposia have fed into and inspired this collection, together with an OGOM special issue of *Gothic Studies*.[9] In this offshoot, we develop the theme of wolf-children, wilderness and werewolves and revisit the story of the Hull werewolf Old Stinker, who, as serendipity would have it, appeared for the first time since the early twentieth century during the period that we were planning and presenting the conference. He became something of a totem figure for OGOM.[10]

This collection then, despite coming under the shadow of the Open Graves, Open Minds Project, is not about undead creatures.[11] Instead, it is about the rather disturbing vitality of the werewolf, and other beings which unsettle the distinction between animal and human, whether wolves themselves figuring as representatives of human nature, other shapeshifters or the curious stories of children discovered in the wild and without language – widely thought to be the unique characteristic of human beings. So, we are cheekily stretching the meaning of 'Open Graves, Open Minds' away from its obvious suggestions of revenants – the phrase comes from *Generation Dead*, Daniel Waters's marvellous novel of unlikely romance between living humans and zombies – just so that it can encompass shapeshifters. We would like the phrase to suggest the uninhibited prying into dark secrets, and an even more strained metaphor of consciousness emerging from the invigoration of dead matter.

Notes

1 OGOM maintains a blog and website that is constantly updated with dialogues around related topics and with additional scholarly resources: <www.opengravesopenminds.com>.
2 The full programme is available on our website: <www.opengravesopenminds.com/company-of-wolves/conference-programme-pdf/>.
3 Kaja gained her PhD in 2016 on 'The Development of the Literary Werewolf: Language, Subjectivity and Animal/Human Boundaries'. She is a now an even bigger part of the project. Matt is completing his doctoral research. His book on the werewolf myth is *The White Devil: The Werewolf in European Culture* (London: Reaktion, 2013).
4 The UK Wolf Conservation Trust is based in Reading. Details can be found at <https://ukwct.org.uk/>.
5 Laurence Cawley, 'University to Host International Werewolf Conference', *BBC News*, 22 August 2015 <www.bbc.co.uk/news/uk-england-beds-bucks-herts-33971546>; Jodie Smith, 'Werewolf Conference: The People Seeking the Company of Wolves', *BBC News*, 4 September 2015 <www.bbc.co.uk/news/uk-england-beds-bucks-herts-34144752>.
6 Kathryn Hughes, 'In Our Dog-Eat-Dog World, It's Time for Werewolves', *The Guardian*, 30 August 2015 <www.theguardian.com/commentisfree/2015/aug/30/werewolves-scarcity-fear-vampires-sexual-anxiety>; Matthew Reisz, 'Werewolf Conference Billed as First for UK Academy', 31 August 2015 <www.timeshighereducation.com/news/werewolf-conference-billed-first-uk-academy>.
7 The Being Human Festival is led by the School of Advanced Study, University of London, in partnership with the Arts and Humanities Research Council

and the British Academy. Our event can be found on the BH site: <https://beinghumanfestival.org/event/redeeming-the-wolf-a-story-of-persecution-loss-and-rediscovery/>.

8   'Little Red Riding Hood Tale Hampers Wolf Debate, Says Academic', *BBC News*, 4 November 2017 <www.bbc.co.uk/news/uk-england-beds-bucks-herts-41845167>.

9   *Gothic Studies*, Werewolves and Wildness special issue, ed. by Sam George and Bill Hughes, 20.1 (May 2019).

10 For Old Stinker, see Dr Sam George, 'Why We Should Welcome the Return of Old Stinker, the English Werewolf', *The Conversation*, 30 October 2016 <https://theconversation.com/why-we-should-welcome-the-return-of-old-stinker-the-english-werewolf-67797>; Sam George, 'Wolves in the Wolds: Late Capitalism, the English Eerie, and the Weird Case of "Old Stinker" the Hull Werewolf', *Gothic Studies*, Werewolves and Wildness special issue, ed. by Sam George and Bill Hughes, 21.1 (May 2019); Kaja Franck and Sam George, 'Contemporary Werewolves', in *Twenty-first-century Gothic: An Edinburgh Companion*, ed. by Maisha Wester and Xavier Aldana Reyes (Edinburgh: Edinburgh University Press, 2019), pp. 144–57.

11 The Open Graves, Open Minds Project began around 2010 with a very successful conference on vampire narratives, followed by the Bram Stoker Centenary Symposium in 2012, and the monograph and special issue of *Gothic Studies* in May 2013. There have been further events, and Dr Sam George has instigated an MA module on vampire fiction at the University of Hertfordshire and an undergraduate one on Young Adult Gothic.

Acknowledgements

We would like to thank Matthew Frost and his team at MUP for enthusiastic support and diligent editing. We are also grateful to all the delegates at the Company of Wolves conference and contributors to this book who made it so unforgettable and seminal. THANK YOU.

We would like to express our gratitude to Sir Chris Frayling for sharing his thoughts on Angela Carter and wolves and for being a long-standing supporter of OGOM, and Catherine Spooner, Stacey Abbott and Garry Marvin for their rare insight and research with bite. Thanks must also be extended to Marcus Sedgwick, whose novel *The Dark Horse* fuelled Sam's obsession with wolf-children. Wild children have fascinated us both down the years and Sam's session on wolf-children with Marcus at Company of Wolves was one of the highlights of her career.

Thanks to the University of Hertfordshire for hosting the OGOM Project and Company of Wolves conference. Thanks are also due to Sam's colleagues in research at the University of Hertfordshire; in particular, Jeremy Ridgman, Rowland Hughes and Andrew Maunder. We would like to thank Louise Akers and April Wilson of the UH press office, Amanda Phipps and Professor Sarah Churchwell at the Being Human Festival, and Chris O'Brien, the genius behind our impact for the 'Redeeming the Wolf' event, and also the BBC for their interest in all the Company of Wolves symposia and events.

OGOM would also like to extend thanks to our UH Humanities helpers at the conference: Daisy, Rachael, Elliot, Janette and Amelia, and to Florence Scott in Creative Arts for her wonderful werewolf sculpture.

Many other people have given support and aided us in our research into wolves and wolf-children. These include but are not limited to Mike Collins and the staff at the UK Wolf Conservation Trust, the Rev. Gordon at St Mary's Church in Northchurch and the staff at Berkhamsted Collegiate School.

Sam would like to send special thanks to Bill Hughes for his inspirational work on the project. The book would never have been completed without his rigorous editing, generosity and support. Kaja Franck was the inspiration behind the project and Sam has fond memories of their conversations about wolves in her role as supervisor for Kaja's PhD. Thank you for lending your boundless energy and lupine expertise to OGOM, Kaja – we are privileged to have you.

Acknowledgements

Finally, last but by no means least, Sam thanks her sisters, Demelza, Rowena and Caroline, and her nephews and nieces, Miranda, Patrick, Joseph, Luke and Lyra. And to her father, David George, and Jonathan: thank you for making me who I am, for believing in me and for keeping the wolves from my door.

Bill would like to thank Avril Horner, Sue Zlosnik, Angela Keane and Hamish Mathison for initiating and guiding him through his academic career. Members of BARS, BSECS and the IGA, along with many other scholars, have all enhanced this through much fruitful discussion. The support of friends including Sarah and Dave Bartlett; Mel and Pete Duxbury, Liz Fox and their lovely families; Martin Green, Kevin Jones, Sue Chaplin and particularly his sister, Caryl, has been invaluable, particularly through difficult times. He owes a huge debt to the beleaguered NHS. Bill would especially like to praise Sam George for shared delights in research and friendship. This book celebrates the memory of Mat Fox and Bill's mother, Barbara Hughes.

This book is dedicated to the wolves and wolf-children who have inspired us, in particular Peter the Wild Boy, whose Hertfordshire grave we visited during the conference, and to our animal friends, gone but not forgotten: Freddie and Jason, Hatty, Buffy and Angel, Morrissey, Spike; and those who continue to delight us in the present: Willow and Teddy, Arrietty, Denny, and Morticia and Gomez (who have made their own delightful contributions to this project despite their aversion to anything vaguely canine).

Introduction: From Preternatural Pastoral to Paranormal Romance

Sam George and Bill Hughes

Amidst concerns about our relationship with nature, in a culture informed by Romanticism and a post-Enlightenment doubt about the centrality of humanity, contemporary fictions often turn to the animal and to transitions between animal and human to interrogate what is special about our species. In her Young Adult werewolf paranormal romance *Linger*, the author Maggie Stiefvater quotes Rilke: 'even the most clever of animals see that we are not surely at home in our interpreted world'.[1] This captures the amphibious nature of being human, of our embodied consciousness and our status as speaking, interpreting animal. It raises the kinds of questions that the essays in this collection respond to and illuminate. Our contributors examine werewolves, wolves, wild children, and other transitions between culture and nature. The chapters below explore how these themes interact and how they shapeshift around different narrative modes from utopian pastoral to Gothic and romance.

Wolves and wilderness

The history of werewolfism is inextricably bound up with humankind's treatment of wolves.[2] Peter Stubbe (variously spelled Stump, Stumpf, or Stube), the Werewolf of Bedburg, is a seminal case. He was executed in Cologne in 1589.[3] A likeness of a wolf was framed in wood and set above a pole which contained his severed head – a permanent monument to both the killing of the werewolf and the destruction of the wolf. Dead wolves were coveted as trophies in Anglo-Saxon Britain, and King Edgar (959–75) demanded that his Welsh subjects pay him three hundred wolf-skins a year; some criminals were encouraged to pay their debts in wolf-tongues.[4] English wolves were almost totally eradicated under the reign of Henry VII (1457–1509). Wolves held out in Ireland until the 1700s (though they were extinct in Scotland by the late 1600s).[5] British and Irish wolves were exterminated much earlier than wolves across Europe; the total extinction there was not completed until the 1800s.

The result is a contemporary landscape constituted more actively by what is missing than by what is present. The spectre-wolf or werewolf has replaced the actual flesh-and-blood animal. This contemporary werewolf is far from being a curse; perhaps it is a gift, for it can reawaken the memory of what humans did to wolves, initiate rewilding debates and redeem the big bad wolf that filled our childhood nightmares, reminding us that it is often humans, not wolves or the supernatural, that we should fear.

Yet wolves have long been the archetypal enemy of human company, preying on the unguarded boundaries of civilisation, threatening the pastoral of ideal sociality and figuring as sexual predators. On the other hand, with their complex pack interactions they have often served as a model for society. Lately, this ancient enemy has been rehabilitated and reappraised, and rewilding projects have attempted to admit them more closely into our lives. Contemporary narratives have aided or hindered this assimilation in various ways.

The blurring of the boundary between animal and human recurs throughout literature. Wolves in particular, ambiguously social animals yet savage outsiders, predators on the community and disruptors of the pastoral, have long played a versatile role in exploring these topographies. They have a close relationship with the pastoral, which in its literal sense concerns the tending of domestic animals, and the wolf is the shepherd's eternal foe from at least the Old Testament onwards (then there is all the additional allegorical weight that arrives with Christianity, with Christ as shepherd of the human flock). The wolf of tradition preys on the pastoral – quite literally, attacking the sheep that the pastoralist cultivates. The wolf is also well known as one who threatens female virtue: hence 'wolf whistles' and Perrault's warning to innocent girls at the end of his version of 'Little Red Riding Hood'.[6]

The idea of pastoral goes a long way back, of course.[7] But our account begins in the eighteenth century, where so much of modernity begins. Then, in the present day, we argue that contemporary werewolf fictions take on peculiarly modern versions of pastoral that emerged in the Enlightenment and that are challenged in various ways now. In that period, writers and thinkers explored certain themes about the origins of language and society, and the complex interplay between the human and nature or the animal.

The eighteenth century is also the moment when vampires emerged from the twilight of superstition to become literary monsters. These creatures play a significant part in the development of werewolf narratives. In our discussion below, we want to avoid the idea of some timeless, universal werewolf archetype that has always existed throughout all cultures (though they are certainly more persistent and have more archaic roots than vampires).[8] We are concerned mainly with the artistic transformation of the folkloric material, although the latter is of interest. Ideals of animality and nature in the eighteenth century display a continuity with those of today, though significant shifts have taken place, and contemporary representations of the wolf are often employed in reaction to Enlightenment.

Wild children in the company of wolves

With this cultural history of the wolf as predator on the pastoral, it seems paradoxical to discover the wolf itself in the role of a pastoral figure. Yet wolves may also be founders and nurturers of culture, raising Romulus and Remus, or fostering into sociality those abandoned feral children that so fascinated Enlightenment thinkers as they probed into the origins of society and language.[9]

The eighteenth century was a fertile time for new ideas about language. Hans Aarsleff points to the uniqueness and intensity of these inquiries; Nicholas Hudson notes a crucial shift to theories of language as intersubjective and dialogical rather than private.[10] Bernard de Mandeville, Étienne Bonnot de Condillac and Jean-Jacques Rousseau are significant figures who all speculated that human language originated in a primal dialogue.[11]

Accounts of wild children feature prominently in these inquiries. Condillac examined many wild children accounts, particularly one of a child thought to have been raised by bears.[12] He too imagined a primal couple, one of each sex, lost in the desert and creating language out of necessity (or perhaps passion). The Scottish Enlightenment thinker James Burnett, Lord Monboddo, took the ideas of Condillac and Rousseau further. Monboddo had visited Marie-Angélique Leblanc and Peter the Wild Boy. Marie-Angélique was found in the woods of Champagne in 1731 and eventually taken into care and socialised by nuns. Peter was found naked and void of speech in the forests of Hanover in 1725 and brought over to England, becoming a court celebrity and an object of interest to thinkers such as the Rousseauvians Richard and Maria Edgeworth. 'Man is a creature of art', claimed Monboddo, and that we need to separate what is natural from what is artificial. He notoriously thought that orang-utans were humans, giving credence to travellers' tales of them living in society, building wooden huts and enslaving women. Crucially, many of these wild children were thought to have been raised by wolves (and such stories persisted long after this period).

Rousseau explores two dialogic ideas of origins, suggesting that children invented language in dialogue with their parents, but also setting forth a theory of dialogue rooted in the passion of a primal couple. But where Mandeville had seen a development of increasing sophistication (though ambivalently spiced with vice), Rousseau sees decline and corruption, leading to the manipulative speech of contemporary civilisation. Casting Rousseau's ideas as regressive back-to-nature fantasy is a simplification. Yet there is an element of pastoral nostalgia in his thoughts on nature and civilisation.

The term 'preternatural pastoral' in the title of this Introduction serves to emphasise the Enlightenment utopianism of pastoral as image of not a lost Golden Age but a reaching beyond nature, that projection into the future and transcendence of present conditions that characterise that period (a position which has come under suspicion in recent decades). These utopian aspects of pastoral feature in the genre of paranormal romance, which will be discussed below.[13] Thus to the eighteenth-century mind, humanity is preternatural in that it is beyond nature, though this lies uncomfortably alongside the birth of mechanically determinist thinking. Later scientific ideologies develop this, eliminating agency and reducing human existence to mere biology. In the twenty-first century, many are less assured of human ambitions, and contemporary wolf and werewolf narratives dramatise this uncertainty. The ubiquity and longevity of the wolf-child can also be seen in the variety of narratives from Kipling, through tales by Angela Carter, to such contemporary fictions as Jill Paton Walsh's *Knowledge of Angels* (1994) and Marcus Sedgwick's Young Adult novel *The Dark Horse* (2002), both compelling stories of wolf-girls.[14] Stories of wild children raised by animals appear in the twentieth and twenty-first centuries in a variety of genres from recasting the lives of such real-life wild children as Peter the Wild Boy, Victor of Aveyron, Amala and Kamala in novelistic form to newly imagined characters in fantasy fictions.[15] There are obvious relationships between these narratives and the werewolf fictions discussed in this collection, not least the preoccupation with wildness and civilisation, culture and nature. Some werewolf narratives assimilate more closely the wolf-child motif, dwelling on the nurturing aspect of the wolf mother within the werewolf colony.[16]

Werewolves and wearing wolves

Werewolves and shapeshifters have served in narrative fiction to question what humanity is; weres tend to reveal the complex affinities and differences between our existence as linguistic, social subjects and our physiological continuity with other animals.[17] They also draw our attention to questions of hierarchy and sexuality, to the instinctive, and to what extent our conceptions of these are ideological.

Werewolves and similar shapeshifters emerge from ancient myth such as the Classical Greek tale of Lycaon, retold by the Roman Ovid in that paradigm of shapeshifting creatures and genres, the *Metamorphoses*; through medieval romances like Marie de France's twelfth-century *lai* 'Bisclavret'; becoming a staple creature of Gothic horror with Victorian penny dreadfuls such as G.W.M. Reynolds's *Wagner the Wehr-wolf* (1846–47) and then, cinematically, in films such as *Werewolf of London* (1935) and *The Wolf Man* (1941).[18] Contemporary incarnations such as Angela Carter's wolf stories and Neil Jordan's adaptations of these as the film *The Company of Wolves* have also referenced the fairy tale 'Little Red Riding Hood' which, in some versions, is a tale of lycanthropy.

However, as we warned earlier, one must be careful not to universalise the shapeshifter and erase its history. Perspectives on our relationship with nature and animality shift dramatically, and readings of werewolf texts should be particularised and placed into context.[19] In the twenty-first century, werewolf fiction is much engaged by questions raised in the Enlightenment and by contemporary counter-currents against that.[20] The werewolf is a Gothic monster, and the Gothic genre has from its inception been in a complex dialectic with Enlightenment principles.

The monster as metaphor for the social Other has been much charted by Jeffrey Jerome Cohen and many more critics.[21] As identity politics became mainstream and otherness, to an extent, assimilated into society around the 1980s, there arose a tendency to humanise, even romanticise, the monster in various kinds of fiction. Thus those creatures that once embodied fear and hostility towards racial or sexual outsiders became unwitting victims and sometimes lovers, and uneasy participants in society rather than its absolute Other. Vampires, soon followed by werewolves, soon became the sympathetic protagonists of narrative, often voiced in the first person. Women, too, became more conspicuously the focalised centre of these stories. Alongside this, late twentieth- and twenty-first-century concerns with the environment have played a part in reshaping Gothic tales of monstrosity.

As with the vampire, werewolves invite analyses about alterity, as this collection demonstrates. And just as the vampire figure both conditions the shape of the subgenres it dwells in and draws other genres into its sphere, so fictions about werewolves, wild humans and human–animal relationships also invoke questions of genre and intertextuality. But within this shift, the specificity of the sympathetic *werewolf* may also be accounted for by our distance from the pastoral model of the human–nature relationship that once presided. The sympathetic werewolf has its own characteristics that draw on the complex history of the wolf in culture that has been outlined above and on the questions around nature, culture and language raised in the Enlightenment with those wild children alleged to have been raised in the company of wolves.

The werewolf in the twenty-first century takes many forms.[22] But by far the dominant arena for them is paranormal romance – a newly emerged genre born from the coupling of two genres themselves thought to be rather unsavoury.[23] Paranormal romance is an uneasy intermodulation of Gothic horror and romance fiction. This alerts us to ideas of genre, and how different literary kinds bring with them different perspectives, with hybrid genres being particularly intriguing in this respect. And, in the background, the genre of pastoral, with its concerns with our relationship to nature, remains crucial.

The new genre of paranormal romance was born, as new forms often are, from a risky mating of earlier genres. It is characterised most of all by a fusion of Gothic with romantic fiction in the everyday sense that we associate with Mills and Boon and the like. These encounters with different forms bring with them discordant perspectives on the world and may reflect the clash of values in our uncertain modern world. The uneasy coupling of horror and romance humanises horror in quite special ways, focusing on agency (which the inexorable doom of horror often denies) and on the human intersubjectivity found in the mainstream novel. At the same time, it desentimentalises romantic fiction, revealing the darker aspects of eroticism and even humanity as a whole.

This form has many of the trappings of Gothic, but the plot is subordinated to the movement towards amatory consummation of romantic fiction; the setting tends to be contemporary; it seems to assume a female readership; and, crucially, it centres on love affairs between humans and supernatural creatures. The typical Gothic text of darkness and evil now flirts with the much-maligned genre of romance fiction. The monster has become tamed, domesticated or feminised, and transformed into the lover. Thus there has been a significant and dramatic shift away from Gothic as pure horror. This must be qualified: on the one hand, the Gothic horror tradition of the werewolf as absolute monster continues alongside this newer incarnation; on the other, the fictional werewolf has always been a somewhat sympathetic creature.

The vampire, with its own fluid crossing of boundaries, has enabled this commingling of genres – leading us, incidentally, to think in broader terms than the Gothic paradigm. It is fair to say that the paranormal romance began with love affairs between tamed, sympathetic vampires and humans. But, since then, all kinds of supernatural species have been found in the arms and beds of humankind, with werewolves a particular favourite. The shapeshifter, especially the werewolf, is particularly suited as an instrument for exploring the boundaries of humanity and animality, culture and nature. The werewolf of this genre is far more tied to animality and the physiological than the present-day vampire, despite the latter's often compulsive blood-lust.[24] The werewolf, too, is bound to a hierarchical pack society; this group membership necessarily evokes a different perspective on the social than the usually solitary vampire.

As noted above, the contemporary werewolf is often female. According to Coudray, in the more recent female-centred werewolf texts of the 1980s and 1990s, there is a background of 'revaluations of the wolf (and the human relationship to the natural world) [which] have paralleled the feminist reclamation of previously degraded values' (p. 128). Alongside a broad critique of the Enlightenment 'in which', Coudray uncritically claims, 'both femininity and nature are systematically othered' (p. 119), 'narratives of female lycanthropy have thus experimented with the positive revaluation of those "negative" qualities traditionally associated with women (such as nature, embodiment, and intuition)' (pp. 128–9). However, Coudray's analysis is too sweeping an approach, and does not elucidate many of the more recent texts.

Questions of gender are among the ideological issues raised by recent werewolf narratives. Many werewolf romances feature the obligatory 'post-feminist' feisty female protagonist, who is present both in order that the text may conform to a generic imperative and owing to what is socially expected in present-day Western society (particularly when a largely female readership is involved). Readers have expectations concerning gender equality, and so on. Yet contradictions emerge between the ideas of the independent woman and of instinctual submission both to pack hierarchy and to the dominant alpha male, to which the heroine half-willingly acquiesces. These narratives thus resonate with contemporary anti-humanist ideologies of sociobiology and genetic determinism.

Contemporary werewolf narratives incorporate the legacies of Romanticism and twenty-first century concerns about the environment, accompanied by currents of thought that are sceptical of the centrality of the human. They often express a longing for a less antagonistic relationship with nature and utopian aspirations towards the heightened powers and imagined intensities of animal existence. This is a new incarnation of pastoral, which modulates these narratives. However, many such fictions adopt an uncritical enthusiasm for the instinctual and a postmodern denigration of agency and subjectivity that can lead to unexpectedly reactionary positions – as when hierarchies become legitimated by an essentialism derived from animal analogies. Generally, werewolves embody determinism more than other paranormal characters, biology inescapably dictating their identity. Kelley Armstrong's *Bitten* (2003) is exemplary here; Armstrong's heroine, Elena Michaels, sums up the overall perspective: 'Nature wins out. It always does.'[25]

A final theme which resonates with contemporary ideological concerns is humanity's relationship to the environment, which is often represented in a post-Romantic manner through the appeal to what is spontaneous and 'natural'.[26] This is represented as unproblematically appealing in many of these fictions. Anne Rice's *The Wolf Gift* (2010) exemplifies this perspective.[27] Rice's text is complex, and she does value human qualities in certain ways, but the novel displays in general an anti-humanist orientation. The dominant devaluation of Enlightenment humanism – and, indeed, humanity – is expressed through the celebration of the instinctual and the animal as being subversive. Other fictions are more ambivalent and potentially more humanist about the dialectic of instinctual fleshliness and the voiced subject (for language is a crucial theme).

Incarnations of the (were)wolf

This book explores crucial questions concerning human social existence and its animal substrate, and the intersection between the human and the wolfishly bestial as expressed in narrative media from a variety of epochs and cultures. Taken together, the essays have a deliberate coherence and are shown to be in dialogue with one another. They represent a substantial body of work, one that makes clear the significance of the relationship between the flesh-and-blood wolf, legends of wolf-children, and the werewolf as the wolf's spectral Other.

The different incarnations of the werewolf quite obviously depend on the cultural representation of wolves themselves and chapters in this collection explore narratives of the real wolf. Our collection also highlights the human term of the werewolf's oscillation between nature and culture by discussing the figure of the wild child, so crucial to speculations on the origins of language and society and what differentiates human from animal.

We begin with the wolf itself as it has been interpreted as a cultural symbol and how it figures in contemporary debates about wilderness and nature. Alongside this, we consider the fictional representation of wild children – often thought to have been raised by wolves and other animals. In Chapter 1, from the perspective of an imaginative writer of fictions and one who tells stories about wolves, the author Marcus Sedgwick performs a dizzying tour of interconnections between stories, lies and the wolf – a creature characterised as the arch-deceiver. Thus, in Aesop's fables the wolf is the pre-eminent deceiver, as in the fairy tale 'Little Red Riding Hood'. From *Gilgamesh* through Classical Greece and Rome to Norse mythology this stereotype persists. (Though, as Marvin also shows, there are cross-cultural differences as well as similarities.)

Turning to the twentieth century, Sedgwick situates Disney's *Three Little Pigs* (1933) in the context of the Depression and the rise of the Nazis, leading to a discussion of anti-Semitism and Stanley Kubrick's *The Shining* (1980), seen by some as an allegory of the Holocaust. Sedgwick moves on to the disputed *Misha: A Mémoire of the Holocaust Years* (1997), with its tale of salvation by wolves, and then to accounts of feral children raised by wolves. Present-day arguments about protecting wolves become part of this narrative, with the problems of distinguishing truth from fiction in the evidence given. One side of the debate invokes the image of the wolf as noble – a particularly modern, and recent, attitude. In Sedgwick's own *The Dark Horse*, the character Mouse is discovered living with wolves. Sedgwick wants to ask questions about what has been lost in our shift away from the wildness that wolves embody. This returns us to the lie, and to fiction, and above all to this consoling fiction that wolves reveal to us a lost authenticity. We are reminded of the importance of language in wolf/human narratives and of the lost pastoral that Sam George also invokes later.

Garry Marvin further elaborates the context of the book through his anthropological account of how the wolf has been experienced and created through culture. He observes differences in the way societies perceive wolves: hunter societies admire them; pastoralists, who have separated areas off from the wild, hate and fear them. The werewolf figure appears in the latter cultures, notably ancient Greece and Rome, then again in medieval Europe. Wolf behaviour is always represented as laden with value judgements. The records of ecologists observing the social behaviour of wolves in the wilderness are themselves bound up with human concerns; the wolf is constructed by science. Thus wolves have a cultural as well as a natural history.

But now wolves are returning across Western Europe. The debates around this are about more than wolves themselves. For pro-wolf advocates, this process is seen as a sign of return to a healthy relationship with a damaged natural world. But others see a risk of dangerous criminal animals roaming. Those opposed to rewilding object to environmentalists and urban animal lovers as people who have lost contact with rural reality. The language also reflects rhetoric over immigration. Thus Marvin analyses the role of the wolf in human culture and casts light on aspects of the unstable oppositions of wildness and humanity that are expressed elsewhere in accounts both of wolf-children and humans who take on lupine form.

Sam George takes up culture itself, looking at how its foundations in and departure from wolfish nature are problematised by the wild children so frequently associated with wolves. The sound of wolves is commonly associated with unsettling, uncanny or sublime moments in literature and film but George begins with a contrary depiction in Ted Hughes's poem 'Life after Death'. Here, the empathic and consoling nature of the wolves' cry is emphasised in a moment of absolute grief. Hughes is seeking solace in the notion that wolves and other animals can become surrogate parents to orphaned human children.

George then turns to wolf-children in Romantic-period poetry, where notions of native innocence prevail, drawing on poems by Wordsworth and Mary Robinson. She interrogates the representation of such children in relation to Locke's *tabula rasa* theory and Rousseau's lost 'state of nature'. Whilst the eighteenth-century wild children Victor of Aveyron and Peter the Wild Boy remain largely mute, literature constructs a history for these children through repeated storytelling. The Rousseauvian ideal of the child of nature is often undermined in such accounts but there is ambiguity too. Abandonment can be seen as a blessing: the child inhabits an animal world, a gap is bridged and something once lost is rediscovered through narrative.

Stacey Abbott foreshadows the later chapters' concern with the transition between human and wolf as werewolves by analysing the eerie howling soundtracks of horror films. She begins with the evocative theme music of *Buffy the Vampire Slayer* (1996–2003), where wolf howls meet Gothic organ and rock 'n' roll. The howl of the wolf has come to be a key signifier of the horror genre. This sound and the noises that accompany the physical metamorphosis of the werewolf are central to this chapter. The wolf's voice is both terrifying and melancholy, and is employed to illuminate the movement between animal and human. Bram Stoker in particular links the wolf to that other classic monster, the vampire (as the title's 'what music they make' suggests); the howls of wolves are the soundtrack to the latter creature.

In film, the lupine howl immediately connotes ideas of wilderness. Abbott briefly outlines the history of sound in cinema, leading up to *Werewolf of London* (1935) and *The Wolf Man* (1941) where this signifier is developed further and an extra ambivalence is introduced as the werewolf becomes both monster and victim. After this classic period, another wave of werewolf films occurred in the 1980s. In *An American Werewolf in London* (1981), the soundscape of wolf howls, close-up personal noises and the sounds of transformation is enhanced by the ironic use of pop music and the screams of the protagonist, eliciting further sympathy through bodily identification. The sounds of the werewolf dismantle distinctions between good victim and evil monster, and between human and animal.

The next four chapters further concentrate on the purported savagery of the wolf – the animal that werewolf fictions employ as metaphorical 'beast within' to indict human nature. In Russian fairy tales, Shannon Scott uncovers one culturally specific attitude to the wolf. As Marcus Sedgwick and others in this volume have noted, we are accustomed to the fairy-tale image of the wolf as vicious and devious and the enemy of pastoral life – this is true in many Russian fairy tales, where they are often also stupid. In the nineteenth century, when many of the tales were collected, wolves were a major threat to livestock. But at the same time a sense of identity between (human) hunters and predators emerges (perhaps recalling the values of pre-agricultural cultures in Marvin's account). As with the nurses of wolf-children that George describes, wolves may have a benevolent role. Thus in some tales, conventionally evil characters such as witches and wolves appear as helpers, and their realm, the forest, is seen as a sanctuary for humans failed by society. For heroines, especially, in these tales the wilderness of the forest can be a refuge from brutally patriarchal practices. Paradoxically, it is the wolves of the forest that act with humanity. In one tale, the Grey Wolf becomes a shapeshifter in order to protect the heroine from rape, in an inversion of the more familiar image of the wolf as sexual predator. In another, he becomes a Christ figure.

Joseph Crawford looks at the legal and medical discourses that are drawn on in Victorian fiction to incarnate the werewolf. The association of the werewolf with insanity and the shifting understandings of that make concrete the abstractions of 'the beast within'. Crawford uses a case study from nineteenth-century Britain to show how contemporaneous werewolf narratives dramatised questions of sanity and moral responsibility. Legislation around insanity had long been founded in the opposition of rationality to the behaviour of the wild animal; Crawford's telling phrase is of madness as a state of 'legal lycanthropy'. But the 'M'Naughton Rules', named after the assassin of the Prime Minister's secretary in 1843, changed this interpretation and no longer saw madness as ferocious animality.

The controversy over the limits of responsibility, argues Crawford, helped give rise to the nineteenth-century popular werewolf narrative, which clearly linked werewolves to both lunacy and criminality. It is G.M.W. Reynolds's *Wagner the Wehr-wolf* (1846–47) which, in this period, established the involuntary aspect of werewolves in fiction, clearly linking it to older ideas of lunacy as savage animality. However, the newer medical understanding of lunacy embraced 'moral insanity' – behaviour that seemed non-animalistic but where the affections had been distorted, as in the narrative of Sweeny Todd. Crawford speculates that the werewolf may have been an oddly consoling creature during panics over insanity and anxieties about the moral wilderness of the industrial city of modernity.

Rebecca Langworthy begins with the premise shared by Crawford that nineteenth-century Britain was marked by concerns over the distinction between animal and human. Analysing George MacDonald's 'The History of Photogen and Nycteris' (1882), she shows how the werewolf or witch figure in a fairy-tale setting questions notions of scientific experimentation in the late Victorian period. She brings in contemporary ideas of evolution and degeneration and the educational theories of Locke, Rousseau and Godwin, recalling the wolf-children discussed by George and the developmental theories of eighteenth-century linguists. Wolfishness in MacDonald's allegorical tale is used to characterise scientific enquiry as cruel and having an irrational, even magical, component, subverting established conventions. There is a subtle reading of how MacDonald uses the modified fairy-tale genre to explore these epistemological issues behind education and scientific knowledge.

Victoria Amador adds a sociological dimension by drawing attention to the class status of the werewolf in cinema and television from *The Wolf Man* to *Twilight* and *True Blood*. In many twentieth- and twenty-first-century representations of the werewolf, it is characterised as working-class. The animality and savagery of the creature is bound up with its lower social status (in contrast to the usually sophisticated vampire). With parallels to the resistance over the reintroduction of real wolves, the werewolf is outcast and unwanted, standing in for various marginalised peoples. In Stephenie Meyers's Twilight books and the subsequent films, the werewolf's outsider status is compounded by its being Native American. Amador looks at apparent exceptions to this tendency and finds that upper-class werewolves are also social outcasts of a kind. But Lon Chaney's Wolf Man is distinctly lower-class. Again, in the television series *True Blood* (2008–14) the werewolves are 'white trash', outsiders in the way that the wolf itself has been vilified.

Werewolves are taken up further in the next three chapters, where they prowl through various media and break through the boundary fences of genre.

Bill Hughes looks at werewolves (and the associated shapeshifters) in the beast tales of Angela Carter's *The Bloody Chamber* (1979) where they appear in a spectrum of manifestations, devouring Gothic, fairy tale and other genres to reveal an equally promiscuous set of human potentialities, exploring human agency, creativity and sexuality by paradoxically shifting them into beast form. Hughes analyses how in Carter's tales flesh, and particularly the flesh of women, is commodified, teasing out the various implications of Carter's phrase 'The price of flesh is love'. Flesh can be object for others but its animal nature can be redeemed as love and pleasure. Hughes argues that Carter's well-known feminist writing is part of a larger humanist project, rooted in a socialist materialism that acknowledges and celebrates the embodied aspect of human consciousness and agency. Her tales adumbrate the emancipation of human flesh from its reification as mere meat under capitalism as well as from patriarchy.

The metamorphoses of animal and human in Carter's beast stories are paralleled by her permutations of textual motifs and intermodulation between genres to examine the topics of flesh and the way it is evaluated from different perspectives, anticipating the recently emerged genre of paranormal romance, whose central figure is the love between bestial monster and human. Inspired partially by the wolf-children that George describes, Carter creates a mode of writing that looks back to questions first raised in the Enlightenment about our relation to nature and animality, bequeathing her explorations to her successors.

Kaja Franck returns to the transformations of Gothic and romance fiction that Hughes argues Carter developed as they appear in the hybrid genre of paranormal romance. Franck points out that the painful transition from one state to another in lycanthropy as depicted in Young Adult paranormal romance is an apt figure of adolescence. But transformations from beast to human also challenge the animal–human dichotomy itself. As previous chapters explore, the idea of 'the beast within' is common in interpretations of werewolf narratives from 'Little Red Riding Hood' onwards. But Franck wants to challenge the derogatory stereotype of the wolf in these incarnations, along with the idea of 'taming' the wolf. The oppositions of nature/culture and animal/human are again dramatised as Franck performs a close reading of two Young Adult paranormal romances, Maggie Stiefvater's Wolves of Mercy Falls series (2009–14) and Annette Curtis Klause's *Blood and Chocolate* (1997). She shows in what ways these novels undermine the hierarchy of human over wolf while exploring the metaphorical relationship between lycanthropy and adolescence.

Ivan Phillips hunts for werewolves through the long career of the television time-traveller Doctor in *Doctor Who* and, allowing generously for variants of the creature (by including shapeshifting between animal and human, wild and civilised), finds quite a handful. The creatures Phillips looks at are hybrid in this sense and also hybrid concoctions out of a whole intertextual lineage of

Gothic monster narratives. For Phillips, werewolves, among other things he charts, including ecological themes of wilderness, play a metafictional role in *Doctor Who*, representing moments of transition in the way the series has developed. Phillips mentions the sexual aspect of lycanthropy but notes that it is mostly repressed in its appearance in the series.

The final section looks at humans performing wolfishness in a way that is not quite werewolf but gains power from the latent image of that creature. Turning to the visual arts, Sarah Wade considers the later sculptures that developed from the 'becoming animal' and shamanistic works of the contemporary artist Marcus Coates. In his earlier works, Coates attempted to experience the world as an animal, or to demonstrate the impossibility of that, and shed light on human identity. Wade shows how Coates's later, more minimalist sculptures continue these themes. Wade approaches shapeshifting in an oblique and revealing manner through the theory of Deleuze and Guattari. These engagements with animals take on a lycanthropic aspect with the sculpture *Running Grey Wolf*. Wade then connects her analysis with themes that run through this collection in a comparison with sculptures and installations by other contemporary artists.

Polly Atkin takes performance into the linguistic realm by undertaking a close reading of a group of contemporary women's poems where a kind of shapeshifting akin to lycanthropy takes place: here, humans take on animal selves as a flight from human consciousness. The poets Liz Berry and Kim Moore employ this trope as a way of understanding female embodiment and as a means of resistance. Atkin also reads Berry's and Moore's poems in an ecofeminist manner, though pointing out that the poems pose challenges to the orthodoxy of that way of thinking. Both Kaja Franck's female werewolves and the wolf-women of Angela Carter in Bill Hughes's chapter are recalled here. The poems are full of metamorphoses; Moore's pieces in particular play with the transformation between human and wolf, challenging patriarchal assumptions but also celebrating the wolf itself. The Otherness of the wolf casts light on gender and raises paradoxes about language and the voicing of animals.

Catherine Spooner, in the final chapter, looks at the transvestitism of humans transformed into wolves by fur and fashion. Examining the signification of wolf imagery and the wearing of fur in fashion advertisements for Ralph Lauren and others, she links this to female werewolf fictions, showing what it means to 'wear the wolf'. This raises questions about the antinomy of culture and nature, gender, whiteness, and also the representation of indigenous peoples (as in the photography of Jimmy Nelson, which Spooner shows are often homologous with his fashion shoots for Lauren). Spooner examines Victorian female werewolves, then early twentieth-century representations of women with dogs in painting, which share this iconography of fur in fashion. The feral child appears again in this chapter in an analysis of the 1990 film *Dances with*

Wolves, where the representation of women, wolves and wilderness resonates with both the later fashion imagery and the earlier female werewolf. Despite uncomfortable ideas about gender and the problematic images of indigenous peoples and of wolves themselves, fashion has a utopian promise of transformation, including our relationships with nature.

Thus, through humans in wolves' clothing we return to the pastoral genre as a utopian vision of our place in nature and to the complex issue of the dialectic of humanity's transcendence of and immersion within the natural world. By integrating analyses of werewolf texts with studies of wild children and wolves themselves, these essays situate the werewolf in a broader context of animality and sociality, leading to interpretations that challenge the simplistic model of the werewolf as 'the beast within'. The contributors here show how, in various ways, the Gothic (were)wolf confronts Enlightenment, traversing genres and illuminating the contradictions of modernity. The attention paid by the following essays to prose fiction alongside such media as cinematic sound, fashion, visual art and poetry, and the range of theoretical positions therein opens up new approaches to these topics. We invite you now into the company of wolves and to listen to their voices as they sound in 'our interpreted world.

Notes

1. From the first *Duino Elegy*, in Stiefvater, *Linger*, p. 223.
2. The best account of the cultural history of the wolf is Marvin, *Wolf*. But see also Lopez, *Of Wolves and Men*.
3. Charlotte F. Otten gives in full the original trial transcript of Peter Stubbe in English, translated from the Dutch in 1590 and supposedly based on eye-witness accounts by Tyse Artyne, William Brewar, Adolf Staedt and George Bores. See 'A Discourse Declaring the Damnable Life and Death of One Stubbe Peeter', in *A Lycanthropy Reader*, pp. 69–76.
4. Marvin, *Wolf*, p. 82.
5. These dates are well documented by Garry Marvin and others. There is not a complete consensus on this but the dates roughly correspond in most accounts. We refer to Marvin's 'Timeline of the Wolf' (*Wolf*, pp. 182–3) for evidence here.
6. Where they are warned that 'the most dangerous wolves of all' are the 'softly-spoken and discreet' men who talk to them on the street (Perrault, 'Little Red Riding-Hood', p. 103).
7. For a brief account, see Gifford, *Pastoral*.
8. That the vampire, as a revenant that sucks blood to survive, is not timeless (as Montague Summers and others claim) but is a creature specific to eighteenth-century Eastern Europe is argued in George and Hughes, Introduction, *Open Graves, Open Minds*, pp. 7–15). But see George, 'How Long Have We Believed in Vampires?'.

9   See Novak, 'The Wild Child Comes to Tea'; Douthwaite, *The Wild Girl, Natural Man and the Monster*; Newton, *Savage Girls and Wild Boys*; Benzaquén, *Encounters with Wild Children*. Newton's is a well-researched but populist account while Douthwaite and Benzaquén provide more academic in-depth analyses. Also very useful is Malson, *Wolf-children and the Problem of Human Nature*; this contains the physician Jean Itard's accounts of his attempt to socialise Victor of Aveyron: *Of the First Developments of the Young Savage of Aveyron* (1799) and *Report on the Progress of Victor of Aveyron* (1806).

10 Aarsleff, 'The Tradition of Condillac', and 'An Outline of Language-origins Theory since the Renaissance', in *From Locke to Saussure: Essays on the Study of Language and Intellectual History*, pp. 146–209, 278–92; Hudson, 'Dialogue and the Origins of Language'.

11 Mandeville, *The Fable of the Bees*, II, pp. 269–89; Condillac, *Essay on the Origin of Human Knowledge*; Rousseau's *Essay on the Origin of Languages* has been published alongside Herder's *Essay on the Origin of Language* in *On the Origin of Language*, trans. by Moran and Gode, pp. 5–74.

12 Condillac, pp. 88–91.

13 But the eighteenth century also saw a moment of anti-pastoral, a reaction against this optimism over modernity itself, which manifests itself in the oppositional genre of satire. Swift and his fellow Scriblerian John Arbuthnot (the doctor to whom Peter the Wild Boy was entrusted) subverted this with their satires. They envisaged Peter as natural and Other and a standard of virtue to measure modern society against. This would be a common device in eighteenth-century satire, but it is interesting that these two chose Peter to act as a foil against the corruptions of modern civilisation. (See Jonathan Swift, *The Most Wonderful Wonder* (1726) and John Arbuthnot, *It Cannot Rain But it Pours* (1726), which has in its subtitle 'Of the Wonderful Wild Man that was nursed in Germany by a Wild Beast'.)

14 Angela Carter's tales 'Wolf-Alice' (1979) and 'Peter and the Wolf' (1985) retell wolf-child narratives as dazzling explorations of sexuality and humanity (see Bill Hughes, Chapter 9 below). Sedgwick's novel is loosely based on the story of Amala and Kamala.

15 See Sam George, Chapter 3 below.

16 Pertinent examples are the Young Adult paranormal romance by Jennifer Lynn Barnes, *Raised by Wolves*, and the enchanting anime film *Wolf Children*.

17 Surprisingly, there are few scholarly books on representations of werewolves, and they tend to be restricted in scope in various ways. None of them explores the connections with the wild child or the wolf itself as mediated through culture (as does this book). Isolated chapters on or references to the werewolf have appeared in academic studies of monsters, paranormal romance and the Gothic generally. There are many popular books on the werewolf phenomenon in general; these tend to focus on the folkloric and the cinematic, do not treat other media or genres and are sometimes rather uncritical. Among the better ones are: Beresford, *The White*

Devil; Douglas, *The Beast Within*; Frost, *The Essential Guide to Werewolf Literature*. This last has more of a literary focus and is comprehensive and useful, but not particularly analytical.

The principal academic monographs are as follows. Coudray, *The Curse of the Werewolf* provides a broad sweep and is perhaps the most analytical and theoretical of competing books in the field, though it is confined to literary texts and does not consider recent Young Adult fiction. McMahon-Coleman and Weaver, *Werewolves and Other Shapeshifters in Popular Culture* focuses on werewolves in contemporary popular culture through the lens of identity. Sconduto, *Metamorphoses of the Werewolf* is mainly confined to medieval and Renaissance literary texts. Stypczynski, *The Modern Literary Werewolf* includes more recent texts but employs a reductive and somewhat questionable Jungian approach.

There are two edited collections to consider. Priest, ed., *She-wolf: A Cultural History of Female Werewolves* is, as the title suggests, focused on female werewolf texts. Then, more recently, *Werewolves, Wolves and the Gothic*, ed. by McKay and Miller, takes a mainly ecocritical approach to werewolves and the representation of wolves; it does not extend the analysis to wild children.

18 A brief but concise general account of the folklore of the werewolf is Russell and Russell, 'The Social Biology of Werewolves'. The werewolf in European folkloric tradition is covered from an anthropological perspective in *Werewolf Histories*, ed. by de Blécourt. For an insightful analysis of the werewolf in Classical Greece, see Buxton, 'Wolves and Werewolves in Greek Thought'.

19 This is one reason why the collection eschews psychoanalytic approaches, which the idea of the werewolf as 'beast within' seems to lend itself to. This has been a frequent move in understanding the werewolf (Freud's own analysis of 'the Wolf Man' being central, of course). However, such readings tend to be reductive and to lose sight of the particularity of the text; our contributors perform close readings, situating the creature in its context. That is not to ignore insights from the psychoanalytic tradition and the essays here do draw on, for example, Marcuse, Kristeva, and Deleuze and Guattari.

20 Perhaps Gothic literature has always been concerned with central issues of Enlightenment rationalism in various, often conflicting ways. However, in that mode's present incarnation, there are clear signs of its involvement with a contemporary counter-Enlightenment exemplified by Lyotard's and other postmodernists' suspicion of 'grand narratives' and the widespread scepticism towards ideas of human progress, universalism, science and rationality in popular and high culture and in political discourse.

21 See Cohen, ed., *Monster Theory*, and Halberstam, *Skin Shows*.

22 See Franck and George, 'Contemporary Werewolves'.

23 Crawford, *The Twilight of the Gothic*.

24 The vampire in its eighteenth-century folkloric origins is grossly bestial and is often not clearly distinct from the werewolf. In its literary development it exhibits a range

of characteristics, from Polidori's rather insubstantial Lord Ruthven to the monstrous Count Dracula, who again shares features with the werewolf (see Franck, '"Something that is either werewolf or vampire"'.

25 Armstrong, *Bitten*, p. 1. Erin S. Young sees more of a subversive side to Armstrong than we do, in her article 'Flexible Heroines, Flexible Narratives'. Typically, shapeshifter heroines' dramas revolve around their search for autonomy against the authority and appeal of a pack dominated by alpha males (who are, adding a requisite narrative tension, often the love interest). Armstrong's Elena and Rachel Vincent's werecat Faythe Sanders are good examples of this tendency; see Vincent, *Stray*.

26 As always in this area, Raymond Williams is illuminating; see 'Ideas of Nature' and 'Culture', in *Keywords*, p. 89; and also Terry Eagleton, 'Culture and Nature', in *The Idea of Culture*, pp. 87–111.

27 Rice, *The Wolf Gift*.

Part I

Cultural images of the wolf, the werewolf and the wolf-child

1

WOLVES AND LIES: A WRITER'S PERSPECTIVE

Marcus Sedgwick

From the wolf in sheep's clothing to the boy who cried wolf, from anti-Semitic propaganda to lupine hoaxes of the Holocaust itself, there has always been a connection between the wolf and untruth. What is it about the wolf that lends itself to the concept of fraudulence, and is there something more positive we also take away from the nature of this particular beast? 'All stories are about wolves. All worth repeating, that is. Anything else is sentimental drivel.' So says Margaret Atwood, or at least, that's what she has her character Alex declare in *The Blind Assassin*.[1] Alex's point is that every story requires a metaphorical wolf – without a problem of some kind, a story is not a story in the truest sense. This exploration of wolves and lies is written from the point of view of a storyteller; my life is invested in stories. I have observed that we do not read books that contain only the positive: stories that recounted only a sequence of wonderful and fulfilling things happening would be, ironically, not at all fulfilling to the reader. From time to time, however, attempts have been made to cast fiction in this mode. We might consider a story such as Ernest Hemingway's 'Big Two-hearted River', in which the protagonist Nick Adams goes on a fishing trip and everything is more or less absolutely fine. If this story succeeds at all it's because of the reader's understanding of implicit jeopardy – themes of warfare and conflict lurk beneath the surface throughout the piece.

A more extreme attempt to write a story without dramatic incident appears *within* another novel. George Gissing's *New Grub Street* of 1891 describes the tribulations of a character called Harold Biffen who writes a novel depicting the everyday, utterly realistic life of *Mr Bailey, Grocer* with no dramatic incident whatsoever. The result is untenably dull and the attempt is a failure.[2]

Such experiments serve only to prove to us that story is not about the representation of human life – story is about the representation of the *conflicts* of human life. This is the sense in which Atwood's Alex declares that all stories worth repeating are about wolves, and yet, although he's speaking metaphorically, very often in the past our stories have been about real wolves.

Wolves are there from the start, and from the start are associated with deception. Of the fables associated with Aesop, around seventy-five of the 725 stories listed in the Perry Index feature wolves – no other animal features as often as the wolf does: eagles have twenty stories; donkeys, twelve; cats, twenty-one; dogs and lions each have fifty-six, for example.[3] Only by combining stories about men, women and children does humankind itself merit more mentions than the wolf. The closest animal rival to the wolf is the fox, with sixty-six fables. A fox is of course a close relative of the wolf, both members of the Canidae family, and yet even in these fables, approximately two and a half thousand years old, there is a distinction. The fox is cunning and wily. The wolf shares these traits, but with a crucial addition – the wolf is often depicted as voracious, rapacious, merciless, even wantonly cruel, as in tales such as 'The Wolf and the Lamb'.[4]

It's interesting to note that in one of the most famous of Aesop's fables, 'The Shepherd Who Cried "Wolf!" in Jest', deception is still part of the tale, even though the lies are now being told by the shepherd, and that, in many stories where the wolf is not depicted as extremely malicious, deceit is once again part of the mix – see 'The Dog and the Sheep', which features a wolf bearing false witness and winding up dead in a ditch for its trouble.[5]

Another very old story, 'The Wolf in Sheep's Clothing', was in the past falsely attributed to Aesop, and indeed bears Perry Index Number 451, though the story is now held to be of biblical origin. In one of his sermons, Jesus declares 'Beware of false prophets, which come to you in sheep's clothing, but inwardly they are ravening wolves' – now a universally popular adage in the English language, when referencing danger disguised as innocence.[6]

It's hard to date fairy tales. It's far from certain who Aesop was, or when he lived, but, if it is indeed the case that he lived between 620 and 564 BCE, we can be far less sure of when the original versions of common fairy tales were first told, and it remains impossible to know who first told them. Whilst it was long assumed that the fairy tales recounted by the likes of Brothers Grimm, Charles Perrault or Marie-Catherine D'Aulnoy were not vastly older than the period in which these famous fairy-tale narrators first wrote them down, recent research challenges this view. In a paper for the Royal Society, Sara Graça da Silva and Jamshid J. Tehrani argue that phylogenetic dating techniques provide robust evidence that stories like 'Beauty and the Beast' (ATU 425C, as per the Aarne-Thompson-Uther fairy-tale classification system) may be as much as four thousand years old, and other familiar fairy tales, such as the 'Jack and the Beanstalk' family, could be even older.[7] To return to wolves, Tehrani argued in earlier work that while ATU 333 – better known to us as 'Little Red Riding Hood' – may be 'only' eleventh century in origin, a closely related tale, ATU 123 ('The Wolf and the Kids') is possibly much older, being evolved from an 'Aesopic' fable and first recorded around 400 CE.[8] What these two tales have in common is the notion of the deceitful wolf: in the former story, the wolf disguises himself as the girl's grandmother; in the latter, as the mother goat to the kids.

It seems, therefore, that for as long as stories have been told and recorded the wolf has been penned not only as voracious but also as deceitful. What is the explanation for these connections? As to traits of supposed cruelty, certain opinions have long been held about the wolf's predation habits. One of the historical accusations made against the wolf has been its tendency to kill more than required for the provision of food. Though argument still occurs on the subject, 'surplus killing' by wolves (the predation of animals that are left uneaten at the time of the kill) beyond immediate need is well documented. The critical point, however, is the word 'immediate'. Wolves, like various other species, will sometimes kill more than they can eat *at one feed*, returning to a kill on several other occasions, or making a cache of the excess.[9] Note also that the leading example of a species that uses 'surplus killing', to considerable benefit, is humankind.

What of the latter aspect: that of deceit? To understand this, we need to consider a little further the supposed ruthless nature of the wolf. It's hard to find anything different said about the animal at first; indeed, in the oldest surviving great story we still have, *The Epic of Gilgamesh*, lies what must be the first mention of a wolf in all literature, and, as we might expect, it is not favourable. Tablet VI of the epic refers to Gilgamesh rejecting the Goddess Ishtar's advances, reminding her that she once turned a shepherd into a wolf, thus threatening the very flocks he should have been protected.[10] From the outside, the threat of the wolf is so apparent it serves without the need for elucidation.

Moving to the Classical period, while both Greek and Roman myth saw the wolf as a predominantly evil creature – consider *'homo homini lupus est'* ('man is a wolf to man') – the Romans did also see better qualities in the wolf: the legend of the very founding of their city state tells the story of Romulus and Remus, suckled by a she-wolf.[11]

If we turn to Norse mythology, we find Fenrir, the monstrous wolf destined to devour Odin himself during Ragnarök, and though we also find other, tamer wolves, such as Geri and Freki, Odin's pets, it should be noted that their names respectively mean 'greedy' and 'voracious'.[12] Many other negative portrayals of the wolf can be found in world mythologies, but this is not the whole story. Some cultures have represented better characteristics of the animal and have even revered them, one such being the First Nations of North America.

Native North American mythologies are notable for their predominantly positive depictions of the wolf, in stories, songs and personal names. In fact, the non-profit organisation Wolf Song of Alaska states 'American tribes have an overwhelming tendency to look upon the wolf in a much more favourable light [than other cultures]', pointing to wolves' strength, courage and independence as favourable traits.[13]

It seems apparent that a culture's depiction of the wolf correlates to its relation to the animal through time and/or across place. Communities at risk of predation of livestock are likely to present the wolf in a different light from those where the wolf has become extinct, such as the bulk of Europe in most of the modern era. In the absence of the real creature, the wolf can attain a symbolic status that, perhaps, displays the 'better' side of its nature. (And, as we will see, the re-emergence of the wolf in such areas has led to a corresponding re-emergence of antipathy in certain locales.) However, this does not explain the more positive attitudes to the wolf in First Nations accounts, given that the wolf was at no time extinct on the continent. It took the coming of the white settlers to inaugurate massive wolf culls (peaking with around twenty-one thousand animals being killed annually in the 1920s) and First Nations' more positive attitudes speak more about a different relationship with wild animals than something cued by their total absence from the landscape.[14] After all, whilst certain tribes revered wolves, they would on occasion hunt them too, for pelts, and for food, though often with a restraint, and infrequently.[15]

In all these accounts of wolf predation, it's not just the viciousness of the wolf that defines it, but its stealth, too. The wolf, a primarily nocturnal animal, will commit its 'atrocities' in the night. Humanity's essential, deep-seated fear of the dark and the creatures that operate within it no doubt contributes to the feeling that the wolf is a creature of deception. It arrives, kills and disappears in the night, all with little trace but the carcasses of its victims to show it was there, and the fact that a wolf can run dozens of miles in a single night can only enhance this sort of belief.

When we turn to literature of the modern era, it becomes easier to find more positive portrayals of the wolf, alongside plenty that persist with the wolf-as-beast motif. So while J.R.R. Tolkien had frequent recourse to the bestial nature of the wolf (deriving from the influence of Germanic myth on his work), and C.S. Lewis gave us Maugrim, the chief of the White Witch's secret police in *The Lion, the Witch and the Wardrobe*, others have brought us a very different animal, even a kind and noble one: the prime examples being Rudyard Kipling's Akela (the leader of the wolf-pack), Raksha (the mother of the pack) and Father Wolf in *The Jungle Books*. Here, far from being at risk of becoming the wolves' next meal, little Mowgli is raised in safety as one of the pack.

Other more or less benign wolves in fiction include 'Two Socks' in *Dances with Wolves*; 'White Fang', three-quarters wolf, one-quarter dog, in the novel of the same name by Jack London; and the nameless she-wolf in Cormac McCarthy's *The Crossing*.[16] In children's fiction, Melvin Burgess's *The Cry of the Wolf* and my own *The Dark Horse* also depict wolves primarily as animals, but ones with the capacity to 'behave' themselves in the right circumstances.[17]

All five examples given here attempt to depict wolves that have not been overtly anthropomorphised, retaining their animal natures, and yet which still come to terms of peace with their human contacts. The question of how realistic these attempts to make stories with apparently more realistic wolves actually are is not for consideration here; instead we merely note the presence of beasts capable of more than the instinct to rip throats and devour all.

Who's afraid of the big bad wolf?

Can wolves ever be trusted? Disney's 1933 animation *The Three Little Pigs* gives a definite answer, and in doing so launched one of the studio's most popular songs.[18] The refrain 'Who's afraid of the big bad wolf?' captures perfectly the mood of the film's three porcine heroes. Full of bluster before they actually see the wolf, two of the pigs dance and sing their defiant song, while the third (Practical Pig) builds a house of bricks. Until the villain of the piece actually appears – at which point all three rush in to the safety of Practical Pig's solid house. We should *all* be afraid of the big, bad wolf, the film suggests, for he comes knocking on our door protesting innocence, while all he wants to do in reality is burst into our most treasured safe space (our home) and consume us.

Viewers of the film in 1933 were left in no doubt of this – the wolf is bad through and through. Above and beyond the film itself, the song became a best-selling single, an ear-worm of national proportions, as well as something of an anthem against the troubles posed by economic turmoil of the era.[19] Critics immediately recognised that 'it bored into the national consciousness, both reflecting and somehow ameliorating anxiety over the Depression.'[20] Such anxiety concerned not just the economic turmoil of the 1930s but the political threats too. The film was released in 1933; events in Europe were taking sinister shape. While the horrors of the prewar period are easily seen in hindsight, they were not obvious to everyone at the time even on the continent, never mind far away across the ocean in the United States. The two complacent pigs, happily singing and dancing while the third prepares for attack, became a perfect metaphorical rallying cry for the need to resist the rise of Hitler's Nazis. That Walt Disney himself was trying to warn anyone about the Nazis or comment on the Depression is disputed; Louise Krasniewicz recounts that the man himself dismissed the latter idea.[21] As is well known, Disney has long been accused of having been an anti-Semite, about which argument rumbles on, long after his death.[22]

It's worth noting, however, that the version of *The Three Little Pigs* seen today is not exactly the one seen in 1933. In the original, when the wolf comes to the door, he's depicted in a disguise that would have been widely recognised to refer to Jewish pedlars, and which we now clearly interpret as anti-Semitic. In 1948 the sequence was reanimated to change the disguise to that of a 'Fuller

Brush man'. In the original version, too, the wolf imitates a Yiddish accent in this scene, something that was also changed in subsequent versions. In whichever version we consider, the wolf is a dissembler, a cunning figure of evil, but the disturbing overtones of the 1933 portrayal remind us of dark territory – namely the relationship between wolves, lies and the Holocaust.

In his book about the psychogeography of Stanley Kubrick's films, *The Wolf at the Door*, Geoffrey Cocks elaborates on the connection between the Disney song and anti-Semitism.[23] Speaking of *The Shining* (1980), Cocks notes how Jack Torrance, having trapped his wife Wendy and son Danny in the bathroom, prepares to axe the door down. But not before he's recited the lines from the rhyme that gave Disney the story for his 1933 animation:

> Little pigs, little pigs, let me come in.
> Not by the hair on my chinny-chin-chin.
> Then I'll huff, and I'll puff, and I'll blow your house in.

One of many differences between Stephen King's book and Kubrick's movie, Cocks cites this as no mere coincidence, but as an example of material planted by Kubrick to give a deeper meaning to his version of the story. The argument of Cocks, a contributing narrator in the documentary *Room 237*, is that, unable to complete his Holocaust project *Aryan Papers*, Kubrick instead used King's novel as a vehicle to tell an allegory of the Holocaust.[24] Cocks claims that:

> any mention of the wolf in The Shining is a(n) (in)direct expression of a growing preoccupation in the 1970s on Kubrick's (and the culture's) part with the subject of Nazis, the Second World War, and the Holocaust.[25]

His views, and those of other *Room 237* contributors, have been scoffed at by people connected to Kubrick: for example, the actor Leon Vitali, who worked as Kubrick's personal assistant during the shooting of *The Shining*, and who noted 'I'm certain that [Kubrick] wouldn't have wanted to listen to about 70, or maybe 80 percent [of] Room 237 ... Because it's pure gibberish.'[26]

While it is hard to see some of the theories expounded in *Room 237* as anything other than very far-fetched, the supposed evidence of Holocaust references in Kubrick's *The Shining* is striking. The number 42 appears in the film more than chance occurrence would explain: it is the number of cars in the parking lot in the establishing shot of the hotel, it is on Danny's sweatshirt, it is the *six* trays of *7Up* caught in shot on more than one occasion, it is the movie *Summer of '42* that Wendy and Danny watch on television one day, it is the result of multiplying 2 × 3 × 7. This last number might seem like a conspiracy theorist's idle fancy, until we learn that in King's novel the haunted room is room 217, and that on Kubrick's own copy of the book he played around with the number 217, and then for the film switched to room 237 – the Holocaust link being that the 'Final Solution' was implemented in 1942.[27] Add this to shots of piles of suitcases, a classic Holocaust image, and frequent shots of Jack's 'Adler' (German for Eagle, a Nazi symbol) typewriter. And add all this to the fact that Kubrick had had to forgo his chance to make the Holocaust film he had been working on for years, and the theory at least deserves consideration. At the very least, Jack becomes 'the wolf at the door', and in doing so becomes the arch dissembler. His attempt to murder Wendy and Danny, the only other people in the hotel, is thus an attempt to murder not only everyone in his family but everyone in his world, and can therefore be considered an act of genocide, just as the Holocaust was.

The ultimate architect of the Final Solution, Adolf Hitler, had his own associations with the wolf. The name of the Nazis' military HQ on the Eastern Front was the *Wolfsschanze*, or Wolf's Lair. Peter Arnds has argued in strong Freudian fashion that Hitler identified deeply with the animal – the name Adolf derives from the Germanic *Adalwolf*, meaning 'noble wolf' – and even that he was familiar with Disney's cartoon and was heard to whistle 'Who's afraid of the big, bad wolf?' to himself frequently.[28] Arnds also refers to one supposed source for Hitler's obsession with wolves. As in Freud's famous case of Sergei Pankejeff, 'The Wolf-Man', the young Hitler is believed to have witnessed his parents in the sexual act at a very early age.[29] Here lies another possible source of the wolf's connection to lies. The wolf has long been a metaphor for the human sexual predator – the insatiable philanderer – and so signifies another form of deceit, in the shape of the Casanova who professes love but who is only really interested in lust.

How much, if any of this, was in Kubrick's mind when he included that fairy-tale element in his movie, we can only conjecture. We can be sure at the very least that Kubrick, the most meticulous of filmmakers, did not put things into his movies without thought. Even if all he wanted was to make Jack Torrance that little bit more menacing, the lines from *The Three Little Pigs* were an unexpected yet powerful way of achieving that.

'The wolf at the door' or 'that will keep the wolf from the door' are of course expressions used to describe life when times are hard, bringing to mind the notion that in a hard winter even the wolves will be forced to enter human communities in their desperate search for sustenance.[30] The privations of the Second World War were one such period in recent human history. Whether or not Kubrick overtly connected wolves to Hitler is open to discussion, yet that very connection had already been made for him thirty-eight years earlier, by MGM Studios.

Blitz Wolf of 1942 is another retelling of *The Three Little Pigs*, but is one that leaves nothing to the imagination in casting the wolf as no less than Hitler himself, in the role of 'Adolf Wolf'.[31] At this point in the war, American cartoons had become explicit in their use of propaganda, and, as Geoffrey Cocks argues, since Kubrick eschewed school for the movie house from an early age, and was faithful in his attendance at this alternative place of education, 'we may therefore assume with great confidence that if a movie played at either the RKO Fordham or Loew's Paradise, in particular between roughly 1936 and 1946, Kubrick most likely saw it'.[32]

It would seem that the only useful depiction of the wolf in a period of warfare such as the Second World War is in its bestial guise, and yet, out of the war in general, and the Holocaust in particular, purportedly true stories later began to emerge of the wolf as friend, not foe. Perhaps the most (in)famous example of such a story is the internationally best-selling book *Misha: A Mémoire of the Holocaust Years*.[33] The author, Misha Defonseca (born Monique de Wael), claimed that the book, published in 1997, was a true account of her survival in Nazi Europe, following the deportation of her parents in 1941. Making her way across the continent at the age of nine, she recounts various adventures escaping the Warsaw ghetto, killing a German soldier in self-defence, and being befriended and protected by a pack of wolves. Even before the book was published its veracity had been called into question. After various exposés and pressure from the media, Defonseca later admitted she had made it up.[34] In defence, Defonseca conceded, 'The book is a story, it's my story. It's not the true reality, but it is my reality. There are times when I find it difficult to differentiate between reality and my inner world.'[35]

The Holocaust is an episode of history that has spawned numerous false accounts and outright hoaxes: *The Painted Bird* by Jerzy Kosinski; *Fragments* by Binjamin Wilkomirski; *Hannah: From Dachau to the Olympics and Beyond* by Jean Goodwin Messenger; and *Angel at the Fence: The True Story of a Love that Survived* by Herman Rosenblat are just four examples of this dubious literary phenomenon.[36] Whether there remains any literary or cultural merit in a work that has been shown to be 'false' is a hotly debated question. Even Elie Wiesel, who won the Nobel Peace Prize in 1986 for his indisputably genuine account of surviving the Holocaust, *Night*, noted, 'Things are not that simple ... Some events do take place but are not true; others are – although they never occurred.'[37] The book, though acclaimed, has always suffered from debate over whether it is an eyewitness account, a fictionalised autobiography, semi-fictional memoir and so on.

We accept that writers make things up. When they're writing novels, that's their job. When they're writing their autobiographies, it's charming at best, disingenuous at worst. When they're writing accounts of the Holocaust, it's offensive to many people, and results in acrimonious disputes – in Misha Defonseca's case resulting in a multi-million-dollar court case. Defonseca's account of being taken in by six adult wolves and four pups raises a wider issue – there have been numerous reports of feral children from across recorded history, from Romulus and Remus on. Put simply, are any of these stories real?

In France, one of Defonseca's denouncers was the surgeon turned self-made expert on feral children, Serge Aroles. Following his revelations about the story of Misha, Aroles investigated accounts of feral children between the years 1304 and 1954.[38] His conclusion was that the vast majority of them were false.[39] Speaking specifically of cases of wolves rearing children, he allowed that in cases of phantom pregnancy (when the production of milk sometimes occurs) there were a handful of genuine cases of she-wolves suckling human infants, but denies that any human child has ever lived in a pack of wolves. Famous cases such as the Indian twins, Amala and Kamala, were no more than scams; these children, and others like them, being victims of brutality, having been beaten with sticks since early childhood and forced into their animal-like behaviour.[40] With regard to feral children in general, Aroles was similarly dismissive, but did allow the veracity of the eighteenth-century case of Marie-Angélique Le Blanc, known as the Wild Girl of Champagne, having studied contemporaneous American and French records.[41]

There are more recent examples of so-called feral children – Ivan Mishukov, a boy of five years, living with wild dogs on the streets of Moscow, or Andrei Tolstyk, a seven-year-old from Siberia who was raised by a dog, though these are just the kind of cases that Aroles disputes the truth of, and equally it must be said that the papers that report them have usually taken the Russia news media's accounts at face value.[42] In the United States, recent examples of something akin to feral children have tended to come in the form of children suffering from extreme neglect and imprisonment – cases such as that of the girl known as 'Genie', an authentic and very disturbing case of a girl kept in isolation from the age of twenty months until the age of thirteen.[43]

Perhaps there are too many accounts of hoax feral children to fully let that idea drop but we are left with that nagging question: are any accounts of feral children real? Whether or not we can ever find the answer to that, however, is irrelevant to the final question I want to consider: genuine or not, why do so many people want such accounts to be true, easily believing them upon uncorroborated hearing?

Wolves and wildness

> That night Max wore his wolf suit and made mischief of one kind and another. His mother called him 'WILD THING!' and Max said 'I'LL EAT YOU UP!'[44]

Today, there are many parties 'crying wolf' in various parts of the world – from Europe to the USA, there is conflict between people who would preserve and protect the wolf, and those who want them killed. As one example, we might browse the Facebook page 'Save Western Wildlife', based in Idaho, which posts about the supposed threat to human life from wolves in the area, and the corresponding Facebook page 'Save Western Wildlife Is a Terrorist Organisation' which seeks to expose 'Save Western Wildlife as a group that uses scare tactics, acts of intimidation, and outright threats in an attempt to destroy any remaining wildlife and wilderness'.[45]

The Haute Savoie, France, sees similar tensions. A resident of Petit-Bornand-les-Glières, Franck Michel, was prosecuted in 2009 for killing a wolf that he claimed had been threatening the hamlet. Freely admitting that he had killed the wolf, he stated 'I did not think I was doing wrong by killing a wolf. For me, I did a good thing ... For everyone.'[46] Michel also stated that he knew that an official request was being considered for a permit to shoot wolves in the area, but felt it was taking too long.

It is hard for the layperson looking on to know how to sort the truth from the lies in many of these instances. It is apparent that self-interest will often guide one's view of the wolf – the French farmer who believes his livestock is being predated by wolves will have a very different view of the wolf from the city dweller with a possibly idealised view of wildlife and its protection – just as it comes as no great surprise that the hunting fraternity in the United States is keen to disseminate the opinion that wolves are a threat to human life. As Ed Bangs, the wolf recovery co-ordinator for the US Fish and Wildlife Service, notes,

> If you live in an urban area where your only exposure to wolves is watching them on TV and seeing them running in a national park, it is very easy to be supportive of wolves. The debate right now isn't about the biology. People think it is morally wrong to kill wolves because it reminds them of pet dogs or people because wolves live in packs like families.[47]

As noted, the view that wolves are noble beasts, with admirable qualities such as freedom and courage, is in the main a more modern one, aside from a few notable exceptions. Wolves therefore hold the somewhat unusual position of being symbolic of very different, even opposite characteristics, depending on your point of view. They are noble to some, but they are the most savage of beasts to others. They are callous, killing without measure, and represent voracious instincts, and yet, in the (possibly never proven) image of the pack rearing a feral child, they represent maternity and/or fraternity. It is this last image, of the child like Mowgli, which persists in fascinating us, something even more remarkable if it is indeed untrue. What is its power, why do we find this idea so appealing?

That is the question lying underneath the character of Mouse in my book *The Dark Horse*, who is found living with wolves on a mountainside and 'rescued' to live with a human community where, despite her and everyone else's efforts, she is never entirely happy. Mouse communicates with animals, in a way no one understands – and is regarded with awe and suspicion as a result. It is also the question underlying the feral child, Amara, in Jill Paton

Walsh's *Knowledge of Angels*.[48] Amara, it is believed, can prove (or disprove) the existence of God by seeing whether, once she develops language, she has innate knowledge of the divine.

What both these books are asking is this: what have we lost? What did we once know that we no longer know? Who were we once, that we can no longer be? In the opening lines of *Civilisation and Its Discontents*, Sigmund Freud put it well:

> It is impossible to escape the impression that people commonly use false standards of measurement – that they seek power, success and wealth for themselves and admire them in others, and that they underestimate what is of true value in life.[49]

Freud's argument in this famous book concerns the feeling of unease we find at being in the world – always seeking something, something largely unspoken and never found. Freud puts his finger on the source of this longing, arguing that in infancy, before the separation of the ego from the surrounding world, we are bathed in a sense of oneness that we will never be able to restore:

> originally the ego includes everything, later it separates off an external world from itself. Our present ego-feeling is, therefore, only a shrunken residue of a much more inclusive – indeed, an all-embracing – feeling which corresponded to a more intimate bond between the ego and the world about it.[50]

Is this what the wolf represents to us? The 'world-as-ego'? Not directly, perhaps, but through what we perceive that it has which we do not. We look at the apparently easy way in which animals operate in the wild, and it serves only to make us wonder why life is so complex to us. The wolf 'knows how' to be a wolf, while we humans all too frequently find life a struggle. As Freud argues, we are consequently motivated to fill what has been lost in us, but, without knowing what that thing is, blindly seek to fill it with money, success, fame and so on.

We consider animals in general and the wolf in particular, with stories of poor children being protected by beasts that are apparently savage and wild, and it reminds us of our lost state, of some Rousseauvian noble savage (who may never have existed), and deep down we never sense that what we have lost is simply this: a sense of complete belonging.[51] It was this that Rudyard Kipling caught exactly in the poem that appears in *The Second Jungle Book*, 'The Law of the Jungle', which begins:

> Now this is the Law of the Jungle – as old and as true as the sky;
> And the Wolf that shall keep it may prosper, but the Wolf that shall break it must die.
>
> As the creeper that girdles the tree-trunk the Law runneth forward and back –
> For the strength of the Pack is the Wolf, and the strength of the Wolf is the Pack.[52]

There seems to be a close relation between wolves and lies. This may be due to their stealth and skill in predation, a trait intensified over time through our telling of fairy tales and horror stories of all kinds. It may have been reinforced by connotations of sexual predation, and accompanying deceit. Yet ultimately, perhaps the most significant lie we tell about wolves is this one – that they have a secret which can connect us to a truer version of ourselves – and this lie is a powerful one, very easily swallowed, simply because we want it to be true.

Notes

1 Atwood, *The Blind Assassin*, p. 344.
2 As related by Jonathan Gottschall, in *The Storytelling Animal*, p. 51.
3 Perry, *Studies in the Text History of the Life and Fables of Aesop*. Perry's is the accepted categorisation system for the stories known as Aesop's fables. Numbers given are approximate, as stories and versions of stories overlap and their separation is debatable at times.
4 Perry Index 155.
5 Perry Index 210; Perry Index 478.
6 Matthew 7:15, King James Version. See Garry Marvin, Chapter 2 below.
7 Silva and Tehrani, 'Comparative Phylogenetic Analyses'. Devised by Antti Aarne, and with successive revisions by Stith Thompson and Hans-Jörg Uther, the ATU index classifies folktales by grouping together those with shared formal properties; for a broad account, see Cara Giaimo, 'The ATU Fable Index'.
8 Tehrani, 'The Phylogeny of Little Red Riding Hood'.
9 Howell, 'Wolves Do Not Kill For Sport'; 'Why Don't Wolves Eat All That They Kill?'.
10 *The Epic of Gilgamesh*, trans. by Kovacs, p. 53.
11 'lupus est homo homini, non homo, quom qualis sit non novit' (Plautus, *Asinaria*, trans. by Henderson, p. 52, line 495).
12 Lindow, *Norse Mythology*, pp. 120, 139.
13 Wollert, 'Wolves in Native American Culture'.
14 Mech and Boitani, *Wolves*, p. 448.
15 Lopez, *Of Wolves and Men*, p. 320.
16 Blake, *Dances with Wolves* (1988); London, *White Fang* (1906); McCarthy, *The Crossing* (1994).
17 Burgess, *The Cry of the Wolf* (1990); Sedgwick, *The Dark Horse* (2002).
18 The song 'Who's Afraid of the Big Bad Wolf?' (by Frank Churchill and Ann Ronell) appears in Disney's *The Three Little Pigs* (1933).
19 'It bursts out you in almost every film theatre; the radio hurls it in your direction; try to escape from it by adjourning to a speakeasy and some unfortunate alcoholic will begin to sing it at you' (Richard Watts Jr, *New York Herald Tribune* film critic, quoted in Gabler, *Walt Disney*, p. 183).

20 Gabler, p. 185.
21 Krasniewicz, *Walt Disney*, p. 63.
22 See, for example, Medoff, 'Was Walt Disney Antisemitic?'.
23 Cocks, *The Wolf at the Door*, pp. 33–9.
24 'Room 237'.
25 Cocks, p. 38.
26 Segal, 'It's Back'.
27 'This Is Uncanny'.
28 Arnds, *Lycanthropy in German Literature*, pp. 122–50.
29 Waite, *Hitler*, pp. 163–5. See Freud, 'From the History of an Infantile Neurosis'.
30 The original saying is thought to have been 'keep the wolf from the gate' and dates from at least 1470, appearing in Hardyng, *The Chronicle of John Hardyng*, ed. by Ellis, p. 181.
31 *Blitz Wolf* (1942).
32 Cocks, p. 40.
33 Defonseca, *Misha*.
34 Bhattacharjee, 'A Pack of …?'.
35 Shields, 'Adopted by Wolves?'.
36 Kosinski, *The Painted Bird*; Wilkomirski, *Fragments*; Messenger, *Hannah*; Rosenblat, *Angel at the Fence*.
37 Wiesel, *Night*; Wiesel, *Legends of Our Time*, p. viii.
38 'Misha Defonseca: tricher avec les loups'.
39 Aroles, 'L'énigme des enfants loups', Loup.org.
40 *Ibid.*
41 Aroles, *Marie-Angélique*.
42 Neary, '"Dog Boy"'; Osborn, 'Siberian Boy'.
43 See Newton, *Savage Girls and Wild Boys*.
44 Sendak, *Where the Wild Things Are*.
45 'Save Western Wildlife'; 'Save Western Wildlife Is a Terrorist Organization'.
46 Le Dauphiné Libéré, 'Franck Michel explique pourquoi il a tué le loup'.
47 Goldenberg, 'Montana and Idaho'.
48 Walsh, *Knowledge of Angels*.
49 Freud, *Civilisation and Its Discontents*, p. 23.
50 *Ibid.*, p. 29.
51 Sam George grapples with the concept of the 'state of nature' and its relationship to wolf children and fictionalised accounts such as Kipling's in Chapter 3 below.
52 Kipling, 'The Law of the Jungle', in *The Second Jungle Book*, in *The Jungle Books*, ed. by Robson, lines 1–4.

2

'MAN IS A WOLF TO MAN': WOLF BEHAVIOUR BECOMING WOLFISH NATURE[1]

Garry Marvin

Wolves, and their behaviours, have always generated strong emotions among the peoples whose societies and cultures intersect with them. They have been admired as powerful and efficient hunters by peoples who live, at least in part, by hunting the same wild animals as they do. However, they have been reviled by pastoralists and other husbanders of domestic livestock whose animals become subject to wolf predation. Equally divided are the responses of different peoples in terms of the threats that wolves are perceived to pose to their own lives. Those who live among wild animals and live by hunting them do not seem to fear that they will be hunted by wolves; although they might be wary of their attention. The powerful fear of wolves attacking people emerged in cultures in which spaces of human habitation were conceptually, perceptually and physically established as separate from the wild. Wolves lived out there, in the uncontrolled wild lands, places from which they might emerge to kill people or where they waited for those who had to enter or traverse those spaces.[2] Werewolves, the monstrous creatures formed out of the human imaginings of wolves, emerged in such societies and cultures; specifically, in the ancient Greek and Roman worlds and then again in medieval and early modern Western Europe. These imaginings were underpinned by, and given cultural sense by, the perceptions of, and attitudes towards, the predatory behaviour of wolves and what was thought to drive their killing. A general theme, throughout this chapter, is that the behaviour of wolves, and particularly their predation, is not simply regarded as a natural, and necessary, part of their social world, but it is construed, by humans, as a moral ecology, and the human judgements of the morality of that ecology construct the nature of wolves.

In order to understand more fully how the werewolf emerged it is necessary to turn to wolves themselves and their behaviours in particular environments and landscapes. However, there is an immediate set of issues with the phrase 'wolves themselves'. When and how can wolves ever be themselves? This has two key elements: that which wolves do amongst themselves to maintain and proliferate their lives – worlds of their own concerns – and how their presence and their worlds are thought about by people who have their own concerns about wolves. I suggest, and will elaborate later, that wolves have never been ignored or left to be themselves.

Perhaps the only way of knowing or understanding them as themselves is when they are physically distant from the daily lives of people. But, even then, any attempt to know them requires human observers who have a close interest in them – wolf scientists, for example. One might imagine these as unobtrusive observers in a wilderness, uninhabited by people, where wolves live and interact with other wolves and predate on other wild creatures. It might be tempting to read the observations, descriptions and analyses of wolf social ecology as accounts of wolves living truly wolfly lives when and where they are free of, or uninterrupted by, intruding humans. Rigorous and carefully crafted field studies do offer insights into the worlds of wolves but, as documents of scientific procedures, understandings and interpretations they are part of a cultural practice – science. Scientific accounts are based on interests and concerns for understanding, among other things, predation and hunting behaviour; reproduction, family structures and pack size; use of territories; conflicts within and between packs; intra- and extra-pack communication; generally, the social ecology of wolves in particular places and what is going on with them and between them in their worlds. As good scientists, different wolf scientists will have different views and interpretations of all the elements that make up wolf worlds but what they are all constructing is *Canis lupus*, a particular creature; the wolf of science. However rigorous and wide-ranging such socioecological studies, they do have a limitation in terms of issues relating to 'wolves themselves'. They are accounts of how wolves are in the world, but they do not, and perhaps cannot, because of the limitations of humans entering the perceptual and communicative worlds of wolves, the subjective world of wolves, offer accounts of how it is to be them as themselves.[3]

Those of us in the humanities and social sciences who are interested in wolves should, I believe, pay close attention to such accounts for they tell us a great deal in their foregrounding of the animals as they are away from humans. However, I suggest that they should not be regarded as neutral, pure or independent bench marks for what wolves are and how they behave. Perhaps lurking here are the terms 'natural' and 'naturally' attached to, and defining, such behaviours; the characteristics of wolves when not impinged on, or intruded on, by humans. This understanding of 'natural' is, however, problematic.[4]

Canis lupus is certainly a wolf in terms of biology, zoology and scientific taxonomy, but it is only one on a spectrum of wolves, all of which are very real to those who encounter them and who configure them in specific social and cultural contexts. As the historian Erica Fudge has commented, 'Humans do not live with biological creatures as much as they live with beings constructed within human cultural frames' and the real creature, at least for them, is the creature they culturally construct and live with.[5] The simplistic scenario I imagined above, with wolves living in a wilderness with unobtrusive human observers, is not one that captures how wolves have been in the world, in much of their ranges, in historical times. When the lives of wolves intersect with those of people they immediately acquire a cultural history as well as a natural history. The *Canis lupus* of the scientists is not the same creature as the wolf for the livestock farmer, for example. I believe it is essential to understand the images and representations of wolves, their social and cultural constructions, because these *are* the wolf for different people. I suggest that there is no such creature as a real or true wolf, an essential wolf. Wolf scientists often speak of the cultural misunderstandings of wolves but apparent misunderstandings from one perspective are understandings from another. Here we are back to issues of 'themselves'. Different cultural configurations and constructions of wolves do not emerge from an attempt to understand wolves in and of themselves but rather as a response to what happens when wolves draw close to, and intrude into, human concerns.

However, before exploring such concerns, it is worth making a comment on an aspect of the predation of wolves on wild animals because this has helped shape attitudes to wolves generally. Wolves, as carnivorous creatures, need the flesh of other animals to survive, and they are also pack animals, hunting together. Unlike cats, which can leap on to, hold and bring down large prey with their sharp claws, wolves do not have sharp retractable claws and must rely only on their teeth to immobilise their prey. Once members of the pack have fixed on a particular animal, they attempt to hold on to it with their teeth in any way possible while avoiding the dangers of kicking legs, sharp hooves and potentially lethal horns or antlers. A wolf kill, particularly of a large animal, is often a prolonged one, with pack members biting into, and eating into, the soft underbelly of the animal before it is dead (see Figure 2.1).[6]

Such killing is, from one perspective, that of wolf ecology, merely natural behaviour, the necessary behaviour of creatures that must kill in order to live. However, from another perspective it is often represented as ferocious and vicious. Such emotive terms seem to relate to a judgement as to the inner nature of wolves, that they are excessively aggressive in their manner of obtaining food and deliberately seek to cause suffering to their prey. Here their manner of predation is characterised and represented in affective terms rather than in terms of efficacy; their behaviour is construed in terms of morality.

In his *Natural History: General and Particular* (1749–88), Georges-Louis Leclerc, Comte de Buffon, described the wolf as 'dastardly', a 'rapacious creature' which 'mangles and devours its prey'. He notes that, although a young wolf can be tamed, 'with age, he resumes his ferocious character and, returns, with the first opportunity to his savage state'.[7] He concludes his particular natural

2.1 Wolf predation on elk

history of the wolf by condemning it as a creature that is 'consummately disagreeable; his aspect is base and savage, his voice dreadful, his odour insupportable, his disposition perverse, his manners ferocious; odious and destructive when living, and, when dead, he is perfectly useless'.[8] Theodore Roosevelt branded the wolf as a 'black-hearted criminal' and 'the arch type of ravin, the beast of waste and desolation'.[9] Roosevelt might perhaps, have been using the term 'ravin', a fierce and frightening form of being ravenous from hunger, from a biblical source where, in Genesis, Jacob describes his son: 'Benjamin shall ravin *as* a wolf; in the morning he shall devour the prey, and at night he shall divide the spoil'.[10]

For William Hornaday, the first director of the New York Zoological Park, a zoologist and a concerned conservationist, the wolf, because of its character and behaviour, should have no place in the wild landscapes of America. His condemnation and denunciation of them was as fierce as the ferocity he attributed to them. 'Of all the wild creatures in North America none are more despicable than wolves. There is no depth of meanness, treachery, or cruelty to which they do not cheerfully descend.'[11] His opinion had not changed in a later text when wolves were judged, universally, to be 'the most degenerate and unmoral mammal species on earth'.[12] Once again, there is here a strong sense that wolves are motivated by ill intention, rather than driven out of necessity by hunger, or that the hunger of wolves is unnatural.

As a general point, I suggest that the wolf has not only been named for its teeth (*canis*/canine), but its teeth, related to killing, have been a major element in its cultural representations. It was not until well into the twentieth century that wolf scientists began to reveal the complexities of the social lives of wolves, their co-operative behaviour in raising offspring, the intricacies of their systems of communication and the richly multifaceted nature of wolf ways.[13] However, for as long as people have been concerned about wolves it has been killing that has been at the centre of such concerns, and wolves are reduced to nothing more than, or nothing less than, dangerous predators.

In Western Europe, the birthplace and the hunting grounds of werewolves, wolves have always lived in close proximity to, or across, lands of human habitation and human use. A significant part of this use has been for pasturing domesticated animals and it is here, and in this context, that a particular set of representations of wolves has been created. These representations cannot be understood simply in terms of human–wolf relations. Rather they need to be understood in terms of the relationships between humans, wolves and other animals. In regimes of domestication humans began to care for animals, for example providing them with food, water and shelter, in ways very different from humans and wild animals in hunting societies. Importantly such animals became the property of particular people and part of that notion of property involved protection. They had to be protected from other people who might seek to steal them, and from wild animals that might prey on them.

In the context of Western Europe, in historical times, there have been few large carnivores that could predate on livestock – foxes, bears, lynx and wolves – and it was the latter that were the most feared, in particular because they were pack animals.[14] When wolves turned their predator attentions to livestock such as sheep and cattle they often moved into flocks and herds and injured or killed many animals at a time without consuming all of them. This was because domestic animals had lost the instincts of defence of their originally wild counterparts or because they were enclosed and could not flee. In the mêlée of panicking animals, wolves might snap and tear at many of them. Wolves could not do otherwise but the owners of livestock thought such behaviour to be evil, greedy and unnatural. In a sense this *was* unnatural predation because humans cut down forests where wolves preyed on wild animals to create fields and pastures in which they developed the systems of amassing difficult-to-protect groups of animals in territories where wolves lived. Wolves merely took the opportunity of the potential for feeding that they encountered. However, this was construed as unacceptable intrusion into human concerns and wolves became thieves that needed to be found and punished. Unlike the case of human thieves, where the individuals responsible for a crime were punished, here the entire species became a collective of thieves and was punished. Across Europe there were campaigns to eradicate wolves. They were hunted, trapped and snared, and poisoned, and bounties were paid to encourage their killing. Such was the campaign against wolves that their numbers were severely reduced by the eighteenth century and wolves were virtually extirpated from their Western European ranges during the nineteenth century.[15]

In the pastoral European context, the wolf very early came to be given a complex character that has had deep and long cultural resonances and implications for how wolves have been responded to and treated. I have touched on the notion of an inner ferocity. To that were added the elements of duplicity and treachery and a related evil nature. Out of the wolf humans created the Big Bad Wolf of folklore, legend, story and literature; a humanly created wolf from which wild wolves have not, until recently, and only in some contexts, been able to escape.[16] Here I will touch on just two examples of duplicity and evil in terms of how they link to the imaginings related to werewolves.

A number of the fables of Aesop feature wolves. In many the focus is on the dissembling nature of the wolf as it attempts to enter the worlds of humans and their domesticated animals. Domesticated animals had been separated from the wild and were not meant to be subject to the predations of wild animals. In one tale a wolf meekly follows a flock of sheep, making no attempt to attack them. The shepherd begins to believe that the wolf is actually acting as a protector of the flock (see Figure 2.2). So great is his misplaced trust that he goes to the city, leaving the sheep in the care of the wolf. At this point, 'The wolf saw its chance and, falling on the sheep tore most of them to pieces'.[17] In another, a shepherd raises a wolf cub with his dogs. If a wolf attacked and took a sheep, the wolf-dog would set off in pursuit with the other dogs. However, if they could not keep up with it, the wolf-dog would continue until he found the predatory wolf and then, 'like the wolf he was – shared the plunder with him'.[18] In this story the wolf-dog is sometimes even more treacherous, killing sheep and sharing them with the dogs, thus corrupting them. In a final example, wolves approach the dogs of a shepherd; they claim that there is no real difference between them, except that they, the wolves, live in freedom, whereas the dogs were merely chained and collared slaves. They suggest that the dogs relinquish the care of the flock to them so that they might 'share them between us and gorge ourselves'.[19] When they allow the wolves into the fold they are immediately killed by their so-called brothers. In these tales dogs emerge as potentially ambiguous in terms of their relatedness to wolves just as wolves are ambiguous as potential dogs.

In such tales Aesop uses the fears of the predations and dangers of wolves within a pastoral society to create a creature through which to tell his tales of morality. The wolf, as a character, is created out of the behaviour of wolves, and it is bound into systems of representation which then feed back into how actual wolves were perceived and responded to: a feedback loop of behaviour, representation, judgement and response.

As a speculative, although hopefully a related, aside, it is intriguing how wolves and dogs are brought into juxtaposition here. Domestic dogs emerged, in complex, evolutionary ways, from wolves and, through processes of domestication, became closely associated with humans in a variety of ways – for hunting,

2.2 Gustave Doré, *Wolf Turned Shepherd*

guarding and companionship. Such creatures are not bred to fulfil their own natures, rather they are bred to fulfil the needs of their human owners. Perhaps part of the concern about wolves is that, although in appearance they are doglike, wolves are un-doglike in their behaviour. Whereas dogs are bred to be docile and unthreatening and should wait to be fed by humans, the wolf is the opposite of that: it is wild and threatening and it takes food from humans. They behave in ways that a dog should not. Humans have bred out qualities of wildness in their domestic dogs, and the continuing wildness of their ancestors becomes disturbing. In a sense wolves are responded to as lapsed dogs, or ancestors of dogs that have fallen from grace because of the threat they are perceived to pose: they violate the established cultural codes that bind humans and dogs. The reverse is also true: the risk that the wolf still lurks within the dog.

Returning to a more central theme, that of the duplicitous wolf and defenceless sheep, in the fables of Aesop the wolf is represented as disguising its intentions through dissembling speech or behaviour. Neither shepherds nor their dogs should be deceived by such ploys. They should know that wolves seek to turn sheep into prey but they must overcome the defences and means of protection that humans should have set. The wolf is present as a wolf in the tales, it can be seen in wolfish form, and humans and their dogs should know what all wolves intend and should not be deceived by their guile. It is the New Testament of the Christian Bible that offers a perhaps more disturbing wolf, the wolf that does not appear as a wolf, the wolf in disguise, the wolf in sheep's clothing.[20]

Here again the context is one of a pastoral society in which people would have a sense of the threat of wolf predations to shepherds and their flocks. Jesus, as in the case of Aesop, uses the wolf to illustrate a set of warnings. His followers are as vulnerable to attack as are sheep are to wolves. Jesus offers the naturalistic image of the shepherd whose duty it is to protect his sheep. The metaphorical image is that Jesus is just such a good shepherd who is there to protect his human flock from harm. He is there for them as they engage with the world but here they are 'as sheep in the midst of wolves'.[21] Here, though, the danger is that which wolflike people pose to other people. He warns, 'Beware of false prophets, which come to you in sheep's clothing, but inwardly they are ravening wolves'.[22] Unlike the wolves in the tales of Aesop, here the dangerous wolf is disguised and the human flock must be alert to the person who might appear to be one of them, a docile sheep among other sheep, but who is actually a predator who seeks to do them harm. Once again we have wolves that are 'ravening', unacceptable, excessive and unnatural, rather than being driven by normal animal hunger. Here the wolf is drawn into a human moral universe. Jesus uses an image that people would understand and respond to. Wolves were already perceived as dangerous, threatening and ill-intentioned creatures.

Wicked people are then seen to be like wolves but that human wickedness is then played back on to the wolf and its image as an essentially, naturally, wicked creature is ratcheted up and reinforced.

The image of the wolf in sheep's clothing is, at one level, an animal one; an animal covering itself with the skin of another to disguise itself. However, Jesus is not actually referring to the manner in which wolves prey on sheep and the image is, therefore, more than animal. All Jesus needs from wolves themselves is that they do prey on sheep and that this must be protected against. He does not offer, for example, a wolf in deer's clothing to comment on its ways of predation. It is domestic predation that is wrong and the image of the wolf in sheep's clothing can work only in that context.

The wolf in sheep's clothing is dangerous because it appears not to be, but it is scarcely fearsome, that is the point, and what is needed is an awareness that things are not what they seem. The wolf, revealed beneath its disguise, can be dealt with as a troublesome predatory carnivore. It is interesting that many older images of how such a wolf is dealt with show shepherds standing next to a tree, from a branch of which a wolf has been hanged with its head clearly protruding from its sheep skin (see Figure 2.3). These are illustrations of executions of criminals, acts of punishment and retribution rather than the

2.3 *A Wolf in Sheep's Clothing*, after Francis Barlow

simple killing of an unwanted pest.[23] In terms of an image relating to dangerous people, the disguise is at the level of surface, as clothes are, and can easily be separated, stripped away. Here the wolf does not transform itself into a sheep; it does not have a dual wolfly-sheeply nature. It is what it is and remains as such – dangerous but always itself – a wolf.

My focus has been on the responses of wolf attacks on other animals but there is a long history of fear of potential and actual wolf attacks on humans and the horror of humans becoming prey to, and food for, wild animals. Natural wolves might prey on humans but even more disturbing, in some cultures and at particular times, is that attacks on humans might be from unnatural wolves – werewolves. Here I do not want to venture far into the territories of my colleagues in this volume who are familiar with the ways of these creatures and responses to them. However, I would like to offer a few comments about these wolves and their relationships with natural wolves. At the time of the emergence of werewolves in Europe, the late Middle Ages and the early modern period, there were other carnivores in the landscapes – bears, foxes, lynx and other wild cats: these were predators on wild animals and domesticated livestock but none of them came to be regarded as unnaturally ferocious, wicked and dangerous as did the wolf. It was only the wolf that was imbued with such a character that people could turn to when they sought to make sense of what were regarded as unnatural attacks on animals or purportedly wild animal attacks on people. Such attacks were seen as monstrous, but people did not seek to explain them in terms of the predations of a monster, in the sense of a mythical or imaginary creature. Rather, they turned to a natural creature that was already thought of as being unnatural. However, the wolf in its behaviour is not beastly, a term that is critical of animal behaviour, it is simply wolfly, but humans might be. In the context of the human, beastly refers to behaviour that is inappropriate for a human, expressed in terms of an animality that is not actually shared with other animals.

A key difference between the wolf in sheep's clothing and the werewolf is in terms of the notion of disguise. With the wolf in sheep's clothing it is the wolf that instigates the subterfuge and it is an animal–animal process in the sense both of the wolf pretending to be another animal and of the wolf, in that disguise, seeking to kill other animals. The sheeply wolf does not attempt to attack humans. Also, there is no sense of a transformation. As noted above, the wolf here is still a wolf even though it is pretending to be something different. Pretence is important here. However, with the werewolf the notion of disguise is more complex because it involves a transformation of bodily form and, to some extent, of character. But the werewolf is not pretending, it attempts to disguise itself when in human form but it is, always, a werewolf. Unlike the wolf in sheep's clothing, the werewolf is a human who is the instigator, willingly or unwillingly, of the transformation into animal form. Importantly, werewolves are not wolves that become human in order to do harm, but humans who transform and take on the culturally perceived character of wolves. Here there is also an important element of inside and outside in terms of cultural spaces. The wolf in sheep's clothing is an animal that attacks from outside. From the wilderness it attempts to enter the human world of the flock and the sheepfold. The werewolf is altogether more disturbing; it lurks within human society but has a wildness that cannot be seen. Crucially, the 'were' (the human) and the wolf cannot be separated because they are one. In either manifestation they are the same creature merely turned inside out or outside in. Each transformation is a manifestation of that which is within, a singular creature, revealing different aspects of its nature.

My comments on the nature of werewolves are thin and refer only to something I think is fundamental about the creature – its elements of the wolf and the human. There is no such creature as a generic werewolf. Werewolves are creatures of particular societies, cultures and times. However, I would like to suggest that their animal nature is configured in terms of how wolves themselves are configured in the cultures where werewolves live. The same would apply to their human aspect and how human nature is configured in different societies, cultures and times; but that is beyond my writ.

My only exposure to these creatures is in literature from Greek and Roman times and up to the early twentieth century. In this long history in Western Europe wolves were generally feared and reviled and the hatred of them is revealed in the very successful attempts to extirpate them from both domesticated and wild landscapes. However, during the twentieth century the wolf gained new champions. Ethological studies of wolves revealed their significance for the flourishing of ecosystems and with the rise of environmental movements the wolf was revalued, as the wild, in all its forms, was revalued. The new wolves that emerged were regarded as necessary in ecological terms and numinous for what they represented about nature. Once again, wolves in themselves became creatures configured in terms of new cultural and social concerns. Across the century new werewolves appeared in literary and cinematic forms that embodied and expressed concerns about human nature and the wild and what, to humans, was a wolf. As the doyen of wolf biologists, L. David Mech, eloquently puts it, 'The wolf is neither a saint nor a sinner except to those who want to make it so'.[24]

In Western Europe wolves are reappearing across the physical landscapes from which they have been absent, often for more than a century. Wolves from Italy moved into France in the 1990s; in Switzerland a wolf appeared in 1995 and in 1998 so did one in Germany. In other countries wolves were later arrivals – in Belgium and the Netherlands in 2011 and in Denmark in 2013.[25] However, they are also emerging in social, cultural and political landscapes, landscapes that are very different from those when they were last present. Into such spaces they bring with them their history, not only their natural history but also their cultural history. Or, as perhaps it might be better expressed, such histories are waiting for them. For some people, for example livestock owners, farmers and hunters, this is certainly not a rewilding that is to be welcomed for it brings with it new fears of, and struggles with, wolf predation and return of an old nature that had been previously brought under proper, human, control. For others, a perhaps more disparate group of conservationists, ecotourists and animal watchers, these are returns that both represent and symbolise a newly authentic nature and redeemed wild.[26] The first group seeks legislative means to halt wolf re-emergence or at least to restrict it. The second also seeks such measures to ensure their continued protection and wolves' rights to exist in their new territories.[27] New narratives, and contested opinions, will also emerge about the ways of these new wolves but, from my social constructivist perspective, it is impossible to discover a true wolf lurking within them, or between them. Karen Jones comments, on the contested positions of science and literature in terms of their claims about wolves, that richer and more inclusive insights might be generated if we adopted the position that

> *all* wolf tales reflect the trappings of contemporary society. As such, the focus of existing scholarship on the diametric oppositions of 'science' and 'sentiment' overlooks a vital point ... by admitting the limits to 'knowing the animal', we allow for the existence of agency in the non-human world and open up to the possibility of a fuller and more provocative deconstruction of wolf tales. Such a project demands acceptance, from both the storyteller and the scientist, that while we might aspire to 'know' the wolf, we can never crawl beneath its skin.[28]

Once again, back to the wolf and its skin and the different potential for what is within.

The wolf has always been a creature too powerful for humans to ignore. Wolves have lives that are normal or natural to them but their fate has always been that these lives are also lived within human cultures and history – something from which they cannot escape.

Notes

1 '*Homo homini lupus est*' (after Plautus). Many thanks to Sam George and Bill Hughes for their careful reading, and suggestions for improvement, of an early version of this chapter. Also, thanks to Kaja Franck and Stephanie Schwandner-Sievers for their invaluable suggestions.

2 As a social anthropologist, my perspectives are drawn from anthropological literature on human–wolf relations or from an anthropological reading of historical and conservation literature on these relations. Ideas relating to how wolves are drawn into human cultures were developed during an ethnographic research project on

how Albanian shepherds respond to wolves (see Marvin, 'Wolves in Sheep's (and Other's) Clothing').

3   However, for a rich encyclopaedic account of wolf worlds, see Mech and Boitani, eds, *Wolves*.
4   As Raymond Williams commented, 'Nature is perhaps the most complex word in the language' (*Keywords*, p. 129). My particular orientation towards nature and understandings of nature is firmly within social constructivist perspectives. See for example, Burningham and Cooper, 'Being Constructive'; Coates, *Nature*; Evernden, *The Social Creation of Nature*; Franklin, *Nature and Social Theory*; and Macnaghten and Urry, *Contested Natures*.
5   Fudge, Book review of Brantz, *Beastly Natures*.
6   For a close set of analyses of the reports of specific wolf hunts, see Mech, Smith, and McNulty, *Wolves on the Hunt*, and, for an analysis of how wolf killing is represented in a popular form, the magazine *National Geographic*, see Kalof 'The Shifting Iconography of Wolves'.
7   Buffon, *Natural History*, vol. v, p. 195.
8   *Ibid.*, p. 210.
9   Roosevelt, *The Wilderness Hunter*, p. 386. For a detailed account of aspects of such representations, see Jones, *Wolf Mountains*, especially pp. 15–26.
10 Genesis 49:27.
11 Hornaday, *The American Natural History*, p. 53.
12 Hornaday, *The Minds and Manners of Wild Animals*, p. 162.
13 For an early formative study, originally published in 1944, see Murie, *The Wolves of Mount McKinley*, and the hugely influential text on the ecology and behaviour of wolves, originally published in 1970, Mech, *The Wolf*.
14 For a superb exploration of wolves in the Middle Ages in Europe, see Pluskowski, *Wolves and the Wilderness*.
15 Marvin, *Wolf*, pp. 81ff.
16 As examples, see Zipes, *The Trials*, and Mitts-Smith, *Picturing the Wolf*.
17 Aesop, 'Misplaced Confidence', in *Fables of Aesop*, trans. by Handsford, p. 34.
18 'Trying to Make a Silk Purse from a Sow's Ear', in *Aesop*, p. 36.
19 'The Wages of Treachery', in *Aesop*, p. 29.
20 Aesop does actually have such a wolf but the notion of disguise is not much focused on in a very short tale. A wolf puts on a sheepskin to get into the fold. In the evening the shepherd decides to slaughter a sheep to eat and it is the sheep-wolf he kills ('A Case of Mistaken Identity', in *Aesop*, p. 38).
21 Matthew 10:16.
22 Matthew 7:15.
23 Intriguingly, when Peter Stumpf, the notorious werewolf was executed in Bedburg, Germany, in 1589, a pole with a carved wooden head of a wolf was erected, 'to show unto all men the shape wherein he executed those cruelties' ('Stubbe Peter:

original trial transcript, 1590', in Otten, ed., *A Lycanthropy Reader*, pp. 69–76 (p. 76)). The display was topped with the head of the werewolf.

24 Mech, 'Is Science in Danger of Sanctifying the Wolf?', p. 143.

25 For detailed information about the status and distribution of wolves in Europe, see Reinhardt, *Current Situation*, and the European Commission Report (2013) on wolves: European Commission, *Status, Management and Distribution*; see especially pp. 40ff.

26 For richly detailed accounts and nuanced analyses of recently emerged wolves in France, see Buller, 'Safe from the Wolf'; and in Norway, Skogen, Krange and Figari, *Wolf Conflicts*.

27 In a European Union directive in 1992, wolves were classified as being of 'community interest', requiring protection and conservation (*Habitats Directive: 92/r43 EEC of 21 May.*

28 Jones, 'Writing the Wolf', p. 201.

3

WHEN WOLVES CRY: WOLF-CHILDREN, STORYTELLING AND THE STATE OF NATURE

Sam George

Stories of human children suckled by wolves have fascinated us down the centuries. The role literature plays in mythologising such children reveals much about shifting ideas of animality and humanity, and of narrative itself. In this chapter, I focus on eighteenth-century encounters with wild children, their representation in the poetry of the Romantic period and the legacy of this in accounts of the twentieth century (particularly following the discovery of the wolf-girls Amala and Kamala in 1920) and the present day. I interrogate the representation of wolf-children in relation to John Locke's *tabula rasa* theory and Jean-Jacques Rousseau's concept of the 'state of nature', together with debates that emerged around these concerning native innocence and the Christian doctrine of original sin. Wolf-children in historical accounts rarely acquire language (or are limited to a few words); I demonstrate how literature constructs a history for these children through repeated storytelling, granting them a voice.

The sound of wolves howling is commonly associated with unsettling, uncanny or sublime moments in literature and film.[1] By contrast, Ted Hughes's poem 'Life after Death' recalls the consoling nature of the wolves' cry during a moment of absolute grief for the poet.[2] Hughes is remembering the suicide of his then wife Sylvia Plath. Consumed by sorrow, Hughes and his young children are 'comforted by wolves' (l. 31), howling nearby from London Zoo.[3] Wild nature is benevolent: 'in spite of the city / Wolves consoled us' (ll. 34–5).

As the raw emotion is unleashed, we discover that the wolves are singing for the poet's two motherless children. The wolf voices become humanised, embracing the human, apparently in empathy:

> The wolves lifted us in their long voices.
> They wound us and enmeshed us
> In their wailing for you, their mourning for us,
> They wove us into their voices.

(ll. 41–4)

Yet there is a certain collapse of humanity, as the poet's individuality merges 'into the folk-tale', in the very act of voicing grief, becoming mythical and perhaps even becoming wolf:

> As my body sank into the folk-tale
> Where the wolves are singing in the forest.
> For two babes, who have turned, in their sleep,
> Into orphans
> Beside the corpse of their mother.
>
> (ll. 46–50)

Animal-parented children are common in folktales, and Hughes seeks solace in the narrative tradition of wolves and other animals becoming surrogate parents to orphaned human children.[4] Against the grain of the familiar image of the wolf as savage marauder, the wolf here protects and nurtures. The wolves' howling voices are not, as conventionally, an ominous threat but a sympathetic presence allied to human sensibilities.

Wolf-children

The mythical history of wild beasts as the nurses of abandoned human children is attested to in Shakespeare's *The Winter's Tale* (1609–11):[5]

> Come on, poor babe
> Some powerful spirit instruct the kites and ravens
> To be thy nurses! Wolves and Bears, they say,
> Casting their savageness aside, have done
> Like offices of pity.[6]

Myths and narratives of benevolently parental animals are legion. The most famous of these are the Bear-boys of Lithuania (found 1661, 1694). The Lithuanian woods were full of bears, and Bernard Connor, an English doctor, recounts the story of a boy of about ten years old who walked on all fours and had been brought to the court, having been raised by bears (*History of Poland*, pp. 388–96); see Figure 3.1. The civilisation of Rome mythically discovers its origins in the story of Romulus and Remus, the twin brothers who were suckled by a she-wolf until a shepherd and his wife fostered them to manhood (Figure 3.2).[7]

But there are many accounts of wolf-children in the modern era which claim to be truthful, though these too become seeds of fictional narrative.[8] 'Wolf-children' has become a catch-all phrase for all wild or feral children, fictional or otherwise.[9] An interesting reversal takes place in such accounts: the she-wolf is increasingly humanised, whereas the human 'wolf' child is likened to the animal. Thus what is striking is the way the wolf is redeemed, yet this newly humanised wolf co-exists with the image of the animal as cunning and cruel.[10]

3.1 'The Bear Boy of Lithuania'

Garry Marvin and Barry Lopez have identified a history of 'lupophobia', and 'lupicide' as evidence of humankind's fear and persecution of the wolf.[11] The naturalist Georges-Louis Leclerc, Comte de Buffon, author of the 36 volumes of the *Histoire naturelle* (1749–88), is typical of the modern era. Here the wolf is 'in every way offensive, a savage aspect, a frightful howl, an insupportable odour, a perverse disposition … he is hateful while living, and useless when dead'.[12] Against such preconceptions, where the slaughter and eventual extinction (in Britain) of wolves evoked little sympathy, nineteenth-century theses on wolf-children suggest an alternative perspective. W.H. Sleeman's *An Account of*

3.2 Wolf Suckling Romulus and Remus, Siena Duomo, Tuscany, Italy

Wolves Nurturing Children in Their Dens (1852) and Robert Sterndale's *Natural History of the Mammalia of India and Ceylon* (1884) humanise and dignify the wolf.[13] These texts are important in being a major influence on Kipling.[14] Sterndale's writing is unusual in that he seeks to make it known that 'stories have been related of wolves sparing and suckling young infants, which, if properly authenticated, will bring the history of Romulus and Remus within the bounds of probability' (p. 233). Inspired by such accounts of the wolves and other mammals of India nurturing children in their dens, Rudyard Kipling first recreated this tradition as fiction in a modern novelistic form in *The Jungle Book* (1894) and *The Second Jungle Book* (1895). Kipling's orphaned protagonist Mowgli is a 'man cub' adopted by a Wolf Mother (Figure 3.3).

He grows up with the pack, hunting with his brother wolves (Figure 3.4), and learning the Law of the Jungle. This is given in verse and is recited in a sort of sing-song by Baloo, the bear:

> Now this is the Law of the Jungle – as old and as true as the sky;
> And the Wolf that shall keep it may prosper, but the Wolf that shall break it must die.
> As the creeper that girdles the tree-trunk the Law runneth forward and back
> For the strength of the Pack is the Wolf, and the strength of the Wolf is the Pack.[15]

3.3 Mother Wolf defends Mowgli and the wolf-cubs from Shere Khan

'WAKE, LITTLE BROTHER; I BRING NEWS.'

3.4 Mowgli receives news from Gray Brother and is told 'thou wilt not forget that thou art a wolf'

The ennobling of the wolf is continued by the Rev. Singh, the missionary who bore witness to the discovery of the wolf-children Amala and Kamala in India in 1920. In Singh's account, the wolves' benevolence is, in fact, more than human:

> It struck me with wonder. I was simply amazed to think that an animal had such a noble feeling, even surpassing even that of mankind – the highest form of creation – to bestow all the love and affection of a fond and ideal mother on these peculiar beings … to permit them to live and to be nurtured … in this fashion is divine.[16]

But while Singh elevates the wolf, her adopted human offspring are demonised by their would-be rescuers and identified as *Manush-Bagha*, or monstrous 'man ghosts'.[17] Even Singh's description takes on this ambiguity, hesitating before confirming that the creature he sees is human:

> Close after the cubs came the ghost – a hideous looking being – hand, foot and body like a human being; but the head was a big ball of something covering the shoulders and the upper portion of the bust, leaving only a sharp contour of the face visible, and it was human. (p. 5)

Then, this certainty collapses on observing the girls' eyes: 'Close at its heels there came another awful creature exactly like the first, but smaller in size. Their eyes were bright and piercing, unlike human eyes' (p. 5). Yet Singh immediately reaffirms their humanity: 'I at once came to the conclusion that these were human beings' (p. 5). But his associates ascribe a supernatural quality to the children:

> Both of them ran on all fours. My friends … would have killed them if they had not been dissuaded by me … I told them that I was sure that these ghosts were human children … all present … agreed with me except Chunarem. He still maintained that they were not human beings, but *Manush-Baghas*. (p. 6)

The children are removed from the ant mound they had shared with the wolves and placed in a wooden cage, but when the Rev Singh returns the villagers have abandoned the children. The wolf-girls are revived and taken to a nearby orphanage, where they are accepted simply as neglected children. The description of the wolf-children in the Rev. Singh's journal in subsequent years resulted in Amala and Kamala becoming 'the two best known cases of zoanthropy' in the twentieth century; a type of madness involving the delusion of being an animal, with correspondingly altered behaviour.[18] The children walked about on all fours, had a taste for carrion, panted and bared their teeth, suffered from day blindness and spent their days crouched in the shade, or standing motionless with their faces turned to the wall. They livened up at night, howling and groaning and hoping to escape. They lapped up liquids and took their food in a crouching position. The diaries reveal that Singh viewed them through a zoomorphic lens, now employing animal imagery to describe their behaviour: 'They had a powerful instinct and could smell meat or anything from a great distance like animals'. They slept 'like little pigs or dog pups, overlapping one another' (see Figure 3.5); 'They never slept after midnight and used to love to prowl at night fearlessly, unlike human children of that age' (p. 31). Yet this

3.5 Amala and Kamala, overlapping in sleep on a bed of leaves

classification as animal is undermined and falls into uncertainty: 'With a ferocious look she tried to grab [meat], her eyes rolling, jaws moving from side to side, and teeth chattering where she made a fearful growling sound, *neither human or animal*' (pp. 23-4; my italics).

Despite his fascination with their animality, Singh kept the history of Amala and Kamala hidden until they were near death, when it became necessary to explain something of their early life to the doctor who was treating them.[19] Sadly, Amala died on 21 September 1921 and Kamala eight years later on 14 November 1929. Singh's nine-year observation of the children (1920–29), was eventually completed in manuscript in 1933 and published in *Wolf Children and Feral Man* (1942). By this time the story of the girls' history as wolf-children had already broken in the world's press. Singh remained something of an unwilling author who died in 1941, one year before the diaries were released.[20] There were attempts to authenticate the diaries in the publication that followed. An affidavit by the District Judge of Midnapore appears on the title page, to which he has affixed his seal and asserted that 'Singh's truthfulness is absolutely to be relied upon'; the prefatory material claims it is a factual record in regard to 'these authentic feral children' (p. xxii).[21] But this empiricism is already being displaced by an interest in narrative for its own pleasures. A year earlier, the clinical psychologist Arnold Gesell compiled his own narrative interpretation of the life history of Kamala, based on his reading of Singh's manuscript. *Wolf Child and Human Child* (1940) is something of a fictionalised biography which attempts to show a trajectory of Kamala's transition from 'wolf ways' to 'human ways'.[22] Gesell does not waver from his belief in wolf-children: 'there can be no doubt whatever that Amala and Kamala early on in life were adopted by a nursing wolf' (p. xvii). However, Gesell's preface informs readers that 'it will be our task to reconstruct the whole story of Kamala from the evidence in hand. To do this we shall have to summon imagination and even invent a few conjectures to fill the gaps of actual knowledge. But our objective is truth rather than fiction' (p. 2). In just over a decade, following her death, the history of Kamala had been transformed by storytelling and myth. Generous quotations from the *Jungle Book* appear as chapter headings in this book, linking Kamala to the fictional wolf-child, Mowgli: '"Come soon" said Mother Wolf ... listen, child of man, I loved thee more than ever I loved my cubs".'[23] The girls later become known as 'the two Mowglis', the fictionalisation of their history seemingly complete.[24]

Feral children of Enlightenment and Romanticism

Crucially, the scholarly forewords to Singh's diary forge connections to earlier accounts of wild children: the history of 'wild Peter' (1726), Itard's reports on Victor of Aveyron (1801, 1806) and Feuerbach's account of Kasper Hauser

(1833).²⁵ It is these histories to which I now turn, examining how these too became transformed into fiction and poetry. Peter of Hanover (Peter the Wild Boy), a child of around eleven years old, was found living wild in forests in Germany, and Victor of Aveyron, known as 'the Savage of Aveyron', was found living naked in the woods of central France in 1800.

Eighteenth-century scholars seized on feral children, hoping to find clues to problems around education, psychological development, language acquisition, sociability and civilisation. The overlapping, often nascent disciplines of natural philosophy, linguistics, anthropology, medicine were spurred by encounters with wolf-children. Jean-Jacques Rousseau argued that humanity's lost 'state of nature' is to be found 'midway between the stupidity of brutes and the fatal enlightenment of civilised man'.²⁶ Wild children were the living embodiment of this threshold between ignorance and knowledge, animal and human, innocence and experience. They could demonstrate what had been lost in the civilising process and provide a link back to the past, to our ancestors. Earlier, John Locke had imagined the mind at birth as blank, claiming that all knowledge comes to us through experience: 'Let us then suppose the mind to be, as we say, white paper, void of all characters, without any ideas ... Whence has it all the materials of reason and Knowledge? To this I answer, in one word, from *Experience*.'²⁷ This developmental view holds that a child is born a *tabula rasa* or blank slate, awaiting inscription by experience in order to become a rational, knowing subject. It opposed the innatist position that the child's character is predetermined at conception, gifted with certain pre-existent notions and powers. Wild children could be used to test out these theories. What ideas, if any, would they possess having grown up without human contact? The question of Original Sin also surfaces in these debates. Are wild children innocent or full of sin? The orthodox Christian view (the most dominant) held that the child is originally sinful and must therefore be ruthlessly subordinated to authority. This is challenged by the view exemplified in Rousseau that the child is born innocent and is corrupted only through contact with society and its institutions. Rousseau is unwavering in his assertion that 'there is no original sin in the human heart'.²⁸

Peter the Wild Boy

Peter of Hanover was one of the first wild children to capture the eighteenth-century imagination. The recorded details concerning Peter's capture in a forest near Hamelin, Germany, in 1725 vary enormously but his wild origins are constant. One account from 1726 indicates that Peter was aged between eleven and fifteen; was quadrupedal at the time of capture, running about on all fours; and that he must have been raised by wolves, pigs or bears.²⁹ Another, published in the year of his death, 1785, maintains that he was wearing the remains of a shirt and subsisting on acorns, berries and tree bark.[30] He could be restrained only by force; he was eventually persuaded to wear clothes but rather than accept the food he was offered preferred to suck the sap from raw wood.[31]

Remarkably, he was sent to London as a guest of the Royal House of Hanover. The court doctor tried and failed to teach him to speak. Each day courtiers would wrestle him into a green velvet suit and each evening they would try to persuade him into bed but he preferred to curl up alone on the floor in a corner of his room.[32] He never learned to speak more than a few words but could imitate animal sounds; he developed some sensitivity to music. His portrait by William Kent still hangs in Kensington Palace. He is pictured in the green velvet suit that was made for him and is shown clutching acorns and oak leaves, symbolic of his wildness. His cupid bow lips and wild unruly hair are characteristic of descriptions in the written accounts and some fingers on his left hand are fused 'like a duck's foot'.[33] This animalistic characteristic is noted with some excitement.[34] Peter used to stray and so was forced to wear a leather collar with a brass plate bearing the inscription 'Peter the Wild Man of Hanover. Whoever will bring him to Mr Fenn at Berkhamsted shall be paid for their trouble' (Figure 3.6).[35]

Though the collar was meant to prevent him coming to any harm it also suggests that he was regarded as nothing more than a human pet. Those who encountered him often questioned his humanity: 'by his behaviour and want of speech, he seems to be more of the Ouran Outang species than of the human'.[36] This classification was reinforced by natural historians of the day; Peter appears under 'feral man' in the tenth edition of Linnaeus's *Systema naturae* (1758).[37] As a sub-species, he is given his own taxonomical name *juvenis Hannoveranus*.[38]

3.6 Peter's collar, housed at Berkhamsted School

3.7 Peter's grave, St Mary's Church, Northchurch, with the simple inscription 'Peter the Wild Boy, 1785'

He was entrusted to Dr John Arbuthnot, the satirist and physician. Arbuthnot abandoned his instruction after only two months and, with interest waning in the boy, Peter was placed with one of the Queen's chamber-women, and later with a yeoman farmer named James Fenn in Berkhamsted, Hertfordshire, where he lived out his existence on a royal pension as a kind of very old child. He died in 1785, aged seventy-two, and is buried in St Mary's churchyard in Northchurch (Figure 3.7).

After witnessing Peter's long-term failure to become socialised, many writers represented the boy as an archetypal primitive. In *The Spirit of the Laws* (1748), Montesquieu mentions the boy as an example of natural man's innate timidity and ignorance.[39] Rousseau uses wolf-children to illustrate how humans learn through imitation. Thus, having been raised by wolves, such children were necessarily (but not innately) quadrupedal; Peter is used as an example.[40]

In *Mere Nature Delineated* (1726), Daniel Defoe rejects the claims that Peter has been nourished by a she-wolf.[41] He asks instead the question of whether he has a soul: 'his soul is naked; he is but the appearance or shadow of a rational creature, a kind of spectre or apparition' (p. 28). Despite his hesitation over whether Peter is properly human, he argues against those 'who tell us he is nothing but an *idiot*, or what we call a *Natural* ... though he may have some degrees of *idiotism* upon him, yet he seems still to have with it some apparent capacities of being restored or improved' (p. 25).

The Rousseauvian educationalists Maria and Richard Edgeworth in their educational treatise *Practical Education* (1798) recount their psychological observations of Peter and how they were disappointed by his lack of development. Having for several years observed the wild boy, they reported that

> [Peter] had all his senses in remarkable perfection ... he could articulate imperfectly a few words, in particular, *King George*, which words he always accompanied with an imitation of the bells, which rang at the coronation of George the Second; he could in a rude manner imitate two or three common tunes, but without words.[42]

Defoe thought that Peter was educable, despite 'degrees of *idiotism*'; others saw him primarily as an 'idiot'.[43] As the Edgeworths contended: 'Though his head ... resembled that of Socrates, he was an idiot' (1, p. 63).

Johnny the Idiot Boy

Wordsworth's 'The Idiot Boy' from *Lyrical Ballads* (1798) might be read as a poetic dramatisation of these themes of wildness and idiocy that had become attached to Peter; a poem about childhood, innocence, idiocy and the state of nature.[44] Locke had used idiocy critically as a crucial example against theories of innate ideas.[45] Wordsworth sees 'idiots' as sacred and mystical, proclaiming that 'their life is hidden with God'.[46] Shielded from corruption or sin, they are locked into a pure childlike state for ever. In Wordsworth's poem idiocy takes on a new meaning, being sympathetically aligned to nature and to animal experience.

The eponymous 'Idiot Boy', Johnny, is another version of the Rousseauvian child of nature, yet one frozen in a state of innocence and inwardness, and incapable of understanding even the simplest instructions. In the poem Johnny is sent out on his pony to fetch the doctor, but he completely forgets his task, losing his way in the forest after becoming absorbed in his adventure and the moonlit night. His journey can be seen as an education according to nature, after Rousseau.[47] He carries a holly bough instead of a whip, an emblem of his wildness, reminiscent of the depictions of Peter clutching acorns and oak leaves. His intellect is unfavourably compared with that of the pony: 'but then he is a horse that thinks'.[48] He has a kind of language, a burring that merges with bird calls: 'The owlets hoot, the owlets curr / And Johnny's lips they burr, burr, burr' (ll. 114–15), but he cannot communicate any facts. At the end of the poem Johnny is asked where he has been and what he has been doing. His language is figurative and shows him to exist in a timeless space where owls and moon are made one with their daytime equivalents: 'The Cocks did crow to-woo, to-woo/ and the Sun did shine so cold' (ll. 460–1). His dialogue is impressionistic and imitative of animal sounds, reminiscent of Peter. He confuses cocks with owls, the sun with the moon, hot with cold and night with day. His mother's anxious questioning at the end of the poem seems to parody the intellectuals who conversed with Peter the Wild Boy, seeking answers to questions about native innocence, the state of nature and animal/human development.[49]

> 'Tell us Johnny do,
> Where all this long night you have been,
> What you have heard, what you have seen:
> And, Johnny, mind you tell us true.'
>
> (ll. 438–41)

Johnny's confused response is like that of an abandoned wolf-child, and he denies us an answer. Wordsworth puts forth his alternative to the mother's failed instruction, a process that works through nature and isolation in the woods and one that requires a sensory responsiveness, apparent in the highly figurative character of Johnny's language.

Unlike such wolf-children as Amala and Kamala, who rarely experienced a moment's joy, the boy is in a happy state of nature. In this idealised version of events he does have some language; is this still idiocy? In Wordsworth's account Johnny is an innocent, apparently without original sin, suffused with simple contentment. It is useful to compare Peter the Wild Boy and Wordsworth's Johnny to another wolf-child, Victor of Aveyron.[50]

Victor of Aveyron (or the little savage)

Victor is the dark 'Other' of the carefree Romantic child; the representation in poetry of him which I examine is a critique rather than a celebration of the 'state of nature'. Victor was found running about on all fours in the rugged forest region of France, and was first captured in 1798. He escaped back into the forest but was forcibly recaptured by hunters fifteen months later. In 1800, he was taken to a hospice in Aveyron (hence his name) and examined by the French zoologist Pierre Joseph Bonnaterre. Bonnaterre brought him to Paris and placed him in an institute for deaf mutes (he was not in fact deaf, merely unresponsive to the human voice). He disliked sleeping in a bed. His body was covered in scars (noticeably knife wounds to his throat).[51] It was reported in the *Morning Post* that the boy

> lived on potatoes, chestnuts and acorns ... his features are regular but without expression, every part of his body is covered with scars; these scars attest the cruelty of persons by whom, it is presumed, he has been abandoned; or perhaps they are attributable only to the dangers of a solitary existence at a tender age, and in a rude tract of country.[52]

He was later entrusted to Jean-Marc-Gaspard Itard, a French doctor who published a two-part treatise on the wild boy.[53] Itard despaired of the boy's backwardness; as others did in other accounts, he resorted to zoomorphism:

> He seemed not to hear music or the sound of the human voice, though he recognised at once the sound of the chestnut being shelled ... He was more helpless than a chimpanzee and could neither open a door by himself nor climb onto a chair to reach what he wanted. He was as incapable of speech as an animal and uttered only a single, formless sound ... his expressions would change rapidly from a sullen scowl to a curious sneer, a muscular contortion meant to be a smile.[54]

He was taught the elements of table manners and a few words and was later cared for by a nurse, Mme Guerin. He died in 1828.

Wild children like Victor did not respond to touch or the human voice. Itard claimed that Victor was dominated by the bodily, by his appetite for food in particular (and would urinate on the spot); 'his whole existence was a life purely animal'.[55] He never sought anything beyond his basic needs, lacked intellectual curiosity, and could not acquire language. The true history of such children, lacking narrative capacity of their own, is mysterious, promoting speculation over whether their lack of development was brought about by trauma or through isolation in the woods, or both. Victor of Aveyron seems to fit this theory because he was found with scars on his throat as if an attempt had been made on his life. Gesell's account reminds us that wolf-children undergo a multiple trauma through their oscillation between animal and human existence:

> [Kamala] was thrice bereft. She was bereft of human care, when she was carried to a wolf's den; she was bereft of the securities of her wolf life when she was rescued ... she was pathetically bereft of the security of reminiscent kinship when her younger 'sister' Amala died. (p. xvii)

And yet she survived, but, despite her resilience, she was never far from trauma: 'if she were left alone she would retire to the darkest corner, crouch down and remain with her face to the wall'.[56] Such trauma would also find literary representation in Romantic poetry.

Romanticism's alienated wolf-child

As with Wordsworth's 'The Idiot Boy', Victor was depicted in Romantic poetry, but in a manner that dramatised the traumatic alienation of the wolf-child noted above. Mary Robinson's poem 'The Savage of Aveyron' appeared in *Lyrical Tales* (1800), a direct response to Wordsworth and Coleridge's *Lyrical Ballads* of 1798.[57] Robinson was inspired by the reports of the 'wild boy of

Aveyron' in October of that year in *The Morning Post*.[58] Her memoir shows that she had been contemplating the history of Victor, 'the little savage'.[59] Robinson had earned the nickname 'Perdita' (or 'lost one') for her role in Shakespeare's *The Winter's Tale* in 1779; she clearly had an affinity with narratives of abandoned children.[60] The play itself is preoccupied with themes of storytelling alongside those of nature, nursing and culture. Using Victor, Robinson was able to construct a story of the most extreme expression of such abandonment. In her poem the boy has been left to fend for himself in the forest after his mother is murdered by ruffians. In fact, we know nothing about Victor's mother (or any of these wild children's parents). Victor's scars suggest his parents may not have been entirely benevolent (but we do not know). In Robinson's fictional representation of him, he is clearly the victim of appalling violence, still in a state of misery, and wounded even by nature – a creature far from the innocent simplicity and tranquillity of Wordsworth's wild child:

> Chequer'd with scars his breast was seen,
> Wounds streaming fresh with anguish keen,
> And marks where other wounds had been
> Torn by the brambles rude.
>
> (ll. 104–7)

The poem contains much Romantic dramatisation of solitary states (the boy is cast as 'The tenant of that solitude' (l. 109)), ambiguously exploring themes of solitude versus sociability. These are topics that are explored with sensibility in 'All Alone' and 'The Alien Boy' elsewhere in the collection. As with Wordsworth's 'The Idiot Boy', Robinson adopts a narrative form but, again like Wordsworth, one that can only tentatively recover the wild protagonist's story. Johnny cannot wield language in a functional, prosaic way and confuses factual particulars; Robinson's 'savage' can only gesture and utter the single word 'alone'. The narrator essentially constructs a story out of their own solitary state and their imaginative sympathy with the child they find in the forest. But their Romantic sense of and yearning for solitude is shown to amount to nothing and when compared to the boy's entire lifetime of isolation. Thus, proclaiming 'I thought myself alone ... weary of the world', they hear the voice of the child. But it is musical rather than articulate, 'a song – / Of nature's melody' (ll. 66–7), expressing pure emotion in its variations from 'a melancholy tone' (l. 3), through 'loud and sad' (l. 16), 'dulcet' (l. 17) to 'a tone of frantic woe' (l. 18). At this point, the narrator wishes for solitude: 'O! wilds of dreary solitude! / Amid your thorny alleys rude / I wish'd myself – a traveller alone' (ll. 25–7). Variants of the last line close each stanza as a refrain while the imagined tale of the wild child slowly unfolds. From his sign language and tonal vocalisations, the narrator infers that great harm has been done to him by other human beings. As Robinson's poem develops, it attempts to construct a history for the lost wild boy. The poem suggests that the boy's mother has been murdered by 'three barbarous ruffians' and her bones are buried under a blasted oak. From his last human interaction, with his dying mother, he acquires his sole token of linguistic competence: 'From HER the WILD BOY learn'd "ALONE"' (l. 160). This word repeats throughout the poem. The boy is now truly isolated in a way that belittles the narrator's conventional dwelling on solitude. Abandoned to nature, he takes on animalistic characteristics, as observed in other wild child narratives above. His appearance lacks humanity or rationality and he is associated with an asocial, even malignant nature:

> Yet dark and sunken was his eye,
> Like a lorn maniac's, wild and shy,
> And scowling, like a winter sky,
> Without one beaming ray!
>
> (ll. 28–31)

The wild boy tries to tell his story to the traveller, using the word 'alone' and a kind of sign language, leading her to the oak where his mother is buried, pointing at three notches on the trunk of the tree (representing the three ruffians) and upwards towards heaven. Robinson conflates two different accounts of wolf-children in the poem, those of Peter of Hanover and Victor of Aveyron. The boy's body is 'chequer'd with scars' (l. 104), as in real-life accounts of Victor, but he is found wearing the remains of a garment (as in accounts of Peter of Hanover). The 'Lady's vest' (l. 124) he is found wrapped in is evidence of the loss of his mother. Robinson's poem imagines a loving nurturing mother killed by 'barb'rous ruffians' (l .134) from the outside of society, in place of a narrative of familial cruelty in which the parents are the perpetrators of the scars on the boy's body and the cause of his abandonment and isolation in the woods. Thus the wild child's origin may be somewhat sentimentalised, yet Robinson's representation of the wild boy debunks the notion of the 'noble savage' and challenges Romantic concepts of the child of nature. The boy is 'fancy-fraught' (l. 173) as opposed to fancy-free, inhuman and wretched, a forlorn 'maniac' (l. 29) wrenched from companionship and sociability. The poem is a critique rather than a celebration of 'the state of nature' but it is another manifestation of Romanticism's interest in primitive states and wild or feral children. There is nothing here of the idealised or utopian longing found elsewhere in this tragic incarnation of the wild child. Robinson's picture of Victor is closer to that of Philippe Pinel, the foremost physician of the day: he saw an abandoned, mentally defective creature, not the Rousseauvian 'child of nature' that his contemporaries in Paris so eagerly conjured up.⁶¹ Yet Robinson renders this outcast with deep sympathy:

> And could a wretch more wretched be,
> More wild, or fancy-fraught than he,
> Whose melancholy tale would pierce AN HEART
> OF STONE.
>
> (ll. 73–6)

Victor and Peter never acquired language and so could not tell their stories (their memory loss possibly the result of trauma). Kamala would repeat the odd word when prompted, but she never used language in a spontaneous way.⁶² Literature has given the wolf-children a voice, a folk history.⁶³ The state of nature from which we have become expelled and where wolf-children appeared to dwell has eluded us. Since the eighteenth century, that sense of loss has been recompensed by storytelling. This returns us to Hughes's consoling voices where I began; romanticised myths of children raised by wolves reappear as fictions and in poetry, establishing a place:

> Where the wolves are singing in the forest
> For two babes, who have turned, in their sleep,
> Into orphans
> Beside the corpse of their mother.⁶⁴

Here abandonment can be seen as a blessing, the child inhabits an animal world, a gap is bridged, something lost is restored. Narratives of wild children reveal what wolves have taught us about human frailty; they animalise the human, but that is not all: wolf-children are significant because they have the power to redeem the wolf as nurturer and source of cultivation.

Notes

1. See Stacey Abbott, Chapter 4 below.
2. Ted Hughes repeatedly used the symbol of the wolf in his poetry, most notably in *Lupercal* (1960), named after the cave where the wolf-children Romulus and Remus were suckled, and *Wolfwatching* (1989). The howling of wolves at Regent's Park zoo could be heard from the flat in Fitzroy Road, Primrose Hill, where, following her separation from Hughes, Sylvia Plath ended her life in 1963. Hughes drew on the image of the wolf in the poem 'The Howling of Wolves' (eventually published in *Wodwo* (1967)); this was one of only two poems he wrote in the three years following Sylvia's death. For Hughes's wolf imagery, see Skea, 'Wolf-masks'.
3. Hughes, 'Life after Death', *Birthday Letters*, pp. 182–3.
4. Hughes initially studied English at Pembroke College, Cambridge, but in his third year he transferred to anthropology and archaeology, both of which informed his

poetry. His poetry shows his fascination with myth, language and folklore and his debt to Robert Graves's *The White Goddess* (a cult anthropological text he devoured at Cambridge). For a recent appraisal of Hughes and myth, see Robert McCrum's memorial lecture on Hughes reprinted as 'To Hell and Back'.

5   The bear boy also features in Linnaeus and Blumenbach. For a detailed history of the bear boy, see Zingg, 'Feral Man', pp. 204-32. Peter the Wild Boy (found 1725) was linked to both wolves and bears. There is much speculation in the accounts as to which animal raised him. One principal source claims that he could have been adopted by a she-wolf or a sow but that it is most likely to have been a 'She-bear' (*An Enquiry How The Wild Youth*, p. 3).
6   Shakespeare, *The Winter's Tale*, 2.3.222-6, p. 190.
7   Sources for Romulus and Remus include the histories of Livy, Plutarch, Dionysius of Halicarnassus and Tacitus as well as the work of Virgil and Ovid. For a comparative study of sources, see Bremmer, 'Romulus and Remus'.
8   See Lucien Malson's table of recorded cases of children with animal parents in *Wolf Children*, pp. 80-2. A critical field has grown up which is broad and interdisciplinary. Seminal studies include, in addition to Malson, and Singh and Zingg: Candland, *Feral Children*; Newton, *Savage Girls and Wild Boys*; Douthwaite, *The Wild Girl*; and Benzaquén, *Encounters with Wild Children*.
9   In that wolf is the animal most conjured up; 'bear-children' does not have the same resonance.
10 Fairy-tale narratives have a part to play in developing the image of 'the big bad wolf' alongside fables and negative biblical images of wolves. Charles Perrault published his version of Little Red Riding Hood, 'Le Petit Chaperon Rouge', in *Histoires ou Contes du temps passé. Avec Moralités* (Paris: Barbin, 1697). The first English translation is reputed to be Robert Samber, *Histories, or Tales of Past Times. By M. Perrault* (1729). Jacob and Wilhelm Grimm published their version of the tale in *Kinder- und Hausmächen* (Berlin: Realschulbuchhandlung, 1812). The tale was translated into English by Edgar Taylor in *German Popular Stories* (1824-26).
11 See Garry Marvin, 'Lupophobia' and 'Lupicide', in *Wolf*, pp. 35-80; 81-118; and Barry Lopez, 'The Beast of Waste and Desolation', in *Of Wolves and Men*, pp. 137-67.
12 Buffon, *Barr's Buffon*, VI, p. 157.
13 Sleeman, 'An Account of Wolves'; Sterndale, *Natural History*.
14 For Sterndale's influence, see Karlin, 'The Jungle Books: Introduction'. For Sleeman, see Robson, Introduction, Kipling, *The Jungle Book*, p. xv.
15 'The Law of the Jungle', Kipling, *The Jungle Book*, p. 165.
16 Singh, 'October 17, 1920', 'The Diary', in Singh and Zingg, *Wolf-children*, p. 7. All further references are to this edition of the journals and are given in parentheses in the text.
17 The Manush-Bagha are what Chunarem, the aboriginal tribesman in Godamuri, on the border between Midnapore and Morbhanja, first called the children. This

is a man/ghost or man/beast, 'like a man in his limbs with a hideous head of a ghost' (3).
18 Malson, *Wolf Children*, p. 68.
19 Singh, Introduction, p. xxxiii.
20 Professor Robert M. Zingg, the co-editor of the journal, claimed that the manuscript had gathered dust and that Singh had no commercial interest in the project. The Rev. Singh sets out his own reasons for delaying publication in the introduction to the journal. These include the difficulty of settling the girls into marriage should their history became known, and the fear of endless visits and enquiries at the orphanage. See Zingg, Introduction, p. xxxv; and Singh, Introduction, pp. xxxii–xxxiii, Singh and Zingg, *Wolf-children*.
21 There are three forewords to the book: by Professor Arnold Gesell, Director of the Clinic of Child Development, School of Medicine, Yale University; by Kingsley Davis, Professor of Sociology, Pennsylvania State College; and by Bishop H. Pakenham-Walsh (pp. xvii–xviii, xix–xx, xxv–xxvii).
22 'Wolf Ways' is Chapter 5 (1920–22) and 'Human Ways' Chapter 7 (1926–29) (Gesell, *Wolf Child*, pp. 30–7, 49–55).
23 Epigraph to Chapter 3, 'With the Wolves, 1912–1920', p. 12
24 Malson, for example, uses this phrase when recounting the story of the wolf girls' capture (*Wolf Children*, p. 68).
25 Feuerbach, *Casper Hause. An Account of an individual kept in a dungeon, separated from all communication with the world, from early childhood to about the age of seventeen* (1833). Wild Peter is described in the *Enquiry* of 1726. Victor of Aveyron is documented in *An Historical Account of the Discovery and Education of a Savage Man: Or, the First Developments, Physical and Moral, of the Young Savage Caught in the Woods Near Aveyron in the Year 1798* (1802).
26 Rousseau, *Discourse*, p. 61.
27 Locke, *Essay*, p. 109.
28 'Jean-Jacques Rousseau, Citizen of Geneva, to Christophe de Beaumont, Archbishop of Paris', p. 170. I am of the opinion that Rousseau, with his theory of the natural goodness of human beings, rejected the doctrine of original sin. For him all derivations from virtue derive from environment and from the mistaken direction of parents and teachers. This is an ongoing debate, however. For a more ambivalent view, see Ahlberg, 'Rousseau and the Original Sin'.
29 *An Enquiry*, p. 2.
30 'A Particular Account of Peter the Wild Boy', p. 43.
31 *Ibid.*, p. 44.
32 These facts are made a lot of in satirical accounts that delight in the wild boy's lack of etiquette and knowledge of the laws of propriety regarding the King. See for example, [Jonathan Swift], *The Most Wonderful Wonder*. For a full list of pamphlets including [John Arbuthnot], *It Cannot Rain But it Pours* (1726) and *The Manifesto*

of Lord Peter (1726), see Newton, who notes that these works 'mock human beings at the expense of the nobility of animals', *Savage Girls*, p. 35.

33 *An Enquiry*, p. 3. New analysis of the portrait suggests Peter had a rare genetic condition known as Pitt-Hopkins Syndrome. This is only speculation, however, and is suggestive of the present-day medicalisation of such deviancy as wild children. See Lane, 'Who Was Peter the Wild Boy'.

34 *An Enquiry*, p. 3.

35 On one occasion he travelled as far as Norwich where he was arrested on a charge of spying and as he did not speak it was assumed he was a Spanish subversive. He was delivered from jail by one of the courtiers and from that day wore around his neck the leather collar with a brass plate. Peter's adventures are documented in a pamphlet produced by the church in which he is buried, 'Peter the Wild Boy'.

36 *The Gentleman's and London Magazine*, November 1751, p. 610; cited incorrectly in Newton, *Savage Girls*, p. 51.

37 Linné, *Systema Naturae*, book 1, p. 20. Seven feral cases are listed.

38 For a discussion of this taxonomical name, see Douthwaite, *The Wild Girl*, p. 15

39 Montesquieu, *The Spirit of Laws*, I, p. 5.

40 Rousseau, *Discourse*, p. 87.

41 'That he was drop'd in the woods by some unnatural mother and left to the mercy of beasts; that providence directed some female brute to nourish him, perhaps a She-Wolf, as Romulus and Remus are famed to be nourished ... I do not believe a word of' (Defoe, *Mere Nature Delienated*, p. 15). All further references are to this edition.

42 Edgeworth and Edgeworth, *Practical Education*, II, p. 63.

43 'Chiefly *Law* and *Psychiatry*. A person so profoundly disabled in mental function or intellect as to be incapable of ordinary acts of reasoning or rational conduct' (*OED*).

44 I am indebted to Alan J. Bewell for bringing together theories of wild children and idiots in his study of Wordsworth in 1983. Bewell analyses 'The Idiot Boy' in relation to the representation of language and memory in *The Recluse* and 'Peter Bell'. However, Bewell associates 'Peter Bell' rather than 'The Idiot Boy' with Peter: 'It is likely that Peter, the aging "wild boy" of Hanover, was in Wordsworth's mind when he described the British counterpart who shares his name, the wild and woodland rover Peter Bell' ('Wordsworth's Primal Scene', p. 331). Coleridge mentions that Victor would have made a welcome addition to Wordsworth's *The Recluse* (*The Notebooks of Samuel Taylor Coleridge*, vol. 3, ed. by Coburn, note 3538, [n. pag.]).

45 'All children and Idiots ... have not the least apprehension or thought' (Locke, *Essay*, I, p. 27).

46 From Wordsworth's 1802 letter to John Wilson. Wilson had written in May 1802 to convey his 'inexpressible disgust' at the subject matter of the poem and Wordsworth responded with a defence of idiocy and an appeal for compassion. Both letters are

supplied as appendices in Wordsworth and Coleridge, *Lyrical Ballads*, ed. by Stafford, pp. 310–21.
47 This is the premise of Rousseau's influential novel-treatise on education, *Emile* (1762).
48 Wordsworth, 'The Idiot Boy', in Wordsworth and Coleridge, *Lyrical Ballads*, pp. 66–79, line 122. All further references are to this edition are given in parenthesis in the text.
49 Bewell argues that in this scene 'an illegitimate mother's urgent questioning of her idiotic son, an age of interrogations of idiocy aimed at recovering the "truth" of human nature would seem to come to its parodic end' (p. 35).
50 Contemporary accounts and representations of Victor include Itard, *Mémoire sur les premiers développements de Victor de l'Aveyron* (Paris, 1801); *Rapport sur les nouveaux développements de Victor de l'Aveyron* (Paris, 1806); *An Historical Account of the Discovery and Education of a Savage Man: Or, the First Developments, Physical and Moral, of the Young Savage Caught in the Woods Near Aveyron in the Year 1798* (London, 1802). He was also the subject of a melodrama by Pixérécourt, *Victor or the Forest's Child* (1797).
51 This is noted by Bonnaterre and others. See Pierre-Joseph Bonnaterre, *Notice historique sur le sauvage de l'Aveyron* (Paris: Chez Panckoucke, 1800), cited in Harlan Lane, *The Wild Boy of Aveyron* (London: Allen & Unwin, 1977), pp. 33–40. For a useful discussion of the significance of Victor's scars, see Newton, *Savage Girls*, p. 99.
52 *Morning Post*, 3 October 1800.
53 Itard's accounts of the wild boy were first published in English in 1802. Itard was supposedly ambivalent to the teachings of Rousseau, preferring the work of the Lockean Etienne Bonnot de Condillac. Critical responses to Itard's teaching of Victor include Shattuck, *The Forbidden Experiment*; Malson, *Wolf Children*; Lane, *The Wild Boy of Aveyron*. In 1969, François Truffaut directed *L'Enfant Sauvage*, a French new-wave film on the life of Victor and the attempts to educate him. Truffaut cast himself in the role of Itard the educator. See Shattuck, 'The Wild Boy in Film', in *The Forbidden Experiment*, pp. 208–14; and Brodski, 'The Cinematic Representation of the Wild Child'.
54 Itard, in Malson, p. 73.
55 *Ibid.*, p. 98.
56 Pakenham-Walsh, Preface, *Wolf-children*, p. xxvi.
57 Robinson, 'The Savage of Aveyron', in *Selected Poems*, ed. by Pascoe, pp. 332–8. All further references are to this edition. When Robinson submitted her *Lyrical Tales* to publishers she acknowledged her debt to Wordsworth in a postscript, where she declared that 'the volume will consist of tales, serious and gay on a variety of subjects in the manner of Wordsworth's Lyrical Ballads' (Mary Robinson, Letter to an unknown publisher, 17 June 1800, cited in Pascoe, Introduction, Mary Robinson, *Selected Poems*, ed. by Pascoe, note 73, p. 54). For further discussions regarding the

overall project and context of the *Lyrical Tales*, see Curran, 'Mary Robinson's *Lyrical Tales* in context'.
58 Robinson was the poetry editor of *The Morning Post* in 1799.
59 *Memoirs of the Late Mrs Robinson*, III, pp. 173–4, cited in Robinson, *Selected Poems*, ed. by Pascoe, note 1, p. 333.
60 Anne Milne goes as far as identifying Robinson herself as feral in 'At the Precipice of Community'.
61 Philippe Pinel's diagnosis was direct and final. To him the boy was an idiot. As he was deprived of that faculty of reason that distinguished humankind from beasts, Pinel classified him alongside lunatics and fools. Pinel's *A Treatise on Insanity* is discussed briefly in relation to Victor in Newton, *Savage Girls*, pp. 101–3.
62 Pakenham-Walsh in Singh and Zingg, *Wolf-children*, p. xxvi.
63 Some present-day narratives that reincarnate the voices of wolf-children are: Jill Dawson, *Wild Boy*; Mordicai Gerstein's novel *Victor: A Novel Based on the Life of the Savage of Aveyron*; Mary Losure's children's book *Wild Boy: The Real Life of the Savage of Aveyron*. T.C. Boyle, *Wild Child and Other Stories* includes Victor and others whilst C.M. Tennant has written *Peter the Wild Boy*. Fictional representations of Amala and Kamala include Jane Yolen's *Children of the Wolf*; Marcus Sedgwick's novel *The Dark Horse* is loosely based on their story.
64 Hughes, 'Life after Death', lines 47–50.

4

'CHILDREN OF THE NIGHT. WHAT MUSIC THEY MAKE!': THE SOUND OF THE CINEMATIC WEREWOLF

Stacey Abbott

The title sequence to the cult horror television series *Buffy the Vampire Slayer* (WB/UPN 1997–2003) begins with the howl of a wolf, underscored by the first four notes of the show's title theme music played on an organ. These two key sounds – the wolf and the organ – position the show within an established history of classic horror, before the organ is replaced by 'an aggressively strummed electric guitar, relocating itself [the title theme] in modern youth culture and relocating the series within an altogether different arena'.[1] In her analysis of the opening title music, the musicologist Janet K. Halfyard acknowledges the horror 'intertextual associations' embedded within this use of the organ, citing the diegetic use of the organ in *The Phantom of the Opera* (Rupert Julien, USA, 1925) and *Dr. Jekyll and Mr. Hyde* (Rouben Mamoulian, USA, 1931) as key referents for this association. *Buffy*'s creator Joss Whedon confirms that the musical aim of the sequence was to 'star[t] out with this scary organ and then devolv[e] instantly into rock 'n' roll, which is basically trying to tell people exactly what this show is in the credits'.[2] Neither Halfyard nor Whedon mentions the sound of the wolf and yet this sound is equally evocative of this sonic history of horror. The wolf's howl provides such a pronounced intertextual association with the genre that it is used frequently to set an atmosphere for horror such as in the *Supernatural* (WB/CW 2005–2020) pastiche 'Monster Movie' (4.5) which matches its black-and-white cinematography with a soundscape filled with wolves, organs and electrical thunderstorms. The sound of the wolf is a recurring feature in haunted-house attractions, Gothic radio programmes and even the DVD menus for classic horror films. It is an immediately recognisable aural signifier for horror.

The aim of this chapter will therefore be to consider the role that sound plays in the construction of the Gothic and horror genres, in particular through the soundscape of the werewolf film. While there is a growing body of work on music in relation to horror and the Gothic, sound still remains a too-often overlooked area of film aesthetics.[3] I will therefore focus my discussion on the sound effects of animality and wildness within these films, particularly the snarls, growls and howls of the wolf and the sound of bodily transformation, alongside the musical scores that accompany the werewolf. In particular, a close analysis of Universal's first werewolf film, *Werewolf of London* (Stuart Walker, USA, 1935), and John Landis's reimagining of the werewolf in *An American Werewolf in London* (also for Universal; 1981), will examine how the werewolf draws upon a tension embedded within the sound of the wolf that causes it to embody both horror and melancholy while also blurring the lines between animal and human. This duality, from the werewolf's earliest appearance through to its modern incarnations, complicates the audience's relationship to horror and the monster within the genre, thus highlighting kinship rather than difference between classic and modern approaches to cinematic horror.

Stoker and the wolf

It is of note that the *Buffy* titles includes a wolf's howl, despite the fact that the show is about a *vampire* slayer and werewolves actually only feature in a few episodes ('Phases', 2.15; 'Beauty and the Beasts', 3.4; and 'Wild at Heart', 4.6). This is because there are no specific sounds that are iconically associated with the vampire in the way that the howl is with the wolf, although the sound of the wolf does have an association with the vampire, particularly in *Dracula*.[4] Bram Stoker's novel *Dracula* (1897) has long been considered a notable prototype for the vampire on film. While by no means the first vampire novel, its influence upon the genre is well established, inspiring numerous adaptations, parodies, copies and spin-offs, spread across a multitude of media.[5] The novel, however, also has a strong relationship with the werewolf, with Stoker interweaving elements of vampire and werewolf folklore within the construction of his story and in his conception of his master vampire. Significantly, Johnathan Harker's journey to, and stay at, Dracula's castle are filled with wolf encounters. While en-route, Harker's coach is repeatedly surrounded by wolves (p. 15), and later, when Count Dracula presents Harker with an opportunity to leave the Castle by his own volition, his escape is blocked by packs of wolves, forcing Harker to retreat back into the vampire's clutch (p. 49). Dracula's attack on Lucy is signalled by newspaper reports of a wolf escaping from the zoo (pp. 127–32) and, on Lucy's final night before succumbing to Dracula's attack, a great grey wolf crashes through her bedroom window, causing her mother to die and leaving Lucy vulnerable to the vampire once more (p. 134). Furthermore, Stoker's short story 'Dracula's Guest' describes one particular adventure while Harker is on his way to Dracula's castle, conjectured to have been cut from Stoker's novel. In this story, Harker's exploration of a deserted village on Walpurgis Night results in ghostly visitation, leaving him passed out in a graveyard only to wake up with a large wolf lying on his chest, licking his neck and keeping him warm until morning, thus ensuring his safe arrival at Castle Dracula. The allusions throughout the book and particularly in this short story highlight Dracula's affinity with wolves and suggest that he is himself a shapeshifter. The presence of the moon is also often described at points when the wolves' activities are more pronounced, thus reinforcing the novel's relationship to werewolf lore.[6]

What is particularly notable in the wolf-related passages in both the novel and the short story is that the presence of the wolves is conveyed through the sound of their howling. Throughout Harker's time in Transylvania, he repeatedly describes not only the fact of the wolves howling but also the emotional impact of this sound. While on the way to Castle Dracula, he describes how 'far off in the distance, from the mountains on each side of us began a louder and sharper howling – that of wolves – which affected both the horses and myself in the same way – for I was minded to jump from the calèche and run, whilst they reared again and plunged madly …' (pp. 11–12). Later he notes the relationship between the wolves and the moon when he explains, 'all at once the wolves began to howl as though the moonlight had had some peculiar effect on them' (p. 13). When he tries to leave Dracula's castle, he explains that 'as the door began to open, the howling of the wolves without grew louder and angrier; their red jaws, with champing teeth, and their blunt-clawed feet as they leaped, came in through the opening door …' (p. 49), causing Harker to acquiesce to Dracula's manipulation. He exclaims 'shut the door; I shall wait till morning!', covering his face with his hands to hide his 'tears of bitter disappointment' (p. 50).

This repeated emphasis upon the howling of the wolves in this section of the book culminates in one of the most iconic moments in the novel when the wolves outside of the castle once again begin to howl and Dracula responds with the following statement: 'Listen to them – the children of the night. What music they make!' (p. 18). This statement is significant at this point in the narrative as it is one of a series of signifiers that tell Harker that something is 'wrong' with Dracula, calling attention (along with his hairy palms, massive eyebrows, profusion of hair, pointed nails and sharp teeth) to his more 'beastly' nature. While Harker describes feeling fear at the sound of the wolves, Dracula refers to them as *children* and their howling as *music*, establishing a tension between their differing perceptions. As this part of the narrative is told from Harker's point of view, the reader is, however, encouraged to share his perspective and read Dracula's comment as odd and unsettling. Yet these tensions surrounding the sound of the wolves embody conflicting emotions often generated by these sounds in the real world as they invoke a sense of danger alongside a melancholy beauty. As Garry Marvin explains,

> a wolf with its head held almost vertical, mouth slightly open and often silhouetted against a full moon, is a ubiquitous, perhaps iconic, image. Fear of and fascination

with the howling of a pack of wolves is a matter of human concerns – a long-held fear that it might signal attack on them or their livestock or a more recent interest and delight in the haunting sounds of the wild.⁷

The wolf is often depicted in art or photography as howling in the manner described by Marvin, while the snarling image of the wolf is also familiar as a figure of horror, from Disney's animated fairy tale *Frozen* (Chris Buck and Jennifer Lee, USA, 2013) to the horror film of the same name (*Frozen*, Adam Green, USA, 2010). In both films, wolves stalk and terrorise people trapped alone in the snow, capturing the way in which wolves 'have been feared and reviled creatures of the wilderness … emblematic of the wild and particularly of the dangerous and threatening qualities of the wild'.⁸ Sound is key to evoking the atmosphere of the wild and infuses our expectations and understanding of the wolf, bringing with it a series of perspectives through which we read and interpret the werewolf.

The conversion to sound and the birth of horror

Debunking a popular myth about cinema, Richard Maltby explains, 'if there was such a thing as silent movies, there was never such a thing as silent cinema, because cinemas were never silent'.⁹ Instead, the sonic landscape of early and silent cinema was a complex and varied one, with pioneers such as Thomas Edison, among others, experimenting with synchronising sound and image, while 'silent films' were accompanied by a wide variety of live musical, as well as sound effects and narrators.¹⁰ There were many different technological formats for film sound and different approaches to the use of sound as filmmakers began to develop a language for its use that would facilitate the mainstream medium's focus on narrative and spectacle.¹¹ The success of *The Jazz Singer* marked, as Jonathan D. Tankel argues, 'the final proof of the success of sound, not the first', whilst Maltby suggests that the film 'establish[ed] the viability of lip-synchronization, and trigger[ed] the wiring of American movie theatres for sound'.¹² By 1928, the industry began the process of converting cinema to sound, a process that took a few years given the need to change not only the production mechanisms and aesthetics of filmmaking but also the exhibition of films. By 1930, the American and European film industry had, however, primarily moved over to sound production and exhibition. This coincides with the rise of the horror genre in film.

The birth of horror is commonly located in 1931 with the successful production and release of three cinematic adaptations of classic Gothic novels: Tod Browning's *Dracula* (1931), followed by James Whale's *Frankenstein* (1931), both for Universal, and Rouben Mamoulian's *Dr. Jekyll and Mr. Hyde* (1931) for Paramount Pictures. Of course, there were films made earlier that have come to be identified as examples of silent horror, such as *The Hunchback of Notre Dame*, *Phantom of the Opera*, *The Unknown*, *The Man Who Laughs*, *The Cat and the Canary*. This is, however, a retrospective categorisation through a recognition of the tropes of horror as they have subsequently been established. In the silent era, these films were generally considered examples of melodrama or crime drama, with a focus on the fantastic, the Gothic and/or the grotesque, although, as Alison Peirse has noted, the critical response to these films often focused on their horror 'effect ... on the audience's sensibilities'.[13] They were not, however, made as 'horror' films. Similarly, when Browning's *Dracula* was released in 1931, it was marketed primarily as a melodrama and a 'vampire thriller' with the tag line 'the strangest passion the world has ever known'. Gary D. Rhodes's detailed study of the production and release of the film, however, shows that early drafts of the *Dracula* press book included numerous references to 'horror', 'shuddering', 'mouldering graveyards', 'the drip-drip-drip of blood' and 'howling of wolves', the latter two phrases evoking what would become familiar to audiences as the sounds of horror. The final press book and press materials for the film, however, included none of these phrases or tag lines, 'making no mention of words like "horror," "terror," "blood," and "mystery"'.[14] It was only when the film went on to general release that the overt association with horror emerged, when critics began describing the film as 'creepy' and 'terrifying', while some cinemas advertised screenings as 'spook shows'. As Rhodes's research has shown, increasingly both exhibitors and critics described the film as '"horror" … during its general release'.[15] In this manner, the horror genre as we know it grew from the reception of *Dracula*. The success of *Dracula*, which led to Universal's follow-up, *Frankenstein*, spawned an initial cycle of horror films in the 1930s and 1940s produced by Universal Studios, as well as other studios and independent production companies.[16]

The confluence of the conversion to sound and the emergence of horror as an established and recognised genre seem significant. These early sound horror films draw from established traditions of silent horror through the visual language of German Expressionism, particularly in the form of chiaroscuro, and the cinematic preoccupation with body horror and the grotesque as typified in the work of Lon Chaney (such as in *Phantom of the Opera*). Additionally, these early sound films continue an established and international tradition of drawing upon recognised examples of Gothic literature (*Frankenstein* (J. Searle Dawley, USA, 1910), *The Sorrows of Satan* (Alexander Butler, UK, 1917), *The Beetle* (Alexander Butler, UK, 1919), *Dr. Jekyll and Mr. Hyde* (John S. Robertson, USA, 1920), *Drakula* (Károly Lajthay, Hungary, 1921), *Nosferatu* (F.W. Murnau, Germany, 1922)). The new element that seems to consolidate the genre in this period is sound. Sound is key for inciting an emotional affect in its audience, a factor that Gothic authors recognised by the emphasis within their descriptions upon sound as a means of immersing the reader within the text. As Isabella van Elferen points out,

> elaborately described soundscapes contribute to the eerie mood of a novel. Such literary soundscapes show remarkable similarities: the advent of terror is generally preceded by an unworldly silence, aided by meteorological (wind, thunder, rain) or technical (rattling fences, hissing pipes) circumstances and announced by sounds that suggest presence (creaks, echoes, voices, music).[17]

All of these effects become the sonic landscape of early horror. In Browning's *Dracula*, however, it is not an overabundance of sound that necessarily generates affect and renders Dracula's castle as uncanny but rather silence. Silence is a recurring trope within the Gothic, as van Elferen notes: 'the silences in Gothic novels are consistently described as the complete absence of sound, which, in its unnatural improbability, functions as a signifier of the unhomely'.[18] In *Dracula*, there is no musical score except over the film's opening credits and so the film is filled with unsettlingly long moments of absolute silence which are then interrupted by bursts of sound, evoking this sense of the unhomely. This is best illustrated in the scene when Renfield arrives at Dracula's castle. The sequence is unusually silent to contemporary ears that are trained to expect musical underscore and sound effects within horror films. It would also have been unusually silent in 1931 to audiences used to live musical accompaniment during silent films but also to the growing movement towards rapid-fire dialogue that characterised much of American early sound cinema. The sound effects and dialogue here are deliberately sparse to render Dracula's castle as uncanny. Sounds like the creaking door, the bats squeaking, the armadillos scurrying across the floor and the wolves howling are emphasised while Dracula's and Renfield's footsteps are absent. Importantly, Dracula's voice is emphasised. As Isabella van Elferen points out:

> A thick Hungarian accent, a bombastic bass voice, and canned sound quality have made the phrase 'I ahm Drrahkuhlah' quite as immortal as the Count himself is supposed to be. This is undead speech to be sure, and Lugosi's accent and vocal timbre only highlight what is most disturbing about the scene: *It speaks*.[19]

Lugosi as Dracula clearly relished his performance of this dialogue – slowly articulating each word to build anticipation not just of what he is saying but also the fact that he speaks. His cadence is unnaturally slow. In particular Lugosi's performance emphasises his accent, in contrast to the book in which Dracula attempts to conceal it, wanting to assimilate in England. In Browning's film, his accent is very present, ensuring, as Nina Auerbach observes, 'after his American transplantation, to be Dracula meant speaking in a different voice'.[20]

All of this signals his strangeness, his foreignness, his Otherness; a fact that is reinforced by Renfield's response to Lugosi as he looks around suspiciously and nervously. Sound here renders this location and this initial meeting as fraught with meaning and dark potential.

When the film moves to England, sound is used to render more familiar or mundane spaces as uncanny, in particular the maniacal laughter of Renfield, now under Dracula's influence, coming from the hold of a ship. Later, Renfield's screams emerge from Dr Seward's seemingly peaceful sanatorium, foreshadowing that this location, as well as the institution of science, will be vulnerable to Dracula's attack. This is also achieved through the transposition to modern London of sounds associated with the Transylvanian location. After Dracula arrives in London, the soundscape deliberately emphasises urban sounds such as motor engines, cars honking and a police whistle when a flower seller is found dead in the fog. Later, however, the soundscape is intruded upon by the squeak of the bat and the sound of the wolf howling in London. Whilst used in the opening sequences to set the Gothic scene when Dracula first emerges from his coffin and when Renfield is picked up by Dracula's carriage at the Borgo Pass, the wolf's howl is later heard repeatedly at sunset outside of Seward's Sanatorium. The sound of the wolf in London is deliberately out of place, offering an uncanny reimagining of the film's modern setting through the intrusion of the wolf. Furthermore, it is the sound of the wolf that alerts the audience to Dracula's presence, an aural reminder of the threat that Dracula embodies. When Renfield begs Dr Seward to let him go, he warns that his screams might disturb Miss Mina and give her bad dreams, and this statement is followed by the sound of the wolf as a warning to Renfield. The next morning, after Dracula's nocturnal visit to the Seward household, Mina does indeed recount her nightmares but they begin with the sound of 'dogs' howling rather than Renfield's screams. Her dreams, along with England, have been invaded and the sound of wolves, although used only a total of seven times in the film, serves to signal the insinuation of the monstrous within the civilised. This repeated use of the sound of the wolf in this film establishes this effect as an element of the emerging Gothic/horror mise-en-scène of cinema. With the release of Universal's first werewolf film, *Werewolf of London* (1935), followed by the subsequent – and far more successful – *The Wolf Man* (1941), the sound of the wolf is further engrained within the aesthetic of horror but also becomes complicated in its representation of the monster.

The Universal werewolf movies – classic horror

The emotional ambivalence that is embedded within the sound of the wolf, although largely denied in *Dracula*, comes to the fore with the rise of the werewolf movie in the 1930s and 1940s through *Werewolf of London* and *The*

Wolf Man (George Waggner, USA, 1941), both for Universal Studios. These films had a lasting impact upon the werewolf films to follow. *Werewolf of London* is the lesser known of the two. Its story of a botanist in search of a rare Tibetan plant that blossoms under moonlight, and who is subsequently attacked by a werewolf while collecting a sample, did not have that lasting impact of *The Wolf Man*'s narrative of gypsy curses, pentagrams and silver-tipped wolf's head canes. Similarly, Henry Hull's performance as Wilfred Glendon, the infected werewolf, lacks the hang-dog quality of Lon Chaney, Jr's Lawrence Talbot, a characteristic that became a significant signifier of the genre for many years. Both men, however, share an arrogance – Talbot's as a result of his class and station within the community and Glendon in terms of his professional obsession with his scientific experiments – that contributes to their undoing. *Werewolf of London* is however the more technically ambitious film and it established the sonic language of the werewolf film, to which so many subsequent films have subscribed.

What is most significant about these early werewolf films is the conflation of the roles of the monster and victim. Many of Universal's monsters are sympathetic – Frankenstein's creature, Imhotep in pursuit of his lost love in *The Mummy* – but they are not the central protagonists and, while they may often be more interesting than the film's actual heroes, fundamentally they are the threat from which the protagonists must be protected. Glendon and Talbot are, however, the central protagonists, the monster, *and* they are also the first victims of the werewolf, suffering an attack by the monster and then facing the nightmarish revelation that they are now cursed. Here the sound of the wolf becomes quite significant in this now complex portrayal of the victim/monster, in which the traditional opposition between the civilised and the animalistic is challenged. The audience's perception of them is *as victim*, first of the werewolf bite and then of their own bodies out of control. The howl of the wolf heard early in both films prior to the first attacks that leave the men afflicted with the werewolf curse, initially speaks of foreboding for what is to come. Later it becomes a signifier of their anguish as well as monstrosity, fostering an emotional ambivalence.

This emotional ambivalence is expressed in *Werewolf of London* through three types of sound which will become regular signifiers of the werewolf in later films. They are the howl of the wolf; the growls, snarls and breathing noises which are generally accompanied by a point-of-view shot from the werewolf's perspective; and the sound of transformation, all of which highlight the breakdown of the human in favour of the wolf. The howl of the wolf is first used at the beginning of the film in Tibet as Glendon is on the hunt for this mysterious flower. Glendon is cautioned not to enter a particular valley 'as it is filled with demons', but his single-minded focus on his research causes him to ignore these warnings. As he enters the valley under a full moon, the sound of a wolf howling is repeatedly heard – reinforcing the warnings not to go further. Once in the valley, he is stalked by a figure in the shadows, conveyed through an over-the-shoulder shot of Glendon, suggesting the point of view of the stalker, the werewolf, but also presenting Glendon as potential victim of the monster. There is, however, no sound but the very quiet strains of the musical score before the werewolf attacks. Once he attacks, there is a loud burst of music to accompany the fight scene. The primary sound effects in the sequence are the sound of the wolf biting Glendon, over a close-up of his arm, and the wolf's howl or whimper when he is stabbed by Glendon. There are no growls or snarls of the wolf at this point in the film. So while the sequence includes a seeming point-of-view shot watching Glendon, the werewolf remains enigmatic, primarily represented via a large shadow that looms over the scientist. The sound of Glendon being bitten and the werewolf being stabbed, however, establishes a symmetry between the two men that is developed throughout the film, for, as Alison Peirse argues, this is a film with two werewolves and much of the narrative drive emerges from the erotic tension between the two men.[21]

A similar werewolf point-of-view sequence is used later in the film when Glendon has transformed, this time offering the perspective of the werewolf as protagonist. The scene begins at a society party, where Glendon's wife and friends are in attendance. Glendon arrives outside, preparing to climb into the house through the window, on the hunt for his first victim. The scene cuts to an interior shot as the howl of the wolf is heard repeatedly, coming from outside. While it is the same sound as in the earlier scene when Glendon was attacked, this time the audience is aware that this is the protagonist howling, and as such it speaks to his human moral agony as well as to the animalistic threat he now represents. At the party, while many guests try to identify the type of animal from its howl, Yogami, the werewolf who turned Glendon but who has been able to use the moon flower to prevent his transformation, describes the howl as the sound of a 'lost soul', emphasising the humanity within the monstrous.

This party scene is followed by Glendon's entrance into the bedroom where an older woman has gone to rest, presented through his point of view in an early example of what Carol Clover describes as the 'I-camera' in which the audience 'see[s] through [the killer]'s eyes and (on the soundtrack) hear [s] his breathing and heartbeat'; a technique most commonly associated with the slasher film.[22] In *Werewolf of London*, the sound of Glendon's rasping breath accompanies the image of his pawlike hands grabbing the edge of the bedroom balcony as the camera cranes up, over and through the doors into the bedroom. The sound reaffirms that the audience is seeing through Glendon's eyes and thus implicates the audience within his point of view. As Clover notes, 'the relation between camera point of view and the processes of viewer identification is poorly understood' and the relationship between audience and killer is often more complicated than the simple formula 'point of view = identification'.[23] Wickham Clayton has made a detailed argument about this particular camera trope, contesting the notion that simply looking through the eyes of the killer forces the audience to identify with him [or her] against the victim.[24] *Werewolf of London* equally suggests a more complex interaction between monster, audience and victim, as well as the division between the civilised and the wild that underpins much of werewolf lore and fiction. In this case, Glendon is driven to commit an act against his own desires. He is driven to kill by the curse and then feels remorse. Suturing the camera to Glendon's perspective, reinforced by use of sound, aligns the audience with his feelings of horror and remorse surrounding his actions, fusing the audience's ambivalence with that of the character.

The transformation from man into wolf in *Werewolf of London* further complicates Glendon's position as a monster. Technically, this scene is far more advanced than the sequences in *The Wolf Man*. In *The Wolf Man* the first transformation is presented by dissolving between a series of close-ups of Talbot's feet as they become hairier with each transition, until they have completely turned into paws. The sequence is accompanied by a dramatic musical score that becomes more foreboding as the transformation progresses. In contrast, *Werewolf of London* shows us the transformation from the waist up. Presented as a single-take tracking shot, the sequence comprises three shots cut together, with each shot containing a stage of the transformation. The cuts are hidden by Glendon's movement behind a series of stone pillars. This approach signals the fluid transformation from man into wolf but it also makes it clear that Glendon is aware of what is happening to him as it happens. In *The Wolf Man*, a close-up of Talbot as the transformation begins indicates that he is aware of what is about to happen, but there is no indication of his perspective as it happens, and the next day he does not appear to remember anything. In contrast, Glendon's perspective is privileged throughout the transition. As Alison Peirse points out, '[h]e holds his paws up to his mouth in horror, he chokes and scrabbles at his throat unable to verbalise the anguish of his transformation. Horror emerges not just from what we have seen – the transformation of man into werewolf – but from Glendon's realisation of what he has become'.[25] Notably, like *The Wolf Man*, the sequence does not use any sound effects but rather conveys the transformation via the music. The stages of his transformation are echoed in the escalation of the tempo of the music, reaching a climax at the end of the transformation. This use of music and this crescendo, in particular, seems to convey the emotional impact for Glendon, capturing his horror at what he has become. Also as Peirse argues, his movements represent his emotional, perhaps even spiritual anguish. This film, much like *Dr. Jekyll and Mr. Hyde*, is largely about the beast beneath the veneer of the civilised, and this transformation allows us a glimpse beneath the veneer.

American werewolf of London – modern horror

The Universal cycle of horror films came to an end in the late 1940s after a series of monster mash-up films, bringing together studio's classic monsters Dracula, Frankenstein's monster and the wolfman (*House of Dracula* and *House of Frankenstein*), and parodies, teaming their monsters up with Universal's hugely successful comedy duo Abbott and Costello (*Abbott and Costello Meet Frankenstein* and *Abbott and Costello meet the Killer, Boris Karloff*). While numerous subsequent werewolf films would be made outside of Universal, including *I Was a Teenage Werewolf* (Gene Folwer Jr, USA, 1957), *The Curse of the Werewolf* (Terence Fisher, UK, 1961), and *The Boy Who Cried Werewolf* (Nathan H. Juran, USA, 1973), the next great cycle of werewolf films to emerge within popular culture came in the early 1980s. This cycle would include films such as *Wolfen* (1981), *An American Werewolf in London* (John Landis, USA, 1981), *The Howling* (Joe Dante, USA, 1981), *The Company of Wolves* (Neil Jordan, UK, 1984), *Silver Bullet* (Dan Attias, USA, 1985), and *Teen Wolf* (Rod Daniel, USA, 1985), all made within a very short period of time. While each of these films approaches the genre in distinct ways, they are unified by a selection of narrative and stylistic conventions that were symptomatic of a new movement of modern horror that began to emerge in the late 1960s and which was hitting its apex in the late 1970s and early 1980s.[26] In particular these conventions include the relocation of horror to a contemporary American setting (in contrast to the Universal werewolf movies which are primarily set in Europe) and their emphasis upon graphic body horror. In the werewolf films, this emphasis upon body horror translated into far more bloody and detailed werewolf attacks and, significantly, the explicit physical transformation into the werewolf achieved through special make-up effects rather than the optical transformations of the earlier films. Each film contributes to the reconception of the werewolf transformation as a violent attack on the body from within as opposed to the external transformation that takes place in the Universal films, characterised by the growth of hair all over the body and the development of canine fangs.

This transformation is best exemplified by *An American Werewolf in London*, a film that is in dialogue with its classic Hollywood precursors. The film was produced by Universal Studios and the title openly alludes to *Werewolf of London* while the film includes direct references to *The Wolf Man*. The film is best known for its modernisation of the werewolf genre and the sophisticated special make-up effects by Rick Baker. This approach to the werewolf was part of a broader cultural moment in which the horror genre was increasingly focused upon the body, its corruption, dissolution and disarray.[27] This movement impacted on other key werewolf films of the period, in particular *The Howling* and *Company of Wolves*. *American Werewolf*, however, signalled a moment when the excesses of the horror genre, which had been building steadily since the 1970s, developed broad mainstream appeal and critical recognition through both this film's box-office success – taking in over $30 million in its domestic market – and its critical acclaim which culminated in the film winning the first Academy award for special make-up effects. The transformation sequence is one of the key elements that has brought the film so much attention, introducing the full body, before-camera transformation, which is presented as 'an invasive procedur[e] that emphasize[s] pain and physical penetration of the skin ... from the inside'.[28] The soundscape equally plays a key role in reimagining the werewolf.

The soundscape of this film includes the three elements that I have outlined above (howling wolves, up-close-and-personal noises, transformation), to which I would add two additional elements. First, a popular music score in which the songs featured on the soundtrack have 'moon' in the title ('Moondance', 'Bad Moon Rising', 'Blue Moon'). This aesthetic choice lends the film an ironic touch that is in keeping with the postmodern quality to much of 1980s horror films, in which horror emerges in a world filled with pop culture references and intertextuality. As Philip Brophy argues, 'the contemporary horror film *knows* you've seen it all before; it *knows* that you know what is about to happen; and it knows that you know it knows you know'.[29] As a result, Landis's film is presented as an American werewolf in London up-to-date with a vengeance. This use of pop music also establishes an unsettling contrast between its upbeat tone and the violence and horror on display. It makes the visuals all the more horrible by contrast to the music. The second element is the screams of David [the werewolf] as he undergoes the transformation. If Glendon is cognitively aware of what is happening to him and horrified by what he has become, David is cognitively, emotionally *and* physically aware of what he is undergoing as he feels the pain of each step of this transformation. While the visuals provide a horrible spectacle, the sounds emphasise the heightened physicality of the process and David's screams highlight his pain and anguish.

The scene begins with David, awaiting the first full moon since his attack, highly sceptical of the werewolf curse. The beginning of the transformation is signalled by a jarring use of sound. The camera zooms into a close-up of the full moon over which Sam Cooke's soulful version of 'Blue Moon' plays. The film cuts to a medium shot of David as the camera tracks into a close of him as he suddenly screams 'Jesus Christ!' before falling to his knees on the floor, holding his head. The abruptness of this transition, shifting from sitting quietly and absolutely still to sudden movement and loud screams, aurally signals a violent attack on his body. It also stands in contrast to the earlier Universal films which built slowly and dramatically to transformation, through the musical underscore as well as signifiers of foreboding, such as Glendon's cat hissing and lashing out at him before he begins to change. Here the poignant quality of 'Blue Moon' deliberately contrasts with the violence of David's reaction, immediately ripping off his clothes, as the transformation begins. The sounds of David screaming and the recording of 'Blue Moon' continue throughout the scene, blurring into an uncomfortable cacophony of noise.

Furthermore, the sequence calls attention to the painful physicality of the change through the sound effects that accompany each stage of the transformation, capturing the sound of skin stretching, bones shifting, hair pushing through the skin, the vertebrae realigning, and the face and ears elongating. These are affective sounds, eliciting a form of 'somatic empathy' relying, as Xavier Aldana Reyes argues, upon 'the human capacity to comprehend pain and physical harm, especially its potential sensations and effects'.[30] While viewers may not understand how it feels to transform into a wolf, the sound conveys torturous physical pains to the body that the audience can comprehend. The sympathy and empathy for David is further elicited by his repeated pleas for help as well as his comic quip to his zombiefied friend Jack – who warned him that he would turn – when he says 'Sorry I called you meatloaf Jack', referring to his decomposition. Sound in this sequence generates cognitive and emotional sympathy for David as well as a somatic empathy, in which the audience feels his pain. What is equally significant about this sequence is that, as the change continues, his screams, which overwhelm the soundtrack throughout, begin to change. They become deeper and huskier until, when his face begins to elongate into a wolf-snout, his voice begins to blur the lines between human screams and animal growls. As he enters the final stage of the transformation and the camera pans along the full body of the wolf, his screams are themselves transformed into the up-close-and-personal snarls and growls of the wolf. As the image of David dissolves to a shot of the moon, the scene concludes with the sound of David howling, reframing this iconic horror sound from one of foreboding, monstrosity and emotional trauma to one of pain and suffering and, importantly, inverting the focus of the genre away from the 'beast within' to the 'man within'. The werewolf film takes the audience further and further within the point of view of the monster, conveying how the howl of the wolf is the howl of the wolf-man screaming. This association of the werewolf with emotional and physical pain and suffering continues to inform representations of the werewolf in film and television from *Ginger Snaps* to *Being Human*.

Conclusion

An American Werewolf in London offers a modern reimagining of the werewolf set within a recognisably contemporaneous world but, rather than highlighting its difference from the classic werewolf films that preceded it, such as *Werewolf of London* and *The Wolf Man*, the film acknowledges its predecessors and builds upon their emotional complexity; complexity that is inherent within the werewolf subgenre. Sound, as I have demonstrated, plays a crucial role in constructing and conveying this complexity that blurs the lines between victim and monster, man and animal, inviting audiences' sympathies as well as horror. So, while classic horror is often marked by a clear-cut notion of good and evil and the monster as Other, this analysis of the sounds of the werewolf highlights the manner in which the genre, from its earliest days, undermined these distinctions through its evocation of the victim/monster duality of the werewolf as conveyed through its iconic howl. So in this manner Dracula was right: if we listen to the children of the night, they do indeed have much to tell.

Notes

1 Halfyard, 'Love, Death, Curses, and Reverses (in E Minor)', p. 16.
2 Whedon, 'Welcome to the Hellmouth' audio commentary.
3 See Halfyard; Hayward, *Terror Tracks*; Lerner, *Music in the Horror Film*; van Elferen, *Gothic Music*.
4 Stoker, *Dracula*, ed. by Luckhurst. All references to *Dracula* are to this edition.
5 See Abbott, 'Dracula on Film and Television, 1960–Present', and Peirse 'Dracula on Film, 1932–1959'.
6 Dracula's shapeshifting ability has been a significant component of many cinematic adaptations of the novel – although perhaps with more attention paid to his ability to transform into a bat rather than a wolf. It was, however most spectacularly used in Francis Ford Coppola's *Bram Stoker's Dracula* (1992), in which Dracula repeatedly appears as both wolf and wolf-man in his attacks on Lucy Westenra. In one scene, he is depicted mounting Lucy, sprawled on a bench in a graveyard. His body is upright, covered in fur and with the beastly visage of the half-man/half-wolf. When he delivers his fatal attack on Lucy, however, he does so in full wolf form, bursting through her bedroom windows and biting down into her neck with his canine fangs.
7 Marvin, *Wolf*, p. 24.
8 *Ibid.*, p. 7.
9 Maltby, *Hollywood Cinema*, p. 238.
10 Altman, *Silent Film Sound*, p. 78. See Rick Altman, *Silent Film Sound*, and Abel and Altman, *The Sounds of Early Cinema*, for detailed discussions of silent film sound.
11 Maltby, pp. 238–41.
12 Tankel, 'The Impact of *The Jazz Singer*', p. 25; Maltby, p. 239.
13 Peirse, *After Dracula*, p. 6.
14 Rhodes, *Dracula*, p. 229.
15 *Ibid.*, p. 258.

16 Peirse, pp. 10–11.
17 Van Elferin, *Gothic Music*, p. 19.
18 *Ibid.*, p. 19.
19 *Ibid.*, p. 45.
20 Auerbach, *Our Vampires, Ourselves*, p. 113.
21 Peirse, pp. 155–9.
22 Clover, *Men, Women and Chainsaws*, p. 45.
23 *Ibid.*, p. 45.
24 Clayton, 'Bearing Witness to a Whole Bunch of Murders'.
25 Peirse, *After Dracula*, p. 159.
26 See Waller, 'Introduction', Wood, *Hollywood from Vietnam to Reagan*; and Brophy 'Horrality'.
27 See Boss, 'Vile Bodies and Bad Medicine'; Brophy; Turner, *The Body and Society*; Aldana Reyes, *Body Gothic*.
28 Abbott, *Celluloid Vampires*, p. 13.
29 Brophy, p. 5. Italics in original.
30 Aldana Reyes, *Horror Film and Affect*, p. 17.

Part II

Innocence and experience: brute creation, wild beast or child of nature

5

WILD SANCTUARY: RUNNING INTO THE FOREST IN RUSSIAN FAIRY TALES

Shannon Scott

In many well-known European folktales, witches and wolves play villainous roles, leading the protagonist into the dark realm of the forest with criminal intent.[1] The wolf becomes symbolic of everything that threatens or harms humans, their pastoral existence and even their faith-based morality. According to the Russian folktale expert Jack V. Haney, 'the wolf seems to be without redeeming features. He is rapacious but stupid, brutal, and feared by all.'[2] One reason the wolf may have been so demonised in Russian folktales is the large number of livestock killed by wolves in the nineteenth century when many of the oral folktales were written down and published. Researching the history of wolves in Russia, Will N. Graves notes that, despite efforts by the Tsarist government, as well as the arming of recently liberated serfs and the exertions of Russian hunting societies, the wolf population, unlike that in Europe in the nineteenth century, was not eradicated; in fact, it was a growing problem for famers living in Russian provinces.[3] The hungry wolf who devours pigs, sheep, calves and colts can be found in folktales like 'The Cock and the Hen' and 'The Wolf', where the wolf is asked by another animal, usually a herbivore: 'Wolf, wolf, why did you carry off the piglet?' And the Wolf responds, 'I was hungry and God told me to eat'.[4] While these tales portray the wolf as an enemy to herders and farmers, they also reflect a necessity for meat that both wolves and humans share. This solidarity between predators and hunters appears in Russian folktales, where traditionally evil characters, such as witches and wolves, become figures of salvation for the human protagonists.

In 'Ivan Tsarevich and the Grey Wolf', typically villainous or antagonistic witches and wolves actually aid heroes or heroines brave and desperate enough to venture into the forest.[5] The witch and the wolf, rulers and recluses in the realm of the *super*-natural forest, abide by their own conception of justice, granting sanctuary to folktale protagonists only when human society or civilisation has failed them utterly. The forest provides a haven from the cruelties of humankind; it offers the hero or heroine a chance to recover their spirits, heal their bodies and return to the world armed with the resolve, skills and wherewithal to demand justice. For example, the character of the Grey Wolf provides Ivan Tsarevich with wise counsel (which he does not always heed), multiple escapes and resurrection from death; the wolf shapeshifts, disappears into thin air and dives into and out of his den 'as if he'd descended into the pits of Hell' (p. 46). However, when events are outside the boundaries of the Grey Wolf's power, he directs Ivan to Baba Yaga, the only other being inhabiting the forest who is equally capable of powerful magic and protection.

In 'Ivan Tsarevich and the Grey Wolf', Baba Yaga becomes the wolf's human counterpart in the wilderness. She is wild, carnivorous and occasionally cannibalistic, living off what the forest provides her. She possesses supernatural powers – a knowledge and control over life and death. Furthermore, like the Grey Wolf, Baba Yaga is never rattled by violence or brutality, either her own or that of others, inflicting no moral judgements on human behaviour with the exception of the behaviours that break her own unique code of ethics. And yet, despite her ferocious demeanour, Baba Yaga often assists the hero or heroine in their quest, as the Grey Wolf does for Ivan Tsarevich.

Fairy tales or folktales featuring Baba Yaga and the Grey Wolf were popular, and continue to be so, in Russian culture. Alexander Afanas'ev, who collected and published over six hundred Russian tales in *Popular Russian Fairy Tales, 1855–64*, found his sources primarily among the 'folk' or 'common people'. According to James Riordan, these were 'village teachers, provincial governors, army officers, and others who had recorded tales for their own amusement'.[6] Unlike Perrault in the seventeenth century, Afanas'ev did not attempt to attach morals to the stories he collected and penned, nor did he, like Jacob and Wilhelm Grimm in the early nineteenth century, clean them up or prettify them for children.[7] His stories, pagan in tone, eventually fell under the scrutiny of the Russian Orthodox Church, and Afanas'ev was punished for failing to censor his material. Fired from his clerical job by Alexander II, subjected to poverty and ignominy, he died of consumption at the age of forty-five.[8] Afanas'ev's fairy tale and folktale collections are still primary source material for Russian folklorists.

In Afanas'ev's tales, the Russian forest features prominently as a wild and liminal space; it also offers the only hope of survival for the fairy-tale protagonist. The beings that inhabit the forest (Baba Yaga, the Grey Wolf and the *Leshii* or forest spirits who can transform into wolves) help the heroes and heroines transform their fate. The venue of the forest is important in folktales and fairy tales since it is one of the few spaces where a protagonist-in-distress can access and request the aid of magical beings. The forest is a space that encourages, fosters and thrives on magic – the home and haven for those with supernatural powers, or those seeking supernatural intervention to their problems.

John W. Ellis Etchison writes about the importance of setting in fairy tales: 'Though the forest is sometimes depicted as the *hinterland*, and thus should be avoided, this is not necessarily the case in fairy tales. Often the forest is regarded with reverence, and when so treated provides supernatural aid to any who tarry there.'[9] Like crossbills feeding on pinecone seeds in the spruce trees of Russia's forests, or moose grazing in near-starvation on pine needles, so the fairy-tale protagonist must demonstrate a certain scrappiness, a willingness to do the tough work required for survival in order to earn the respect and subsequent relief of the forest's resident guardians. This business of salvation demands a complete turning over of control to the wild, which is a necessary act of humility and courage for which the protagonist is rewarded. Robert Pogue Harrison describes the effects fairy-tale forests have on the hero or heroine:

> Anyone familiar with the Grimms' fairy tales knows how prominently forests figure in the collection as a whole. These forests typically lie beyond the bounds of the familiar world. They are the places where protagonists get lost, meet unusual creatures, undergo spells and transformations, and confront their destinies … The forests are sometimes places of the illicit … yet more often than not they are places of weird enchantment.[10]

This 'weird enchantment' proves true for the likes of Hansel and Gretel as they bite into the mirage-like structure of the witch's gingerbread home, or even Little Red Cap as she wanders off the path in search of flowers and finds instead a talking wolf, but the 'enchantment' in Russian folktales and fairy tales often reads more like magical realism, where the wolf may be capable of magical feats, yet also exhibits the traits of a natural wolf. The Grey Wolf hunts and devours Ivan's horse like a real wolf, but he also speaks, tricks tsars, and shapeshifts. Baba Yaga lives in a hut that stands on cock's legs and flies around in a mortar that she steers with a pestle, but she also serves teacakes, responds to 'granny', and farts emphatically (p. 52). Grounded in the practical, and rudely physical, minutiae of life, the magic feels the more real – less of an enchantment than a type of magical realism where the supernatural and uncanny are inextricably woven into the fabric of the material world.

This strikingly naturalist interpretation of the *super*-natural may stem from early Russian observations of the *taiga*, the swampy and coniferous forests of the northern latitudes. Sibelan Forrester notes how 'the forest lies at the heart of Russian civilization, holding riches (the honey, wax and furs that early Slavs traded along routes from the Black Sea to Scandinavia) as well as terrors'.[11] The Russian historian Vasili Kliuchevskii similarly describes the forest as a paradoxical place of danger and succour for early settlers of Rus', providing shelter and food but also challenging them with dangers:

> [The forest] seemed to harbour something evil in the fearful, soundless twilights of its ancient summits. The momentary expectation of sudden, unexpected, unforeseen danger strained his nerves, excited his imagination. And the ancient Russian peopled the forest with all kinds of fantastic creatures.[12]

In this way, the forest is a refuge where one can hunt and forage, but it is also a place where one may become prey through encounters with fellow hunters, such as wolves, bears and lynx. The predators who inhabit the *taiga* were viewed not only as competitors for food but as significant threats to human life, inspiring folktales of 'fantastic creatures', such as spirits and witches, who also inhabited the forest – inciting first fear, then hope for the fairy-tale protagonist.

It is in populated areas – farming villages and imperial cities – where the heroes and heroines of Russian fairy tales are most imperilled. For female protagonists, this is especially true as most are beaten and killed by husbands, brothers or fathers who wish them dead. The rampant misogyny in Russian fairy tales and folktales has been studied by Ireneusz Szarycz: 'Woman here is a property to be acquired, an enemy to overcome, a cross to be borne or lawbreaker to be punished'.[13] In other words, if Little Red Cap wandered into a Russian fairy tale, her doom would come not from a witch riding in a mortar, or a wolf in the forest, or even a handsome aristocrat ruining her virginal reputation, but from her own immediate family, where she might be beaten with whips and rods, harnessed to a sledge in place of horses, spat on, tossed into a blazing oven, thrown into a pit to be forgotten or hurled to the earth with such force that only her braid would be found.[14]

For example, Szarycz views the fairy tale 'The Mayoress' as a 'cautionary tale for wives', particularly ambitious ones.[15] The female protagonist/antagonist in 'The Mayoress' desires to be elected mayor by the village council; however, by the end of the tale: 'The Cossack gave her a good thrashing and left, and thereafter the woman no longer wanted to be mayoress, and obeyed her husband'.[16] Yet the mayoress fares better than many women in Russian fairy tales and folktales that 'feature wives beaten or killed by their husbands for assorted crimes'.[17] In Afanas'ev's version of 'The Armless Maiden', 'The husband took the best mare from the stable, tied his wife to its tail, and let it run in the open field. The mare dragged her on the ground until she brought back only her braid; the rest was strewn across the field'.[18] But it is not only husbands who dole out punishments to wicked or ambitious wives in these tales: brothers can also rebuke their sisters. In 'The Milk of Wild Beasts', Prince Ivan ties his sister, Princess Elena, 'naked to a tree, so that her body might be devoured by mosquitoes and flies'.[19] In each case, be it a municipal village, small farming community or tsardom, women are most at risk in 'civilisation' – in communities away from the wild and solitary protection of the forest. Likewise, Ivan Tsarevich, although he is male and allowed much more liberty, is also in jeopardy within his father's tsardom. Eyed jealously by his murderous and competitive brothers, and overlooked by a clueless and impotent father/king, Ivan leaves for the forest at a particularly low point in his beleaguered career as the youngest son in a long line for succession.

So, if the Russian hero or heroine is to survive, they must flee the civilised world, escape the domestic sphere, and make haste for the *taiga*. The wolf's domain is the forest, as is Baba Yaga's, thus the deep woods become the logical destination for the fairy-tale protagonist. They must go into the forest and place themselves into the paws of the wolf or the ancient hands of Baba Yaga, and seek wild sanctuary in order not only to stay alive but to emerge victorious in the human world, equipped with the knowledge and skills acquired in the wild.

In 'Ivan Tsarevich and the Grey Wolf', the Grey Wolf repeatedly saves Ivan on his quest for the fire bird, the gold-maned horse and Iakuta the Beautiful. Ivan must escape a number of tsars, who all wish to cut off his head, while Iakuta must escape Khoshchei the Deathless, who abducts her and wishes to marry her against her will. The threat to Ivan repeatedly comes from inside a tsardom – his own or others' – and the wolf is always there to rescue him. On their first meeting, the Grey Wolf tells Ivan, 'I want only the good, and I'll teach only wisdom' (p. 47). It is a promise the Grey Wolf keeps throughout the story, saving Ivan, but also teaching him how to take care of himself.

When Ivan holds the Grey Wolf's fur tightly in his fists, allowing the wolf to carry him away from danger, it is the first benevolent and heroic act in the fairy tale, where 'humane' acts come only from non-humans: '[the] grey wolf sprang forward, he flew along faster than the whirlwind and hurricane, like a tempered arrow let loose from a tautly drawn bow' (p. 47). Later, when the beautiful maiden, Iakuta, joins their small team, the Grey Wolf continues to serve as protector: 'And off the grey wolf flew. Mountains and rivers passed between his feet, and he dusted the steppe with his tail' (p. 48). The scene where the wolf escapes with Ivan and Iakuta on his back is one of the most popularly illustrated scenes in the tale. It has been depicted by artists such as Viktor Vasnetsov, Boris Vasilyevich Zvorykin and Ivan Bilibin. In Vasnetsov's 1889 illustration (see Figure 5.1), the young lovers escape on the back of the Grey Wolf. The extraordinary size of the wolf is revealed so that he appears more akin to a horse, capable of jumping over a stream and galloping over a muddy forest floor, all with two grown humans seated comfortably on his back. And whilst the wolf appears as sturdily built as any gallant horse, he has the fierceness of a carnivore who can fight with sharp teeth and claws. It is significant that it is not a horse, an animal domesticated by man, which facilitates their escape, but a wild predator. As a result, the Grey Wolf is depicted in both fairy tale and illustration as a more intelligent, independent and intimidating protector for the young couple. In Zvorykin's illustration, the Grey Wolf pushes through sharp branches and dodges pine trees, then leaps over a fen, an owl swerving between his paws. The lovers are secure on the wolf's back, clutching each other, Iakuta on Ivan's lap, the daring escape providing the couple a rare moment of respite for romance.

5.1 Viktor Vasnetsov, *Ivan Tsarevich Riding the Grey Wolf* (1889)

The scene of the lovers' flight in 'Ivan Tsarevich and the Grey Wolf' is also the subject of Russian lacquer boxes – both past and present. Capturing the same bold escape, lacquer artists focus on the mystical capabilities of the Grey Wolf, as well as his loyalty and willingness to risk his own life for the hero and the hero's future bride, Iakuta. In the same way that forests serve as refuges for protagonists in Russian fairy tales, Russian fairy tales served as refuges artistically for early lacquer artists, such as those in Palekh, who could no longer paint religious icons after years of revolution and civil war brought an end to the imperial era and the beginning of a communist one.[20] Instead of painting the now-forbidden saints and biblical figures, they painted the more acceptable fairy tales to escape persecution from a government that closely monitored their work for subversive material. Interestingly, Russian lacquer artists, after painting with egg-tempera-based colours and layers of lacquer, use a giant wolf's fang to burnish the twenty-four-carat gold that finishes the design.[21] These boxes, typically small enough to be held in the palm, are sometimes painted with a single hair, or a paintbrush made from the hair of a squirrel. In one box painted by an unknown artist in the 1920s, and another box painted by a contemporary artist, Sergey Knyazev, one can see that lacquer artists study fairy tales as part of their education and select the same key sequence in 'Ivan Tsarevich'. The lovers ride on the back of the Grey Wolf, who bounds through the forest, a tsardom fading in the distance, a full moon above in the sky and the brilliantly red firebird gliding behind. In art, as well as in the tale, the Grey Wolf does not warn readers or viewers to be careful of wolves; instead, the wolf is depicted as a noble, devoted and potent ally against the cruelty of tsars who wish Ivan and Iakuta dead or separated.

And yet the role of the Grey Wolf is not always so serious. In many Russian folktales, the earthiness extends to bawdy humour, relieving the tension of a daunting scene and catering to an audience that expects laughs as well as romance and adventure. When Tsar Raflet takes Iakuta away from Ivan in order to rape her, Tsar Raflet is surprised to discover that Iakuta is, in fact, the Grey Wolf:

> The tsar Rafley ordered Iakuta the Beautiful to go into his bedroom, where he kissed and caressed her, and grasped her full breasts. But suddenly a wolf's muzzle was stuck in his face, grinding its teeth. (49)

The Grey Wolf spares Iakuta the humiliation, pain and scandal of rape. Furthermore, in a sequence worthy of Bugs Bunny's best drag, the seduction, or groping, is thwarted by the wolf whose shape, including sex, is conveniently fluid. Besides the comedic aspect of a randy tsar grasping the breasts of an angry wolf, there is the satisfying comeuppance of the tsar receiving his just deserts. There is also a reversal of expectation since the fairy-tale wolf is often portrayed as sexually rapacious, whereas the Grey Wolf is not filled with lust but instead protects virginity. In Perrault's 'Little Red Riding Hood', the protagonist is the victim of the wolf's appetites, both sexual and of the stomach, but the Grey Wolf is neither a glutton nor a sexual predator; he is the knight-in-shining-fur. In the end, there is no dead girl. No dead grandma. No didactic lesson on sexual misbehaviour. There is only one terrified tsar who may think twice before he orders another girl into his royal love-nest.

Although Tsar Raflet desires Ivan in the grave and Iakuta in his bed, the threat to Ivan is not always imperial. Ivan's family, his brothers Lopai and Krutin, agree to kill Ivan in order to obtain the treasures he has acquired with the help of the Grey Wolf, including Iakuta: 'They decided to kill their blood brother. They chopped off his head, and then they started dividing up the booty' (p. 53). Although the brothers are in turn killed by Khoshchei the Deathless, who then takes the treasures for himself, Ivan is left dead for two days. On the third day, the Grey Wolf arrives and obtains life-restoring water from the ravens:

> So then the raven and the little ravens flapped their wings and the grey wolf went up to Ivan Tsarevich and sprinkled him with some water from the first bag in which the living water was, and immediately his head grew together with his body, and then he sprinkled him a second time, and Ivan sighed, so then he sprinkled him a third time and this time Ivan Tsarevich sat up on his butt and said, 'Oh, how long I've slept!'
>
> Then the grey wolf said to him, 'Yes, Ivan Tsarevich, you would have had to sleep forever if not for me.' (p. 51)

The Grey Wolf becomes more than a means of escape, or even a lucky charm to obtain rare and beautiful objects: he becomes a saviour, able to perform a resurrection, which is a type of magic that borders on the spiritual. Blessed water that is sprinkled or poured is used both baptismally and to cleanse the dead – and the Grey Wolf utilises it three times to bring Ivan back from the dead. The threefold repetition is a common numerical fairy-tale motif, yet the number three can also represent the Holy Trinity of the Father, Son and Holy Spirit. This may have been one of the reasons the Russian Orthodox Church found Afanas'ev's tales immoral and offensive to religious doctrine in the nineteenth century. The Grey Wolf as a helper is one thing, but the Grey Wolf as a Christ-figure is quite another.

After Ivan's resurrection from death, the fairy tale is half over; Ivan Tsarevich has lost most of what he has obtained, but he has his life owing to the wolf. However, the Grey Wolf admits that he can no longer accompany Ivan on his quest because his powers are geographically limited. He tells Ivan: 'I would go with you to get back your treasure, but I am not permitted to go further than here. This is my legal limit' (51). He then directs Ivan to Baba Yaga's house – an *izba* or log cabin on cock's legs where the witch waits. The wolf gives him sage advice on how to handle the Yaga, who has a well-earned reputation for being a terror: 'At first she'll be angry with you and even seek to eat you up. But you tell her that grey wolf has sent you. She knows me and will teach you how to bring about the death of Khoshchei' (51).

Now that the protective role of the wolf has ended and that of the witch begun, the distinction between animal behaviour and human behaviour is pronounced. The wolf commits violence in order to live – he eats prey during the course of the tale, but he kills for sustenance and survival; he has no ulterior motive. In fact, the Grey Wolf is made distinct from, perhaps even superior to, human nature since he never feels or expresses the most explicitly featured human emotions in the tale: envy, greed and lust. He never attempts to steal, except to aid Ivan; he prevents the rape of the princess, and restores life when it is taken away by homicidal and covetous brothers. He is both a teacher and a helper to the end: even his final act is to send Ivan to the only being who can help him defeat Khoshchei the Deathless – Baba Yaga.

Many scholars of Russian history and folklore, such as Andreas Johns, trace Baba Yaga's origins to natural forces or ancient pagan religions. The Yaga has been associated with winter and rainbows, along with demons and the East Slavic goddess Mokosh.[22] Szarycz believes that Baba Yaga transitioned from a goddess or nature deity to a witch as a result of 'the introduction of Christianity to 10th-century Russia'; she writes, '[Baba Yaga] offers aid because she is part of a pagan community and functions within that community as a sort of shaman. It is her role to help those in need.'[23] Thus, in some fairy tales and folktales, Baba Yaga is unfairly demonised because the community that told the tale came to view goddesses, paganism and witches with fear and disdain. However, Baba Yaga's destructive power does not necessarily have to be regarded as negative since she is meant to be a liminal figure – frequently on the border between life and death. Helena Goscilo examines the paradoxes Baba Yaga exhibits in Russian fairy tales: 'A composite of contradictory traits, [Baba Yaga] encompasses the paradoxes of nature: life and death, destruction and renewal, the feminine and the masculine'.[24] And still, despite her deadly skills and predilections, Baba Yaga is indeed a helper in many tales, as she is for Ivan Tsarevich. However, Ivan's connection to the Grey Wolf is what provides him with acceptance from this wise and temperamental witch of the forest, since, at first, and somewhat characteristically, Baba Yaga does try to eat him. But then Ivan quickly divulges his connection to the Grey Wolf, instantly quelling her cannibalistic appetites: '"Grey wolf?" she says. "I know him. He is a friend and relation"' (p. 52).

Traditionally, Baba Yaga has been associated with animals of the forest. She can command them at will, and they will obey her, and yet there is no master/servant dynamic. Perhaps this is due to her deep connection to animals, which is hinted at in her response – the wolf is her 'relation', not simply a friend, ally or fellow forest dweller and meat eater. Sibelan Forrester describes Baba Yaga's role 'as an initiatrix, a vestigial goddess, a forest power and a mistress of birds and animals'.[25] In this tale, and others where Baba Yaga aids the protagonist, 'forest power' and 'mistress of animals' are her most significant roles in terms of her connection to the forest, which offers sanctuary to worthy heroes and heroines.

In fairy tales and folktales, animals (wolves, mice, cats, bears, for instance) often take on the role of helpers. Olga Gradinaru notes that Baba Yaga in her 'sympathetic position' functions exactly like an animal helper or donor.[26] For example, in a version of the tale, 'Go I Don't Know Where, Bring I Don't Know What', the hero, Fedot, goes to three Baba Yagas in search of help, much like Ivan Tsarevich. In order to assist him, all three Baba Yagas call on animals for service. To gather the animals, 'The old woman called out in a loud voice and gave a manly whistle, and all the birds came flying to her', while the second Yaga gathered the beasts, and the third, 'all the reptiles of every name [who] came crawling, both the hissing snakes and the jumping frogs'.[27] Thus the rescue inspires and requires a family reunion. And what makes Baba Yaga so terrible – her gory cravings, her unpredictability, her wildness – are also what make her such an enormous asset to the fairy-tale protagonist. If the hero or heroine needs someone to have their back in a fight against humanity's evils, a predatory wolf or a terrifying witch is probably their best bet.

The trinity of Yagas may be more willing to help Fedot because the girl he wishes to rescue is their niece – a young woman, or Yagishna, who can shapeshift into a mourning dove – another hereditary human/animal alliance with Baba Yaga. In 'Go I Don't Know Where, Bring I Don't Know What', Baba Yaga's niece transforms as a means of protection since her human beauty attracts unwanted attention. However, Szarycz claims that the niece's transformation is meant to 'ensure [her] own faithfulness during [her] husband's absence'.[28] While there is an unmistakable vein of misogyny in this tale, as in many Russian fairy tales and folktales, the niece may just as well become unfaithful to her husband in her animal form – surely there is no lack of male mourning doves in the vicinity. Furthermore, physical transformation is a gift and skill, an ability that makes her arguably more powerful than the general population as well as her fiancé. However, there is peril for female shapeshifters in fairy tales from all cultures. Although male shapeshifters, with the exception of the Grey Wolf, are often cursed to take the form of beasts or boars or frogs, women simply change their form because they can. Unfortunately, however, Scandinavian swan maidens and Celtic selkies often have their feathers or skins captured by men who force them to stay in their human form in order to wed them. Similarly, in the Russian fairy tale 'The Frog Princess', the prince takes a frog as his wife because of a lost bet, only to find that she is a witch who can be a woman if and when she chooses. Delighted with this turn of events, the prince takes matters into his own hands: 'The ball was over. Prince Ivan went home first, found his wife's skin somewhere, took and burned it. She arrived, looked for the skin, but it was gone, burned.'[29] So, while young women in fairy tales may have the ability to become mourning doves and frogs, they still fall prey to men who forcibly take away their wildness in order to become their husbands.

Baba Yaga, as a formidable witch and aged spinster, encounters no such opposition from men. Instead, she either helps them – that is, if they have the proper reference – or has them for dinner. Luckily, in the case of both Fedot and Ivan, animals guide her to aid them. For Ivan Tsarevich, Baba Yaga does not need to consult animals in order to discover what she already knows and what Ivan must learn in order to win back his possessions and Iakuta, which is how to kill Khoshchei the Deathless. Although Khoshchei is often considered a male counterpart to Baba Yaga, unlike Baba Yaga, he is not immortal; his death is simply located and hidden outside of himself. The Yaga tells Ivan exactly where to find it – on an island inside a tree inside a hare inside a duck inside an egg. The success of the quest is up to Ivan (he succeeds, of course), but the knowledge must be obtained by a witch wise enough to know Khoshchei's secret.

Although Baba Yaga occasionally supports the male protagonist in his quest (usually only if he is referred by a forest creature), she can be especially helpful to girls, particularly those escaping the brutality of their families. In his study of 'Tales of Magic' or 'Wonder Tales', Vladimir Propp uses the tale of 'Morozko', in which a tormented stepdaughter is sent into the woods by her stepmother, to illustrate how wild sanctuary is provided by the forest and its inhabitants: 'Thus Baba Yaga, Morozko, the bear, the forest spirit, and the mare's head test and reward the stepdaughter.'[30] In another famous tale of an imperilled stepdaughter, 'Vasilisa the Beautiful', Baba Yaga again offers aid to a worthy heroine, who, like Ivan Tsarevich, leaves the dwelling of her cruel family and heads off into the 'deep, dark forest'. Ellis-Etchison views Baba Yaga in this fairy tale as a 'monstrous mother-figure' since her lessons are harsh but life-saving.[31] After putting Vasilisa through several trials, Baba Yaga rewards her nerve and stoicism by giving her a skull from her illuminated fence of skulls, which Vasilisa carries home and which incinerates her entire stepfamily: 'They tried to hide, but no matter where they ran, the eyes kept following them. Toward morning it had burned them entirely to ashes.'[32] In 1899, Ivan Bilibin illustrated the scene where Vasilisa carries the skeletal torch home (see Figure 5.2). With ferns and mushrooms at her feet, cedar and spruce over her head, and a fence of skulls at her back, Vasilisa seems to glow with confidence, much like her torch. She has earned this gift from the Yaga: not simply the gift of a fiery torch to relight the hearth but the wisdom and steeliness she has gained from her stay. Baba Yaga's knowledge and gifts are not given lightly to the ignorant or uninitiated. And they always result in a harsh, but fair, code of justice – one that rewards patience and practicality while disdaining whining and simpering and calculated malice.

5.2 Ivan Bilibin, *Vasilisa the Beautiful* (1899)

In 1947, the Russian expatriate author Nadezhda Teffi recognised the unique power of Baba Yaga:

> The word 'goddess' conjured up images of beauty – of Venus or Diana. We'd seen statues of them, images of perfection. We'd heard people say, 'She looks like a goddess.' And then it turned out that our own goddess, our own Russian goddess,

is this terrible witch – this hideous, vicious old woman. It seemed ridiculous and absurd ... But Baba Yaga is the most terrifying of them all, and the most interesting. And the most Russian. Other nations did not have goddesses like Baba Yaga.[33]

Teffi adds that Baba Yaga lives alone in the forest because she distrusts humanity: '[Baba Yaga] knew only too well that every human approach brought with it deception and hurt. "I can smell the smell of a Russian" meant that she could expect trouble.'[34] And even though protagonists like Ivan or Vasilisa or Fedot do complicate the Yaga's life, and jeopardise the lives of the Grey Wolf or other animal helpers, the helpers know that it is their responsibility to help when humanity has failed – when lustful tsars, greedy families and violent menfolk want to beat the young protagonists into submission, or perhaps to death. The forest, and those who inhabit it, offer asylum from the evils of the world, a chance to regroup, to heal, and to achieve a kind of justice not possible without wild, supernatural intervention.

Notes

1 I am thinking primarily of such familiar fairy tales and folktales as those from Charles Perrault's *Tales and Stories of the Past with Morals, or Tales of Mother Goose* (1697) and Jacob and Wilhelm Grimm's *Children's and Household Tales* (1812).
2 Haney, 'Introduction', *An Anthology of Russian Folktales*, p. xxi.
3 Graves, *Wolves in Russia*, pp. 24–5; 29.
4 Afanas'ev, *Russian Fairy Tales*, pp. 309–12.
5 This Russian folktale, a combination of SUS 550 and 328, appears as 'Prince Ivan, the Firebird, and the Grey Wolf', in Afanas'ev's *Russian Fairy Tales*, pp. 612–24. However, it does not include Baba Yaga and Koshcheii. The version of 'Ivan Tsarevitch and the Grey Wolf' that appears in Haney, *An Anthology of Russian Folktales* does feature Baba Yaga in the second half of the tale. 'Ivan Tsarevitch and the Grey Wolf' was recounted by E.I. Sorokovikov in 1938 and published in *Staryi fol'klor Pribaikal'ia* by A.V. Gurevich and L.E. Eliasov in 1939. For this chapter, I will use the translation by Haney in *An Anthology of Russian Folktales*, pp. 44–56. Further references to this story are given in parentheses in the body of the text.
6 Riordan, 'Russian Fairy Tales', p. 222.
7 *Ibid.*
8 *Ibid.*, p. 224.
9 Ellis-Etchison, '"But Not Every Question Has a Good Answer"', in *Turning Points*, ed. by DeVine and Hendry, p. 84.
10 Harrison, *Forests*, p. 169.
11 Forrester, 'The Wild Witch of the East', in *Russian Magic Tales*, p. 431.
12 Kliuchevskii and Shatz, *A Course of Russian History*, pp. 36–7.

13 Szarycz, 'Morsels on the Tongue', p. 65.
14 I am thinking of well-known Russian folktales such as 'The Mayoress', 'The Frog Princess', 'Daughter and Stepdaughter' and 'The Milk of Wild Beasts'.
15 Szarycz, p. 65.
16 Afanas'ev, 'The Mayoress', in *Russian Fairy Tales*, p. 141.
17 Szarycz, p. 65.
18 Afanas'ev, 'The Armless Maiden', in *Russian Fairy Tales*, pp. 298–9.
19 Afanas'ev, 'The Milk of Wild Beasts', in *Russian Fairy Tales*, p. 306.
20 Jenks, *Russia in a Box*, p. 84.
21 Mutch, 'A Russian Lacquer Revival'.
22 Johns, *Baba Yaga*, pp. 12, 29.
23 Szarycz, pp. 68, 70.
24 Goscilo, 'Introduction', p. 13.
25 Forrester, 'The Wild Witch of the East', p. 429.
26 Gradinaru, 'Myth and Rationality in Russian Popular Fairy Tales', p. 321.
27 Afanas'ev, 'Go I Don't Know Where, Bring I Don't Know What', in *Baba Yaga*, n. 25, p. 189.
28 Szarycz, p. 66.
29 Afanas'ev, 'The Frog Princess', in *Russian Fairy Tales*, p. 122.
30 Propp, *Morphology of the Folktale*, p. 20.
31 Ellis-Etchison, p. 81.
32 Afanas'ev, 'Vasilisa the Beautiful', in *Baba Yaga*, pp. 170–82 (p. 180).
33 Teffi, 'Baba Yaga', in Chandler, ed., *Russian Magic Tales*, pp. 213–17 (pp. 213–14).
34 Teffi, pp. 214–15.

6

'NO MORE THAN A BRUTE OR A WILD BEAST':
Wagner the Wehr-wolf, *Sweeney Todd* AND THE LIMITS OF HUMAN RESPONSIBILITY

Joseph Crawford

On the afternoon of 20 January 1843, Mr Edward Drummond, personal secretary to the then-Prime Minister Robert Peel, left his offices at Whitehall and set off on his daily walk home. Unbeknownst to him, a politically radical Glaswegian wood-turner named Daniel M'Naghten or McNaghten was lurking outside, waiting for the Prime Minister himself. At his subsequent trial, McNaghten, who seems to have suffered from paranoid delusions, insisted that Robert Peel was the leader of a conspiracy by which he had been persecuted for years; that day he had come to Whitehall with a pair of loaded pistols hidden in his coat, determined to put an end to Peel's persecutions once and for all. In 1843, with daguerreotype technology still in its infancy, most people still had only the vaguest idea of what the public figures of the day actually looked like; and so, mistaking Drummond for Peel, McNaghten stepped up behind him and shot him in the back. Drummond died of his injuries five days later.

The police grabbed McNaghten before he'd even finished drawing his second pistol, and his case was rushed to trial; but to the surprise of many, and the extreme displeasure of Queen Victoria – who was herself the subject of assassination attempts by lunatics on a semi-regular basis – he was found 'not guilty by reason of insanity'. Having thus cheated the gallows, he spent the rest of his life first in Bedlam and then in Broadmoor, ultimately dying in Broadmoor Hospital twenty-two years after his initial confinement.[1]

To understand why this verdict came as such a shock to many people, it is necessary to understand the contemporary state of lunacy legislation in Britain. According to British law, an individual could plead innocence due to insanity only if they committed their crimes while in a state of such extreme mental disorder that they had no idea what they were doing, and no control over their actions. More specifically, a whole sequence of legal authorities from the thirteenth century all the way up to the eighteenth asserted that the test for criminal responsibility was essentially this: when the accused committed their crime, were they behaving like a rational human being, or like a wild animal?

In his classic work on English law, written in about 1265, Henry De Bracton defined the *furiosus*, the man who was too far gone in madness to be held responsible for his actions, as one who was 'lacking in reason and not far from the brutes'.[2] Four and a half centuries later, lawyers were still defining the limits of responsibility in very similar language: in the summing-up for the important 1724 case of *Rex* v. *Arnold*, it was specified that in order to be 'exempted from punishment' a madman needed to be someone who is 'deprived of his reason and memory, and doth not know what he is doing, no more than an infant, than a brute or a wild beast', and in 1736 Sir Matthew Hale explained that the insane 'act not as reasonable creatures', and 'are in effect in the condition of brutes'.[3] The law thus envisioned madness as a kind of state of legal lycanthropy: the mad person was an individual who, while still human, was afflicted with a condition which meant that they spent some or all of their life behaving like a wild beast instead. It was only while in this beastlike state that the lunatic, the *furiosus*, was held to be exempt from normal legal responsibility and hence from punishment.

In cases of violent crime, the kind of madness envisioned by the law, here, is clearly a form of frenzy: the lunatic is not legally responsible for their actions so long as they are carried out in a fit or paroxysm of insanity. In such cases, the 'brute' that the lunatic needs to resemble in order to avoid punishment is not just any animal but some traditionally aggressive 'wild beast', such as a tiger, wolf or rabid dog. It was for this reason that when Mary Lamb stabbed her mother in 1796 she was held to be exempt from punishment, as was Richard Dadd after he killed his father in 1843: having murdered their loved ones in mad outbursts of uncharacteristic violence and aggression, they were judged not to have been responsible for their actions, and thus to deserve pity (and medical treatment) rather than condemnation and execution. When *The Times* reported the murder of Elizabeth Lamb, it stressed the wildness of her daughter's behaviour during the murder:

> The child, by her cries, quickly brought up the landlord of the house, but too late. The dreadful scene presented to him the mother lifeless, pierced to the heart, on a chair, her daughter yet wildly standing over her with the fatal knife, and the old man her father weeping by her side, himself bleeding at the forehead from the effects of a severe blow he received from one of the forks she had been madly hurling about the room ... It seems the young lady had been once before deranged. The Jury of course brought in their verdict, *Lunacy*.[4]

'Madly hurling' carving forks at her father, stabbing her mother to death with a case knife, acting in such a state of frenzy that even when she stood still she did so 'wildly': this was exactly the kind of behaviour which legal writers had in mind when they described the *furiosus* (or *furiosa*, in this case) as behaving like 'a brute or a wild beast'. The fact that Mary wasn't normally like this, that just minutes before the murder she had been attending to her ordinary household tasks, made it easy for the jury to accept that this beastlike state represented an aberrant transformation of an otherwise normal human being, rather than a revelation of her own true and authentic criminal nature. Like the jurymen who tried her, the anonymous author of this article seems to have taken it for granted that Mary Lamb was not responsible for what she did while thus transformed, and did not deserve to be punished for it. 'The Jury of course brought in their verdict, *Lunacy.*'

The case of Richard Dadd, while more extreme, was basically similar in this respect. Before going to Egypt in 1842, Dadd had been friendly, well-liked and at most mildly eccentric; but he returned a disturbingly changed man, convinced that the Devil was lurking everywhere and that the ancient Egyptian god Osiris had given him the sacred task of killing those demons who disguised themselves as human beings. Concluding that his own father was one of these demons in human form, Dadd lured him out to a chalk pit in Cobham Park and hacked him to death with a razor and a clasp knife; he then fled to France, where he was arrested after attempting to murder a complete stranger in the belief that the unfortunate Frenchman was yet another demon in disguise. Both the French and British authorities immediately classed Dadd as a madman rather than a criminal, and his case was judged via a medical assessment rather than a criminal trial, leading him to spend the rest of his life in lunatic asylums.[5] (In fact, both at Bedlam and at Broadmoor, Dadd would have been one of McNaghten's fellow-inmates.) The irrationality of his claims, the savagery and apparent randomness of his attacks, and the shocking change in his personality and behaviour after his journey to Egypt allowed him, like Lamb, to be classed as a *furiosus:* one who no longer acted like a 'reasonable creature', and who, at least during the attacks themselves, was 'in effect in the condition of brutes'. The *Illustrated London News* even described him in terms reminiscent of a predatory animal:

> A rumour was prevalent during the week that he ... had been arrested at Calais by one of the Bow Street officers on Monday last, but we regret to state that this is not the fact, and that the savage maniac is still prowling about in quest perhaps, of other victims.[6]

Just as Lamb had been 'wild', so Dadd was described as being 'savage', their ferocity linking them to wild animals and beasts of prey. He is described as 'prowling', like a wolf or tiger, and the suggestion that he is 'prowling about in quest perhaps, of other victims' is reminiscent of the description of the Devil as a wild animal in 1 Peter 5:8, where it is said that 'as a roaring lion, [he] walketh about, seeking whom he may devour'. In other respects, Dadd's behaviour was not really animalistic at all: he was able to deliver a clear (if not exactly rational) account of his belief that he was the chosen instrument of the god Osiris, and while in Bedlam and Broadmoor he remained devoted to the very un-beastlike activity of painting, producing many of his most famous works during his asylum years. But the frenzied violence of his unprovoked attacks was enough to ensure that he, like Lamb, was classed as a lunatic requiring medical treatment rather than as a criminal requiring trial and punishment.

Essentially, the more beastlike the lunatic's behaviour, and the greater the discontinuity between their behaviour before and during their fit of madness, the less likely they were to be found guilty of any crimes they might commit while the frenzy was on them. The fact that both Lamb and Dadd had previously had positive, loving relationships with their parents before their respective mental breakdowns, and that they carried out their murders in what seemed to be sudden outbursts of animalistic fury, using forks, knives and razors much as a wild animal might use its teeth and claws, made it easier for them to be classed as lunatics rather than criminals. The McNaghten verdict came as a surprise precisely because he *hadn't* behaved in this way: rather than falling upon Drummond in a beastlike rage, roaring and howling and foaming at the mouth, he had coolly walked up behind him and shot him in the back. This was hardly the behaviour of 'a brute or a wild beast'; and, indeed, the legal precedent established by his case led to the reformulation of the rules governing lunacy and criminality in Britain.

The new rules, known as the 'McNaghten Rules' after the man whose trial had led to their creation, no longer required mad people to sink to the level of a wild animal before deeming them to be no longer responsible for their actions: instead it would suffice if they were sufficiently deluded to genuinely believe that they were doing nothing wrong at the moment they committed the crimes. (The fact that James Hadfield, a brain-damaged ex-soldier who attempted to assassinate George III in 1800, was also found not guilty by reason of insanity demonstrated that such standards had, in practice, sometimes been used in the past: Hadfield's behaviour both during and after the attack was deeply odd, but he clearly knew what he was doing when he attempted to shoot the king.)[7] The new test was defined as follows:

> To establish a defence on the ground of insanity, it must be clearly proved that, at the time of the committing of the act, the party accused was labouring under such a defect of reason, from disease of the mind, as not to know the nature and quality of the act he was doing; or, if he did know it, that he did not know he was doing what was wrong.[8]

It was on the second of these grounds that McNaghten, like Hadfield before him, was held to have not been responsible for his misdeeds: not because he did not know what he was doing when he pulled the trigger of his pistol but because he was so disconnected from reality that he really thought he was righteously avenging himself on a man who had spent years spying on him and persecuting him, rather than murdering a man who had no idea who he was whatsoever.[9]

The reason I have dredged up all this legal history in a chapter about werewolves is that this controversy over the limits of criminal responsibility forms part of the cultural context in which the popular werewolf narrative in English was born. The first wave of modern English-language werewolf fiction was written between 1827 and 1847, and it repeatedly associated lycanthropy with both criminality and madness. H. Laurence's 'Norman of the Strong Arm' (1827), Richard Thomson's 'The Wehr-Wolf' (1828) and Sutherland Menzies's 'Hughes, the Wer-Wolf' (1838) all feature outlaws who are or pretend to be werewolves, and both Thomson's and Menzies's stories, like Leitch Ritchie's 'The Man-Wolf' (1830), feature characters who *believe* themselves to be werewolves due to episodes of mental disturbance. In his 1865 *Book of Were-wolves*, Sabine Baring-Gould even asserted that most European werewolf stories had their origins in the real histories of individuals who had been maniacs, outlaws, or both, arguing that

> [W]e may rest assured that there is a solid core of fact, round which popular superstition has crystallized; and that fact is the existence of a species of madness, during the accesses of which the person afflicted believes himself to be a wild beast, and acts like a wild beast[.][10]

And also that

> The word *vargr*, a wolf, had a double significance, which would be the means of originating many a were-wolf story. *Vargr* is the same as *u-argr*, restless; *argr* being the same as the Anglo-Saxon *earg*. *Vargr* had its double signification in Norse. It signified a wolf, and also a godless man ... The Anglo-Saxons regarded him as an evil man: *wearg*, a scoundrel; Gothic *varys*, a fiend. But very often the word meant no more than an outlaw.[11]

The werewolf, then, could be a symbolic or garbled description of a man who behaved like a wild beast: because he was evil, and/or because he was insane and/or because he had been outlawed and driven from society into the wilds, thus forcing him to live like an animal. The idea that the outlaw might be a kind of honorary werewolf surfaces in Thomson's 'The Wehr-Wolf', in which Count Gaspar de Marcanville, the 'wehr-wolf' of the title, reassures his daughter that he has nothing to fear from robbers, because 'wolves, thou trowest, will not prey upon wolves'; and the related idea that simply living in the forest like a wild beast might suffice to turn a man into an animal is evident from his subsequent insistence that he himself would welcome such a fate:

> 'I tell thee Adéle, that but for thy sake I should never again quit the forest, but would remain there in a savage life, till I forgot my language and my species, and became a Wehr-wolf, or a wild buck!'[12]

Gaspar feels this antisocial desire to sink into a purely bestial state because he is 'half frenzied', having 'work[ed] himself almost to madness' by ceaselessly repeating the narrative of his own misfortunes. In this particular story his lycanthropy turns out to be literal – he really *can* transform himself into a giant wolf – but his language strongly suggests that others might become almost equally wolflike despite not experiencing any actual physical transformation. The forest-dwelling 'robbers' feared by his daughter, whom she describes as being 'still more cruel' than 'fierce howling wolves', may have become almost interchangeable with actual 'Wehr-wolves' simply through undergoing some combination of outlawry, exile and insanity.[13]

This connection between insanity, criminality and lycanthropy is drawn particularly clearly by Sutherland Menzies in a scene from his 1838 story 'Hughes, the Wer-Wolf'. Like Thomson's Count Gaspar, the eponymous Hughes has already been reduced to a semi-animal condition by being forced to live out in the woods, but his true transformation does not come until the moment when, starving and grief-stricken, he discovers the werewolf costume of his grandfather:

> Hunger and despair conjointly hurried him away: he saw objects no longer save through a bloody prism: he felt his very teeth on edge with an avidity for biting; he experienced an inconceivable desire to run: he set himself to howl as though he had practised wer-wolfery all his life, and began thoroughly to invest himself with the guise and attributes of his novel vocation. A more startling change could scarcely have been wrought in him, had that so horribly grotesque metamorphosis really been the effect of enchantment; aided, too, as it was, by the fever which generated a temporary insanity in his frenzied brain.[14]

In the throes of this 'insanity', Hughes dresses himself in wolf-skins and goes out to extort meat from the local butcher, threatening to eat him alive if he does not comply. He does not actually turn into a wolf, but the text makes clear that the 'temporary insanity in his frenzied brain' has wrought a 'horribly grotesque metamorphosis' in him none the less, effectively transforming him into another person for the duration of his adventure. His wolf-skin garments thus serve as a kind of literalised metaphor, an externalised advertisement of the fact that a criminal in the grip of insanity is more like a wild beast than a man.

The most famous werewolf narrative written in this period is, of course, *Wagner the Were-wolf* by G.M.W. Reynolds. Written four years after the

McNaghten case, it provided the blueprint for most subsequent werewolf fiction in English; crucially, unlike all the previous narratives, it introduced the idea of the werewolf's transformation as entirely involuntary, occurring each month at the full moon. (This connection with the moon, so central to most subsequent werewolf fiction, also serves to connect the werewolf's curse more directly to the condition of 'lunacy', which was traditionally thought to be aggravated by the light of the full moon; in *Jane Eyre*, for example, the beastlike madwoman Bertha Mason, who 'growled like some strange wild animal', is at her most destructive when the full moon is in the sky.)[15] In many of the earlier fictions from the 1820s and 1830s, the decision of the werewolves to transform themselves seems to be sometimes voluntary (usually a matter of deliberately donning an enchanted garment), sometimes involuntary and sometimes in-between, as when Hughes chooses to don the wolf-skin because he is under the influence of a 'temporary insanity' and 'inconceivable desire'. In *Wagner the Wehr-wolf*, however, the transformation is always and only involuntary: each month, Wagner succumbs to a fit in which, like the *furiosus* of English law, he becomes 'a brute or a wild beast' without 'understanding and memory', waking up the following morning with no idea what he has done during the night. The kinship between werewolf and lunatic, already implicit in the fact that his transformations are linked to the lunar cycle, is emphasised by the first description of his transformation from man to wolf:

> In the midst of a wood of evergreens on the banks of the Arno, a man – young, handsome, and splendidly attired – has thrown himself upon the ground, where he writhes like a stricken serpent.
>
> He is the prey of a demoniac excitement: an appalling consternation is on him – madness is in his brain – his mind is on fire.
>
> Lightnings appear to gleam from his eyes – as if his soul were dismayed, and withering within his breast.
>
> 'Oh! No, no!' he cries, with a piercing shriek, as if wrestling madly – furiously – but vainly, against some unseen fiend that holds him in his grasp.
>
> And the wood echoes to that terrible wail: and the startled bird flies fluttering from its bough.
>
> But, lo! What awful change is taking place in the form of that doomed being? His handsome countenance elongates into one of savage and brute-like shape.[16]

This whole passage could easily be describing the collapse of a madman into a manic fit, rather than the transformation of a man into a wolf. All his initial symptoms are mental rather than physical: he feels excitement, madness and a burning in his brain, and he responds by falling on the floor writhing and shrieking 'madly – furiously'. Even the initial change of his 'handsome countenance' into a 'savage and brute-like shape' could describe the changing expression of the victim of lunacy as their frenzy-fit came over them, rather than the shift of a human face into the face of a wolf; and it is only in the following line, which describes his clothes turning into fur, that any kind of overt supernatural transformation starts to take place.

Wagner, then, is basically an extremely literal version of the pre-McNaghten lunatic: indeed, he resembles the *furiosus* of English law rather more than he resembles the werewolf of continental tradition, even dispensing with the magical ointments and wolf-skin garment which most of them required to bring about their transformations.[17] Like the madman, Wagner suffers fits in which he behaves like a wild animal, during which he is 'totally deprived of his understanding and memory'; and in this state he carries out crimes which he would otherwise never dream of performing. (In this chapter, for example, he murders a small child, although he is not aware of this when he returns to human form.)[18] He embodies the older, eighteenth-century conception of madness as a state of total otherness, in which the lunatic becomes mentally inhuman in their frenzy-fit. Like Wagner in his wolf form, such a person cannot be reasoned with, and cannot be restrained by either the teachings of morality or the fear of punishment: instead, they must simply be locked away until such time as they return to something like their right mind.[19]

However, as I have discussed, the years in which this and other werewolf stories were starting to appear in England was a period in which this view of insanity was increasingly being challenged by the medical profession, in favour of a much more capacious interpretation of madness which included far more than just the raving and violent convulsions of the *furiosus*. The McNaghten rules were an expression of this change, as such a ruling – that individuals could know full well who they were and what they were doing when they committed an act of murder, and yet still be found not guilty by virtue of insanity – was able to pass successfully through the court only because the weight of expert medical opinion was already behind it. Indeed, by 1843, many British doctors had already extended their definitions of insanity far beyond even those used in the McNaughten rules. Already, medical writers such as James Cowles Pritchard had started to write about cases of what they called 'moral insanity', a form of madness whose only symptom was a disregard for moral norms, thus opening the way for virtually all kinds of wickedness and criminality to be understood as medical rather than moral issues. In his 1835 *Treatise on Insanity,* Pritchard defined 'moral insanity' as follows:

> *Moral Insanity,* or madness consisting in a morbid perversion of the natural feelings, affections, inclinations, temper, habits, moral dispositions, and natural impulses, without any remarkable disorder or defect of the intellect or knowing and reasoning faculties, and particularly without any insane illusion or hallucination.[20]

Before the McNaghten rules, the law recognised madness as superseding criminal guilt only in cases of what Pritchard calls 'remarkable disorder or defect of the intellect or knowing and reasoning faculties', as when Mary Lamb stabbed her mother to death in a fit of sudden and apparently irrational rage: a human being behaving like a wild beast because their higher faculties had been temporarily suspended by insanity. After the new rules, the law also explicitly recognised that criminal guilt was inapplicable in cases of what he calls 'insane illusion or hallucination', such as that of McNaghten himself: so an individual might understand that they were committing murder, and even make elaborate plans and preparations to do so, and yet still be found not guilty if their reasons for carrying out the murder were based on insane delusions or hallucinations of their own. But Pritchard's concept of 'moral insanity' went further than either of these, arguing that people who took rational (but immoral) actions for rational (but immoral) reasons should *still* be classed as insane if their 'natural feelings' and 'moral dispositions' bore sufficient signs of 'morbid perversion'.

It was in this sense that a figure such as Wagner's fictional near-contemporary Sweeney Todd could be understood as insane despite his lack of frenzies: he might not suffer from 'insane illusion or hallucination', but his 'affections' and 'inclinations' have suffered such severe 'morbid perversion' that he is willing to make his living by murdering people, looting their bodies and using their corpses as the filling for meat pies. 'Todd' was an old word for fox, and Todd is indeed vulpine in his treatment of his victims: but his bestial inhumanity is expressed through his predatory immorality rather than by his actually behaving like an animal, let alone physically turning into one. (His name may be an allusion to the English fairy-tale villain Mr Fox, who, like Todd, murders and robs a whole succession of victims; in the German version of the same story, 'The Robber Bridegroom', he eats their corpses, too.)[21] Similarly, in his description of historical cannibals and serial killers in his *Book of Were-wolves*, Baring-Gould moves fluidly between killers who carried out their crimes in paroxysms of insanity, often while believing themselves to actually be wolves, and those who committed them simply because they felt an overpowering desire for blood, violence or human flesh.[22] For Baring-Gould, writing in 1865, both types could equally be held up as examples of insanity: but, for an earlier generation, the killer who carries out murders because they sincerely believe that they have been transformed into a frenzied wolf would have been seen as a mad person worthy of compassion, while the killer who kills simply because they take great joy in the infliction of suffering would have been viewed as evil rather than insane, deserving the full punishment of the law. (Robert Browning plays on this ambiguity when, in his 1868 poem *The Ring and the Book*, he describes the murderer Guido and his men as 'a pack of were-wolves', complete with 'blood-bright eyes' and 'tongues that lolled': their deeds of violence are brutal and bestial enough, but the extent to which they should be considered morally culpable for them is precisely the question with which the poem is concerned.)[23]

It was only the mid-nineteenth-century expansion of the concept of madness which allowed Baring-Gould to lump together the crazed, hallucinating *furiosus* with the cruel-but-rational sadist as near-interchangeable examples of werewolf-like insanity.

Why, then, might the werewolf appear in British literature at the very point in history when British doctors, lawyers and juries were losing faith in the *furiosus*, his human equivalent, as an adequate depiction of insanity? My guess is highly conjectural; but I would speculate that, within the context of the 1830s and 1840s, the werewolf, odd though this may sound, may actually have been a rather reassuring figure. These were years in which the medical profession was aggressively redefining the boundaries of insanity, asserting that madness was far more subtle, insidious and widespread than had ever been previously recognised, and noting with alarm the apparently rapidly increasing number of lunatics in Britain. Their warnings would lead, in 1845, to the passing of the Lunacy and Asylums Acts, which made compulsory the construction of the enormous county lunatic asylums of the high Victorian period to house what was seen as a rapidly ballooning population of British lunatics. These insanity panics were also intertwined with contemporary anxieties about urban criminality, of the kind articulated in Reynolds's earlier work, *The Mysteries of London*; the anonymous vastness of the industrial city was seen as being a mentally and morally unhealthy environment, in which criminality and insanity were bound to flourish at unprecedented rates.[24]

In the Gothic literature of the period, these fears were embodied by characters such as Sweeny Todd and the Resurrection Man: urban mass-murderers whose native habitat was the modern cityscape, whose inhabitants they were able to massacre with impunity precisely because they were not obviously mad, only 'morally insane'. If they went around behaving like wild beasts, like Wagner the Were-wolf or the *furiosus* of pre-McNaghten lunacy legislation, then they would actually be much less dangerous; for the werewolf, unlike them, wears its murderous nature openly. It may be dangerous, but its danger is of a clear and obvious kind, signalled by its transformation from man to wolf; all that one needs to do in order to survive its depredations is stay out of its way until its transformation is over. It is probably not coincidental that most of the earliest werewolf stories in English are set in the Middle Ages, or that the werewolves in them are so commonly associated with the forest-dwelling outlaws of medieval folklore, articulating an almost nostalgic vision of a world in which criminality existed *out there*, in a clearly demarcated zone outside the community, rather than *in here*, living secretly alongside us. By comparison, Sweeney Todd is a much more unsettling figure: he looks human, seems rational, lives and walks openly amongst us, and yet is able to carry out deeds of predation that surpass those of the most savage of wild beasts. Like the lunatics defined by the McNaghten rules, or the victims of 'moral insanity', he cannot be easily identified by his howling, raving and animalistic behaviour, allowing him to deceive his victims until it is far too late.

This association between werewolves and the agrarian rural past, as opposed to the industrial urban present, would probably have been reinforced by the fact that these were the same years in which the Eurasian wolf was being hunted to extinction across most of Western Europe. The last wolf in Ireland was shot in 1786, which by 1843 would have been barely in living memory; and 1847, the year of *Wagner*'s publication, even saw the death of the last wolf in the once famously wolf-haunted forests of Bavaria.[25] The days when violence and predation wore the literal or figurative face of the wolf were passing; the future belonged to wolves in sheep's clothing, whose criminal madness could only be detected with the aid of professional expertise, rather than being obvious to all and sundry. It was in this cultural context that the werewolf narrative appeared in English: not as a fearsome embodiment of the dangers of the present, like the serial killer, or even as a representation of the persisting power of the past, like the vampire, but as something which was always already consigned to history. In *The Book of Were-wolves*, Baring-Gould warned his readers against assuming that the werewolf could be safely consigned to the past, reminding them that such creatures 'may still prowl in Abyssinian forests, range still over Asiatic steppes, and be found howling dismally in some padded room of a Hanwell or a Bedlam':

> From this time [i.e. the seventeenth century] medical men seem to have regarded it [i.e. lycanthropy] as a medical malady to be brought under their treatment, rather than as a crime to be punished by law. But it is very fearful to contemplate that there may still exist persons in this world filled with a morbid craving for human blood, which is ready to impel them to commit the most horrible atrocities, should they escape the vigilance of their guards, or break the bars of the madhouse which restrains them.[26]

'Fearful to contemplate', no doubt: but it remains no more than contemplation. '[T]here may still exist' such creatures, but, then again, there may not; and even if they *do* exist, it sounds as though they are locked away safe and sound, imprisoned behind 'the bars of the madhouse' (one of the new county asylums, most likely) or 'in some padded room'. It was perhaps something more than mere historical coincidence that the General Inclosure Act, which cleared the way for the enclosure of much of the remaining common and waste land in Britain, was passed in 1845, the same year as the Asylums Act: both represented aspects of the legislative tidying-up of Victorian Britain, through which both the wild places in the landscape and the wild, beastlike people who once inhabited them were to be contained, enclosed and brought under rational control.[27] The wasteland that the werewolf once roamed was to be fenced in and broken up for the purposes of arable agriculture; the werewolf itself, now safely identified as no more or less than a mere lunatic vagrant, was to be packed off to the nearest asylum. As even Baring-Gould was forced to admit, 'perhaps like the dodo or the dinornis, the werewolf may have become extinct in our age'.[28]

Notes

1. Moran, 'Daniel M'Naughtan', *ODNB Online*; Whitlock, *Criminal Responsibility*, pp. 17–20.
2. Prins, *Offenders, Deviants or Patients?*, p. 12.
3. Jacobs, *Criminal Responsibility*, p. 27.
4. *The Times*, 26 September 1796, quoted in Hitchcock, *Mad Mary*, p. 32.
5. On Dadd's murder of his father, see Allderidge, *Richard Dadd*, pp. 22–4, and Greysmith, *Richard Dadd*, pp. 52–62.
6. *Illustrated London News*, quoted in Greysmith, p. 61.
7. Whitlock, pp. 15–16; Eigen, 'James Hadfield', *ODNB Online*.
8. Quoted in Whitlock, p. 20.
9. Prins, p. 14.
10. Baring-Gould, *The Book of Were-wolves* (London: Smith, Elder and Co., 1865), p. 52.
11. *Ibid.*, p. 48.
12. Thomson, 'The Wehr-Wolf', in *Tales of an Antiquary*, I, pp. 237–8.
13. *Ibid.*
14. Menzies, 'Hughes, the Wer-Wolf'.
15. Charlotte Brontë, *Jane Eyre*, pp. 180, 258, 271.
16. Reynolds, *Wagner the Werewolf*, p. 63. The 2006 edition modernises the original title *Wagner the Wehr-wolf*.
17. For examples of this tradition, see Otten, ed., *A Lycanthropy Reader*, pp. 9, 51–2, 65, 87, 89, 116, 164.
18. Reynolds, pp. 64–5, 75.
19. Ingram, *The Madhouse of Language*, pp. 17–30.
20. Pritchard, *Treatise on Insanity*, p. 6.
21. 'Mr Fox', in Jacobs, *English Fairy Tales*, pp. 148–51; 'The Robber Bridegroom', in *Grimm's Complete Fairy Tales*, pp. 52–5.
22. Baring-Gould, chapters 6, 9 and 14.
23. Browning, *The Ring and the Book*, I, lines 611–18, p. 39.
24. Scull, ed., *The Asylum as Utopia*, pp. xxx–xxxiii; Wright, *Mental Disability in Victorian England*, pp. 17–19.
25. Fisher, 'The Last Irish Wolf', p. 41; Thorpe, *The Danube*, p. 249.
26. Baring-Gould, pp. 6, 98–9.
27. Howkins, 'The Commons, Enclosure, and Radical Histories', p. 121.
28. Baring-Gould, p. 6.

7

The inner beast: scientific experimentation in George MacDonald's 'The History of Photogen and Nycteris'

Rebecca Langworthy

The tension between the concepts of human and animal haunted the eighteenth and nineteenth centuries; Mary Shelley's *Frankenstein* (1818) offers an imaginative extension of the implications of vivisection and dissection practices of the time through Victor Frankenstein's experiments on both human and animal corpses.[1] By 1859, Darwin's scientific theory of evolution appeared, challenging the distinction between humans and animals. Towards the end of the century, Ray Lankester popularised the concept of degeneration in his 1880 book *Degeneration: A Chapter in Darwinism*. These tensions can be found in George MacDonald's 'The History of Photogen and Nycteris', the tale of Watho, a witch with '[a] wolf in her mind' (p. 304) who experiments with the development of two children by controlling their environments from birth.[2] The children are placed in the role of animals. As Watho loses control of her test subjects, she also loses control of her inner wolf, ultimately transforming into that wolf and being killed. In 'Photogen and Nycteris', MacDonald uses a fairy-tale setting alongside a werewolf antagonist not only to explore the human/animal divide but also to question the motivations underlying scientific enquiry towards the end of the Victorian era; by extension, MacDonald questions what humanity actually is through his representation of a Rousseauvian child-rearing experiment. This chapter will focus on the role of science and knowledge within the tale by looking at the underlying influence of theories of evolution and degeneration on the narrative before exploring the significance of the educational approaches enforced on Photogen and Nycteris.

MacDonald presents the reader not with a conventionally maternal figure but an egotistical and selfish one that allows discussions of gender roles to be explored in relation to child-rearing, scientific research and the advancement of knowledge. As the central antagonist of the tale, Watho is a deeply complicated figure; though she is a woman raising children, she does not conform to Victorian or more current conceptions of motherhood. Her child-rearing does not fit Alison M. Jaggar's definition of mothering 'as a historically and culturally variable relationship in which one individual nurtures and cares for another'.[3] Nor does it adhere to Sarah Ruddick's suggestion that 'to be a "mother" is to take upon oneself the responsibility of child care, making its work a regular and substantial part of one's working life'.[4] Watho dictates the environment and education of the children but allows other servants to directly engage with them to care for their day-to-day needs. Indeed, Watho is antithetical to Victorian norms of motherhood. Elaine Tuttle argues that 'Women's very power as mother, given the possibilities for egotism and selfishness, had to be denied by norms of Victorian motherhood'.[5] Watho's role is not as a mother but as scientist. This allows for the full expression of her egotism and cruelty towards the children.

MacDonald's tale first appeared in serialised form in 1879. It is the story of a witch who is, on occasion, possessed by a wolf named Watho. The witch persuades two pregnant women to stay in her house before stealing their babies and raising them in strictly controlled environments. The boy, Photogen, is exposed to constant light while the girl, Nycteris, is exposed to darkness to shape their development. As the children become teenagers, they begin to break the constraints of their environments and eventually meet. By supporting each other through the respective terrors of night and day, the children are able to leave the castle they have been living in, defeat the witch and get married.

Whilst the tale was written for a young audience, it touched on a number of adult themes and issues which were prevalent in contemporary Victorian society. The way in which adult themes are presented within this children's tale is examined by focusing on four key aspects: the implications of Watho's designation as a witch and a wolf, the role of scientific experimentation in the tale, the significance of Watho's child-rearing experiment, and MacDonald's goals in depicting a protagonist with a lupine nature. An examination of these aspects reveals the complexity of this apparently simple fairy tale and allows us to reflect on the way MacDonald uses the supernatural to comment on social debates and shifting attitudes towards science. Watho's location in a fantasy world, her pursuit of knowledge and the desire driving that pursuit are the bases of my exploration of the blurred boundaries between humans and animals, the child/adult divide and the tensions surrounding the development of knowledge brought to light in this complex tale.

The fairy-tale elements of 'Photogen and Nycteris' are immediately apparent, even in the brief plot outline above. The narrative is framed by fairy-tale motifs such as a witch and a castle; MacDonald's use of these places his readers in a frame of mind where they accept what in the real world would be illogical or impossible. In his book *Breaking the Magic Spell*, Jack Zipes suggests that writers such as MacDonald use this genre to subvert its conventions and to provide social critiques:

> Serious artists created new fairy tales from folk motifs and basic plot situations. They sought to use fantasy as a means for criticizing social conditions and expressing the need to develop alternative models to the established social orders.[6]

This subversion of the fairy tale is embraced by MacDonald in 'Photogen and Nycteris'. Although it uses aspects of traditional fairy tales, MacDonald's work is a relatively late example of a literary fairy tale, having a multifaceted plot that can be interpreted on multiple levels akin to those in the works of such writers as E.T.A. Hoffmann and Hans Christian Andersen. 'Photogen and Nycteris' explores social shifts and conceptions surrounding scientific advances in the period, but this critique runs parallel to what is ostensibly a tale for children, thereby creating a dual readership.

From the first line of MacDonald's tale, the interplay between the adult and child readers is set up in relation to Watho: 'There was once a witch who desired to know everything' (p. 304). In this opening line a number of expectations are developed. Three aspects of Watho are revealed. Firstly, she is a witch, and as such is a representative of a system of magic, which has two aspects: it 'rests on empirically untested belief and ... it is an effort to control. The first aspect distinguishes it from science, the second from religion.'[7] Watho, as a witch, is engaged in a practice which is distinct from both religious and scientific approaches of interpreting the world. Secondly, we are told that her goal is to 'know everything', thus aligning the pursuit of knowledge with the negative connotations of a witch.[8] Watho's pursuit of knowledge is part of her identity as a witch; therefore, her need to gain knowledge is not part of a religious or scientific striving to comprehend the world around her but is something other. Thirdly, we are told that the pursuit of knowledge is a 'desire' (p. 304), suggesting not only that the witch is seeking knowledge but that there is an irrational or emotional aspect to that pursuit. This allows Watho's accumulation of knowledge to become untethered from scientific methodological constraints and the moral framework of religious faith. This is contrasted with Nycteris's knowledge-seeking later in the tale, which is depicted positively, and suggests that MacDonald is not making a gendered statement about women seeking knowledge. The aspects of her character that are driven by emotional responses allow for the exploration of paths which are morally ambiguous. The suggestion that Watho is driven by emotional considerations places her, according to Victorian thought, in the feminine sphere, where 'women were nothing more than overly emotional and mindless creatures ruled by their sexuality, or simply "the Sex".[9] The psychological profiling of women as overly emotional was directly tied to their reproductive system, as Stephanie A. Shields explains:

> The human female's nervous system was limited (or prevented from its full development) either because of earlier achievement of full maturity and/or because of the biological demands of development and maturation of the female reproductive system. At maturity, women's brain and nervous system were limited in their capacity to support the higher mental processes, specifically objective rationality and true creativity. The lower mental processes (emotion and certain perceptual skills) thus appeared to be or were comparatively stronger. Then, at menarche, the female's mental future was sealed: blood that might have promoted further brain development was diverted to the uterus and sustaining fertility. The result of this abbreviated course of development and the demands of female reproductive physiology were limited intellectual capacity in comparison to men and a triad of interlocking traits: sensitivity, perceptual acumen, and, more important, emotionality.[10]

Watho's emotional desires conflict with her potential to be a mother. Watho has been shown to eschew the role of mother, placing the pursuit of knowledge above any social or biological imperative to nurture the children. She is further distanced from these roles because, rather than bearing the children herself, Watho steals them from other women. MacDonald's decision to distance Watho from a direct link between her gender and child-rearing allows him to explore Watho's emotional state in relation to the fantastic and fairy-tale elements of his tale, These emotional aspects are of particular significance in MacDonald's revelation that Watho has 'A wolf in her mind' which 'makes her cruel' (p. 304). This wolf embodies Watho's loss of control over her magical abilities. Her wolf form makes the otherwise tall and elegant Watho look like a stereotypical, hunched, fairy-tale witch in the depiction of her falling, 'bent together', as the wolf possesses her (p. 304).

The inner wolf is separate from Watho's witch nature but also stems from the loss of control over the magical power that Watho attempts to harness as a witch. Watho's pursuit of knowledge is directly attributed to her as a character flaw which has drawn her to witchcraft: 'she cared for nothing in itself only for knowing it' (p. 304). The combination of this pursuit of knowledge via witchcraft with the cruelty and hunger of the inner wolf becomes the basis from which she engages in experiments, with an insatiable desire to gain knowledge, controlling the development of two children by manipulating their environments from birth. The practice of magic is inherently antithetical to the practice of science and it is the combination of Watho's witch nature with her wolf one which sanctions this protracted experimentation.[11] She places the children in the role of animals or test subjects, as they are kept in controlled environments, fed specific foods and selectively educated and trained.

The figure of Watho becomes the point of contrast between fantasy and the real world, drawing both the fairy tale and reality together. The tale is full of binary oppositions such as light and dark, male and female, good and bad; Watho herself becomes a synthesis of such oppositions: she is a witch and wolf, a parental figure and a captor, a human and an ab-human. She represents magic, which is antithetical to the scientific pursuit of knowledge, yet she becomes involved in a protracted scientific experiment in child-rearing. Watho has the potential for both good and evil and this is most clearly demonstrated in her ability to be either human or wolf in appearance. As a witch, Watho's nature is morally neutral. This appears incongruous; however, her magic abilities place Watho alongside other magically gifted female figures in MacDonald's corpus who use their magic positively. The possession of magical ability is not itself imbued with a moral status, it is up to the practitioner to use their abilities for good or ill. In the case of Watho, the negativity of her use of magic is associated with the wolf within her mind rather than the magical practices themselves. Her desire to pursue knowledge and engage in acts of cruelty, urged on by her wolf nature, forces her magical ability into negative or evil applications.[12] Not only is Watho the antagonist of the tale; she also embodies the duality which becomes the key to the story's development. Watho's experimentation and control of Photogen and Nycteris become an outward signifier of her inner duality. The struggle between witch and world becomes enmeshed with her ability to control her test subjects. Just as she loses control of her outer world when the children escape the castle, Watho also loses control of her inner wolf by fully transforming into a werewolf before finally being killed by Photogen (pp. 338–9).

The fairy-tale setting and werewolf antagonist suggest an exploration of the motivation and implications of scientific enquiry towards the end of the Victorian era. A clear example of how the fantasy aspects of the tale occlude the social critique of the tale is through the description of the children's eyes. Watho lures two women, Aurora and Vesper, to her castle and once these women have given birth their children are taken; Vesper dies, and Aurora is told that her child has died (pp. 306, 307). When the children are born, MacDonald draws attention to their eyes. Photogen's 'eyes grew darker as he grew until they were as black as vespers' (p. 306) while Nycteris '[h]ad just the eyes of Aurora, the mother of Photogen' (p. 307). Each child has the eyes of the other child's mother. This feature is a way of reinforcing the link between the two children and in a fantasy setting does not require further explanation. However, MacDonald repeatedly draws attention to the children's eyes, inviting a closer examination of this link. By way of this, the adult reader is guided towards a deeper social reflection, based on their ability to relate the fantasy world of the tale to issues that were discussed prominently in Victorian society. This is significantly so in the way MacDonald frames the discussion of Nycteris's eyes in specifically scientific terms:

> Watho ... took the greatest possible care of her – in every way consistent with her plans, that is, – the main point in which was that she should never see any light but what came from the lamp. Hence her optic nerves, and indeed her whole apparatus for seeing, grew both larger and more sensitive; her eyes, indeed, stopped short only of being too large. (p. 307)

This explanation of the changes in Nycteris's eyes moves beyond the conventional bounds of the fairy-tale setting by providing reasons for what would otherwise be accepted as part of a fantasy world. Victorian society was especially focused on the eye and its functions, as discussed by Chris Otter in *The Victorian Eye*. MacDonald is appealing to popular aspects of science through his decision to focus on the children's eyes, encouraging adult readers of the tale to engage in scientific speculation.[13] The suggestion that Nycteris's eyes have physically changed in response to her environment links this description to one of the most consequential scientific theories of the Victorian age, Charles Darwin's theory of evolution. The reasoning given for Nycteris's change echoes Darwin's concept of natural selection, albeit in an unrealistic and magical way:

> Thus, as I believe, natural selection will tend in the long run to reduce any part of the organisation, as soon as it becomes, through changed habits, superfluous, without by any means causing some other part to be largely developed in a corresponding degree. And conversely, that natural selection may perfectly well succeed in largely developing an organ without requiring as a necessary compensation the reduction of some adjoining part.[14]

It is not only MacDonald's descriptions of the children's eyes that links to Darwinian theory. The fact that each child has the eyes of the other's mother is mentioned at both the beginning and end of the tale (pp. 306, 307, 340). By repeatedly calling attention to the significance of the children's eyes, it appears that some kind of cross-inheritance has taken place, as Vesper's and Aurora's eyes have been inherited by the other woman's child. We are told that 'Watho at length had her desire, for witches often get what they want' (p. 306). This suggests that Watho's magical abilities are involved in the conception of the children as her status as a witch is what allows her desires to be fulfilled. The use of the term 'desire', as I have argued, shows the emotional facet to her pursuit of knowledge, a position which does not readily attach itself to a moral or ethical framework. Beyond the fantastic aspects of the children's eyes, MacDonald's focus on them draws attention to the significant role played by visual apparatus and the imagination in the public's understanding of new scientific discoveries.[15] When exploring the significance of the children's eyes, this literary fairy tale can be read as a conduit for larger, ongoing debates and controversies regarding the limits of scientific experimentation and the place of humanity within the world.[16] It functions on the level of fantasy to strengthen the link in the reader's mind between Photogen and Nycteris; this also offers the reader the possibility of a dual reading of the tale in which what in a fantasy setting is considered magical can be seen as a veiled allusion to science. Watho, read as a fantastic character, is the witch who has caused this by magic, while, read through realism, the tale casts Watho as a scientist who has physically changed the children. The witch of the fairy-tale world becomes the scientist of a real-world reading of the tale.

MacDonald uses his literary fairy tale to provide a critique of science during the Victorian period. In this project, once again Watho's inner wolf becomes significant. A contemporary adult reader's awareness of Darwinian theory becomes an underlying factor which imports significance to moments of transformation, for example when MacDonald shows Watho transforming into a wolf on losing control of her test subjects:

> At the very moment when Photogen caught up Nycteris, the telescope of Watho was angrily sweeping the tableland. She swung it from her in rage and, running to her room, shut herself up. There she anointed herself from top to toe with a certain ointment; shook down her long red hair, and tied it around her waist; then began to dance, whirling around and around faster and faster, growing angrier and angrier, until she was foaming at the mouth with fury. (p. 338)

Watho's physical transformation into the wolf has three distinct stages, the first of which is her rejection of science by throwing away the telescope. Secondly, she turns to magical means to transform herself by conflating two forms of transformation found in traditional werewolf lore through anointing herself and wearing a hair belt.[17] Thirdly, the transformation is dominated by a growing uncontrollable rage. This transformation is a form of degeneration, a theory put forward by Ray Lankester in 1880 as an extension of Darwin's theory whereby evolutionary advantage can be lost through the lack of use. Here, this atrophy occurs through a rejection of the rational (scientific) faculty in favour of the uncontrollable and emotional (magical) parts of Watho's self. Lankester directly associated scientific knowledge with the prevention of degeneration: 'The full and earnest cultivation of science – the Knowledge of Causes – is that to which we have to look for the protection of our race – even of this English branch of it – from relapse and degeneration'.[18] Lankester's theory was often cited in relation to the lower classes of society, who could then be categorised as being less human. 'Photogen and Nycteris' appears to be prescient in regard to this later development of evolutionary theory and its implications for humans. Watho directly represents Lankester's cultivation of 'the Knowledge of Causes'; however, she subverts it through her willing rejection of purely scientific knowledge. The subsequent loss of control she experiences when the children disobey her initiates her degeneration into a wolf. Watho is then both an observer of these theories and a victim of degeneration. In the tale, her transformation allows the children to kill her without hesitation because she is less than human.[19] 'I've killed it … It is a great red wolf … It *was* a monster!' (p. 339). The other or animal form of Watho provides the justification for Photogen's killing of her; however, the italicised 'was' indicates that her transformation back into human form once dead renders her death an ambiguous action whereby Photogen has both killed a monster and murdered a human.

There is a tension within the tale: Watho's active pursuit of knowledge is portrayed negatively, causing her ultimate degeneration into her wolf form. However, it is Photogen's and Nycteris's discovery of new knowledge which disrupts the environments which Watho had created for the children. Thus knowledge lies at the root of both negative and positive character development in the tale. Photogen and Nycteris are reared, or 'trained' as the tale calls it, in very different ways. As the term 'trained' suggests, they are being dehumanised during this process, or at least are seen as being non-human by Watho.

MacDonald never provides a clear motive for Watho's experiment. In these educational experiments, Watho makes clear binary choices, most obviously in her decision to keep one child in light and one in dark. The use of different educational practices also corresponds to the light/dark imagery, with Photogen learning though external experience (in the light of the world) and Nycteris learning through introspection (within the darkness of her own mind). By enforcing this dichotomy, Watho makes the children more like herself in that they are fragmented beings, unable to fully develop aspects of their personality. This can be read as a critique of gendered education, as neither child is well equipped to deal with their surroundings until they engage with the complementary education of their peer. Just as the witch and werewolf are held in a battle for control of Watho, the children are fractured as only half of their natures have been nurtured. By approaching the tale as a critique of the scientific debates surrounding evolution and degeneration, the pursuit of knowledge through the rearing of Photogen and Nycteris becomes a counterpoint to Watho's multifaceted and incompatible aspects of personality represented by the witch, the wolf and the woman. During the course of this experiment, MacDonald demonstrates the educational principles suggested by both John Locke in *Some Thoughts Concerning Education* (1693) and Rousseau in *Emile* (1763), both seminal texts in the discussion of child-rearing. Locke argues that a child has no innate ideas but needs to have their empty mind filled with experiences of the world. 'I think I may say that of all the men we meet with, nine parts of ten are what they are, good or evil, useful or not, by their education.'[20] Rousseau, however, argues that a child is naturally good and that society can corrupt what is innately present in the child. 'Everything is good as it leaves the hands of the Author of things; everything degenerates in the hands of man'.[21] Watho's control of Photogen's and Nycteris's environment explores both of these theoretical approaches to child-rearing but at no point are these educational practices directly attributed to the children's gender.

Photogen's education is a purely empirical one in which he is taught to hunt, ride, and grow strong while being constantly mentored. His knowledge comes from his direct experience of the world surrounding him. This strictly experiential approach to gaining knowledge echoes Locke's concept of the *tabula rasa* where the association of ideas becomes the principal way in which the child develops an understanding of the world around them: 'Let us then suppose the mind to be, as we say, white paper void of all characters, without any ideas. How comes it to be furnished? … To this I answer, in one word, from *Experience*.'[22] As Photogen grows older, Watho attempts to curb his activity to ensure he never sees the sun set. To do this, she '[a]ccompan[ies] the prohibition with hints of consequences, none the less awful than they were obscure' (p. 309). This appeal to his imagination in an attempt to control him is deeply flawed because his unruly nature and fearlessness stem from his inability to conceive of what is beyond the experiences impressed upon his *tabula rasa*. Watho fails to incite fear as it is beyond the scope of Photogen's experience. It is only when he encounters a nocturnal big cat during the day that Photogen directly experiences the terrors of night which Watho has evoked, and even then his lack of fear only provokes the desire to break those rules (pp. 308–9). However, when faced with the entirely new and unknown world of night-time, Photogen is unable to comprehend what he discovers and so is overcome with fear.

While Photogen's education is reminiscent of Lockean principles, that of Nycteris is more akin to what Rousseau's Emile undergoes, where the child draws inferences from their own surroundings and develops an understanding of the world based on their innate understanding of what they encounter. In terms of education, this innate ability to learn forms the basis of knowledge and underpins any formal learning:

> If one divided all of human science into two parts – the one common to all men, the other particular to the learned – the latter would be quite small in comparison with the former. But we are hardly aware of what is generally attained, because it is attained without thought and even before the age of reason; because, moreover, learning is noticed only by its differences, and as in algebraic equations, common quantities count for nothing. (p. 62)

This is a shift away from the idea of the mind as a blank slate that gains impressions only from the external world. For Rousseau, the mind has an innate ability to allow space for conceptual and speculative learning rather than purely observational learning. Rousseau suggests that boys and girls have the same needs in early life:

> Until the nubile age children of both sexes have nothing apparent which distinguishes them; the same face, the same figure, the same complexion, the same voice, everything is equal; girls are children, boys are children; the same name suffices for beings so similar. (p. 211)

MacDonald appears to embrace a gender-neutral version of Rousseau's theories. The question of gender is not raised in the children's early education. Any gendered aspect of the children's education comes from adherence to differing educational systems, with Photogen following a Lockean approach and Nycteris a Rousseauvian one. The two children are not bound by the strictures of gendered education of these systems. The lack of recourse to the gendered aspects of these education systems is strengthened through the contrasting conditions the children are placed in, which become the defining difference between them. Although the children are treated differently, the decision to do so is not made on the basis of their gender. Photogen, the boy, is raised outside and in the sunlight with an emphasis on physical activities and Nycteris, the girl, is raised inside, in the dark, with an emphasis on music and reflection. While this appears to represent a gendered education, it is it is an arbitrary opposition since the children are unaware of their gender and it is not factored into their early education. As we will see, in their first encounter Nycteris comes to believe that she must be a boy and Photogen a girl.

Nycteris's formal education is severely limited (Watho teaches her only music) and she is confined, alone, to a tomb attached to the castle (p. 309). She persuades a servant to teach her to read as her eyesight is so used to the dark (p. 309). Thus, when Nycteris does escape from her room and faces the unknown she is able to relate what she experiences to what she has previously read or experienced. Nycteris initially thinks the moon is a lamp when she first sees it; however, we are told later in the story that she also believes it to be the sun of which she has knowledge through her reading (p. 315). New knowledge and experiences are shown to be valuable; the children's new experiences and illicitly gained knowledge become the tools by which they escape from Watho. Indeed, Nycteris demonstrates an ability to draw connections not only to her prior experiences but also to her imagination, an imagination which has developed through illicit reading, highlighting the significance of acquiring new knowledge when attempting to comprehend newly discovered aspects of the world.

Nycteris is also associated with William Godwin's modification of Rousseau's theory; as Donelle Ruwe notes, Godwin's approach includes 'a mixing of Rousseau's Emile, associationist philosophy, and Adam Smith's version of the sympathetic imagination'.[23] The concept of the sympathetic imagination as being one of the innate qualities a child is born with becomes central to the development of Nycteris. In Godwin's essay 'Of Choice of Reading', he argues that reading is an important part of a child's education:

> As, relative to the question of social intercourse, the child should early begin in some degree to live in the world, that is, with his species; so should he do as to the books he is to read ... Trust him in a certain degree with himself. Suffer him in some instances to select his own course of reading.[24]

Nycteris chooses her own course of reading through which she becomes aware of the external world. Indeed, through her self-selected course of reading, Nycteris has developed the ability to imagine things beyond her own experience. Godwin argued that children require to read widely and freely in order to enable social intercourse. This concept is demonstrated by Nycteris as her reading engages her imagination, allowing her to fill in the gaps in her life experience, as is demonstrated when she initially interprets the lamp in her room and later the moon as the sun. This allows her to cope with her discovery of the outside world and her interactions with Photogen.

When Photogen and Nycteris finally meet, there is an inversion of fairy-tale convention, with the girl saving the boy. MacDonald draws attention to this in a conversation regarding gender which ends with Nycteris saying: 'No, of course! – you can't be a girl: girls are not afraid – without reason. I understand now: It is because you are not a girl that you are so frightened' (p. 325). Not only is Nycteris unaware of her own gender, this represents an inversion of the expectations attached to the received fairy-tale genre, where the prince saves the princess.[25] As Osama Jarrar argues, this interaction between Nycteris and Photogen is intentionally undermining conventional gender roles; he says of Nycteris's statement that 'girls are not afraid: 'Indeed, the radicalism of this acknowledgement had socio-political implications in 1870s England because it challenged the ideology of the privileged sex.'[26] Nycteris's ignorance of her gender displays how MacDonald's use of Rousseauvian child-rearing is limited to a formula for prepubescent education, without imposing gender roles on the child. Fear and weakness are not just associated with the feminine but become the definition of it. Nycteris places herself in the male role as the role most suited to her self-perception based on her extra-curricular reading. Photogen has been brought up primarily by men with Watho acting as a maternal figure. He has gained empirical evidence of his gender role through this domestic setup rather than through a theoretical knowledge of what qualities are male or female. This challenge to the reader's expectations of the tale extends to the equal nature of Photogen and Nycteris, as they support each other through a day and a night, alternately displaying fear during the night or day. In so doing they are learning from each other, and the isolation in which Watho has been raising them is broken. Photogen and Nycteris occupy a space of co-existence where they depend on each other for support. Indeed, Nycteris, who has no concept of her own gender as her knowledge comes from books, becomes the stronger figure by rescuing Photogen whereas Photogen initially leaves Nycteris in the daylight (p. 328).[27]

There is a final subversion, which works on both literary and social levels. The genre of the fairy tale conventionally arouses expectations of happy endings (though this is not universally so), and Victorian social codes frowned upon interracial marriage.[28] MacDonald depicts a mixed-race marriage, as Photogen is white and Nycteris black-skinned. The idea that this marriage may be controversial is briefly suggested when Photogen refuses to see the king: 'until he had married Nycteris; "for then," he said, "the king himself can't part us"' (p. 340). This is a much overlooked aspect of the tale: the illustrations accompanying the original serialisation and one subsequent book version of the tale (with illustrations by Maurice Sendak) both depict Nycteris as being white-skinned with dark hair. This convention of depicting Nycteris as white has continued most recently with the cover image of the forthcoming edition from Edinburgh Napier University. It is only when viewed in light of the scientific debates surrounding evolution and degeneration which form the subtext of the tale that the significance of the marriage is fully exposed. In Victorian society miscegenation, while not illegal, was a socially charged subject with a complex relationship to colonialism.[29]

MacDonald's use of a fantasy setting for 'The History of Photogen and Nycteris' dictates how visible many of the issues he raises are to the casual reader. The genre allows readers to accept otherwise illogical or troubling aspects of the tale. As a story with a hero and heroine, it is conventional that the story will end with a marriage. By engaging with the reader on this level, uncertainties are circumvented through what the critic Darko Suvin refers to as 'cognitive estrangement'. Suvin suggests that the unfamiliar or fantastic aspects of the text (designated 'the Novum') are balanced by the real world or 'the empirical environment' as Suvin terms it.[30] This cognitive estrangement opens a space where the reader's imagination can be engaged by placing the Novum alongside the recognisable empirical environment. In the case of 'Photogen and Nycteris', this environment can mean one of two things to the reader. Their previous knowledge of the form and function of fairy tales can be used so that they accept new aspects of the tale within the scope of their preconceptions. An alternative reading is that this fictional environment is constructed as a representation of contemporary debates surrounding evolution and degeneration.

In MacDonald's essay 'The Imagination: Its Functions and Its Culture' (1867), he claims that all works of imagination are divine because 'Man is but a thought of God', implying that any imaginative or creative output by a human is merely a channelling of God's thoughts and thus, by extension, is divine. This concept encompasses the reader's engagement with and interpretation of literature.

MacDonald 'dare[s] to claim for the true, childlike, humble imagination, such an inward oneness with the laws of the universe that it possesses in itself an insight in to the very nature of things'.[31] The imagination allows a deeper insight into the natural order of the world and, by linking that imaginative engagement to the debates surrounding evolution, MacDonald invites his readers to discover that natural order for themselves. This is hinted at through Nycteris's education, which includes the development of a sympathetic imagination as a way to get closer to a true understanding of the world.

The setting not only allows readers to accept the fantastic, it also allows readers to understand aspects of the real world in new ways because they are using their imagination to discover the divine centre of reality. This is clearly stated in MacDonald's later essay 'The Fantastic Imagination' (1893), where he encourages all readers to engage imaginatively with, and read their own meanings into, his works:

> It may be better that you should read your own meaning into it [a text] that may be a higher operation of your intellect than the mere reading of mine out of it: Your meaning may be superior to mine.[32]

There is a deliberate attempt on MacDonald's part to excite the imagination and to create tales which the reader can interpret in new ways. This insistence that readers can find their own meanings within the texts lies alongside MacDonald's view of the imagination as a way for the divine to be expressed:

> The greatest forces lie in the region of the uncomprehended. I will go farther. The best thing you can do for your fellow, next to rousing his conscience, is not to give him things to think about, but to wake things up that are in him; or say, to make him think things for himself. (p. 319)

By awakening the imagination and inspiring readers to think for themselves, MacDonald hopes to do the most good for his readership. MacDonald's idea of good is to bring the reader closer to God and this is done by awaking the imagination, which comes from a divine source. The reference to the power of the uncomprehended is intriguing as it allows a space to develop which only the individual's imagination can fill. Although MacDonald appears to give up his control over the text by handing imaginative control to the reader, he guides the reader's newly awakened imagination so that readers may think for themselves. The awakening of the imagination becomes a defining feature of MacDonald's engagement with his readership.

In the light of MacDonald's conception of the imagination and the function of the fairy-tale genre in 'The History of Photogen and Nycteris', the figure of Watho gains another level of tension. This is a tale which encourages its readers to think outside of convention with regard to evolution, gender, knowledge, morality and race, and all of this relies on a fairy-tale, fantastic conception of

Watho. The reader accepts Watho's status as a witch and wolf by acknowledging that she is the antagonist of the tale. She functions as the fantastic wicked witch who is also closely associated with the wolf, a figure of fear. There is no ambiguity in Watho's presentation as a negative figure in the text as the reader's sympathy is not evoked on her behalf. To break out of the traditional modes of fairy tale, MacDonald uses Watho as a foil so that other characters can defy fairy-tale convention. Thus the aspects of the story which challenge the conventional thought of the period (for example, the marriage of Photogen and Nycteris), though caused by Watho's experimentation, rely on the reader accepting Watho's place as a fantastic figure who conforms to fairy-tale conventions as a wicked witch who can be overcome. She is the literary foil to the imaginative reconsideration of issues raised in the tale.

'The History of Photogen and Nycteris' is a deliberately multifaceted tale which requires readers to engage with it on a number of levels. MacDonald's use of a fantasy setting for this tale allows adult readers to understand aspects of the real world in new ways. He declares in 'The Fantastic Imagination' that: 'For my part I do not write for children but for the childlike whether of five or fifty or seventy five' (p. 317). The childlike, for MacDonald, is anyone who is prepared to use their imagination in order to engage with a text and, therefore, is prepared to find multiple meanings and layers to his texts.

This chapter has shown how the tensions between empirical knowledge and imagination are explored by MacDonald in relation to a range of wider topics. These range from the issues raised by Darwin's theory of evolution to the theory of degeneration, and to the continued influence of Locke, Rousseau and Godwin on ideas of how to educate children. In MacDonald's account of the rearing of Photogen and Nycteris, different educational systems are represented but the tale also functions as a demonstration of how these pedagogies shape how MacDonald's readership interacts with 'The History of Photogen and Nycteris'. The readers are encouraged to seek their own meanings and imaginatively engage with the tale. Conventional notions of good and bad are disrupted by the end of the tale, for example, when Photogen kills Watho. Knowledge is shown to have both positive and negative aspects. Photogen's and Nycteris's education allows them to escape from Watho's experiment; knowledge here has a positive value. By contrast, Watho's pursuit of knowledge by experimenting on the children is portrayed as negative without a clear purpose beyond the acquisition of knowledge. The figure of Watho is divided between the witch and the wolf, the rational and the emotional. In a tale full of binary oppositions such as light and dark, or male and female, MacDonald takes pleasure in exposing the tensions between these poles and exploring their interrelation. This is most clearly shown in the marriage of Photogen and Nycteris, a joining of light and dark, male and female, empiricism and imagination. This text, which yields multiple interpretations, enables MacDonald to critique social debates and trends; the fantasy setting of the tale creates the mental space for readers to engage in thought experiments which examine the implications of debates over Darwinian theory.

Notes

1. Guerrini, 'Animal Experiments', p. 71.
2. All quotations from 'The History of Photogen and Nycteris' are taken from George MacDonald, *The Complete Fairy Tales*, pp. 304–41. Page numbers are given in parentheses in the body of the text.
3. Jaggar, *Feminist Politics and Human Nature*, p. 256.
4. Ruddick, *Maternal Thinking: Toward a Politics of Peace*, p. 17.
5. Hansen, *Mother without Child*, p. 12.
6. Zipes, *Breaking the Magic Spell*, pp. 18–19.
7. Leach, *A Dictionary of Social Sciences*, p. 398.
8. The conflation of a desire for knowledge in women and the negative results of that pursuit can be traced back at least as far as Milton's representation of the Fall in *Paradise Lost*, in which Eve is depicted as longing for knowledge prior to her temptation by Satan. This view of the Fall is not commonly found in Victorian religious thought, which tends to view Eve as being tricked or deceived rather than actively seeking knowledge prior to Satan's temptation. Although MacDonald had read Milton, I do not think that he is intentionally drawing this parallel as female pursuit of knowledge is depicted positively later in the tale.
9. Vickery, 'Golden Age to Separate Spheres?', p. 389.
10. Shields, 'Passionate Men, Emotional Women', p. 96.
11. Björn Sundmark argues that it is Watho's wolf aspect which makes her evil: 'for a human to possess the animal nature of a wolf is … not only evil but unnatural' ('"Traveling Beastward"', pp. 11–12).
12. MacDonald often represents magical women in a positive light, and the recurrent motif of a wise magical woman can be found in many of his works.
13. Otter, *The Victorian Eye*, pp. 22–61.
14. Darwin, *The Origin of Species*, p. 147.
15. This, especially in relation to the popular understanding of fossils and Darwinian theory, has been discussed at length in: Beer, *Darwin's Plots*; O'Connor, *The Earth on Show*; Levine, *Darwin and the Novelists*.
16. James Krasner's *The Entangled Eye* focuses on how Darwin drew attention to the limitations of the human observer when representing evolution as the process happens over inconceivably long timescales. MacDonald is here shortening the timescale of the adaptation of the children's eyes to bring evolutionary changes into one imaginable for the reader or observer of his tale.
17. For more details on werewolf transformations, see O'Donnell, *Werewolves*, pp. 40–50.

18 Lankester, *Degeneration*, p. 62.
19 The idea that humans have an inner animal into which they might degenerate appears elsewhere in MacDonald's works. For example, in *The Princess and Curdie* (1883), a young boy, Curdie is given the ability to discern a person's inner animal by shaking their hand.
20 Locke, *Some Thoughts Concerning Education*, ed. by the Rev. R.H. Quick, p. 1.
21 Rousseau, *Emile*, p. 37.
22 Locke, *Essay Concerning Human Understanding*, p. 109.
23 Ruwe, 'Guarding the British Bible for Rousseau', p. 4.
24 Godwin, 'On Choice of Reading', pp. 134–5.
25 That is, expectations raised by the fairy-tale genre as they have been constructed in Anglophone culture since the eighteenth century on the basis of such European fairy tales as those of the collections of the Grimm brothers and Charles Perrault.
26 Jarrar, 'Language, Ideology, and Fairy Tales', p. 45.
27 Kerry Dearborn argues that 'MacDonald is urging us to rethink femininity and that which is associated with it – the night and the imaginative' ('Bridge over the River Why', p. 30). This conflation of Nycteris's upbringing and her imaginative abilities with gender ignores that Nycteris is, in fact, unaware of her gender, so gendered assertions regarding her imagination or the night are imposed upon the text by the reader. As this chapter shows, MacDonald's exploration of educational practice and the importance of imagination goes beyond their symbolic attachment to the feminine.
28 Bruno Bettelheim argues that this happy ending is a form of consolation and that 'at its end [the heroes] are ready not only to rescue each other, but to make a good life one for the other': *The Uses of Enchantment*, p. 150.
29 The complexity of race relations in Victorian Britain is explored in depth by Robert J.C. Young in *Colonial Desire*.
30 'Definitions of SF', in *The Encyclopaedia of Science Fiction*, ed. by Nicholls and Clute, pp. 311–14.
31 MacDonald, 'The Imagination, its functions and culture', in *A Dish of Orts*, pp. 12-13.
32 MacDonald, 'The Fantastic Imagination', in *A Dish of Orts*, pp. 316–17.

8

WEREWOLVES AND WHITE TRASH: BRUTISHNESS, DISCRIMINATION AND THE LOWER-CLASS WOLF-MAN FROM *The Wolf Man* TO *True Blood*

Victoria Amador

In the 1935 Universal Studios film *Werewolf of London*, the aristocratic scientist Dr Wilfred Glendon (Henry Hull), while on an expedition in mysterious Tibet, is attacked and bitten by a werewolf, the enigmatic Dr Yogami (Warner Oland). Dr Yogami may seem Westernised, yet, after finding another murdered girl in Yogami's hotel room, one of the lower-class policemen notes, 'The place smelled like a kennel when we came in'. Mark Vieira observes that 'John Colton's literate and sensitive screenplay … likened a werewolf curse to episodes of binge drinking. Colton, a homosexual with a penchant for lower-class types, set the monster's attacks in tawdry milieus that he himself was known to frequent.'[1]

Glendon's own transformation into a wolf can be halted – temporarily – by the rare plant *mariphasa*, but this disease contracted in the sinister East cannot be permanently cured. Glendon has sacrificed himself for British science, but he has been infected by an Asian infidel for trying to engage in civilised research in a perilous land. However, his suffering is terribly refined, expressed in the finest Received Pronunciation accent, and when he stalks his prey, he wears a tweed stalking cap and top coat.

What a shift there is from this effete British lycanthrope to all-American Larry Talbot a mere six years later in 1941's *The Wolf Man*. Talbot, although born in Britain, was raised in the United States, adopting a mid-Atlantic accent and the bulk of a manual labourer. Green and pleasant Britain has been infected by alien creatures, by werewolves – outsiders, foreigners – who must be dispatched to restored order; they can never assimilate.

That social class shift in the werewolf persona, from gentleman victim to low-status monster, has continued in many popular media depictions of the creature ever since *The Wolf Man*. This chapter will explore this lesser position of the werewolf by first briefly examining that seminal film. Then, in an effort to contextualise the personification of the werewolf as *la bête* rather than a beauty, I draw briefly on texts from the seventeenth century through the Victorian era to the new millennium. Finally, two more recent depictions, in the Twilight series and in *True Blood*, will further illustrate the werewolf's decline as not only Other but a lower-class, unwanted, unredeemable Other.

The werewolf is, more often than not, not a pampered pooch but a junkyard dog. Granted, werewolves are hairy killers, but they are victims as well, attacked only to go on to attack, abused only to abuse. Nevertheless, their link to the canine, their loud howling, their smooth-to-shaggy evolution and their messiness in a kill appear too animalistic, too drooling, too outwardly violent to be humanely integrated within society, even with compassionate control.

Ironically, unlike the vampire, who feeds every night in many incarnations, this beast only transforms on three nights of the full moon each month. The rest of the time, the werewolf retains a contrite human form and presents as far more assimilable than vampires. But as a kind of iconographic representation of the unclean Other, or the unwanted immigrant, or the importunate wannabe, this monster remains a marginalised demographic, ultimately destroyed not solely to conquer evil but in order to preserve the status quo.

Thus, the vampire has generally been presented during its enormous resurgence in film, television and prose fiction in recent years as a stylish and well-groomed, if dangerous, potential spouse/lover/neighbour. The vampire is familiar. To paraphrase Nina Auerbach, the vampire is ourselves. This monster can 'pass' and, presented as it is frequently as a superior being, this revenant is one of us as we would envision ourselves – immutable, impervious, protected with impunity through social status.

Just as there are multiple classes, castes, races and ethnicities, there are varieties of classic monsters. Thus, accompanying this elevated vampiric renaissance has been the werewolf, taking a subordinate place usually, like a familiar or loyal canine accompanying a more elegant master. Rather than being the privileged, evening-clothed, public-school creature of the night, the werewolf is undistinguished, lower-class, often relegated to the equivalent of a kennel rather than a castle.

Horror films and the Gothic genre have often 'serve[d] as a means of acknowledging social difference without addressing it directly'.[2] While the werewolf has shared social parity with the vampire on occasion (as in the British television programme *Being Human*, where a trio of bright young things, a vampire, werewolf and ghost, share a flat), generally the furry beast plays a secondary role without style, without status, without class in all permutations of that word.[3] The werewolf is the Other without agency, the immigrant recipient of xenophobic superiority, the monster which will never be admitted into the inner sanctum of acceptable societal normativity.

Rather like the misrepresented wolf packs currently being reintroduced in various wilderness locations, contravening the reluctance of many groups to allow these animal immigrants into their locality, these filmic werewolves are equally unwanted and undermined, uncouth and untrustworthy. They function frequently therefore as representatives of countless marginalised peoples whose difference symbolises a threat as great to the local populace as that of a beast on the moors. If Donna Haraway is correct when she says, 'Monsters have always defined the limits of community in Western imaginations', the animality of the werewolf cannot penetrate those imaginative limits in most media depictions.[4] Rather, we often find that many texts offering werewolves in particular, but shapeshifters in general, 'have associations with race and class, [and] it is important to pay attention to the issues because of the implications of aligning specific groups to monsters'.[5]

Social class, popular culture and liminal lycanthropes

The werewolf of this chapter is marginalised in many contexts – class, ethnicity, economic status, urbanity, intelligence – even when presented as ostensibly 'civilised' in terms of dominant hegemonic membership. Given the current situations in the USA and UK concerning immigration, border control, rising numbers of hate crimes and white nationalist rhetoric, the werewolf has become a perfect metaphor for discrimination against those who are not members of a dominant population, whose demographic signifies Other. The evolution of this curious discrimination appears in many examples in addition to the three primary cinematic texts addressed in this chapter.

Diego Rossello addresses lycanthropy and its relevance to social critique and analysis by linking the folkloric belief to Thomas Hobbes's seventeenth-century 'Epistle Dedicatory' of *De Cive* (1642). Rossello notes that Hobbes's discussion of melancholy and animality argues that individuals driven by concerns about the English Civil War demonstrated 'wolfish humours' which might be assuaged by 'building a frontier between animal and human, casting the former as non-political and the latter as political'.[6] The non-political is, in its animal body, an undesirable, unwashed, incapable lower class; the human who controls the political is its social and intellectual superior. This elitist philosophy certainly underscores aristocratic and hierarchical systems both in Britain and the USA. Consequently, the werewolf lurks on the fringes of society, but, unlike the superior vampire, we will never invite the beast into our homes, and certainly not through the front door.

Sabine Baring-Gould explored werewolf narratives and collected a variety of folktales for his 1865 *The Book of Were-wolves*, in which, according to Gregory Reece, he 'reports that [in France] it was believed that bastards were especially prone to being werewolves and should be watched more carefully than men of a better pedigree. [They] would often have unusually broad hands, short fingers and hairy palms.'[7] It follows that the folkloric creature therefore represents a masturbatory bastard creature which must remain marginalised; the animality of this particular monster is reflected in its lowly status – or lower race, gender, ethnicity or sexual preference and practice, as determined by a contemporary context – rendering it inappropriate for any kind of assimilation into mainstream respectability.

We can trace this social discrimination trope more directly to the archetypal werewolf template created by Robert Louis Stevenson's *Dr Jekyll and Mr Hyde*, first published to great acclaim in 1886. The novella itself only hinted at Mr Hyde's nocturnal adventures, but from the first 1887 theatrical adaptation Dr Jekyll was given an aristocratic ingénue fiancée, while Mr Hyde kept a bar girl as a mistress. In the majority of subsequent theatrical and filmic adaptations, Dr Jekyll is dapper, respectable and upper-middle-class, but Mr Hyde is hirsute and lascivious, 'a diminutive, broken, corrupt monster … far beyond the parameters of civilized humanity … an unknown other', and disturbingly fascinating to watch as he explores the seamier sides of urban corruption.[8]

Stevenson's Hyde explores the horrors of London; Dr Jekyll maintains propriety; Count Dracula buys an abbey. The location of a metropolitan area suggests urbane sophistication in more 'familiar' monsters than those who haunt impoverished locations, reiterating the same distinctions as the civilised city dweller versus the countryside bumpkin. Here the positing of the city represents the locus for potential corruption through invasion by a being who refuses to conform to prescribed behaviour and adopt the dominant culture. The natural countryside signifies animality; sophisticated urbanity signifies humanity, even in a vampire. This baseness within the werewolf typology therefore reiterates the class division between the human, the urbane aristocrat, the vampire and the beast, the animalistic serf, the werewolf, who will be destroyed by the ruling class for its sin of difference.

There are many other films and television programmes which have linked the werewolf Other to issues contemporary to the time of filming, demonising the werewolf beyond its monster status through its shameful associations: some examples follow. *The Undying Monster* (1942) gives us the upper-crust, Victorian Hammond family trying to address the curse – lycanthropy – with which they live when a series of murders and attacks occurs. Rather like the treatment of epilepsy and syphilis in middle-class English society of the time, the disease and diseased are hidden away until the sympathetic but expeditious conclusion – bad behaviour must be controlled, even through death.

The post-Second World War *She-wolf of London* (1946) presents the monstrous female. Portrayed by the demure June Lockhart, the she-wolf is a sweet, upper-class English heiress who believes she is turning into a werewolf because of an ancient family curse. Any monster is in itself a disruptive nightmare, but a woman makes the possibility of such unbridled animality even more terrifying. This sort of film can be seen in fact as a parable of the working war woman who must now revert to her proper role, and class, and restore the patriarchal and economic status quo.

In a charming break with this tradition of social dismissal, in 1997 the Canadian postal system issued (in part as a nod to the hundredth publication anniversary of *Dracula*) a whimsical series of 'The Supernatural / Le Supernaturel' stamps which depicted the werewolf/*loup garou* in a suit and tie, his hat perched jauntily as he transforms under the moon. Perhaps it is in the nature of Canada – not American, not French, not British, and yet all of those – that the Canadian werewolf is celebrated for his stylish outsider status. In the USA in 1997, on the other hand, the Classic Movie Monsters stamps gave us Lon Chaney, Jr, sans chapeau, sans charm, sans elegance.

Even the 2010 remake of Chaney's film, now entitled *The Wolfman*, presented Benicio Del Toro's doomed Lawrence Talbot as a Victorian actor, still a disreputable profession for the son of a titled patrician (Anthony Hopkins). The patrician may act with impunity; he mated with a gypsy woman who produced his dark-haired, hirsute progeny; but his corrupted offspring must pay. There is no way to lie down with this werewolf and not catch fleas.

The purpose of these examples is to establish a trend in werewolf depictions in film over the last decades of the creature as exotic, as strange, as lower in class, status and position. This historical overview of various werewolves in North American and British popular culture demonstrates that uneasy locus of the werewolf as not only Other but as a lower-class Other.

Thus, 1941's *The Wolf Man* begins the distinct departure from the drawing-room melodrama of *Werewolf of London*, in the depiction of its protagonist as less than polished and whose presence must be obliterated to maintain the supercilious condescension of the privileged class. With few exceptions, from the nerdy Michael J. Fox in *Teen Wolf* (1985) to Kate Beckinsale's outlaw brother in *Van Helsing* (2004), from Jack Nicholson's feral editor in *Wolf* (1994) to Kate Beckinsale (again) in her fight against the Lycans in the 2003–16 *Underworld* series, the werewolf lacks stature in its society, its class, its culture. Its position has continued to decline in two of the most popular productions of the new millennium: the Twilight series and *True Blood*. The caravan of the gypsies is the caravan approaching the US border through Mexico, or the UK border through the EU.

The ugly American: *The Wolf Man* (1941)

The first major film to illustrate the placement of the werewolf on a lower scale of self-realisation to that of the vampire is 1941's *The Wolf Man*. Lon Chaney, Jr's portrayal of Larry Talbot places him, in terms of both script and performance, as a poor relation out of his depth who will pay for his immigrant crudity.

While this classic Universal Horror character is a significant part of that studio's monster pantheon, its presentation of the werewolf by a sweetly sincere but rather graceless Chaney shows him unable to maintain the elegance and bearing of the tuxedoed werewolf in *Werewolf of London*. In 1940 and 1941, many actors were already volunteering for service in the Second World War, and many studios were short on handsome leading men. That may have led to casting Chaney as the clearly improbable son of the Welsh scientist and lord of the manor Sir John Talbot, portrayed with typical sophistication by Claude Rains. America was still neutral in the war in 1941 as well, so one might also see the story of the US lad going to Britain to aid that country as a warning against involvement in the war. A further interpretation, given the number of refugees working in Hollywood at that time, could also see Larry Talbot as the immigrant whose innocence is punished unfairly in a foreign land which was once his home. However one may read his presence in *The Wolf Man*, Lon Chaney, Jr's beast offers a template for the werewolf as a socially inferior interloper.

Chaney was Hollywood royalty and the only actor to have portrayed the monster in all five of his original incarnations, but his persona was that of a working-class hero, not an aristocrat.[9] Chaney had just played Lenny in *Of Mice and Men* and would become typecast as 'hulking' at Universal.[10] The combination of his portrayal and the direction of his performance helped cement that image. Even the scriptwriter, Curt Siodmak, acknowledged the discomfiture of Chaney in the role. He remembered that in his original script, 'I had an American mechanic coming to install a telescope. And [producer/director George Waggner] changed him into the son of a lord. I couldn't imagine that – Lon Chaney as the son of a lord, hm?'[11] Chaney is therefore Larry Talbot, not Lawrence. And what is the ultimate stake in the heart of propriety represented by this wild colonial boy? Talbot upon transformation stalks his prey barefooted/bare-pawed in blue jeans and a work shirt.

In some ways Talbot's fall from aristocratic grace prefigures Sirius Black in the Harry Potter novels and films; Sirius is 'seamless, simultaneously both human and animal' and at the same time a falsely accused criminal, living as a wild thing despite his Animagus abilities.[12] Both Larry and Sirius are the outsiders, the outlaws and, although essentially moral characters, they must be isolated and dehumanised for their unintentional and anarchic displacements or transformations. Indeed, they have been victimised by those who live beyond the limits of accepted Western civilisation. The werewolves have no control over what they have become, but there is no reprieve possible for these overt misfits from the ruling, 'civilised' class. Anyone who transforms, who is threatening or who challenges the elite will perish; sharing an ironically terrifying connection to the werewolf's uncontrollable violence, the elite *choose* to slash and destroy the interloper.

Larry towers over his effete father, his rounded features the antithesis of chiselled genetics; even his necktie appears rather loud. Larry is a kind of tradesman; as he installs a huge lens on his father's huge telescope, and he mentions the 'precision work' he did for an optical company in California, but he admits, 'I'm good with tools and astronomical instruments, but not theory'.[13] In other words, he's no British intellectual.

To compound his dubiety, Talbot has a very casual, colloquially American way of speaking, and his friendliness seems incongruent in this Welsh village, despite his role as a man who 'is pure at heart and says his prayers at night' (to quote the Curt Siodmak-penned rhyme about the wolf curse). Thus, it is rather implausible that he would have the ability to run Sir John's estate after the death of his brother. His large, bulky build even suggests – when juxtaposed with the equally American but far more louche Ralph Bellamy as Chief Constable of the district, Colonel Montford (referred to by Larry in slang as 'a cop') and the trim Rains – a labourer whose suits are not bespoke like those of the rest of the cast. In fact, Rains and Bellamy discuss Larry's return: 'Big boy, isn't he?' says Bellamy. 'Huge!' Rains responds.[14] Larry may carry a walking stick with a silver-headed wolf and star, but that does not make him a gentleman.

His position will also make his wooing of the woman he loves, Gwen Conliffe (Evelyn Ankers), impossible. Gwen is engaged to the British, predictably handsome Frank Andrews (Patric Knowles, often the bland supporting man in Errol Flynn films), and while drawn to Larry, their kisses are always interrupted. He has actually used his father's telescope to peer into Gwen's bedroom – hardly the action of a nobleman. Their one date is not a charming dinner but rather a visit to a disreputable gypsy camp, and the visit leads to the death of Gwen's friend Jenny (Fay Helm) as well as to the attack upon Larry. This hirsute colonial is as inappropriate in this proper British world as the Romany visitors.

Larry Talbot's transformation into a werewolf by a gypsy reiterates his inferior outlander's status. The experience of the gypsy across Europe, along with Travellers in the UK, is one of enduring discrimination. In many films, the gypsies arrive in the village in ramshackle carts and caravans, ready to tell fortunes and drink and dance tarantellas, spreading the infection of their ferality; they are uncivilised, undeveloped, horse-driven interlopers, their presence only ever accepted on the fringes of a community, and not for long.

In keeping with Bram Stoker's view of those from Eastern Europe, the gypsies represent a people who are less evolved than Western Europeans, particularly the British. *Dracula*'s Jonathan Harker notes as he travels into the Carpathians, 'It seems to me that the further east you go the more unpunctual are the trains. What ought they to be in China?'[15] Our visual impression of the film's gypsies also reflects that of Harker's rather patronising view of the local Transylvanians, reiterating again the innate superiority of the native Englishman over all other nationalities:

> The women looked pretty, except when you got near them, but they were very clumsy about the waist ... The strangest figures we saw were the Slovaks, who

> were more barbarian than the rest, with their big cow-boy hats ... and [they] had long black hair and heavy black moustaches ... On the stage they would be set down at once as some old Oriental band of brigands ... rather wanting in natural self-assertion.[16]

That characterisation continues to echo xenophobically in contemporary illustrations of immigrants across Europe, and of the long march of refugees 'threatening' the US/Mexican border in the present day.

That Larry Talbot is bitten by the ultimate Hollywood horror film outsider who was once King of the Vampires and by 1941 was relegated to supporting roles – Bela Lugosi – further establishes the marginalisation of this wolf-man. Lugosi's gypsy werewolf is even named Bela, certainly to capitalise on his Dracula fame but also, ironically, equating the actor with a peasant by bestowing this significant appellation upon him. Bela Lugosi as Bela the gypsy is beaten to death, a particularly personal and brutal kind of violence, by the next generation of actors, by Lon Chaney, Jr, by Larry Talbot, with the silver-headed cane. Continuing this tradition of class warfare, Larry's father will beat him to death with the silver cane as well; the upper classes will defeat the lower to maintain their superior position; the subordinate cannot survive, in reality or in cinema. That triumph of status and position is clear when Larry's silver stick is found by Bela's body. Larry is not arrested as would be normal in such a situation because of his father's status. Even though he admits, 'That's the one I killed the wolf with', and he also proclaims his guilt, crying out in colloquial American dialect, 'They're treatin' me like I was crazy!', he remains free due to his family's privileged position, not his own credibility.[17]

Even after his tragic end, when, after killing the local gravedigger, his own father beats him to death, Larry's last rites are pronounced not by a vicar or minister but rather by the symbolically named Maleva (the divine Maria Ouspenskaya), Bela the Gypsy's mother: 'The way you walked was thorny, through no fault of your own ... Now you will find peace for eternity.'[18] He can receive no Christian rites; he is damned both by his supernatural curse and by his colonial social status. Lord Talbot will get away with the murder – 'The wolf must have attacked her and Larry came to the rescue.'[19] Larry's torment and fate are distinctly earthy and common; the colonial Other is dead.

Twilight at 'the Rez'

The almost steady social diminution of the werewolf would continue to mirror class distinctions in contemporary culture. In terms of the evolution of the monster as marginalised, lower- or working-class, we have seen a trend towards its typification as a metaphor for an unwanted citizen, a stranger in a strange land, a stray animal. If Lon Chaney, Jr's wolf-man ever had a grandson, he might be the unrequited lover Jacob Black, in the novels and films in Stephenie Meyer's Twilight novels and the Twilight Saga film series, who is in some ways as unwanted as his predecessor Larry Talbot.[20] However, in this case, the unwanted American becomes an American Indian. Just as Talbot represents a dangerous interloper into a more civilised, elite society, the Native American shapeshifter, Jacob Black (Taylor Lautner), lives outside the Caucasian community on the reservation and cannot compete against the elegant vampiric Cullen family for the hand of Bella Swan.

Jacob is a Native American member of the Quileute tribe, living on the reservation in western Washington, near the setting of the action, the small town of Forks. The attitude toward 'The Rez' in some US towns is informed by stereotypical impressions of Indians as drunken casino owners living in the wild. Too, the difficulties in many Native American communities continue. From underemployment to education difficulties, addiction issues, resentment and prejudice from predominantly white or Caucasian populations, as well as ongoing challenges to their integration into mainstream culture through educational, socioeconomic and political opportunities, there is a continuing marginalisation of Native Americans. In fact, in the November 2018 US elections, headlines were made when two Native American congresswomen were elected, as well as a lieutenant governor, 'in a country where indigenous people were not granted the right to vote until 1924'.[21] This triumph, despite dubious voting laws in a variety of states, including North Dakota, which rely on residential addresses rather than post office boxes as is typical on reservations, is a victory but a delayed one.

Thus, Jacob's role in the novels and films reflects that xenophobia by whites, for, while he is a loyal friend who facilitates and protects Bella's growing awareness of a supernatural world, his growing affection for her cannot be realised because of his ethnicity and social position.

In his cinematic incarnation, Jacob's glossy, flowing dark locks, his brown skin and his rather obvious last name mark him, despite actor Taylor Lautner's Hollywood white teeth, as a minority in a world of pale Caucasians. Jacob is a mechanic who works on Bella's beat-up pick-up truck, a typically lower-class vocation. Jacob is educated on the reservation, rather than attending the local high school. His father is in a wheelchair, and their financial situation cannot compare to that of his rival for Bella's heart, Edward Cullen, whose doctor father and extended family are wealthy, well groomed, chic and uniformly pale in appearance.

The difference between the 'townies' of Forks and the Native American kids is emblematised in the shapeshifting of Jacob and his friends and family. Viewed as animals of sorts anyway, that they turn into wolves is representative of their social status among the townsfolk; not getting a break, these wolves are also misunderstood and alien, as many country people view wolves in the wild.

Unlike Lon Chaney, Jr's Larry Talbot, the cinematic Jacob Black has control over his transformations into a wolf, his shifting a gift rather than a curse like Talbot's. Interestingly, however, Jacob transforms while wearing jeans as does Talbot, a signifier of a lower-class male. Even more significantly, Jacob spends much of his time in the films shirtless, like some primeval warrior or manual labourer. Much was made in the media of Taylor Lautner's washboard abdominals and short haircut in the later films, and the 'Team Jacob' versus 'Team Edward' fans hoped Bella would choose their particular dreamboat, but crossing class and species lines was a worse fate than becoming a vampire.

Rather like the archetypal, Adonis-like, working-class shirtless drifter of a Tennessee Williams script who doesn't commune with the local *hoi polloi*, Jacob is made even more suspect by his natural state. That he grows his hair long again in the novels and develops to the height of six foot seven implies not only his animality but also a coarseness which would never be displayed in the diamond-like Edward. Bella's body changes, of course, as she grows from teenager to woman to vampire to mother, but this is all done within a context of normative heterosexual maturity. Jacob's body on the other hand, and its 'size, heat, and muscularity' as well as his cutting 'his hair off when he changes into a werewolf/shape-shifter' and the addition of a tattoo in *New Moon*, further identify him as earthy, natural and uncivilised despite the haircut.[22]

The author, Stephenie Meyer, does give Jacob a voice in the text of *Eclipse*, and he has more prominence cinematically in part two of *Breaking Dawn*, so his status is elevated as the written series continues. Also, in both the novels and the films, Bella comes to love Jacob and rely on his friendship. He is not, however, patrician enough to become her husband. Rather, the enervated, suicidal Edward Cullen, whose wealth and sparkling beauty, as well as his accomplished family and links to the vampire leadership, the Volturi, will give Bella a room with a view which Jacob couldn't possibly provide. In the pastiche of the *Twilight* film *Vampires Suck* (2010), Becca/Bella asks who the tall young man in the cafeteria is, describing him as '[T]he really pale dude with big hair and constipated look'. Edward Sullen/Cullen, the vampire, contravenes the living, breathing, *canis lupus* warmth of Jacob, whose black cannot compete with Edward's white.

Rather disturbingly, Jacob imprints (finds his soulmate) upon Renesmee, the daughter of Bella and Edward, for not only is he condescendingly granted second best rather than his great love, it also implies a discomfiting paedophiliac kind of affection. If Jacob cannot have Bella, he will take her daughter. His Native American werewolf has been accepted into the vampire fold, but only tangentially. Jacob becomes the best friend in the romcom, not to mention the avuncular future husband of a far-too-young family friend. The thought of his cross-species mating at a later date with Renesmee perhaps offers true assimilation, but only for a later generation.

True Blood's true trash

Finally, while the stereotypical notion of American Southern white/trailer trash permeates the television adaptation of Charlaine Harris's Sookie Stackhouse novels, HBO's *True Blood*, the series portrays the wolf packs as the crudest of rednecks, deplorables living in the 'boondocks' – the wrong side of town. Despite his kindness and loyalty, the werewolf Alcide Herveaux (Joe Manganiello) must lose to Confederate hero Vampire Bill for Sookie Stackhouse's affections.[23]

The werewolf as marginalised Other is seen as far lower on the fantasy food chain than vampires as well as other fantastic beings in the series. Ranked below the distinctly, foully aromatic maenad Maryann Forrester and the lascivious fae, werewolves truly embody the stereotypes of Southern US, white/trailer trash status. Like Jacob Black, they occasionally interact with higher classes, or to continue the Southern stereotype, those from better families – including vampires; authentic assimilation is impossible.

Even the sweet shapeshifter Sam Merlotte, who spends the first season as a dog, looks down on the werewolves. After revealing his supernatural nature to Sookie, who asks him if he's a werewolf, he replies, 'Werewolves are dangerous, nasty creatures. Do not call me a werewolf.'[24] There are clearly 'hierarchies … [and] distinction[s] between shifters and werewolves'.[25]

Werewolves do not even make their appearance until season three of the television series or the third novel, and then they first appear as bodyguards for Sookie, acting under orders from the vampire Eric Northman.[26] Many creatures appear throughout the series, but the werewolves distinctly lack the romance of a vampire or the iridescence of a fairy.

Alcide Herveaux is treated more thoughtfully than this in Harris's novels and in *True Blood* by author Charlaine Harris and show creator Alan Ball, but he is still a lesser being than the other supernatural beings because of his werewolf nature. In his first appearance in the series, in the novel *Club Dead*, Alcide is assigned (as in *True Blood*) the protection of Sookie Stackhouse by Eric the vampire, to whom he owes a favour. Immediately he is subservient to the more human monster. His physical prowess is appreciated by Sookie, describing him as:

> a big rough man [who] was eating real food … He was big as a boulder, with biceps that I could do pullups on. He would have to shave a second time if he planned on going out in the evening. He would fit right in on a construction site or a wharf. He was a proper man.[27]

This is a positive description, but it is also a description of Alcide as working-class; his pleasures, his size, his 'proper man'-hood almost reflect the lyrics to a country-and-western song.

Alcide himself acknowledges that, as a werewolf, he is not nearly as attractive or tolerable as a vampire: "'We just can't tell the world we exist, like the vampires did. We'd be locked up in zoos, sterilized, ghettoized – because we're sometimes animals. Going public just seems to make the vampires glamourous and rich.' He sounded more than a little bitter."[28]

Even with the first view in *True Blood* of Alcide Herveaux, portrayed by the handsome, impossibly built Joe Manganiello, the werewolves of the series further represent the social stratifications in the small Louisiana town of Bon Temps and its environs. The Stackhouses are Bon Temps natives, their lineage and respectability thanks to their ancestors and Sookie's grandmother.[29] After the Civil War, family became vitally important in many Southern communities; there was nothing to hold onto but lineage. The werewolves, on the other hand, are not accorded such tolerance.

Alcide's pack, the Long Tooths, is centred outside Shreveport, a large port city not unlike New Orleans, but without that city's charm. The Shreveport of *True Blood* implies an urban nightmare and lacks the small-town, communal commitment of Bon Temps. Furthermore, Long Tooths live not even in the city but out in the countryside in shacks. Wearing black leather and stripping down to total nudity when they run, their battles for pack leader are brutally vicious and far less stylish than the same battles among vampires. Their accents represent the most uneducated of the rural Southern US lower classes. The women appear hard-used, and the men ignorant. No wonder the business owner Sam Merlotte looks down upon them; he may live in a trailer behind his bar, but he is no werewolf.

Alcide, on the other hand, works in his father's construction business rather than in a saloon, yet he is still viewed as having more brawn than brain. The images in the opening title sequence of the programme which 'evoke[] a number of stereotypes that portray Southerners as poor, rural, violent, drunken … highly sexualised' are all centralised in the werewolf bodies of Alcide and his pack.[30] Alcide is a serial monogamist and a good guy, but he is a werewolf.

In comparison, Sookie Stackhouse's brother Jason is a man-whore of the first degree, and Sookie gains a reputation not only as bizarre for her telepathic powers but also as a 'fangbanger' for dating Bill Compton. But the Stackhouses are legitimately a part of their society. Alcide and his kind are the sort the great Southern Gothic author and satirist Flannery O'Connor would describe as 'kind of vacant and white-trashy'.[31]

The arc of Alcide's story in the novels and in *True Blood* offers a character who, like Jacob Black and like Larry Talbot, adores the leading lady unrequitedly. The vampires look down upon Alcide because he is a werewolf, and their powers outstrip his physical might. When he does come to Sookie's rescue, he is always bested by or abandoned for Bill or Eric.

When Alcide has relationships with other female wolves, the women present a 'biker chick' aesthetic, perfect candidates for the Jerry Springer or Jeremy Kyle programmes. His girlfriend, the furrily named Debbie Pelt, is the ultimate bar bitch who does not love Alcide so much as want dominance over him like an alpha dog. Sookie kills Debbie in self-defence, certainly, but, in an echo of contemporary American racial injustices, the blonde white girl gets away with killing the big bad wolf.

Even in the final season of *True Blood*, where we see that 'the distinct sexual tension between Sookie and the werewolf Alcide' has developed into something profoundly stable and quite human, Alcide is not allowed to see that love to a happy ending.[32] Rather, he is shot dead early in season seven, episode 3, 'Fire in the Hole', defending Sookie.[33] As actor Joe Manganiello noted, 'I die naked in the woods with nothing but my sock on. Given Alcide's track record on the show, I was like, "That's about right".'[34] That season ends with Sookie happily pregnant and married to a human, eschewing all of the supernatural creatures she once loved and by whom she was loved. Why she could not have married Alcide and have had the same ending reiterates the marginalisation of the werewolves in the HBO adaptation while reassuring the audience that the status quo has been restored; no inappropriate cross-pollination between classes or races has proved sustainable.

Conclusion

The werewolf struggles for respect in the pantheon of mythic monsters. Dogs may be humans' best friend, but, in terms of most contemporary portrayals, werewolves are generally second-class citizens. They are loyal but will not be invited to the ball, and they certainly will not get the girl. They are working-class rather than aspirational middle-class professionals. They wear Levis, not tweeds or Savile Row suits.

Even the dysfunctional vampire roommates of 2014's *What We Do in the Shadows*, and its 2019 reboot on FX Network, discriminate against werewolves on the basis of class, specifically appearance. On a lads' evening out in their hometown of Wellington, New Zealand, film vampire Deacon (Jonathan Brugh) inhales deeply and pronounces, 'I can smell werewolves'. The werewolves are presented as middle-class guys dressed in track suits and trainers, unlike the overtly romantic vampire dandies. There are several clashes throughout the film, with the vampire Vlad affirming, 'I'm not racist, I just don't like werewolves.' They hurl insults at the werewolves, taunting, 'Why don't you go smell your own crotches?'[35] In the film and the television series, an uneasy truce is made between the vampires and werewolves, but, even then, the vampires maintain an aristocratic front, while the werewolves dress like everyday humans.

As in reel life, also in real life. Despite the efforts to reintroduce wolves to the wild in real life, such efforts 'have to overcome "enormous" challenges to be successful, a major study of the UK's largest "rewilding" project has found, for there are many reservations about these species and their creation of "conflicts with other land users", amid local concerns over "disruption to rural business".[36]

Hence, the werewolf remains a version of the awkward interloper, of the indigenous native whose manifest destiny was to be conquered by a superior Caucasian, of the lower class, of the monster against whom one must build a tall wall constructed of powerful materials: fear of difference, disgust with those of lower status and hatred of the unfamiliar. The werewolf has metamorphosed into a metaphor for the marginalised Other. These scary, hairy monsters represent super-creeps, seemingly doomed for ever to the dog house, 'when the wolfbane blooms, and the autumn moon is bright'.[37]

Notes

1. Vieira, *Hollywood Horror*, pp. 94–6 (p. 96).
2. Hudson, 'Of Course There Are Werewolves and Vampires', p. 661.
3. *Being Human* (2008–13).
4. Haraway, 'A Manifesto for Cyborgs', p. 222, cited in Batty, 'Harry Potter', p. 26.
5. McMahon-Coleman and Weaver, 'The Alpha Race', p. 92.
6. Rossello, 'Hobbes and the Wolf-man', p. 256.
7. Reece, 'Oh Grandmother, What Big Teeth You Have!', p. 104.
8. *Ibid.*, p. 106.
9. As David Skal relates in his documentary *Monster by Moonlight*.
10. *Ibid.*
11. *Universal Horror* (1998).
12. Batty, 'Harry Potter', p. 26.
13. *The Wolf Man*.
14. *Ibid.*
15. Stoker, *Dracula*, ed. by Auerbach and Skal, p. 11.
16. *Ibid.*
17. *The Wolf Man*.
18. *Ibid.*
19. *Ibid.*
20. Meyer's Twilight series consists of: *Twilight* (2005), *New Moon* (2006), *Eclipse* (2007), *Breaking Dawn* (2008). The Twilight Saga films are: *Twilight* (2008), *New Moon* (2009), *Eclipse* (2010), *Breaking Dawn – Part 1* (2011), *Breaking Dawn – Part 2* (2012).
21. Romero, 'Native Americans Score Historic Wins'.

22 Nykvist, 'The Body Project', p. 35.
23 *True Blood* (2008–14).
24 'I Don't Wanna Know', *True Blood*, 1.10.
25 McMahon-Coleman and Weaver, p. 106.
26 Harris, *Club Dead*; 'It Hurts Me Too', *True Blood*, 3.3.
27 Harris, pp. 55–6.
28 *Ibid.*, p. 56.
29 'Fang-banger' is the appellation given in the books to humans who engage in sexual relations with vampires.
30 Anderson, '*True Blood* Title Sequence'.
31 O'Connor, 'Revelation', p. 320.
32 Ruddell and Cherry, 'More than Cold and Heartless', p. 51.
33 'Fire in the Hole', *True Blood*, 7.3.
34 Siegemund-Broka, '"True Blood" Star on Shocker'.
35 *What We Do in the Shadows* (2014).
36 Merrill, 'Rewilding'.
37 *The Wolf Man*.

Part III

Reinventing the wolf: intertextual and metafictional manifestations

9

'THE PRICE OF FLESH IS LOVE': COMMODIFICATION, CORPOREALITY AND PARANORMAL ROMANCE IN ANGELA CARTER'S BEAST TALES

Bill Hughes

Of all the monsters that haunt the Gothic tradition, the werewolf, drawing on the cultural history of the wolf itself as singularly predatory and antisocial, is the most apt for representing our conflicted relationship with nature. This hybrid creature, shifting between mute instinctual savagery and the negation of this as speaking, suffering subject, can serve to dramatise our existence as simultaneously flesh-bound animal and a transcendental consciousness beyond nature. Werewolf fictions have recently taken a sympathetic turn and, following the vampires of paranormal romance, have emphasised the subjectivity of the werewolf, casting them as victims of ineluctable urges and as lovers, very often female.[1] This turn was anticipated by Angela Carter in her 'beast tales', by which I mean 'Peter and the Wolf' and most of the tales in the 1979 collection of transformed fairy tales, *The Bloody Chamber and Other Stories*. In these tales, metamorphoses between animal (often wolf) and human explore what costs are incurred in being animated, conscious flesh, particularly when that flesh is female. Animals enable Carter to assert a radical humanism that yet recognises our fleshly animality. Thus, as Jessica Tiffin points out, beasts

> are probably Carter's most potent symbols, the space in which she can most powerfully explore the notion of sexuality as an animal urge quite apart from its constructions through culture … they are … figures of transgressive eroticism redeemed by the trappings of intellect (speech).[2]

This emphasis on an embodied consciousness where flesh both speaks and desires is a central concern of Carter's fictions.

In this chapter I will show how Carter stages her own kind of paranormal romance, where encounters with werewolfish figures liberate human beings by way of the flesh from their reification as mere meat. This will involve some examination of how Carter variously uses 'meat' and 'flesh' to characterise bodies and of the ideas of cost, price and value that she associates with them. Alongside this, I look at Carter's multifarious perspectives on love and how it interacts with both economy and the flesh.

'Peter and the Wolf': flesh and the price of humanity

Carter's tale 'Peter and the Wolf' (from Carter's later collection, *Black Venus* (1985)) is a successor to the wolf stories of *The Bloody Chamber*, especially 'Wolf-Alice', which similarly features a wild child raised by wolves.[3] In this story, Carter dramatises the costs of renunciation of the flesh and a process of emancipation through the flesh. Flesh is opposed to spirit in Christian dualism, where the price to pay for being human is the mortification of the flesh. But Carter overturns this.

'Peter and the Wolf' takes place in a feudal world before the onset of generalised commodity exchange that is capitalism, yet it is at the threshold of modernity. In the tale, an old village woman goes up to see her daughter in the mountains as she is due to give birth. She finds the mother dead and no child but traces of wolves. Some years later, her grandson Peter goes up into the mountains with his father. They see a pack of wolves, among them a strange, naked creature on all fours. This is his lost cousin, who had been taken and raised by wolves. They capture her, taking them back to their home to try and return her to human life.

Peter, like his world itself, is perched on a threshold. He catches sight of the wolf girl's 'forbidden book' (p. 87) – her genitals – which fills him with 'absolute fascination' (p. 86), 'drawing him into an inner, secret place … his first … intimation of infinity' (pp. 86–7). Raw unclothed nature paradoxically incites Peter's desire to read, leading him to Bible readings with the priest. Thus flesh leads to the chastisement of flesh; the wild 'language' of the wolves to the literary. Equating flesh to text in this way already suggests Carter's refusal to see the body as purely natural; it is always caught up in that most artificial of processes, language. Peter's awareness of the raw femaleness of the wolf girl is a desublimation.[4] This desublimation is a moment in reinvention; a non-repressive *re*-sublimation will follow, yielding a transformed consciousness.[5] This pattern will occur throughout the beast tales – descent and stripping away; re-emergence and re-creation. But this takes place in the service of anti-essentialism, rather than subjection to any putative 'natural' essence. Betty Moss says, 'Carter insists that gender and sexuality are not fixed according to anatomy or essences'.[6] I would claim that it is not just gender and sexuality at stake here; these stories warn us that our entire human existence should not be reduced to meat by the 'anatomical reductionism' of which Carter speaks in *The Sadeian Woman*.[7]

Carter hints that it is this text, this 'forbidden book', paradoxically inscribed upon the flesh of a creature radically exiled from culture, which individuates Peter, setting him apart from the rest of the village and inciting him to learn to read, to ask the village priest to teach him to read the Bible, with its own promises of infinity. He is the 'first of his flock' (p. 89) who had ever wanted to read; the Biblical-pastoral image is significant, denoting the absolute distinction of Peter from the girl through the age-old opposition of sheep and wolf. He becomes pious and mortifies his now-alienated flesh through self-flagellation (p. 89).

However, some years later, on his way to the seminary to become a priest, Peter has a second encounter with his lupine cousin by the river. Now, her nakedness, which is 'that of our first parents, before the Fall' (p. 90), induces a collapse into a pre-symbolic state, the Kristevan semiotic, where 'Language crumbled into dust under the weight of her speechlessness' (p. 90).[8] But, in a movement akin to his earlier revelation, falling into this precultural state, akin to animality itself, is the necessary prelude to a re-emergence and a reshaping of subjectivity. He continues towards his destination but dizzy now with doubts about his vocation: 'He experienced the vertigo of freedom' (p. 91). It is important to note that Peter has not abandoned himself to instinctual, animal life; he has in part freed himself from what Marcuse calls *surplus* repression.[9]

Hope Jennings sees this tale as challenging the patriarchal Eve myth in Genesis, with 'female flesh as representative of an economy of desire that disrupts the repressive authority of the paternal law or word'.[10] The sight of female genitalia, in a revision of Freud, offers 'plenitude and plurality' rather than absence.[11] Peter is 'free to construct his future without the burdens of sin or shame'.[12] But Carter does not show Peter as completely emancipated; this is a utopian potential that is suggested rather than explicitly delineated.[13] Rather, he steps into a world open to reinvention.

History is enacted in miniature as he moves from a feudal worldview to Enlightenment modernity, where 'The cool, rational sun surprised him' (p. 92). There is a hint of the new world of commodification, and a certain sense of loss is registered too as the mountain of his childhood 'began to acquire a flat, two-dimensional look', transformed into 'the postcard hastily bought as a souvenir of childhood at a railway station' (p. 92). Carter's dialectical treatment renders Peter's enlightenment as highly ambivalent: there are costs as well as gains. His consciousness of nature has a new detachment; he sees the mountain now as 'primitive', 'barren' and 'unkind' (p. 92) – nature as inimical to humanity. The enchantment of folk culture has been lost as even his own tale, with the mountain now as 'a wonderful backcloth for an old country tale, tale of a child suckled by wolves, perhaps, or of wolves nursed by a woman' (p. 92) (Carter turning recursively on her own art). But in this state of alienation from his roots, there is also emancipation: he will acquire a polyglossal virtuosity and new landscapes open up to him, 'strange cities, other countries' where he will speak 'in strange languages' (p. 92). This existentialist sense of human agency is central to Carter's values; she does not want the subject dissolved into animal flesh.[14]

Wolfish and naked flesh, though clearly menacing to the sociality of village life, can awaken consciousness and foster autonomy. By the end of the tale, Peter is able to rewrite his own narrative away from what had been predetermined, and marches 'into a different story' (92). There is a clear dialectical movement from nature, to a civilisation based on repression and renunciation of the fleshly, then to a partial desublimation of the gains of literacy that allows the human to reshape themselves. He has become emancipated as a bourgeois. As Marx and Engels say in *The Communist Manifesto*, 'everlasting uncertainty and agitation distinguish the bourgeois epoch from all earlier ones … [the bourgeoisie] must get a footing everywhere, settle everywhere, establish connections everywhere'.[15] Note that there is ambivalence here; there are positive aspects to this transformation and Carter registers these too. Thus Peter's flesh has been granted voice by the flesh of the Other and embarks upon a vertiginous and uncertain liberty. The plunge into or encounter into animality, as often in these tales, is the route to emancipation, though it is not animality itself that is freedom. Carter is, I think, a humanist, though one who acknowledges our material animality and the ways in which its repression can bind us.

The Bloody Chamber

Angela Carter's *The Bloody Chamber* is a delirious whirl of metamorphoses, between animal and human akin to those of the werewolf, but also of texts.[16] Variations on the same tales and themes allow Carter to examine the same problems in various ways from different angles. All the tales in *The Bloody Chamber* are connected, alluding to each other, and though the wolf tales are obviously most pertinent for this collection, the other stories involve beast–human transformations and interactions.[17] They are formally involved with the werewolf theme. Motifs from 'Little Red Riding Hood' recur throughout. The connecting theme of the essays featured in this collection is the dialectic of wildness and culture, and this theme dominates Carter's tales too. The ambiguous quotation in my title – 'The price of flesh is love' – could characterise *The Bloody Chamber*; all the conventional meanings attached to 'price', 'flesh' and 'love' are unsettled in turn throughout Angela Carter's interlinked collection of tales.[18] I will examine each of these three terms in turn to see what Carter's tales do with them in the hope that I can convey something of how they depict the commodification of flesh, most often female. But alongside this, I reveal counter-currents that envisage paths of erotic mutuality and emancipation from the reification of the flesh

Price

The Erl-King in the tale of that name has a mane, linking him in a series with the lion and tiger stories. The heroine is enticed into the wood, following the birdsong. The trees 'stir with a noise like taffeta skirts of women who have lost themselves in the woods' (pp. 96–7), and the narrator/protagonist does indeed 'go into the wood as trustingly as Red Riding Hood' (p. 97) only to be seduced by an alluring monster. The Erl-King is vampiric – 'you sink your teeth into my throat and make me scream' (p. 101) – but with the sexualised vampirism of the demonic lover of paranormal romance who is simultaneously alluring and repulsive. Crucially, the Erl-King, as the Red Riding Hood allusions announce, is also another avatar of the werewolves that will appear in the final group of stories; as the heroine perceives: 'What big eyes you have. Eyes [having] the numinous phosphorescence of the eyes of lycanthropes' (p. 103). She repeatedly visits him for sex: 'He is the tender butcher who showed me how the price of love is flesh; skin the rabbit, he says! Off come all my clothes' (p. 100). Here, 'skin' or clothing is what demarcates her from the natural. In contrast, he is vegetable, tree-like, as well as animal: 'his flesh is of the same substance as those leaves that are slowly turning into earth' (p. 100).

The phrase 'the price of flesh' urges us to examine different senses of price and raises such questions as whether flesh *should* be bought and sold. In the context of the quotation, the Erl-King is a 'tender butcher' (p. 100), revealing the ambivalence of love in patriarchal relationships, for he *can* offer tenderness – at a price. But she has become bestialised, made meat, turned into the cattle that serve as prey or the commodities of the butcher's shop. The price of love, it seems, is submission, and this love is the inevitable cost of being flesh. But Carter will lead us into evaluating the forms that love can take and positing alternatives where flesh is emancipated from the market and from the inert heteronomy of meat.

It is not hard to read this as, in part, an allegory of the predatory but irresistibly alluring male who diminishes the selfhood of those captivated by his charm. The price, or cost, of love here is the autonomous self. This is connected to the flesh/skin theme: her skin here represents her individuality; he has stripped her even of that and clothed her in something that is simultaneously sensual and menacing. She loses her self in hyperarousal: 'He strips me to my last nakedness … like a skinned rabbit; … his fingers strip the last tattered skin away and clothe me in his dress of water [with] its capacity for drowning' (p. 102). However, the woman ultimately resents her captivity; unlike the birds, she will not spontaneously, artlessly sing; she will 'be dumb, from spite' (p. 103).

Cost and value

Price leads me to talk of value and, following the Marxist analysis, of exchange value, from which the price of commodified goods is derived.[19] Exchanges – as cash transactions, but of other, alternative kinds, and often of flesh itself – are prevalent in the stories. It is a consequence, for Marx, of exchange value that commodities are rendered abstract; all material particularity is stripped away as goods are equated to each other in the exchange process.[20] Carter restores particularity to the flesh that has been abstracted thus. This leads me to the other face of value in Marx – *use value*; the concrete, fleshly if you like, qualities of goods.[21] Carter returns flesh from spirit, from abstract exchange to concrete use. We must not let 'use' mislead us into thinking of a base utilitarianism – Marx's idea is to return to the human needs that commodities serve, thus a work of art, though purposeless according to narrowly functionalist values, has use value. But there *is* a repressive sense of 'use' that Marx does not distinguish overtly but which is certainly in line with his thought. Under capitalism and within patriarchy human beings are reduced to objects of 'use' in the narrow and imprisoning sense; Carter's tales challenge this through a 'useless' playfulness which re-evaluates notions of cost and price.[22]

Flesh

The 'moral pornographer' that Carter anticipates in *The Sadeian Woman* seeks a 'demystification of the flesh' (pp. 19–20). Carter also talks of 'skin' in contrast to 'flesh':

> the pleasures of the flesh are vulgar and unrefined, even with an element of beastliness about them … flesh plus skin equals sensuality. But, if flesh plus skin equals sensuality, then flesh minus skin equals meat.[23]

Merja Makinen says of this passage that 'this motif of skin and flesh as signifying pleasure, and of meat as signifying economic objectification, recurs throughout the ten tales'.[24] Skin may symbolise the restoration of authentic human needs to the concept of use value. 'Meat' represents a further stage of dehumanisation than flesh (which is ambiguously alive yet animal; not always or not quite human). Carter's reading of Sade is that 'he writes about sexual relations in terms of butchery and meat'.[25] Likewise, Bluebeard, in the title story, 'The Bloody Chamber', eyes up his young bride with, she tells us, 'the assessing eye of a connoisseur inspecting horseflesh'. Thus his gaze is enough to transform her into animal. She adds: 'or even of a housewife in the market, inspecting cuts on the slab' (6), where animal meat is a commodity.

When the girl in 'The Tiger's Bride' strips for the Beast figure as part of the price she pays for her father's transgression, she tells us that she was 'so unused to her own skin that to take off all my clothes involved a kind of flaying' (p. 73). Clothing, of course, is distinctively human and is another recurring motif in the stories. Here, garments blend with skin; she is stripping off her sensuality as well as her culture as she 'peel[s] down to the cold white meat of contract' (p. 73). The childhood fears of being devoured, of losing one's self, are 'made flesh and sinew' (p. 74). The precarious acquisition of human subjectivity is threatened by commodification. Yet she offers herself in the utopian hope that 'his appetite need not be my extinction' (p. 74). And finally, she is literally stripped of her skin, as the tiger flays her tenderly with his tongue, and she acquires an animal skin, of 'beautiful fur' (p. 75). Carter shows the ambiguous pleasures of submission, where 'everything will disintegrate' (p. 75). Here, becoming animal has a utopian appeal. But this is only one of many possibilities Carter imagines; the submerging of the self into wildness may in addition be the precursor of a reconstructed subjectivity, as in Peter's resublimation via the wolf-girl.

Flesh in *The Bloody Chamber* is *animated*; it talks, sings, moves, desires as well as being desired, and wants to consume as well as to be passively consumed. (Carter's assertion of female desire has, of course, been pointed out in many feminist readings.)[26] Carter explores what motivates these bodies: instinct or subjectivity, art or nature. Carter is concerned with not just flesh but embodied consciousness. She is, as she herself proclaims, a materialist.[27] But she is not a reductionist, nor, I think, is she a dualist. She is a humanist materialist whose concerns with autonomy rescue her from the first charge, and her stories point to the full humanity of a conscious flesh that acts freely and is bestowed with speech. The tongue that liberates the Tiger's Bride by restoring a repressed animality is also the tongue of language.[28] It could also be said that she is a historical materialist: in *The Sadeian Woman* she declares, 'our flesh comes to us out of history' (p. 9).[29] This awareness of the contingent nature of our bodies and the appetites and speech for which they are a substrate is emancipatory, recognising the possibility of transformation and flight from any fixed essence.

Language is central to Carter's visions of autonomy and humanity. The Lady in 'The Lady of the House of Love' is 'a system of repetitions' (p .108), a prisoner of a linguistic system that cannot account for creativity.[30] In the same way, the innate mechanisms behind animal signals cannot generate the open-endedness that characterises human language. The Lady considers her captive bird: 'Can a bird sing only the song it knows or can it learn a new song?' (p. 108). Likewise, the birds in 'The Erl-King' 'don't sing, they only cry because they can't find their way out [they] have lost their flesh in the corrosive pools of [the Erl-King's] regard' (pp. 103–4). Real song is art, voluntary; the bird's cry is instinctual, from the flesh (and 'cry' here bears the extra meaning of sorrow). In that story, Carter exposes the dangers of passively submitting to sexual allure and becoming a price-bearing commodity of flesh in the Goblin Market of love.[31]

The Lady's vampiric flesh does not decay. In this tale, it is the woman who is Beast, preying on vulnerable human males. But she is also, in direct opposition to the fleshliness of beasts, mechanical like the maid in 'The Tiger's Bride'; she resembles 'a great ingenious piece of clockwork' with a 'curiously disembodied [that is, fleshless] voice' (p. 118). Love might 'free her from the shadows' (p. 119), she speculates, just as 'A single kiss woke up the Sleeping Beauty in the Wood' (p. 116). Flesh decays and dies, but it is a precondition of humanity and of the joys that come from embodied consciousness. The price of love, and of being 'fully human' (p. 124), is flesh.

Carter is a writer of freedom. Makinen rightly quotes from 'The Bloody Chamber' to illustrate that in what she calls Carter's 'feminist re-write, Bluebeard's victimization of women is overturned'.[32] Thus, 'The puppet master ... saw his dolls break free of their strings' (p. 39). But the freedom Carter delineates is not women's emancipation alone; she is arguing against all reification, against dehumanising ideologies and against the alienation of capitalist society.

Love

I turn now to love. Carter employs the romance between beast and human to anticipate a transcendence of these oppositions, where animated, desiring (beastly) flesh is fully humanised, and where monstrous males are tamed by a newly independent femininity. This is the twentieth- and twenty-first-century secret of 'Beauty and the Beast', and of Carter's various reworkings of it, and it motivates paranormal romance.[33] In these stories Carter traces many varieties of love and exchange between the sexes: the self-deceptions of romance, enchainment and submissiveness, practicality and visions of mutuality.

In the tale 'The Company of Wolves', the wolf begins as absolute Other; dangerous, 'cunning' and 'ferocious' (p. 129). He is driven by 'the taste of flesh' (p. 129). Wolves are 'forest assassins', drawn by 'the smell of meat' of those who risk the wildness of the forest at night (p. 129). So, meat and flesh are the same to the undiscriminating senses of the animal, who is unaware of the market. Wolves sing, but the 'wolfsong' is an 'aria of fear' (p. 129). Of all the creatures of superstition that comprise the 'perils of the night and the forest', 'the wolf is the worst for he cannot listen to reason' (p. 130). Thus the Beast here is uncompromisingly inhuman. All of nature allies itself with the wolf: 'it seems as if the vegetation itself were in a plot with the wolves' (p. 130), and it is profoundly asocial: 'You are always in danger in the forest, where no people are' (p. 130). 'If you stray from the path, the wolves will eat you', the narrator says, recalling the Grimms' version of 'Little Red Riding Hood' with its hint of moral transgression, but also suggesting a plunge into nature.[34]

Thus the prelude sets up a stark opposition between human and natural, with wolf firmly aligned with the latter. Then Carter hints that she will upset all of this: 'for, worst of all, the wolf may be more than he seems' (p. 130). This is followed by four embedded tales, all variations on 'Little Red Riding Hood' and the werewolf theme.[35] Here, humanity and wolfhood become confused, with the wolf taking on different shades of malevolence and benignity in each.

In the fourth embedded story, the 'strong-minded child insists she will go off through the wood' p. (132). She has just entered puberty and the paradoxical initiation into regular chronology of 'her woman's bleeding, the clock inside her' (p. 133) that strikes once a month (clocks and time are another recurring theme of the tales). She meets in the forest a handsome young man who carries a compass; like the clock, the compass is an instrument for imposing regularity on the natural world. Unsurprisingly, this seductive man is a wolf, elemental and belonging to nature, and 'one of the worst wolves', those who 'are hairy on the inside' (p. 137).[36] He negotiates a price for her flesh in the form of a bet that he reaches her grandmother's before her; the stake is a kiss from her. As the knowing fairy-tale reader would expect, his wiles trump her innocence. She arrives at her grandmother's cottage and discovers him in the bed (he has eaten the grandmother). The girl, at his command, strips before the man-wolf until she is 'clothed only in her untainted integument of flesh' (p. 138) – a strange image; the girl is naked and vulnerable, yet 'integument' can mean a 'tough, outer protective layer'.[37] This initiates a free exchange, of flesh that is both tender and tough, a marriage of equals beyond the illusionary equality of commodity exchange.

Now, the wolves outside the grandmother's cottage sing once more: a 'prothalamion' (p. 138) as another inversion of the marriage ceremony, nature appropriating culture, that is also a 'Liebestod' (p. 138), where Eros and Thanatos are united.[38] Yet life and love triumph over the death urge; the fearless girl laughs at his threat to devour her, with the much-quoted phrase 'she knew she was nobody's meat' (p. 138).[39] The girl has 'freely' given 'the kiss she owed him' (p. 138). '[O]nly immaculate flesh' (p. 138), free from flaws, stain or sin, can satisfy the wolf's innate desire. But this immaculacy is not necessarily virginal: it exists either below or beyond the social stain of sin; that is, natural and presocial or instead lying in a transformed sinless economy. He is 'carnivore incarnate' – meat eater made flesh. 'Flesh' here is repeated in two senses, revealing the duality that is present throughout: in 'carnivore' it is meat to be consumed; 'incarnate' shows flesh as the embodiment of human qualities. However, the man-wolf's voraciousness is sublimated by the girl's conscious agency into an amatory mutuality where, as the clock of midnight strikes, 'sweet and sound, she sleeps in granny's bed, between the paws of the tender love' (p. 139). Nature has been tamed and, in a parallel allegorical thread, masculinity has been made authentically human instead of modelling itself on the rapaciousness of forces that render flesh as meat.

In the final tale of the collection, 'Wolf-Alice', Carter creates two more hybrid beast-humans with very different natures. The wild girl raised by wolves who becomes Wolf-Alice could well be Peter's lycanthropic cousin from 'Peter and the Wolf'. At home in neither nature nor culture, Wolf-Alice is a werewolf without the compensations of either life; she is estranged from the wolves: 'she would have called herself a wolf, but she cannot speak, although she howls because she is lonely' (p. 140). She does not understand wolf 'language' either, 'for she is not a wolf herself, although suckled by wolves' (p. 140). Her flesh and skin is an ambiguous substance as befits her confused nature: 'Nothing about her is human except that she is *not* a wolf; it is as if the fur she thought she wore had melted into her skin' (p. 141). But she dwells still in the timeless wolf world: 'She inhabits only the present tense ... a world of sensual immediacy as without hope as it is without despair' (p. 141), whereas to be authentically human is to have projects, to envisage futures where desires may be realised or which may fall to despair. The sense of futurity facilitates the making of social bonds, even of contracts for the exchange of goods or for reciprocal relations, whether free or exploitative. So nature is not utopia here, despite its promise of 'sensual immediacy' (p. 141), since it constrains human possibility.

Carter describes the attempts by nuns to socialise the girl in a way that recalls those eighteenth-century narratives of wild children, who were found living in the wilderness, unsocialised and without language. They were often assumed to have been raised by wolves or other beasts; attempts were made to teach them language and assimilate them to human society.[40] In particular the story of Marie-Angelique Le Blanc (who, like Wolf-Alice, was raised by nuns) is a likely source.[41] Tired of her wildness, the nuns hand her over to the local aristocrat, the Duke, for whom she is able to perform 'the few small tasks to which the nuns trained her' (p. 143). 'Trained' here suggests the repetitive routines that an automaton or domesticated animal can perform rather than creative, conscious labour.

The Duke is another Beast figure, but one whose status seems hard to pin down. He is another Bluebeard; like him, a connoisseur and marketer of flesh – his bedroom is like a 'butcher's shop' (p. 142), linking him with the rabbit-skinning Erl-King but also with Bluebeard via 'bloody chamber' (p. 144). He is lycanthropic: 'the moon, the governess of transformations' (p. 142) wakes him. (The moon is governess of Wolf-Alice's own menstrual metamorphosis too, revealing a kinship through the rhythms of the flesh.) Bestial, 'his eyes see only appetite' (p. 142). He raids the graveyards for meat. Flesh, for him, is reduced to meat in commodity form, to 'items on [his] menu' (p. 144). He is vampiric, casting no reflection, and rapacious, 'eyes open to devour the world in which he sees, nowhere, a reflection of himself' (p. 142). Thus, despite his bestial appetites, which suggest a complete immersion in nature, he is simultaneously set *against* nature, alienated from the animated, thinking flesh of the human body. His is a distorted Cartesian consciousness, psyche divided from body in a way that sees fleshly matter only in terms of consumption and abstract exchange and that rests on the division of labour that, for Marx, is involved in alienation.

Though wolflike in his voracity, he is not truly of the wolf world; the wolves themselves 'howl, as if they know his transformation is their parody' (p. 141). Here, Carter knowingly equates the multifarious transformations of beast and human in her stories to the dazzling generic metamorphoses she performs; parody is but one of many forms she experiments with and intertextual devices she employs. Her formal variations are as important for her shifting, kaleidoscopic exploration as the content of her work, where each beast incarnation conjures a different perspective.

Carter briefly suggests a lost Golden Age where animality and humanity were once reconciled (though this utopianism is undermined by a touch of Carterian mockery). The girl would have been at home in 'the Eden of our first beginnings where Eve and grunting Adam' pick 'lice from one another's pelts' (p. 143).[42] In this Paradise, 'her silence and her howling' would be 'a language as authentic as any language of nature' (p. 143). 'In a world of talking beasts and flowers [this is Looking-Glass World] she would be the bud of flesh in the kind lion's mouth' (p. 143). This is an image of gentle oral eroticism and is akin to the young woman lying 'between the paws of the tender wolf' (p. 139) in the earlier tale. But the only signal she can utter is 'an involuntary rustle of sound' (p. 143). It is an instinctive response, like the birds' song. If there is music here, it is like that of 'a wind-harp that moved with the random impulses of the air' (p. 143) like one of Carter's automata; it is not composed consciously.

Then menstruation initiates her into the human symbolic order. In Carter, animal fleshliness is also the bedrock of human consciousness which, in turn, facilitates the regulation of nature. Carter here retraces some of those speculations on the origins of thought, language and society that so fascinated Enlightenment thinkers such as Lord Monboddo, Condillac and Rousseau, who often looked at wild children as test cases.[43] And her recognition of herself in the mirror (the Lacanian trope is perhaps too obvious to dwell on) accompanies her dawning humanity and ego. It is at this stage that she is first named by the narrator; appropriately, as 'Wolf-Alice' (p. 145). Prior to this she is nameless; naming invites her into human social life. She has not only passed through the mirror and dwelt briefly in the land of talking beasts and flowers, but she has emerged from a dreamlike underworld into humanity. She now perceives herself as separate from the world; her bleeding seems to have given her a 'new skin' (p. 146), a transformed interface with the sensuous world.

In contrast, the Duke is 'locked half and half between such strange states, in an aborted transformation' (p. 148). Carter's project is to envision the completion of such metamorphoses, to rescue them from stasis, so that oppositions such as use and exchange, animality and consciousness, flesh and spirit, masculine and feminine are transcended. All these transformations are 'impartially recorded' by the mirror, the 'rational glass, the master of the visible' (pp. 148–9). This may be Carter's far from impartial image of the realist mode of writing she subverts.[44] For the mirror itself is transformed: as Wolf-Alice licks the wounded Duke, within this speculative looking-glass appears, 'as vivid as real life itself, as if brought into being by her soft, moist, gentle tongue, finally, the face of the Duke' (p. 149). As with the Tiger's Bride, her tongue brings the Beast into human life. This final, willed transformation restores the reflection – that is, the self-consciousness of humanity – of the now resurrected and humanised Duke. Carter's loving writing, woman's tongue, has effected this marvellous metamorphosis.

The Bloody Chamber is full of metamorphoses, of animal and human, but also of texts. Carter's set of variations on the same tales and themes and adoption of different genres, perspectives and styles creates a truly polyphonic and dialectical style. She prefigures the generic hybridity of present-day paranormal romance, where the monster of traditional Gothic becomes a sympathetic lover, forming an architext for the later form. Makinen acknowledges the commercial appeal of Carter; sex sells 'in this commodified age', according to her, and the book covers drew attention to 'bizarre romance'.[45] She also tells us that 'beast marriage' stories fascinated Carter. Both these phrases might stand in for 'paranormal romance', which plays in a like manner with affects of mutual 'awe and fear'.[46] Carter's 'bizarre romance' is paranormal in another sense than that denoting erotic encounters with the supernatural. That is, that it lies outside 'normal' romance, with its deviance, but also its utopian possibilities, which may well work against 'this commodified age' which makes meat even out of books.[47]

I think it is questionable to say, as some do, that Carter's beast romance collapses the boundary of animal/human (as if this were an emancipatory event anyway).[48] Rather, she explores this avenue among many other possibilities and temptations. Overall, her tales of metamorphosis between animal and human tend more to dissolve social constructions of the self only to rebuild them as *more* human, as liberated from the chains of essence, biology, or history, less bound to nature. Yet Carter's ebullient, highly artificial, and ornamental language explicitly distances art from nature; even if she had wished to dissolve the distinctions between animal and human she, perhaps inadvertently, establishes a paradox where what is uniquely human is revelled in while celebrating the animality at its core. Her characters' passages into animal life are but the first stage and suggest the possibility of further transformations and a non-repressive resublimation that liberates the flesh.

Carter's tales depict flesh (usually female) as in the marketplace. Flesh is commodified, but exchange value becomes transformed into use value (that is, following Marx, its sensuous particularity is restored) through her miraculous metamorphoses. Her writing achieves the goal of the 'total demystification of the flesh and the subsequent revelation, through the infinite modulations of the sexual act, of the real relations of man and his kind'.[49] Carter performs 'infinite modulations' of the narrative act, permutations as ingeniously various as Sade's. Her 'moral pornography' is akin to Marcuse's 'libidinal morality', which envisages the abolition of surplus repression in the service of that fleshly pleasure which 'contains an element of self-determination which is the token of human triumph over blind necessity'.[50] Carter has a vision of utopian mutuality in desire, emancipated and enhanced by immersion into and return from the non-human – a liberation not only from patriarchy but also from the capitalist commodification of those bodies. The plunge into chaos through transformation emancipates one from the past and enables the construction of future projects. Carter's humanist materialism acknowledges the embodied, fleshly, yet autonomous nature of human consciousness, with all its 'blood and mire', and re-evaluates the price of love.

Notes

1 Many paranormal romances feature werewolves as lovers, often with female werewolf protagonists. For analyses, see Kaja Franck, Chapter 10 below; McMahon-Coleman and Weaver, *Werewolves and Other Shapeshifters*; Bodart, *They Suck*, pp. 75–138; Priest, 'I Was a Teenage She-wolf'; and Hughes, '"But by Blood no Wolf am I"'. For paranormal romance as a genre, see Crawford, *The Twilight of the Gothic*.
2 Tiffin, *Marvelous Geometry*, p. 91.
3 Carter, 'Peter and the Wolf'. All further references are to this edition, with page numbers in parentheses in the text.
4 As Jean Wyatt puts it, 'the vision of real difference ... opens the mind to the previously unsignified, springing the subject free from established categories of thought' ('The Violence of Gendering', p. 552). And this revisioning is spurred by flesh; as Betty Moss says, 'Peter has experienced a material transcendence ... as effected via the flesh, the body' ('Desire', p. 198).
5 This is what the Frankfurt School philosopher Herbert Marcuse calls 'self-sublimation', 'a non-repressive mode of sublimation which results from an extension rather than from a constraining deflection of the libido' (*Eros and Civilization*, pp. 169–70). Such transformational moments are visible throughout the tales.
6 Moss, p. 192.

7 Cited here by Moss (p. 192) from *The Sadeian Woman*, p. 4.
8 In Julia Kristeva's work, the semiotic is associated with the instinctual. It precedes the signification in language that occurs through the symbolic process but is a precondition of it, and its rhythms, rooted in the flesh, permeate the later phase as poetic language. See 'Revolution in Poetic Language', pp. 92ff.
9 Marcuse defines surplus repression as 'the restrictions necessitated by social domination' over and above 'the "modifications" of the instincts necessary for the perpetuation of the human race in civilization' (*Eros and Civilization*, p. 35). Carter acknowledges Marcuse's influence: 'Marcuse and Adorno were ... part of my personal process of maturing into feminism' ('Notes from the Front Line', in *Shaking a Leg*, pp. 45–53 (p. 46)).
10 Jennings, 'Genesis and Gender', p. 165.
11 *Ibid.*, p. 169.
12 *Ibid.*, p. 170.
13 I mean 'utopian' in the sense that Fredric Jameson, following Ernst Bloch, uses when identifying the emancipatory forces within a text (see 'Conclusion: The Dialectic of Utopia and Ideology', in *The Political Unconscious*, pp. 281–99).
14 'History tells us that every oppressed class gained true liberation from its masters through its own efforts' (Carter, *Sadeian Woman*, p. 151). Julia Kristeva, whose awareness of the precariousness of the subject and the animality it rests upon resembles Carter's, similarly insists on the need for agency in political revolution, summarised by Toril Moi as: 'without some kind of subject structure, meaningful subversive or creative action is impossible' ('Introduction', p. 14).
15 Marx and Engels, *The Communist Manifesto*, p. 223.
16 The secondary literature on *The Bloody Chamber*, and on Carter generally, is voluminous. Important criticism on the beast and wolf tales can be found in: Bacchilega, *Postmodern Fairy Tales*; *Angela Carter*, ed. by Roemer and Bacchilega; Tiffin, 'The Bloodied Text'; Lau, *Erotic Infidelities*.
17 Lucie Armitt argues that the transformations are not only within the tales but between them, the lion becoming the wolf, 'who is simultaneously both man and woman' ('The Fragile Frames', p. 96). Jessica Tiffin: 'each tale in the collection offering a different possible response to the difficulties of patriarchy encoded within fairy-tale situations' (p. 68). I argue Carter is responding not to patriarchy alone but to reification under capitalism.
18 *The Bloody Chamber*, p. 100. All further references are to this edition, with page numbers in parentheses in the text.
19 Exchange-value is 'the proportion, in which use-values of one kind exchange for use-values of another kind' (Marx, *Capital*, p. 126).
20 '[T]he exchange relation of commodities is characterized precisely by its abstraction from their use-value ... All its sensuous characteristics are extinguished' (*ibid.*, pp. 127, 128).
21 'The usefulness of a thing makes it a use-value' (*ibid.*, p. 126).

22 Marcuse argues that 'play is *unproductive* and *useless* precisely because it cancels the repressive and exploitative traits of labor and leisure; it "just plays" with reality' (*Eros and Civilization*, p. 195).
23 *Sadeian Woman*, pp. 137–8.
24 Makinen, 'Angela Carter's "The Bloody Chamber"', p. 10.
25 *Sadeian Woman*, p. 138.
26 Carter's complex affiliations with feminism are well documented. Jessica Tiffin enumerates the shifting feminist responses to Carter (pp. 69–70). I strongly recognise Carter's feminism but want to explore how, through that feminism, she articulates also her own firmly avowed materialist socialism as a humanist critique of reification in capitalist society.
27 Her project has been 'the product of an absolute and *committed materialism*' (Carter, 'Notes from the Front Line', in *Shaking a Leg*, p. 47).
28 Likewise, in the final story, Wolf-Alice's recuperative tongue gains its potency only after she has acquired language; see below.
29 And 'Carter was completely committed to historically rooted socialist materialism' (Dimovitz, *Angela Carter*, p. 5).
30 As perhaps Saussure's *langue* is; there is an implicit and humanist critique of structuralism here. Carter was not sympathetic to the methodology of such as Barthes, suggesting his mind functioned 'like clockwork'; 'clockwork' conjures up the automata in Carter's tales, who are the antithesis of flesh and humanity ('Roland Barthes: *The Fashion System*', in *Shaking a Leg*, pp. 175–7 (p. 177)).
31 Carter alludes heavily to Rossetti's poem in this tale.
32 Makinen, p. 10.
33 The fairy tale of 'Beauty and the Beast' binds all the stories in *The Bloody Chamber* together. In each of the tales (all of which are also variations on other classic fairy tales), Beauty and Beast undergo various kinds of exchange. Beasts are beastly to greater or lesser degrees; Beauty overcomes or tames Beast, or is herself subjugated; Beauties may even themselves turn bestial. Angela Carter added a translation of Madame Leprince de Beaumont's 1756 version of the tale to those she had made of Perrault in 1977 (*Sleeping Beauty*); her translation emphases the story's materialist concerns with exchange. See Rochère's careful attention to the relationship between Carter's translations and her refashionings: *Reading, Translating, Rewriting*. For 'Beauty and the Beast', see Hearne, *Beauty and the Beast*; Warner, *From the Beast to the Blonde*, pp. 273–318; and Tatar, ed., *Beauty and the Beast*. Warner discusses Carter's specific uses of 'Beauty and the Beast' (pp. 307–10).
34 'Little Redcap', in Grimm, *Selected Tales*, p. 90.
35 It may seem odd not to treat the preceding tale, 'The Werewolf', given this book's theme, but this brief story says little about the aspects of flesh that are so interesting elsewhere.
36 Recalling Perrault's moral to young women and the more overtly sexual werewolf (or *bzou*) of the oral variant which Carter likely used as a source. In Perrault,

'softly-spoken' lecherous men are 'the most dangerous wolves of all' ('Little Red Riding-Hood', p. 103). The earthy qualities in Carter's tale can be found in Delarue, 'The Story of Grandmother', in Dundes, ed., *Little Red Riding Hood*, pp. 13–20.

37 From *Oxford Living Dictionaries*; the *OED* has 'The natural covering or investment of the body, or of some part or organ, of an animal or plant; a skin, shell, husk, rind, etc.' but the connotation of toughness is common.
38 For Marcuse, through the reconciliation of Eros and Thanatos, a transfigured eroticism 'pacifies the animal world, reconciles the lion with the lamb and the lion with man. The world of nature is a world of oppression, cruelty, and pain, as is the human world; like the latter, it awaits its liberation' (*Eros and Civilization*, p. 166). Carter beckons towards the liberation of both.
39 What Red Riding Hood does with her laughter is to demolish and transcend the Romantic or Wagnerian equation of Love and Death as well as resisting her reification as meat; through loving, flesh becomes a living subject, not dead and thing-like.
40 See Sam George, Chapter 3 above.
41 See Douthwaite, *The Wild Girl*, pp. 29–53.
42 This image of domestic mutuality also figures in the conclusion of 'The Company of Wolves', with the granddaughter picking 'out the lice from [the wolf's] pelt' (p. 138).
43 Aidan Day sees Carter as being firmly in the Enlightenment tradition (in *Angela Carter*).
44 On realism, Carter said, 'I've got nothing against realism. But there's realism and there's realism. The questions that I ask myself I think are very much to do with reality' (Frayling, 'We Live in Gothic Times', in *Inside the Bloody Chamber*, pp. 235–46 (p. 235)).
45 Makinen, p. 9.
46 Lorna Jowett notes the revision of horror in Neil Jordan's film adaptation of Carter's text *The Company of Wolves* (1984) towards female concerns, aligning this with the popularity of 'Dark Romance' (or paranormal romance) ('Between the Paws: Of the Tender Wolf: Authorship, Adaptation and Audience', in *Angela Carter*, ed. by Andermahr and Phillips, pp. 39–40). I have not the space to examine the further complexities of the transformation of the stories into film, but Jowett's article is an excellent starting point. Tiffin, too, draws attention to the intertextual relationship with romance fiction (pp. 81–2).
47 As Marcuse says, 'Against a society which employs sexuality as means for a useful end, the perversions uphold sexuality as an end in itself; they thus place themselves outside the dominion of the performance principle and challenge its very foundation' (*Eros and Civilization*, p. 50).
48 For example, see Margot Young, 'Everybody Eats Somebody', in McKay and Miller, eds, *Werewolves*, pp. 203–26.
49 *Sadeian Woman*, p. 9.
50 *Sadeian Woman*, p. 9; *Eros and Civilization*, pp. 228, 227.

10

Growing pains of the teenage werewolf: Young Adult literature and the metaphorical wolf

Kaja Franck

The werewolf has become an increasingly familiar figure in the worlds of Young Adult literature and popular culture as a means of representing the transition to adulthood and the sense of isolation that is felt by many teenagers.[1] Yet, the relationship between human and animal identity in children's literature is not a new phenomenon. Using the example of 'Beauty and the Beast' and its adaptation by Disney, which was aimed at a young audience, Susan Z. Swann argues that animal characters in fairy tales typically symbolise the aggressive, uncontrolled wilderness.[2] In this tale, the goal of the Beast is to return from a state of animality to a civilised, human form.[3] Bruno Bettelheim argues that in 'animal groom' fairy tales, such as 'Beauty and the Beast', the narrative resolves itself when 'a beast is turned into a magnificent person' through the power of love.[4] The animal state is only temporary and human identity is redeemed. Regarding Gothic literature, Kelly Hurley suggests that the presence of the non-human or the possibility of hybrid human–animal monsters challenges human systems of order over the natural world, threatening to bring chaos into the realms of human society.[5] Thus, hybrid or species-shifting creatures such as werewolves are depicted as monstrous because they threaten the stability of categorisation. Alternatively, in breaking these boundaries, werewolves also offer the possibility of freedom from the binary structure of human versus animal.

Yet this complex potential tends to be simplified in the comparisons between werewolves and teenagers by framing the relationship as a metaphor. I want to look first at how the teenage werewolf as metaphor for adolescence functions as part of a system for understanding humanity's relationship with the animal Other, before considering how language constructs and maintains this separateness even as the narrative werewolf breaks down this boundary. Jodi Richards Bodart claims that

> Teens are struggling with controlling themselves, as they learn to cope with the new sexual and emotional drives that are coming alive inside them. Their brains

have not matured enough to allow them rational, logical decision making, and are instead controlled by a more primitive part, the amygdala ... The 'inner beast' breaks out to overcome the 'human side' of the individual. It is all too easy for teens to respond as 'beasts' with high levels of emotion triggered by the amygdala, even when they don't actually feel all that emotional ... The werewolf, snarling at danger, may also feel an emotional disconnect between its animal and human sides.[6]

Bodart's reductive explanation contrasts the human with the animal in order to depict the werewolf and by extension the teenager as aggressive and uncontrollable. This approach, as I will show, exemplifies the model that has been used to read the werewolf in Young Adult literature. Bodart relates the physical and emotional experience of transforming from child to adult to the werewolf's transformation. The human or adult side is more highly evolved and represents control, whilst the wolf or child side is seen as instinctive and violent. The teenager vacillates between the two. Alison Waller argues more broadly about teenage animal transformations that there 'is a clear correspondence between metamorphosis and the physical changes at puberty'.[7] She goes on to suggest that animal transformations in Young Adult novels can be 'natural' or 'unnatural'.[8] 'Natural' transformations allow the adolescent to use their metamorphic powers to successfully navigate becoming a human adult; 'unnatural' transformations see the teenage protagonist reject 'development as a human' in preference for the animal state.[9]

Waller notes that there is an overlap between the figure of the shapeshifter and the genre of adolescent literature. Both can be described as liminal: the shapeshifter is between two categories just as Young Adult literature is neither children's nor adults' literature.[10] Waller's use of the word 'liminal' expresses an uncertainty over identity, placing the teenage werewolf on the outskirts of subjectivity. Adolescence, and, therefore, the werewolf, is shown to be unstable. Bodart's invocation of the animal as instinctive and Waller's discussion of metamorphosis build on the idea of the werewolf as symbolising 'the beast within'.[11] The werewolf represents the human subject as split between 'the wolf [who] represents nature and the animal within, whereas the clean and proper body of the human represents culture, rationality and reason'.[12] The animal Other, in this case symbolised by the wolf, stands in direct conflict to the emergence of the human subject.

Though 'Little Red Riding Hood' is not explicitly about werewolves, the fairy tale has been read as using certain beliefs about the wolf and the pubescent child to explore the fragility of transitioning from child to adult. As I will show, the sexuality of the teenage werewolf in romance narratives is often rooted in this fairy tale. Both Jack Zipes and Bruno Bettelheim acknowledge the latent sexuality in 'Little Red Riding Hood', both the Grimms' and Charles Perrault's versions.[13] This sexuality is gendered as the virginal female versus rapacious masculinity. The negligence of Red Riding Hood in straying from the path leads to her falling prey to the wolf. In Bettelheim's reading of 'Little Red Riding Hood', he proposes that the wolf represents 'the selfish, asocial, violent, potentially destructive tendencies of the id', drawing on negative portrayals of this animal.[14] This description suggests that the anthropomorphic Big Bad Wolf symbolising the malign aspects of humanity is, like the werewolf, an embodiment of the 'beast within'. In the fairy tale the wolf is an externalised symbol of the 'beast' whereas for the teenage werewolf this is embodied in their experience of lycanthropy.

Many retellings of 'Little Red Riding Hood', following second-wave feminism, expose the danger of gender stereotypes that assume women are passive and men are aggressive while accepting the notion of the wolf as symbolising violent animality. Angela Carter's most famous revision of this fairy tale, which draws on its many variants, 'The Company of Wolves' (1979), shows Red Riding Hood as the wolf's equal who, rather than being threatened by his attempts to eat her, laughs as 'she knew she was nobody's meat'.[15] Carter refers to the wolf as 'carnivore incarnate' and it is only after he has been 'tamed' by Red Riding Hood that he becomes 'the tender wolf'.[16] The wolf conforms to being a vicious creature that must be overcome by the human protagonist, although, for Carter, the wolf symbolises violent masculine sexuality. In this example, Carter interrogates primarily the depiction of gender roles in the fairy tale, though she is not entirely unsympathetic to the treatment of the wolf. In Suzy McKee Charnas's 'Boobs' (1989), the teenage girl and the wolf are combined in the figure of the werewolf, and Charnas draws on the relationship between menstruation, puberty, werewolves and female sexuality. In this short story, a pubescent girl transforms into a werewolf each month rather than menstruating.[17] The unnamed female protagonist is depicted as equally as aggressive as her male counterparts, consuming the young men who mock the sudden onset of her 'boobs'. Whilst this short story celebrates the expression of active femininity and deconstructs gender stereotypes regarding the passivity of women, it does so at the expense of the wolf. Lycanthropy is still connected with the unleashing of the 'beast within'.

The connection between puberty and the emergence of lycanthropy recurs in male teenage werewolves. The premise of *Teen Wolf* (both the film from 1985 and the television series which premiered in 2011) is that 'PUBERTY IS WEREWOLFISM', as exhibited in the parallels between the increase in body hair, speed and physical prowess that come with both puberty in young men and turning into a werewolf.[18] As in 'Boobs' and 'The Company of Wolves', the acceptance and, concomitantly, control of your inner wolf is the key to navigating the dangerous terrain of puberty and lycanthropy. Puberty may 'unleash the beast within' but the beast cannot be allowed to take over. Whilst there are potential benefits of being a wolf, these must be tamed and domesticated by the human aspect of the werewolf. The contrast between being at once physically superior but psychologically unstable due to lycanthropy and puberty is presented in the character of Jacob Black in the Twilight series. His transformation is manifested by sudden growth spurts and changes to his temperature; Bella comments: 'His skin was burning hot ... He looked *huge*.'[19] His lycanthropy forces him to undergo a fast-forwarded version of puberty and the novel repeatedly compares his physical changes from man to wolf to his increased musculature. The stress on the word 'huge' and body heat correlates to the relationship between wolves, werewolves and monstrosity. Jacob's size is a potential threat and his heightened temperature is in stark contrast to the cool, elegant physique of his love rival, the vampire Edward Cullen.[20] In his transformed state, Jacob is a 'gigantic black monster' but also 'just an animal'.[21] As a large wolf, and a large man, Jacob's size is potentially monstrous because of the possible threat to the safety of Bella. In this way, his ability to shapeshift suggests he is greater or more powerful than a human. However, as an animal, he is also less than human. Animals are associated with violence and lack of control. Within the novels this is shown when Sam Uley, the Alpha of the pack, accidentally transforms and attacks the woman he loves while in a heightened emotional state. Unless the beast is controlled by the human, the werewolf is a figure of violence and a threat to the human subject.

Recent studies on the differences between female and male lycanthropes in fiction have acknowledged the varying portrayals of the two and how these reflect gender stereotypes in human society.[22] However, using an animal to explore the creation of human identity during puberty is informed by an assumption of human superiority rather than equality. Though referring to the depiction of lycanthropy in medieval literature, Jeffrey J. Cohen describes the werewolf as 'not an identity-robbing degradation of the human, nor the yielding to a submerged and interior animality, but the staging of a conversation in which the human always triumphs'.[23] His description suggests there is the potential for incorporating both the wolf and the human equally in the figure of the werewolf. The word 'conversation' suggests that this is based on the concept of communication. However, ultimately, Cohen concludes that this equal engagement is undercut by the hierarchy of the human subject over the animal Other. The power and failings of human language in the experience of the teenage werewolf are central to Maggie Stiefvater's Wolves of Mercy Falls series (2009–11) and Annette Curtis Klause's *Blood and Chocolate* (1997).[24] Both texts explore similar ideas regarding the relationship between lycanthropy and adolescence but, in addition, critique certain ideas regarding the human subject and the animal Other. The novels suggest that human language fails as a means of expressing hybridity, causing an irreparable separation of the human and the (were)wolf.

The Wolves of Mercy Falls is centred on Grace and Sam and their romantic relationship. Whilst the series introduces Sam as a werewolf and Grace as a human, this is complicated throughout the novels as both move from being human to being (were)wolf. In these novels, lycanthropy is a disease that is passed through blood and saliva. *Blood and Chocolate* centres on the love affair between Vivian, a werewolf, and Aiden, a human. In contrast to Stiefvater's novels, Vivian's werewolfism is hereditary: it is something into which she was born. The difference between Sam's lycanthropy, which is forced on him through a bite, and Vivian's, which is present from birth, is encompassed in their differing experiences of transformation. Sam's changes are painful and caused by a drop in temperature rather than his volition; in one scene, narrated from Grace's point of view, she describes how he 'seized violently … and threw up'.[25] There is no possibility of controlling these transformations so the human subject is always victim to the natural surroundings and the sudden, unwanted emergence of the wolf. In comparison, Vivian's transformations are pleasurable and she is able to choose when she wants to transform.[26] Yet the wolf will also emerge during times of emotional stress, conforming to Bodart's model of the teenage werewolf; thus Vivian's narrative is about learning to control her wolf within. Though Vivian celebrates her identity as a werewolf, referring to herself as 'a beautiful *loup-garou*' (p. 12), she is aware that this alienates her from her peers. She wonders whether her peers can 'see the forest in her eyes, the shadow of her pelt? Were her teeth too sharp?' (p. 12). Her lycanthropy functions as a metaphor for puberty by expressing the isolation that can come with changing identities. Despite the more celebratory regard for the experience of being a werewolf, the novel still ends with the separation of the couple. Where Sam and Grace choose to reject the wolf from their human identity, *Blood and Chocolate* ends with Vivian embracing her wolfishness and accepting that she cannot be with Aiden because he is human rather than a werewolf.

Both texts acknowledge the influence of 'Little Red Riding Hood' in the expression of the wolfish Other, puberty and sexuality. Vivian's question about her teeth echoes the questions posed by Red Riding Hood to the Wolf. Just as the Wolf is unable to hide his true nature from Red Riding Hood, Vivian believes that she is unable to hide her animality from her peers. Her physical attributes betray her as 'Other'. Even Aiden, the human who falls in love with her, is tacitly aware of her animal-otherness, predicting their eventual separation. Their first kiss is precipitated by the following exchange:

> 'What red lips you have', he said in her ear.
> Did she dare say it? 'All the better to kiss you with, my dear', she replied.
> And then their lips met.
> He was gentle. She hadn't expected that. (p. 51)

This interaction draws on the latent sexuality in 'Little Red Riding Hood'. However, the gender of the characters is inverted so that it is the human boy who is 'gentle', undermining Vivian's expectations. This reinforces the idea that it is the werewolf, with the addition of the wolf element, who is related to aggressive sexuality, regardless of the gender of the character themselves. In his discussion of monstrous animals, Jeffrey Weinstock suggests that animals become more monstrous the closer they come to humans:

> sometimes because of the animal's lack of humanity, but even at times because the animals represent amplifications of 'human' characteristics. The metaphorical relation to being human is often a site where the literal boundary between human and animal is transgressed through scientific or metaphysical means.[27]

Weinstock's comments open the multiple ways in which the werewolf's relationship with the human can be considered.

First, the wolf aspect of the werewolf draws attention to the potential monstrosity of the animal as the Other. The wolf is 'just an animal', as Bella refers to Jacob when he is in wolf form; it is less than human, suggesting the comparative superiority of humanity. Alternatively, the wolf stands in for malign human characteristics as suggested by Bettelheim's reading of 'Little Red Riding Hood' and the symbolism of the werewolf as the 'beast within'. Finally, the proximity of wolves to humans relates to two types of physical transgressions: the wolf can move from wilderness to domestic spaces, rupturing the boundary between the two, and, in werewolf narratives, the wolf can destroy the somatic integrity of the human subject. The werewolf is both human and animal just as the teenager is adult and child. This 'metaphorical relation' predicates the treatment of lycanthropy within the two novels. Vivian's interactions with other humans show that her belief that she can form a healthy relationship with Aiden is naive. The proximity of the animal to human contained within her lycanthropy is apparent to fully human subjects. She is prevented from being accepted because she is partially animal Other. Here the metaphor of lycanthropy for the isolation felt during puberty disintegrates. Pubescent isolation will pass once healthy adulthood is achieved. Vivian will never be able to stop being a werewolf and become a stable human subject. Thus she must reject and be rejected from human society.

'Little Red Riding Hood' is used to explore the proximity between human and animal and the possible transgression this implies in the opening sequence of *Shiver*, the first in her Wolves of Mercy Falls series. The scene opens with Sam's pack, who are starving due to a cold winter, attacking Grace as a child while she plays in her backyard. Grace remembers 'lying in the snow, a small red spot of warm going cold, surrounded by wolves' (*Shiver*, p. 1). The use of the colour red invokes the colour of Red Riding Hood's cloak, and the location of the attack, Grace's backyard, recalls the narrative of travelling through the woods away from the family home. Grace's house is located at the boundary of Mercy Falls and her garden bleeds into the aptly named Border Woods. With no clear demarcation between the human habitation and domesticated garden, the wolves are able to get close to Grace and threaten her. Without distance, they become monstrous. Stiefvater's use of the imagery from 'Little Red Riding Hood' and her opposition of the wolfish woods to human homes links the text to the various negative discourses that have dogged the wolf and informed the figure of the werewolf.

The idea of animality, sexuality and Sam's rejection of the wolf surfaces later in the novel as Grace and Sam discuss having sex. As in *Blood and Chocolate*, the male partner eschews the role of sexual aggressor but in this case because he wants to reject that which makes him wolf. Grace asks Sam why he is 'so careful with me [Grace]', to which he replies, 'I – it's – I'm not an animal' (*Shiver*, p. 326). Sam correlates the wolf with aggressive sexuality and violence, which he rejects. His struggle to express himself leads him to swap between 'I', the human subject, and 'it's', suggesting that he refers to the wolf side of his nature as 'it' – an animal object that is not part of him. Sam demarcates between the 'animal' and the 'human' and is unable to accept that, like all humans, he is an animal. Rather, he can only define being human by being 'not animal'. Grace, despite knowing he transforms into a wolf, is not afraid of him. Rather than rejecting the wolves, Grace's encounter leads her to become infatuated with Sam. The first transgression of the boundaries between human and animal, woods and domesticity opens the possibility of breaking that boundary again. Yet this occurs only once Grace has reached puberty and is herself in a liminal zone between child and adult.

Both texts assume prior knowledge of the nature of werewolves and wolves. The decision to invoke 'Little Red Riding Hood' suggests that the authors assume readers have a certain amount of familiarity with the wolves, werewolves and the tropes attached to the animal and its monstrous counterpart. In his discussion of metaphor, Max Black uses the phrase 'Man is a wolf to man' to explore how metaphor functions. He argues that this metaphor can work only if there is a common concept of the wolf. Thus a 'speaker who says "wolf" is normally taken to be implying in some sense of that word that he is referring to something fierce, carnivorous, treacherous, and so on'.[28] It is noticeable that Black, as in Bettelheim's reading of the wolf, accepts that this particular animal is considered to be an embodiment of aggression. In reaction to this proverb, Serge Bouchard comments: 'Man is a wolf to man, which you will agree, is not very kind to the wolf'.[29] Though there is a flippancy to this comment that wolves are no worse than humans, there is also an acknowledgement of how humans use the animal Other as a means of distinguishing and creating the human subject. Barbara Creed suggests that 'the human subject sees nature and the animal world as abject – dirty, diseased, mute. Yet, the human subject is drawn to myth and legends, fairy tales and literary narratives, painting and sculpture, film and media which continue to explore the fragile boundary between human and animal.'[30] In structuring the werewolf as a metaphor for human, the real wolf is replaced by a symbolic structure of 'wolfishness' that serves only to highlight what befits a proper human. The wolf is, to use Julia Kristeva's term, abjected; it is pushed away, literally and linguistically. Its proximity is deemed to be threatening to the boundaries between human and animal. In the figure of the werewolf, caught between human and wolf, the wolf is denigrated and must be rejected, controlled and/or removed from the human sphere. Creed's use of the word 'mute' draws attention to the perception that animals lack language. This 'muteness' or lack of vocalised language prevents the animal, in this case the wolf, from being the subject, as usually understood, as it cannot express itself as 'I'. Sam's shift from 'I' to 'it' when discussing his desire for Grace draws attention to the inherent problem of expressing non-human subjectivity: is it possible to represent animal subjectivity using literary language? Furthermore, can animals be considered an 'I' without verbalised language? Here, fiction gives a space for imagination to think beyond the human 'I', thereby acknowledging differing forms of subjectivity. The werewolf, as a hybrid creature, creates a space to consider non-human identity, a hybrid 'I'.

By allowing their werewolves to be protagonists, both novels offer the possibility for the wolves to speak. In doing so they react to the idea that werewolves, and by extension wolves, can only be objects of observation and not themselves be narrators since they lack the self-reflexive consciousness needed to relate their existence.[31] Both texts acknowledge the difficulty of expressing the wolfish aspect of the werewolf as successfully as they do the human. The failure of human language within the novels to articulate the experience of being a wolf denies the possibility of a meaningful relationship between humans and werewolves. The following lines from Rilke, quoted in *Shiver*, encapsulate how language becomes an impassable boundary in the novels: 'and even the most clever of animals see that we are not surely at home in our interpreted world.'[32] This poem is discovered amongst Sam's belongings. He is the character who finds the tension of being wolf and being human the most difficult to accept. Sam's aim in the novel is to find a cure for his werewolfism so that he can stay human. If left untreated, the werewolf will stop transforming and stay as a wolf. The werewolves must settle into one state: either wolf or human. Even the transition of the titles of the novels, *Shiver*, *Linger* and *Forever*, follows this movement from one state to another. From the involuntary 'shiver', to the indecisive 'linger', the novels end in the eternal and never-changing state of 'forever'; Sam and Grace's happy ending comes with the destruction of their inner wolf. For Sam, the wolf is an infectious, foreign 'Other' which has invaded the human subject. The human subject is civilised by rejecting the animal within just as a teenager becomes an adult by rejecting their childishness and reaching the more stable state of adulthood. Sam's love of literature and language exemplifies his desire to remain human. Bill Hughes argues that Sam's engagement with language is the means by which he can return to humanity and is emancipated, through choice, from his animal identity.[33] Yet this also opens the question of the possibility of depicting animal subjectivity through human language, which is addressed in the novels.

In *Blood and Chocolate*, Vivian is first attracted to Aiden when she reads his poem 'Wolf Change' because it seems to express successfully the experience of being wolf. The poem encapsulate the sensations of becoming a wolf to the extent that Vivian believes '*He knows*' (p. 16). The lines he writes transcend the boundaries between human, wolf and werewolf and translate the experience of being a werewolf into human language. This informs Vivian's belief that he would be able to love her not despite but because of her lycanthropy. Moreover, throughout the novel, Aiden's behaviour suggests that he rejects mainstream culture and morality and is interested in exploring the boundaries between the natural and civilised world. He reads witchcraft books and believes that 'we shouldn't close ourselves to possibilities' (p. 77) regarding the supernatural. With regard to the relationship between humans and animals, he rejects the hunting practices of his father, protesting that there 'should be more to being with your father than going out and killing something together' (79). This rejection of violence towards animals and his open-minded attitude towards non-scientific explanations of phenomena suggest his potential to accept lycanthropy. These elements of his personality and his writing abilities convince Vivian that, unlike other humans, he will not reject her; thus she decides to show him her transformation.

It is at this point that human, vocalised language fails within the novel. Aiden is shown to be unable to accept the proximity of Vivian's wolf-self because she loses the ability to speak. As she transforms, she senses his fear and tries to reassure him: '"I know. I look odd now but the end is gorgeous." But the words came out in a hollow growl from a mouth not meant to speak' (p. 168). Her wolf form is unable to express itself adequately and Aiden fails to understand what is happening. Aiden's experience of the world is entirely tied to his ability to vocalise and express himself within human notions of language. As Vivian cannot speak to him, he can only interpret her transformation through the language of horror movies and his fear of the monstrous. To return to Rilke's poem, Vivian is the 'most clever of animals' who can see Aiden's horror as he (mis)interprets her. Though she is non-human, she is still the subject of the scene and it is Aiden's fear and horror which is made Other to the reader. Despite the reader's empathy towards the werewolf protagonist, this scene is pivotal in reinforcing humanity's need to separate human from werewolf, in order to reassert the dominance of the human subject. Towards the end of the scene, Vivian tries to behave as a dog, a creature familiar to

Aiden and one with connotations of being 'man's best friend', in order to help him realise she is not a threat. She uses her body language to communicate how unthreatening she is: '*Look, I am lovely*, she begged. She whimpered and wagged her tail like a dog. He flung a mug at her head' (p. 169). His aggressive action shows that he fails to understand her use of non-verbal language. Instead, he returns to violence in order to control the animal Other, despite his previous rejection of hunting practices.

Ultimately, Aiden is so trapped as a human subject within his interpreted world that he fails to expand towards the acceptance of other forms of existence. By attempting to transform in his room, Vivian closes the proximity between the animal Other and the human. Firstly, she brings the wolf into the domestic sphere, and secondly she shows the fragility of the boundary between animal and human. Aiden, unlike Grace in *Shiver*, rejects both these transgressions. By the end of the novel, he convinces himself that the only thing to do is kill Vivian despite his feelings for her. As Vivian realises, 'all he saw was a savage beast' (p. 169) which he must destroy. He turns to familiar texts such as horror movies in order to gain the information he requires to kill a werewolf – by forging a silver bullet and shooting her. In returning to textual versions of the werewolf rather than communicating with Vivian herself, he betrays his inability to see the fault lines of human language and the possibility that it cannot explain everything that he experiences. These fictions are comforting because they offer, as Creed suggests, a safe place to be enticed and explore the boundary between human and animal.[34] They also offer a solution should the monstrous occur.

In *Shiver*, it is Sam who explains how humanity has demonised the wolf. He claims that 'Humans made monsters out of us' (p. 279). Humans make 'monsters' out of wolves through narratives such as 'Little Red Riding Hood' which depict the wolf as a cunning predator intent on killing humans. His comments suggest that he is aware of the bloody history between man and wolf.[35] Conversely, though Sam acknowledges the cruelty of humans towards wolves, he is also the character most invested in his own humanity, which centres on his love of language. He is described as 'the most human' (*Shiver*, p. 130). Whilst this is meant as a compliment, it also shows how, like Aiden, he is invested in being a stable human subject. He works in a bookshop, reads poetry (such as that of Rilke) and writes lyrics. Sam is highly conscious of how human language enables him to understand and interpret the world around him. He tells Grace: 'I have words. I can say anything I want to you' (*Shiver*, p. 162). He refers to the way in which the werewolves communicate through sharing images as a 'wordless, futile language' (*Shiver*, p. 60), and is frustrated by its limitations. Though Sam enjoys translated poetry, he cannot translate his wolfish experience into human words. The werewolves' lack of verbal language is translated into voicelessness in the sense of not being a subject, or 'I'. Though

Sam acknowledges the ways in which human language can 'make monsters' out of animals, he cannot separate his sense of self from his identity as a thinking, speaking subject of language. Mary Midgley explains that one of the great obstacles to animal rights is the belief that, without language, animals cannot be subjects; she suggests that the human imagination is one way of overcoming this boundary between animals and humans.[36] Despite Sam's wolf-memories of saving Grace at the beginning of the series, he does not accept the possibility of being a lupine subject.

Like those of *Blood and Chocolate,* Stiefvater's werewolves are not able to use human language once transformed and, as I have argued, this lack of language is portrayed as the greatest obstacle in the relationship between man and (were) wolf, something which both novels find insurmountable. The moments in which Sam and Grace regard each other when in different forms is described as 'an impossible void' (*Shiver*, p. 9). John Berger describes the gaze between human and animal as across 'a narrow abyss of non-comprehension', one that is echoed by Stiefvater's description of the 'impossible void'.[37] Though the abyss cannot be bridged by language as it can between two humans, the animal's gaze forces humans to consider themselves as the 'Other' – we are the object of the animal's gaze.[38] Berger's statement depicts the gaze as shared between the human and animal: the human regards the animal and the animal regards the human. The gaze becomes, to use Cohen's previous description of the werewolf, a conversation – an engagement between two species, though not one that is vocalised. The werewolf, as human and wolf, embodies this engagement. To return to *Blood and Chocolate*, the moment when Aiden watches Vivian transform allows the reader to enter the role of the 'animal' being regarded, the animal which Aiden can define only as being a 'savage beast'. Thus Aiden's reaction does not support the situation – Vivian is not a threat to him – and his reliance on the 'interpreted world' is flawed as it misinforms him about the violence of the wolf. It is Vivian who realises this in the end. She refers to the word 'wolf' as 'her animal shape with its imperfect name' (p. 249). The word itself, as human language, cannot contain all that she is and the reality of her existence.

Aiden's rejection of Vivian and the subsequent emotional upheaval leaves her caught mid-transformation between being a wolf and being a human. Unable to accept that she cannot exist in human society and that humans will always react to her with fear, she remains between states until she is visited by her werewolf suitor, Gabriel. He informs her that, like Vivian, as a young werewolf he fell in love with a human woman and transformed in front of her. Her response was terror: 'She screamed and called me a filthy beast' (p. 260). Gabriel's human suitor echoes Creeds comments about the abjected animal as 'dirty, diseased'. Gabriel reacts by hitting her and, as she is much weaker than a werewolf, he kills her. Like Sam Uley and the other werewolves in the Twilight series, he is physically stronger than a human but acts emotionally and unpredictably on his aggressive instincts. Though this incident is highly problematic and reads as extreme domestic abuse, Vivian understands Gabriel's behaviour. In doing so, she accepts that humans and werewolves can never have prolonged contact because werewolves are undomesticated and violent. This realisation allows her to transform again. By focalising through Vivian, the novel allows the reader to partially experience being a werewolf but, despite this, the narrative ends with an impasse: human and werewolf are shown to be in opposition to one another. For the reader, neither Aiden nor Gabriel seems a satisfactory partner for Vivian.

Though 'the impossible void' is maintained more firmly in *Shiver*, Sam and Grace engage with one another in both human and wolf forms. In these moments, the text blurs the line between wolf and human. While in wolf form, Sam 'watched her, like I'd always watched her' (*Shiver*, p. 431) and Grace, once transformed, explains, 'I watched him'.[39] Both quotations use 'I' as the subject of the sentence, which suggests that, even in wolf form, Grace and Sam maintain an identity. However, the rejection of their human names in these sections suggests that it is a sense of identity that destabilises the conventional notion of the subject. At the end of the series, Grace is forced to make a decision between being human and being werewolf, leading to her killing her inner wolf. Her transformation allows her to disengage from her emotionally distant parents, consolidate new friendships and find love with Sam. However, 'she realises that if she remains that way [as a werewolf] for too long, these relationships will descend into stasis and eventually disintegration'.[40] She chooses to be injected with meningitis in order to destroy the infection that causes her to transform into a wolf, despite the risk to her life. Once lycanthropy has served its purpose in supporting her movement into adulthood, it is no longer needed.

Yet, as with *Blood and Chocolate*, *Shiver* is never entirely able to deaden the voice of the wolf. It is only Sam's repeated conjectures regarding the importance of human language and the negation of lupine subjectivity in the narrative which tend towards this. By the end of the series, Sam realises that the distinction between the human and wolf mind is 'getting less true every day[,] like finding out that gravity no longer worked on Mondays' (*Forever*, p. 289). This description betrays how Sam has interpreted the experience of lycanthropy. The distinct categories between humans and wolves, on which Sam relies and which he believes to be based on language, are dissolving. Though the narrative of the Sam and Grace's love story seems to reject the possibility of successfully and happily being werewolf, the language undercuts this, suggesting that the werewolf can bridge the 'impossible void'. As Rob Boddice argues, a text 'may convincingly be constructed against an anthropocentr*ist* world view, but its starting point will be no less based in the anthropocentric'.[41] Despite being an imperfect tool to represent lycanthropic and lupine subjectivity, the literary imagination and language offer a space to reconsider what it is to be a subject, an 'I'.

The character of Olivia challenges the notion that there is no slippage between wolf and human. Introduced as one of Grace's friends who, like Grace, is concerned for the future of the wolves living in Boundary Woods, Olivia is bitten and becomes a werewolf. She is bitten in the first book and offered the 'cure' at the end. Unlike Sam, she chooses to transform into a wolf, telling Grace, '"I can't say that I'd rather die than be this way"' (*Shiver*, p. 408). When the cold weather arrives and it is time for her to become a wolf, she admits that '"I'm actually looking forward to it"' (*Shiver*, p. 422). Olivia notices that the other wolves in the pack are waiting for her to transform and welcome her new form. By the end of the first novel, even her human form is transformed as Grace describes her pre-transformation as 'a strange, light creature that I didn't recognise' (*Shiver*, p. 423), who becomes 'a light, light wolf, joyful and leaping' (*Shiver*, p. 423). The echo between the language used to describe the girl and that which characterises the wolf proposes a continuity between the human and animal form, making Olivia reject the liminality of human/animal transformations suggested by Waller. Unlike the other wolves, she suffers no pain in transformation, suggesting that Sam's pain during transformation is not a necessary part of lycanthropy; rather, it is a symptom of his hatred at losing his human identity. Olivia's pleasure in transforming is based not on the potential loss of self to be found in the 'void' but rather in accepting her dual nature. Yet she is killed in the third book before she is able to become a protagonist of the novel and she is never given a first-person narrative.

Though both texts use the werewolf metaphorically to explore the teenage experience, their exploration of the power of human language also offers a way of reclaiming the animal experience within these novels. Although the novels' endings reinforce the idea of separate existences, it is possible to find moments that truly blur the division between human and wolf despite their lacking a common language. On this reading, it is not human language which fails to communicate the werewolf experience but that, in considering the werewolf only as a metaphor for adolescence, we fail to recognise the power of the werewolf to bridge Berger's 'narrow abyss of non-comprehension'. Reducing the werewolf to this metaphor may only reflect back humanity's fear of the wolf as an animal Other and not the real creature itself. At the end of *Blood and Chocolate*, Gabriel argues:

> They [humans] can't change ... But I do believe they have a beast within. In some it's buried so deep they'll never feel it; in others it stirs, and if a person can't give it a safe voice it warps and rots and breaks out in evil ways. (p. 261)

What these novels show is that the 'safe voice' might not be one that is entirely human.

Notes

1. For examples of teenage werewolves, see *Teen Wolf* (1985); the character of Oz in *Buffy the Vampire Slayer* ('Phases', 2.15; 'Wild at Heart', 4.6; and 'New Moon Rising', 4.19); *Teen Wolf* (2011–); Cremer, *Nightshade*; and *Red Riding Hood* (2011).
2. Swan, 'Gothic Drama in Disney's Beauty and the Beast', p. 354.
3. *Ibid.*, p. 354.
4. Bettelheim, *The Uses of Enchantment*, p. 282.
5. Hurley, *The Gothic Body*, pp. 24–5.
6. Bodart, *They Suck, They Bite, They Eat, They Kill*, pp. 83–4.
7. Waller, *Constructing Adolescence*, p. 44.
8. *Ibid.*, p. 49.
9. *Ibid.*, p. 49.
10. *Ibid.*, p. 33.
11. Coudray, *The Curse of the Werewolf*, pp. 91–7; Stypczynski, *The Modern Literary Werewolf*, p. 52; and Sconduto, *Metamorphoses of the Werewolf*, pp. 183–5.
12. Wilson, 'Dans ma peau', p. 200.
13. Bettelheim, pp. 166–83; and Zipes, *The Trials and Tribulations*, pp. 17–81.
14. Bettelheim, p. 172.
15. Angela Carter, 'The Company of Wolves', in *The Bloody Chamber*, p. 138.
16. *Ibid.*, pp. 138, 139.
17. Charnas, 'Boobs'.
18. Koetsier and Forceville, 'Embodied Identity', pp. 50–1.
19. Meyer, *New Moon*, p. 281.
20. Commentators on the Twilight series have noted the imperialist and racist implications of the text. As a Native American, Jacob Black's connection to animality has been critiqued as racially insensitive. See Wilson, 'It's a Wolf Thing', and Leggatt and Burnett, 'Biting Bella'.
21. *New Moon*, pp. 242, 243.
22. See Sibielski, 'Gendering the Monster Within', and Coudray, pp. 91–129.
23. Cohen, 'The Werewolf's Indifference', p. 352.
24. The Wolves of Mercy Fall series consists of *Shiver* (2009), *Linger* (2010) and *Forever* (2011). There is a further novel, *Sinner* (2014), which follows one of the secondary characters from the trilogy, Cole St Clair. However, for this chapter I will be considering the first three novels only.
25. Stiefvater, *Shiver*, p. 412. Further references are to this edition, placed in parentheses in the main body of the text.
26. Klause, *Blood and Chocolate*, p. 30. Further references are to this edition, placed in parentheses in the main body of the text.

27 Weinstock, *The Ashgate Encyclopaedia of Literary and Cinematic Monsters*, p. 14.
28 Black, *Models and Metaphors*, p. 40.
29 Bouchard, *Quinze lieux communs les armes*, p. 177 (my translation).
30 Creed, 'Ginger Snaps', p. 188.
31 Gutenberg, 'Shape-shifters from the Wilderness', p. 172.
32 Rilke, 'The First Elegy', in *Duino Elegies*, cited in Maggie Stiefvater, *Linger*, p. 223.
33 Hughes, '"But by Blood no Wolf am I"'.
34 Creed, p. 198.
35 Mech, *The Wolf*, pp. 334–5; and Marvin, *Wolf*, pp. 81–118.
36 Midgley, *Animals and Why They Matter*, pp. 54–5.
37 Berger, 'Why Look at Animals', p. 5.
38 *Ibid.*, pp. 5–7.
39 Stiefvater, *Forever*, p. 35. Further references will be in parentheses in the main body of the text.
40 Priest, 'I Was a Teenage She-wolf', p. 143.
41 Boddice, 'Introduction', *Anthropocentrism*, p. 13.

11

'I AM THE BAD WOLF. I CREATE MYSELF': THE METAFICTIONAL MEANINGS OF LYCANTHROPIC TRANSFORMATIONS IN *Doctor Who*

Ivan Phillips

At first glance, werewolves seem to be thin on the ground in *Doctor Who*. In 1981, a year after the vampire tale 'State of Decay', and eighteen years after the television series began, the incumbent producer, John Nathan-Turner, reported that he 'would love to see a werewolf story in the programme'.[1] Even so, it took another seven years for the punk lycanthrope Mags to menace Sylvester McCoy's Doctor in the ring of the Psychic Circus in 'The Greatest Show in the Galaxy' (1988–89). And for an out-and-out werewolf story – as opposed to a story with a werewolf in it – viewers would need to wait until Russell T. Davies's 'Tooth and Claw' during the second season of the revived series in 2006.

Looking beyond televised stories, the *Doctor Who* werewolf pack swells to include creatures from the Eighth Doctor Adventures novel *Kursaal* (1998), the Past Doctor Adventures novel *Wolfsbane* (2003) and the Big Finish audio dramas 'Loup-Garoux' (2001) and 'Legend of the Cybermen' (2010). Then there are the Werelox, Wardog and the Windigo from the pages of *Doctor Who Weekly* and *Doctor Who Monthly*, and Flinthair, the prehistoric werewolf encountered by the Second Doctor in the story 'Loop the Loup' in the *Doctor Who Yearbook 1994*.[2] It would seem that the lupine infection is heavy in the blood of the franchise after all, which might send us back to the small screen for a closer study. As werewolf lore tells us, we need to look for the fur beneath the skin; specifically, we need to look for the werewolf by any other name.

If we approach the genus of werewolf in an inclusive spirit, allowing for complexity and ambiguity, Mags and the foundling host of 'Tooth and Claw' are soon joined by other wild contenders. Placing the emphasis on shapeshifting transformations between naked ape and hairy beast, or between other oppositional variations (cultural/natural, civilised/savage, domesticated/feral and so on), reveals a number of monsters in the werewolf mould, none of them explicitly referred to as such but all of them drawing on the same mythology. There are the Primords of 'Inferno' (1970), for instance, the Anti-Man from 'Planet of Evil' (1975) and Dorf, or the Lukoser, from the 'Mindwarp' episodes of *The Trial of a Time Lord* (1986). These creatures are, if not strictly lycanthropic, at least lycanthrope-ish and they are certainly influenced by the long iconographic and mythopoeic traditions of the werewolf. This company might also, at a push, include the Tharils from 'Warriors Gate' (1981), the Cheetah People from 'Survival' (1989) and even the Cybershades from 'The Next Doctor' (2008).[3] The Tharils are distinctly leonine rather than lupine and they are a discrete race of alien beings, not transformed humans, but – with a design based closely on that of the Beast from Jean Cocteau's film *La Belle et la Bête* (1946) – they have a lineage that connects them to myths of the accursed bestial hybrid. The Cheetah People, appearing in the final story of the classic series, are humans who have been mutated into a kind of savage nobility by the primal influence of an unnamed but dying planet. As their name suggests, they are human–cat rather than human–wolf hybrids but they exhibit many of the physical and thematic attributes of the werewolf. The Cybershades, described by David Tennant's Doctor as '[s]ome sort of primitive conversion, like they took the brain of a cat or a dog', are part animal and part Cyberman, which implies that in some aspects they might also be part human, so can be located somewhere – *somewhere* – on the hybrid nexus between human, beast and machine.[4]

In his transformation from obsessed geologist to flickering, hairy Anti-Man, Professor Sorenson of 'Planet of Evil' (1975) shares numerous features with the classic cinematic werewolf (burning eyes, coarse grey hair, fangs, claws, hunched back and loping walk) but he is also a version of the Id creature from *Forbidden Planet* (1958) – itself, of course, a version of Shakespeare's wild-man from *The Tempest*, Caliban. Clearly, the Sorenson/Anti-Man monster is most explicitly a rendering of the Jekyll/Hyde character, especially as it has been realised in successive film adaptations of Robert Louis Stevenson's 1886 novella. Merging visual tropes from both John Barrymore's 1920 depiction of Hyde and that of Fredric March from Rouben Mamoulian's 1931 version, and almost comically reliant on regular swigs from a smoking beaker of anti-matter potion, the Anti-Man, played with relish by Frederick Jaeger, reminds us that – as Ken Gelder notes – *The Strange Case of Dr Jekyll and Mr Hyde* can be 'understood as a version of the werewolf myth'.[5] Infected, in effect possessed, by the planet Zeta Minor while leading a scientific expedition, Sorenson's condition is analogous to that of Henry Hull's botanist Wilfred Glendon in Universal's *Werewolf of London* of 1935.

The intertextual tangle of 'Planet of Evil' is typical of a period in the history of *Doctor Who* that has often been described as a 'golden age'. The first three years of Tom Baker's seven in the role were presided over by Philip Hinchcliffe as producer and Robert Holmes as script editor and mark the beginning of the classic programme's greatest and most consistent popularity, at least in terms of audience ratings and public profile. The Hinchcliffe–Holmes era was characterised by its Gothic tone and styling, its dark wit and its indebtedness to horror film traditions. Strikingly, it was in 'Planet of Evil' (the second story of Tom Baker's second season) that the mode favoured by Hinchcliffe and Holmes established itself fully. It is also notable that, although their creative ransacking of the horror-film back catalogue was extensive, they steered clear of explicit borrowings from werewolf and vampire cinema during their tenure. The Anti-Man, however, as already observed, contains traces of the lycanthrope and, in its ability to drain the life-force from its victims, of the vampire too.

What the Anti-Man shows, crucially, is an intensification of themes of possession and transformation within the series, frequently in conjunction with body horror. Figures of hybrid monstrousness dominated as never before or since in *Doctor Who*: not just the metallic hybridity of the Daleks and the Cybermen, but a more gruesomely organic variety epitomised by the Wirrn ('The Ark in Space', 1975) and the Krynoid ('The Seeds of Doom', 1976).[6] Clearly, although not werewolves, such mutations occupy an equivalent imaginative territory where the limits of human being and self-knowledge are destabilised by the invading 'Other'. Both ontology and epistemology are implicated here and, linked (via Chantal Bourgault du Coudray) with Slavoj Žižek's reading of the modern monster as a 'spectral' challenge to Enlightenment rationality, these hybrids point to something intriguing about the frequent use of Gothic motifs in the series.[7]

Given *Doctor Who*'s ostensible status as science fiction, it is unsurprising that these motifs should be validated through scientific (or *pseudo*-scientific) narrative mechanisms rather than through supernatural or metaphysical ones. The Anti-Man, the Krynoid and the Wirrn might well signify anxieties of the self and what it is to be human, unease about the things that take shape in the anomalous zone between society and wilderness, kindness and cruelty, reason and instinct, sanity and insanity, but they do so in a specific context. The hybrids of *Doctor Who* tell a mutable tale about our relationship with technology, one which can be mapped against the evolution of the programme itself. This is evident if we look from the Anti-Man to the monster that he most closely resembles in the television series, the Primords of 'Inferno'.

'Inferno' is a seven-part story that was broadcast in May and June 1970, the final tale in Jon Pertwee's first season as the Doctor. A vital phase in the show's development, this had seen, among other significant changes, the transition from black-and-white to colour. James Chapman has argued, persuasively, that the shift to a full palette coincided with a shift in the paradigm of monstrosity within *Doctor Who*, the robotic giving way to the organic, silver-white to a greater variability of hue and texture.[8] This meant that those ubiquitous enemies of the 1960s, the Daleks and the Cybermen, were to be used far more sparingly in the 1970s. Stacey Abbott reflects in Chapter 4 above on the importance of the arrival of cinematic sound within the development of the horror-film genre and, in a more specific context, the coming of colour to *Doctor Who* can be seen as comparably influential. The Primords are emblematic in this respect.

Never actually named in the story on screen (instead, they are identified in the closing credits), the Primords are humans who have suffered mutation as a result of Project Inferno, an attempt by the fanatical Professor Stahlman to mine the energy resources at the Earth's core. They have sometimes been referred to as apelike in commentaries on the story and, as their name suggests, they seem to represent some kind of regression to a primordial state of bestiality. Their realisation on screen is wolfish rather than simian, however, and is clearly inspired by the classic werewolf designs of Jack Pierce and others.[9] Terrance Dicks's descriptions of the creatures in his novelisation of the story tend to reinforce this impression. This is the Doctor's encounter with 'the most advanced case of the mutation':

> The face and hands were entirely covered with hair. The whole shape of the jaw had changed and the teeth were great yellow fangs. The eyes glared redly, bestial and savage.[10]

In a sense, apelike or wolflike is beside the point: the Primords are a race of shapeshifting monsters, unlike anything seen previously in *Doctor Who*. Although Jon Pertwee is known to have been dismissive of them – 'these ridiculous werewolf things with great false teeth and fur-covered rubber gloves'[11]– they embody, as Graham Sleight suggests, a different and more complex approach to questions of human identity and technological ethics than had been conveyed by the mechanical hybrids of the first decade of the series.[12] A monstrous outcome of ecological meddling, the Primords are also a correlative of the fascist brutality that the Doctor encounters in a parallel version of Earth that features in the story, where they are literally harbingers of apocalypse. They enact a movement towards the themes of human identity crisis that would become prevalent during the Hinchcliffe–Holmes years, characterised by tales of transformation, possession and body horror.

Leslie Sconduto has written that '[w]erewolves, as a cultural product, have been and always will be a reflection of their time'.[13] This might seem self-evident to many, but the nature and meaning of the Gothic is easily oversimplified or misread. It is worth reminding ourselves that, as Fred Botting, Nick Groom, David Punter, Catherine Spooner and others have observed, the Gothic's playful adaptation of resources from the past is a critical and imaginative way of engaging with the present.[14] Its flirtation with modes of nostalgia is, in essence, a defining aspect of its modernity. Regarded as a species of werewolf, the Primords of *Doctor Who* are consistent with this, a screaming brute atavism transposed to a *Doomwatch*-style science fiction environment. Those of a technologically deterministic inclination might align this with cultural models from Marshall McLuhan and Walter Ong to argue that the mythologies of an age are formed in response to the media that communicate them.¹⁵ In other words, there is something metafictional about the Primords: they embody not only familiar cultural narratives but also transformations (technological, ontological, mythical) in the format of *Doctor Who* itself. At a time of major change for the series, its audience and the wider culture, here are monsters that make both the possibilities and the anxieties manifest. Other creations from Pertwee's first season (a very 'grown up' season) can also be read in this way – the plastic Autons, the prehistoric Silurians, the radioactive Martian ambassadors – but it is the lycanthropic Primords who most vividly contain the evolving moment.

This would seem a rather abstruse point if it was restricted to the Primords but forms of lycanthropic monstrosity seem to recur at points of strain or transformation in *Doctor Who*. Notably, the delayed appearance of werewolf creatures under Nathan-Turner – two in relatively quick succession, three if we count the Cheetah People – coincided with a period of decline and fall that would culminate in the indefinite suspension of the series after the final episode of 'Survival' aired on 6 December 1989. The Lukoser, the mutant outcome of genetic experimentation, featured in the story 'Mindwarp' as part of the fourteen-episode *Trial of a Time Lord* story arc which followed an ominous eighteen-month hiatus in the programme's production (a metafictional season if ever there was one). Philip Martin, in the novelisation of his own script, refers to the creature as 'the Wolfman' and describes it in unmistakable terms:

> The head of the Lukoser lifted. Wild bloodshot eyes stared at them from out of a once-human face that had elongated into the muzzle of a wolf. On his bare torso large patches of fur grew at random. The slavering mouth opened, revealing long canine teeth, while from his throat came a rolling growl that made the hairs lift on Peri's neck. At the same time compassion made her somehow want to reach out to this hybrid creature, in chains and so obviously in torment.¹⁶

The pitiful but spirited and strangely noble creature, movingly performed on screen by Thomas Branch, reminds us of the association between horror and melancholy discussed by Abbott, and looks compellingly like a metaphor of the series itself. The appearance of the exploited Mags two years later in 'The Greatest Show in the Galaxy' offers a return to werewolf mythology in conjunction with a similarly self-reflexive and anxiously ironic title. That Mags, unlike the Lukoser, survives the story, proposing to establish a new Psychic Circus – a new show on a new planet – seems to combine the newfound confidence of the show in the final two seasons of Sylvester McCoy's Doctor with a sense of its inexorable doom.

Doctor Who would, as it turned out, survive its own death to be regenerated in the twenty-first century, but only after years of quiet transformation beyond the public eye, the ultimate hybridisation resulting in fan-producers such as

Russell T. Davies, Steven Moffat and Chris Chibnall, and fan-performers such as David Tennant and Peter Capaldi. The professionals who now create *Doctor Who* are, conspicuously, the amateur enthusiasts inspired and enabled to develop their careers by the classic series that they kept alive when no one else was looking.[17]

Given the restlessly hybrid, endlessly transformational character of *Doctor Who*, it seems both fitting and perhaps oddly inevitable that Russell T. Davies, setting in place the foundations of *Torchwood*, should have delivered a full-blown werewolf story only one season into his period as show runner. As the Primords exhibited the progression from black-and-white to colour, so the werewolf of 'Tooth and Claw' reflected (not uncontroversially) the technological parameters of its own day, being rendered in CGI but containing the transformed essence of traditional lycanthropic folklore. And as the Primords incorporated the ecological concerns of 'Inferno', so the lycanthrope of the Torchwood Estate provided the basis for a degree of social satire at the expense of the Church (the belligerent monks of St Catherine's Glen) and the Royal Family:

> THE DOCTOR: No, but the funny thing is, Queen Victoria actually did suffer a mutation of the blood. It's historical record. She was haemophiliac. They used to call it the Royal Disease. But it's always been a mystery because she didn't inherit it. Her mum didn't have it, her dad didn't have it. It came from nowhere.
> ROSE: What, and you're saying that's a wolf bite?
> THE DOCTOR: Well, maybe haemophilia is just a Victorian euphemism.
> ROSE: For werewolf?
> THE DOCTOR: Could be.
> ROSE: Queen Victoria is a werewolf?
> THE DOCTOR: Could be. And her children had the royal disease. Maybe she gave them a quick nip.
> ROSE: So the royal family are werewolves?
> THE DOCTOR: Well, maybe not yet. I mean a single wolf cell could take a hundred years to mature. Might be ready by, erm, early twenty-first century.
> ROSE: Nah, that's just ridiculous. Mind you, Princess Anne …
> THE DOCTOR: Oh, say no more![18]

This cheerful (some might say childish) badinage was not Davies's first attempt to use lupine material as a vehicle for satire in the series. The 'Bad Wolf' story arc of his debut season had been a more prolonged and less explicit manifestation of the same wild dog allegory.

First mentioned in the second episode of the revived series, 'The End of the World', the phrase recurred in various forms and languages throughout the 2005 season. This led to enthusiastic speculation among fans and in the media about its possible meaning, Ladbrokes even opening a book on the subject.[19] The season finale, 'The Parting of the Ways', revealed that the Bad

Wolf was actually Rose. Sent back to the safety of the Powell Estate in London in the twenty-first century by the Doctor, she was determined to return to support him in his battle against the Daleks aboard the Game Station orbiting the Earth in the year 200,000. Forcing open the TARDIS console, she stared into its heart, absorbing the lethal energies of the Time Vortex. Transmuted into an entity of god-like powers, a creature with acute consciousness of 'all that is, all that was, all that ever could be', and absolute power over life and death, she dispersed the 'Bad Wolf' meme through time as a message to draw herself back to the Game Station as the Doctor's avenging angel: 'I am the Bad Wolf. I create myself.'

Rose as the Bad Wolf is a distinct and dangerous hybrid, a human merged with the uncontrollable forces of space and time. The inherent contradiction of this *sui generis* super-being, a version of the 'bootstrap paradox' which has been an enduring premise in science fiction since its original designation in Robert A. Heinlein's 1941 tale 'By His Bootstraps', has also been described by Hills as an effective reversal of the 'grandfather paradox'.[20] Rose doesn't destroy her own past, in other words; instead, she creates the future that will affect a past that will create the future that will affect a past that will create the future that will … and so on. The causal loop that encircles this story depends on a form of ontological uncertainty that is at least loosely analogous to the unsettled condition of lycanthropy. It also depends on the kind of narrative contrivance, *deus ex machina*, that some saw as unsatisfyingly prevalent within Davies's *Doctor Who*, finding a more intricately developed (but no less contentious) counterpart in the shaggy-dog-story arcs of the Moffat era.[21] Hills has argued that this attraction to tales of temporal paradox in new *Who* is symbolic, representative of life in the twenty-first century. As well as being very much the matter of the particular mythology – a mythology 'about time', as Alec Charles has noted, but also about 'timelessness' – it is a representation, too, of the putatively 'postmodern' condition of contemporary life in which 'we are all everyday time-travellers'.[22] This is true of how *Doctor Who* is watched, and otherwise engaged with, in a culture of on-demand digital services, transmedia proliferation, intensified nostalgia and encyclopaedic capacity. It also corresponds to the restlessness with which the mythology relates to its own past. Just as the modern werewolf wears its ancestry beneath the skin – Ovid's Lycaon lurks within the *Underworld* franchise (2003–16) and MTV's *Teen Wolf* (2011–present) as surely as it did within Henry MacRae's *The Werewolf* (1913) – so *Doctor Who* in the twenty-first century must always contain the rough, brilliant beast of its twentieth-century forerunner. It is not surprising, then, that the Doctor's werewolves might – in their many and variant forms, and in a certain lunar light – present themselves as metaphors of the series itself.

Lucie Armitt, citing James B. Twitchell's privileging of the vampire over the werewolf, has noted the latter's tendency to 'fall into abeyance' while the former 'retains its currency'.²³ The werewolf, seen as unambiguous in its bestial monstrosity, lacks the uncanny elusiveness of the vampire, its more subtle questioning of cultural categories. Crucial to this reading is an assumption that the werewolf, because of its overt carnality, misses the erotic allure of the vampire, at least as it has been evident from Polidori's Lord Ruthven onwards. Many of the most successful werewolf tales subvert this pattern, notably Angela Carter's 'The Company of Wolves' (1979) and John Landis's *An American Werewolf in London* (1981), but others seem to confirm it. Neither Henry Hull's stiff (in the non-priapic sense) Glendon in *Werewolf of London* nor Lon Chaney, Jr's 'lumbering, affable' and 'repressed' Larry Talbot in *The Wolf Man* (1941) can be said to generate much sensual potential.²⁴ Interestingly, many narratives of recent decades have foregrounded the carnal intensity of the lycanthropic mythos, including John Fawcett's film *Ginger Snaps* (2000) and Toby Whithouse's television series *Being Human* (2008–13).

Questions of carnality and eroticism have never troubled the lycanthropic creatures in *Doctor Who*, although Rona Munro, author of 'Survival', has complained about the diminution of her script's sexual themes in its realisation on screen:

> Because the Cheetah People shouldn't have looked like that! ... [They] should have just had cheetah eyes and a very faint pigmentation round of cheetah spots, and big canine teeth. And in fact, I think the actors that were cast, from what I was told, were doing all this wonderful expressive facial work, and then these 'Puss In Boots' things were dropped on them – and so then you can't see what they're doing under there. Particularly Karra and Ace, there were whole amazing scenes between them and for me, that was supposed to be my lesbian subtext – and you can't see it!²⁵

There is nothing sexy about the Primords, the Anti-Man or even the Lupine Wavelength Haemovariform of *Tooth and Claw*. Not even Mags (my own teenage predilection for the actress Jessica Stevens notwithstanding) is able to channel the libidinous energies of the Carterian werewolf, although it hardly requires a mind kinked by the prurient obsessions of tabloid journalism to read uncomfortable innuendo into her situation as the travelling companion of the leery old explorer Captain Cook:

THE DOCTOR: Do you often travel together?
CAPTAIN: Of late, yes. I found her on the planet Vulpana. Between you and me, old boy, she's rather an unusual little specimen.
THE DOCTOR: Of what?
CAPTAIN: Ah, that would be telling, old boy. What about yours?
THE DOCTOR: I never think of Ace as a specimen of anything.²⁶

The Captain is referring to Mags's condition as a werewolf but the sexually predatory insinuation is clear.

When the amatory and the narrative finally, briefly, merged within an allusively lycanthropic context in *Doctor Who*, it was nearly twenty years later, in the first season of the rebooted series. Rose, having 'created herself' as the Bad Wolf, is about to be destroyed by her own raging godlike powers:

> THE DOCTOR: But this is wrong! You can't control life and death.
> ROSE: But I can. The sun and the moon, the day and night. But why do they hurt?
> THE DOCTOR: The power's going to kill you and it's my fault.
> ROSE: I can see everything. All that is, all that was, all that ever could be.
> THE DOCTOR: That's what I see. All the time. And doesn't it drive you mad?
> ROSE: My head.
> THE DOCTOR: Come here.
> ROSE: It's killing me.
> THE DOCTOR: I think you need a Doctor.
> *The Doctor kisses Rose. The golden energy transfers from her eyes to his, then she faints in his arms.*[27]

Little Rose Riding Hood, who has given herself to the Big Bad Wolf in order to save her hero, is here set free by the kiss that will kill him, or at least force him to regenerate.[28]

Suggestively, the most recent televisual occurrence of the lupine in *Doctor Who* alludes to the same fairy-tale sources but treats them rather differently. Frank Cottrell Boyce's 'In the Forest of the Night', first broadcast in October 2014, is an eccentric and strangely low-key, even gentle, tale about the vegetation of the Earth enveloping it overnight in order to protect it from solar flares. Lost in the sudden forests of London with a party of children from Coal Hill School and two of their teachers, Clara Oswald (his latest companion) and Danny Pink (her boyfriend), the Doctor is increasingly intrigued by the behaviour of the red-coated Maebh, a girl troubled by the recent disappearance of her older sister. At one point, Maebh, the Doctor and Clara are chased by a (small) pack of wolves:

> CLARA: Was that a howl?
> (*A second animal replies.*)
> CLARA: Was that a wolf? No. That is impossible. We're in London.
> THE DOCTOR: Would that be the London with the zoo? The zoo with the pack of wolves? The zoo whose barriers and gates have probably been mangled by the trees? No, wolves are not impossible. Stick to the path, Red Riding Hood.
> CLARA: There is no path.
> (*The pack howls.*)
> THE DOCTOR: Then we're lunch.[29]

In the event, the wolves are frightened by the arrival of an escaped tiger, a Blakean beast that is itself mesmerised by Danny and driven away. Apart from perpetuating the myth of their threat to humans, the story is remarkable for featuring wolves rather than werewolves: not representations of unsettled hybridity, in other words, but agents of the natural world, set free from their cultural confinement by a vegetable love that seems almost supernatural. Maebh, whose medication for anxiety has been wearing off, is revealed to have a connection to 'the life that prevails', the eternal spirit of the trees that appears as a busy cluster of glowworm lights in the air: 'We are here, here, always, since the beginning and until the end'.

The appearance of wolves, however briefly, in Cottrell Boyce's poetically understated parable of apocalypse is revealing in the context of their meaning within the narratives of *Doctor Who*. 'Catastrophe is the metabolism of the universe', the Doctor comments at one point; 'I can fight monsters. I can't fight physics.' The story has not proved popular with fans (it came last in the *Doctor Who Magazine* poll for 2014) and many have complained that it lacks a recognisable foe or threat, with no alien invasion, no monsters to fight. These memorably troubling words, however, expressing helplessness in the face of physics, contain a peril at least as potent as that signalled by 'Exterminate'. Furthermore, the wolves, like the tiger, like the trees and the solar flares, have a collective symbolic significance that connects this singular addition to the *Doctor Who* mythos with the wider world of stories being told in recent times and discussed in the pages of this book. Beyond the easy reputation of the wolf as the epitome of dangerous wilderness, there are more recent narratives which see the creature as an index of humanity's reformed relationship with a damaged natural world. If the Doctor's glib misreading of the lupine predator is corrected through a message of global redemption channelled through a child, then the wolf begins to resemble a figure of salvation.

The ecological theme of 'In the Forest of the Night' has precedents in earlier wolfish tales in *Doctor Who*. Sorenson's transformation into the Anti-Man in 'Planet of Evil' is, after all, brought about by his removal of samples from Zeta Major and the planet's refusal to allow him to leave with them. Similarly, Stahlman's mutation into a Primord is the consequence of his unrestrained mining of the Earth's resources. These two professors are cautionary examples of exploitative obsession at the limits of scientific knowledge, excessive rationality reversing into destructive irrationality. A parallel case can be seen in Chris Chibnall's episode '42' (2007), in which an agonising mutation among the crew of the *SS Pentallian* is discovered to be the result of possession by a sentient sun whose energy reserves have been plundered.[30]

The narratives of *Doctor Who* are typically those of redress or restoration, frequently interwoven with tales of deliverance and self-discovery. These elements are rarely unambiguous, however, and the mythology itself is intrinsically unsettled, riddled with contradictions, tensions, instabilities. The central character, after all, is an unknowable, shapeshifting wanderer, with a vehicle that defies the laws of physics and is also supposed to be able to transform its appearance. It is perhaps unsurprising, then, to discover that themes so often embodied in the protean mythologies of the wolf are recurrent.

When the Doctor and Ace walked off into the distance, arm-in-arm, in the final episode of the original run of the television series, it was at the end of a story (Munro's 'Survival') in which ideas that are rehearsed throughout the discourses of the wolf and the werewolf had been prominent, albeit in a more subdued form than its author had hoped. Ace, removed from suburban Perivale to a burning alien world on the verge of extinction, partially transformed into a werecat, rejecting her civilised conditioning and relishing a wild, violent, implicitly lesbian-erotic freedom, is representative of the kind of rough epiphany that abounds in readings of the lupine, whether in accounts of feral children or analyses of carnality in the regenerated folk tales of Angela Carter. Ace, hunting with the Cheetah People, and with her self-defined 'sister' Karra in particular, approaches a condition of almost-desirable ferocity that is familiar to anyone who has kept the company of wolves: 'Smell the blood on the wind. Hear the blood in your ears. Run, run beyond the horizon and catch your hunger!'[31] It seems significant, suddenly, that the 'distance' the Doctor and Ace walk towards at the end of the episode is actually a forest, one of those endangered sites of primal hazard that are also places of quiet leisure, arcadian fascination and, of course, fairy stories.

Notes

1 Bentham, 'Interview', p. 33.
2 Anghelides, *Kursaal*; Rayner, *Wolfsbane*; Platt, 'Loup-Garoux'; Maddox, 'Legend of the Cybermen'; Mills, Wagner and Gibbons, 'The Dogs of Doom'; Gray, Geraghty and Roach, 'Bad Blood'; Platt and Vyse, 'Loop the Loup', pp. 16–20.
3 'Inferno'; 'Planet of Evil'; 'Warriors' Gate'; 'Survival'; 'The Next Doctor'.
4 'The Next Doctor' [transcript].
5 Gelder, *Reading the Vampire*, p. 127.
6 'Ark in Space'; 'The Seeds of Doom'.
7 Coudray, *The Curse of the Werewolf*, p. 4. See also Žižek, *Enjoy Your Symptom!*, p. 136.
8 Chapman, *Inside the TARDIS*, p. 76.
9 Pierce (1889–1968) was the pioneering head of make-up design at Universal Studios during the 1930s and 1940s, responsible for creations including Boris Karloff as Frankenstein's monster (*Frankenstein*, 1931; *Bride of Frankenstein*, 1935; *Son of Frankenstein*, 1939) and the werewolf make-up of Henry Hull (*Werewolf of London*, 1935) and Lon Chaney, Jr (*The Wolf Man*, 1941). Among his admirers is Rick Baker,

who was responsible for make-up in John Landis's *An American Werewolf in London* (1981).
10. Dicks, *Doctor Who – Inferno*, p. 86.
11. 'Posts Tagged "Jon Pertwee"', *The Doctor Who Interviews*.
12. Sleight, *The Doctor's Monsters*, pp. 34–8.
13. Sconduto, *Metamorphoses of the Werewolf*, p. 200.
14. Botting, *Limits of Horror*; Groom, *The Gothic*; Punter, ed., *A New Companion to the Gothic*; Spooner, *Contemporary Gothic*.
15. McLuhan, *Understanding Media*, pp. 62–4; McLuhan and Zingrone, eds, *Essential McLuhan*, pp. 67, 114–15, 141; Ong, *Orality and Literacy*, pp. 41, 47–8, 67.
16. Martin, *Doctor Who – Mindwarp*, pp. 17–18.
17. See Hills, *Triumph of a Time Lord*, pp. 55–8; Chapman, pp. 185–7; Booy, *Love and Monsters*, pp. 250–2.
18. 'Tooth and Claw'.
19. Perryman, 'Doctor Who and the Convergence of Media'.
20. Hills, p. 87. Heinlein's story was originally published in the October 1941 edition of *Astounding Science Fiction* magazine, under the pseudonym Anson MacDonald. It was subsequently included in his 1959 collection *The Menace from Earth*.
21. Chapman, pp. 207, 278.
22. Hills, p. 87; Charles, 'The Ideology of Anachronism'.
23. Armitt, 'Twentieth-century Gothic'. See also Twitchell, *The Living Dead*.
24. Kehr, review of *The Wolf Man* (1941); Mooney, 'Non-review Review: *The Wolf Man* (1941)'.
25. Darlington, 'You're Killing My Lesbian Subtext …!!'.
26. 'The Greatest Show in the Galaxy' [transcript].
27. 'The Parting of the Ways' [transcript].
28. 'Little Rose Riding Hood' is one of the stories in Justin Richards's *Time Lord Fairy Tales*, where the *Märchen* of so many human childhoods are reworked, almost *à la* Carter, as fables from Gallifrey.
29. 'In the Forest of the Night' [transcript].
30. '42' [transcript].
31. 'Survival' [transcript].

Part IV

Animal selves: becoming wolf

12

A RUNNING WOLF AND OTHER GREY ANIMALS: THE VARIOUS SHAPES OF MARCUS COATES

Sarah Wade

For over twenty years, the contemporary artist Marcus Coates's fascination with wildlife has been reflected in what the artist calls his 'becoming-animal' works, and in socially engaged performances where Coates utilises these 'becoming' skills to assume the role of the shaman, or, more recently, 'Unconscious Reasoning' consultant.[1] These performances are often presented to viewers in the form of photographs, videos or video installations, although some of the props and costumes fashioned by Coates for these works have also been exhibited. However, a sculpture entitled *Platonic Spirit: Running Grey Wolf* (2012), which takes the form of a single grey rectangular prism, and the installation *All the Grey Animals* (2012), comprising similarly grey cuboids arranged in close proximity to one another in the gallery space, appear to make a puzzling visual departure from many of the artist's earlier works. Whereas Coates's 'becoming-animal' and shamanic performances are well known and have been frequently written about, these more recent sculptural installations have received comparatively little critical attention.[2] I will consider these works in the context of Coates's wider practice to reveal that, whilst initially appearing as a far cry from the artist's earlier work, they nevertheless demonstrate a preoccupation with the same concerns.

Marcus Coates and 'becoming-animal'

In a grainy photograph, Marcus Coates appears in the middle distance of the landscape, kneeling on all fours in a costume comprised of a bright orange jumpsuit complete with orange headpiece. This is *Red Fox (Self-portrait)* (1998), a work documenting the artist disguised as a fox walking through the countryside, and one of the first in a series of works in which Coates explored imitating British wildlife, adopting various approaches that highlight the difficulty – and humour – of trying to do so. For instance, in *Stoat* (1999) Coates was filmed trying to walk on crudely made stilts in an attempt to move with the same

12.1 Marcus Coates, *Stoat* (1999)

gait as this creature (Figure 12.1). Clumsily attached to the artist's feet with a chaotic arrangement of elastic bands, the stilts appear ramshackle, yet they are based on careful studies Coates made of stoat footprints, so that the distance between the stilts reproduces the gap between the feet of this small British mammal, and the diameter of the rods replicates the spread of the stoat's paws.[3] Whilst such proportions are perfectly suited to stoats, they are clearly far from an ideal means of human mobility, which becomes immediately apparent through Coates's stumbling, twisted ankles and audible emissions of pain during the film, as he struggles to walk like a stoat.[4]

In *Goshawk (Self-portrait)* (1999), the artist adopted another tactic in his attempt to become animal and had himself attached to the top of a Scots pine to attain the perspective of this predatory bird (Figure 12.2). Precariously placed beneath the highest branches of this tree, Coates may have achieved the same view as a goshawk, but he was looking through very different eyes and, furthermore, prohibited from diving for any prey he might spy since he was firmly fixed in place, and obviously unable to fly. Conversely, in *Sparrowhawk Bait* (1999), the artist inverted this idea, filming himself running through a forest

12.2 Marcus Coates, *Goshawk (Self-portrait)* (1999)

with dead songbirds haphazardly tied to his hair in an attempt to attract a sparrowhawk, and, as a result, empathise from the perspective of the prey. With no discernible predator in pursuit, the degree to which Coates achieved this remains open to question.[5]

In 'What Is It Like to Be a Bat?' (1974) the philosopher Thomas Nagel recognised the impossibility of definitively understanding the subjective experiences of other animals, because human imagination is formed from human senses and perception and therefore, he suggests, inadequate to the task.[6] Coates disagreed with Nagel because he 'felt there were at least degrees to which we could understand what it was like to be any non-human'.[7] Accordingly, the artist remains undeterred, taking solace, or perhaps inspiration, from the fact that whilst Nagel believed that we are unable to imagine what it is like for a bat to be a bat, he did concede we might instead behave as a bat behaves.[8] In each of the aforementioned works, Coates imitates various non-human animal behaviours with the aim of experiencing the world as a fox, a stoat or a bird, employing a makeshift and comic aesthetic that serves to highlight the absurdity – and even the impossibility – of the task the artist has set himself. Whereas the philosophers Gilles Deleuze and Félix Guattari position imitation as an ineffective means of becoming-animal (since 'becoming animal does not consist in playing animal or imitating an animal'), and imitation offers no genuine insight to the lifeworlds (*umwelten*) of other animals, it nevertheless remains central to Coates's attempts to understand the world from a perspective other than human.[9]

The art historian Steve Baker claims that imitation offers artists the opportunity to imaginatively perform animals, sloughing human identities and approximating animal ones to produce artworks where animals emerge as beings that must be 'thought actively' and performed, therefore approaching 'that genuinely experimental state of becoming-animal where things "cease to be subjects to become events"'.[10] It is precisely this performative approach that Coates exemplifies through his work. Furthermore, the theatre and performance studies scholar Laura Cull has argued that any total disassociation of imitation from becoming in performance practice is 'misleading', noting that it is the 'being/mimesis opposition' that Deleuze and Guattari appear to refute when they claim 'We fall into a false alternative if we say that you either imitate or you are'.[11] Instead Cull suggests that performance practice may function 'along a kind of continuum, with some tending further towards mimesis … and others, like … Coates's … tending towards becoming', leaving room for some elements of imitation to inhabit Deleuze and Guattari's model of becoming-animal.[12] Cull recognises becoming-animal as inextricably bound with a Deleuzian model of affect, in which encounters between bodies and what a body can do achieve primacy over personal feelings, and she goes on to suggest that imitation enacted by movement – as an instance of what a body can do – 'resonates with Deleuze and Guattari's positioning of the animal as a verb rather than a noun'.[13] The philosophers claim not to be interested in characteristics of specific animals, stating that every animal is instead a pack: 'The wolf is not fundamentally a characteristic or a certain number of characteristics; it is a wolfing'.[14] It follows that through these becoming-animal works Coates has the potential to achieve a 'foxing', a 'stoating', a 'goshawking' and so on. The artist retains an affinity with Deleuze and Guattari despite imitating these animals, since in doing so he 'establishes the relations of movement and rest, speed and slowness that are *closest* to what one is becoming, and through which one becomes'.[15]

However, this reading of Coates's work is not without contradictions. The artist appears to display a particular fascination with the characteristics of specific animals, as shown by his careful measurements of stoat gait and footprints in advance of building the stilts for this work. This information would most likely be found in a natural history book, a book with the role of imparting knowledge relating to particular species. However, for Deleuze and Guattari, unlike becoming-animal, '[n]atural history can think only in terms of relationships (between A and B), not in terms of production (from A to x)'.[16] Furthermore, Coates makes a statement of intent that seems to contravene the fluidity inherent in Deleuze and Guattari's model of becoming-animal, when he claims that through these performances his aim is 'to try and locate what it is to be human by attempting to embody a nonhuman perspective'.[17] Any dissolution of a human/non-human animal dichotomy achieved through becoming is foiled by the artist's desire to experience the world from the perspective of a specific animal, be it a goshawk or anything else, with the ultimate aim of arriving at a more certain sense of human identity. The artist has recognised that his aim to achieve this may be impossible, and, despite the artist's apparent sincerity, the difficulties such an endeavour presents are manifested in the comic nature of these performances, in the ridiculousness of the artist's attempts, in the humour inherent to their failings.[18] In this way Coates's work reinforces one of the numerous ways a differentiation between humans and other animals has been proposed in philosophy, since according to Henri Bergson 'the comic does not exist outside the pale of what is strictly *human* ... Several have defined man as "an animal which laughs." They might equally well have defined him as an animal which is laughed at.'[19] It is to this risk that Coates subjected himself when he assumed the role of shaman.

Marcus Coates as shaman

Western philosophy and thought have repeatedly placed a border between humans and non-human animals, which the art critic and writer John Berger positioned as an 'abyss of non-comprehension', and with the philosopher Jacques Derrida expressing what he felt to be the 'absolute alterity' of the animal 'Other', for instance.[20] However, in shamanic cultures, animals are frequently regarded as sources of wisdom, respected as equals, even ancestors, and as a result human–animal relations are conceived quite differently.[21] Recognising the potential the shaman offered for considering an alternative perspective in this regard, and with the desire to use his 'becoming' skills for social good, Coates developed a body of work where he assumed this role, travelling to the 'lower world' to encounter animals in search of answers to dilemmas facing various communities. Perhaps nervous of the ethical implications of appropriating rituals from other cultures for artistic ends, Coates eschews problematic criticisms of his work through his refusal to use authentic equipment and dress from other cultures. Instead, he has created his own from what is local and encountered in everyday life, assembling costumes and making his own ritualised objects for use in these works.[22] Despite the humour of the resultant performances, they were intended not as parodies but instead earnest attempts to offer help to those in need.

In *Journey to the Lower World* (2004), Coates tried to offer solutions to questions posed by the residents of a Liverpool tower block destined for demolition.[23] Standing in the living room of a high-rise flat wearing a stag-skin and with 'bells' in the form of house keys tied to his shoelaces, Coates 'descended to the lower world' performing his becoming-animal skills to a drum soundtrack playing from an outmoded portable stereo (Figure 12.3). On returning from his 'journey', Coates revealed that he met a sparrowhawk whose individual wing feathers were moving independently, making it impossible to fly. The artist interpreted this as the need for this community to stick together at this time of uncertainty. Various elements of this performance exuded a similar sense of the comic and makeshift aesthetic I observed in relation to the becoming-animal works. For instance, there is the moment when the antlers

12.3 Marcus Coates, *Journey to the Lower World* (2004)

of Coates's deer-skin accidently bump into the lampshade, or the inauthentic cleansing of the site of this ritual, which involved the artist vacuuming the carpet and spitting water on the floor from a mug. Furthermore there is the fact that the deer-skin is prominently attached to the artist's body with a combination of adjustable straps and elastic bands. Despite the humorous qualities of his shamanism, Coates uses the performance to offer helpful insights to this community.

Such works have been read alongside the shamanistic aspects in the work of artist Joseph Beuys (1921–86).[24] It has been argued that, like many shamans, both Coates and Beuys have undergone a healing from ill-health that often leads to the assumption of this role – Coates from severe childhood eczema, and Beuys famously following his 1943 plane crash in Crimea, for instance.[25] Both artists, according to the artist and academic Victoria Walters, 'frame their engagements with shamanism in relation to attempts to communicate with, and learn from, other animals'.[26] In doing so, these artists place emphasis on mammals indigenous to their respective British and German contexts. Beuys is also in step with Coates's interest in seeing from the perspective of non-human animals in order to understand what it means to be human, claiming that in 'Using the example of an animal you can get to an answer to the question: what is the human being, how is he meant?'[27] Furthermore, in relation to Beuys, the curator and critic Robert Storr suggested that viewers might 'suspect that his myth was pure hokum ... and yet ... readily succumb to its lyricism', being moved by the artist's vision for social change.[28] It is in this way that Coates's shamanic performances function. What is central to this argument, however, is that the shaman has provided Coates with an alternative model for conceiving of human relations to non-human animals.

The other shapes of Marcus Coates

In stark visual contrast to this body of performance work, Coates's installation *All the Grey Animals* (2012) consists of an arrangement of grey rectangular prisms, which have been fabricated from MDF in various sizes, painted grey and placed directly on the floor in the gallery space (Figure 12.4). The work seemingly replaces mimicry with minimalism, recalling the visual simplicity of the early grey plywood works produced by the artist Robert Morris at the beginning of the 1960s, such as *Two Columns* (1961) (Figure 12.5). However, Coates's cuboids instead represent a menagerie of eighty animals bound by an alternative taxonomy – that of their greyness.[29] Whilst the colour and dimensions of the various shapes correspond to their animal referents, they are stripped of the more characterful and tactile features of these creatures, which might ordinarily instil a sense of fascination, fear or even wonder in viewers.[30] Instead, each animal is consistently represented as a monochrome cuboid, visually

12.4 Marcus Coates, *All the Grey Animals* (2012)

differentiated from each other by size and scale alone and identifiable only by the small labels placed on the floor beside them, which indicate the creature's common name. *All the Grey Animals* ignores traditional zoological classifications, and various phyla from the kingdom *animalia* are placed side by side so that the wide variety of creatures represented in this work – which range from a grey reef shark to a comparatively much smaller great grey slug – inhabit the same space in close proximity to one another.[31]

This installation initially appears to be a far cry from Coates's earlier performance work, but a biographical detail becomes illuminating in this context. Recalling how he and his brother were fascinated with endangered species as children, Coates described how the only reference the boys had to these creatures were the drawings and measurements in wildlife books.[32] As a result, the brothers manifested their interest in these animals in a game where they paced out their sizes in the living room of their family home.[33] Coates recalled that the Siberian tiger was a particular favourite at this time, and when the brothers paced out the size of this creature they simply could not believe how big it was.[34] This game became a way for the artist to develop relationships with wild animals, and form attachments to creatures despite their faraway habitats by allowing him to consider the size of various creatures in relation to his own body, thereby serving as a means of bringing this wildlife into the artist's suburban realm of experience.[35] Coates recalled how subsequently seeing a Siberian tiger in the flesh at a zoo as a child was a disappointment and he

12.5 Robert Morris, *Two Columns* (1961)

reported how his fascination with this creature ebbed away.[36] It became apparent to Coates that what fascinated him was not just these animals themselves but the relationships humans have with them – a realisation that went on to inform his practice.[37]

This originary tale goes some way to explaining *All the Grey Animals*. Viewers of Coates's installation stand in close proximity to cuboids sized according to the animals they represent. By considering these animal referents in physical relation to their own body, viewers are provided with a way to relate to animals inaccessible in everyday life due to their impenetrable or distant habitats. As a result, viewers are offered the chance to forge a relationship with wildlife in a manner that recalls Coates's childhood game. The way in which these abstracted animals visually recall the early minimalism of Robert Morris's grey sculptures allows for a link to be made between the experiential qualities of sculpture that preoccupied Morris at this time and the ways viewers can develop relationships with the creatures represented in Coates's installation.

Writing about Robert Morris, the art historian Annette Michelson reveals how the artist began working with simple shapes made from plywood that he painted grey, eliding colour and texture in order to shift the viewer's attention to the form and experience of his works instead.[38] Believing that colour emphasised the optical and subverted the physical qualities of a work, Morris elected to use a consistent, neutral shade of light grey to paint his sculptures, which he felt served to draw maximum attention to the qualities specific to sculpture itself, such as shape, scale and proportion.[39] Morris preferred to use simple regular and irregular polyhedrons in his work – what the artist referred to as 'unitary forms' – since he thought they were more resistant to being perceived as shapes with separate parts, consistent with his interest in the gestalt.[40] It is the viewer's resultant experience of Morris's sculptures that is so crucial in relation to *All the Grey Animals*, and Annette Michelson's commentary on these works by Morris offers a valuable insight into why this might be the case:

> In these instances ... the central focus of attention is the manner of the solicitation – through placing, scale, unity of shape, volume, the nature of materials and of the spectator's sensed relationship of the self as a perceiving, corporeal presence, to the object in question: a sense of copresence ... Confronting sculptures such as those by Robert Morris, the beholder perceives an object whose mass and volume, whose scale and structure are, in their compactness and clarity, perceived as providing not a focus for a synthetic reading, but as being copresent with himself.[41]

It is this sense of 'copresence', which is central to the functioning of Coates's installation. By making a visual analogy to minimalism through the use of smooth-surfaced, light grey 'unitary forms', Coates's installation simultaneously borrows from the way these works were perceived to function. However, unlike the 'unitary forms' of Morris, Coates's cuboids are representations of animals, pared back and abstracted to the extreme. As a result, the sense of copresence that Michelson argues to be so integral to the experience of Morris's sculptures is harnessed in *All the Grey Animals* to draw attention to the bodily relationship between viewers and the various animals represented in Coates's installation.

Indeed, Coates's decision to base his taxonomy on grey animals lends itself generously to this reading, since the artist could equally well have selected red or brown as the thematic colour for this work, with animals likewise abounding in these categories: red admiral, red deer, red fox, red mullet, red panda, red squirrel, red wolf, brown bear, brown hare, brown hyena, brown lemur, brown pelican, brown trout ... However, the artist chose grey, and this colour, together with the use of simple geometric prisms that visually reference the physical attributes of 'unitary forms', offers an immediate link to Morris and the issues occupying him in this body of work. In pursuit of this comparison it seems that Morris's concern with the placement of objects further resonates with Coates's installation. Speaking of *Two Columns* (1961), Robert Morris insisted that 'A beam on its end is not the same thing as the beam on its side'.[42] This simple assumption is demonstrated in *All the Grey Animals* by the way various prisms have been positioned: the grey mullet represented by a horizontally placed rectangular form, and upright animals represented by prisms positioned on their vertical axis.

However, these allusions to minimalism have their limits. This installation is not intended to be considered in an all-at-once encounter, as extolled by the minimalist Donald Judd, but instead part-by-part, as viewers move between various shapes denoting an array of different species.[43] Furthermore, these geometric prisms are not *Untitled* like many minimalist works, but named, with small labels placed beside each block to indicate the species to which the abstracted grey shape refers. Accordingly, these are not, as Judd would say, 'specific objects', but instead represent specific species.[44] Yet the knowledge of this is entirely dependent upon the titling of the work and the provision of the creatures' common names.

Platonic Spirit: Running Grey Wolf

Platonic Spirit: Running Grey Wolf (2012) is another rectangular prism made out of MDF which is sized according to the dimensions of its lupine referent and painted in a neutral shade of grey, recalling the measured monochromy of *All the Grey Animals* (Figure 12.6).[45] The grey wolf is one of the creatures inhabiting Coates's abstracted menagerie, but in this instance it is presented as a stand-alone sculpture, identifiable only by its title and subsequently recognisable through its colour and wolf-sized measurements.[46]

Since Coates's work interrogates human–animal relations, the wolf is a potent creature for this artist – the manifold ways human–wolf relationships are conceived in human societies offer a rich resource for him to draw from. Wolves are frequently found inhabiting the grey areas between nature and culture, re-emerging in landscapes from where these creatures had long been

12.6 Marcus Coates, *Platonic Spirit: Running Grey Wolf* (2012)

extinct – territories now inhabited by humans and livestock – and featuring in discussions about rewilding.[47] Throughout history, wolves have been variously feared and revered, venerated and preserved, and such is the appeal of this transgressive animal to the artistic imagination that these creatures have frequently featured in folktales, myths, films, literary fiction and visual art. Humanity's historic affinity with, and proximity to, wolves resulted in the emergence of stories of people becoming wolf, taking on the feared and beastly characteristics of these creatures in the form of werewolves – a shapeshifting subject matter that clearly maintains its allure today.[48] More recently, the wolf is considered by many to be an icon of wilderness, representative of an idealised and untouched fiction of nature, which humans seek to protect and preserve.[49] Human–wolf relations are therefore as complex as they are contradictory, and today, as much as at other periods in history, attitudes towards this animal are manifested in many different ways. The social anthropologist Garry Marvin has examined human–wolf relations via the various attitudes and representations of this creature throughout history, using the diversity of responses to wolves to structure his book *Wolf* (2012), which evolves from lupophobia to lupicide, through lupophilia, and towards rewilding. Of course such distinctions are not so chronologically discrete (as Marvin makes clear), and today attitudes towards wolves remain equally ambiguous – rewilding being just one example where opposing attitudes about wolves collide. However, Marvin's book serves to reinforce what Steve Baker has proposed elsewhere, that 'Any understanding of the animal, and of what the animal means to us, will be informed by and inseparable from our knowledge of its cultural representation'.[50]

Throughout art history, visual representations of wolves have frequently reflected contemporaneous attitudes held towards these creatures, giving form to the guise of wolves as they existed in the collective imagination of the time. Today, no less than in previous eras, society's attitudes and imaginings of wolves are expressed by artists who capture the full suite of sensibilities from lupophobia to lupophilia. For instance, there is Mircea Cantor's *Deeparture* (2005), a video work replaying the result of an encounter between a live deer and a wolf in a white cube gallery space. Throughout the duration of the film, predator and prey remain wary of one another's presence, shifting their bodies in response to each other's movements and throwing watchful glances at one another, in a situation perceived by viewers to become increasingly intense as the film unfolds. Whilst the visible stress of the deer makes the work ethically dubious (the animal's quick breathing is clearly apparent), the piece nevertheless serves to challenge viewers' expectations of wolves, since this predator comes across as a cautious creature, unsettled by both the artificial environment of the gallery and the contrived encounter with an animal it would commonly regard as prey.

Then, for example, Mark Dion's *Mobile Wilderness Unit – Wolf* (2006) is constructed from a car trailer covered with artificial foliage, a tree trunk, a rock and a taxidermied grey wolf, which, apart from the unusual display base, is reminiscent of a museum diorama (Figure 12.7). The work offers a wry take on the American model of wilderness preservation, and through its artificiality seems to echo the environmental historian William Cronon's well-versed critique that wilderness, 'Far from being the one place on earth that stands apart from humanity ... is quite profoundly a human creation'.[51] The mobility of Dion's trailer-mounted display also comments on rewilding, since this wolf can be moved from one location to another. However, Dion's work also highlights the allure of wilderness by offering a mobile display, which can be towed from place to place to be experienced by viewers like the spectacle of a travelling circus.[52]

Finally, Nicholas Galanin's work *Inert* (2009) is a wolf-skin rug, in which it seems that the animal is becoming reanimated, its head and forelegs appearing in the midst of a struggle to creep forwards. Assuming the form of a trophy, Galanin's modified wolf-skin rug evokes two opposing human responses to these creatures: on one hand, hunting, trapping and poisoning of wolves and the eradication of these creatures from many territories where they were viewed as pests and competing predators. On the other, the work alludes to the

12.7 Mark Dion, *Mobile Wilderness Unit – Wolf* (2006)

conservation efforts and reintroduction programmes that began following the recognition of the pivotal role wolves play in ecosystems, and a shift in attitude that positioned wolves as icons of 'wilderness'. This selection of contemporary artworks is by no means exhaustive, but demonstrates the ways attitudes and concerns regarding wolves have seeped into work being made recently.

Unlike these examples, Coates's lupine-sized prism, *Platonic Spirit: Running Grey Wolf*, is not only bereft of physical features such as fur, fangs and claws but is also marked by the absence of any projected attitude or idea of the wolf *per se*. Coates's wolf is not a vicious animal or a 'benign eco-wolf'.[53] Neither is Coates's wolf-sized prism a loaded vehicle for any particular comment on the history of wolves and human relations to these creatures. Instead, Coates plays with ambiguity. By referring to this specific animal and naming it to be identifiable to viewers, Coates is able to invoke the numerous incarnations of human–wolf relations and the various iterations of 'wolf', which exist in the collective imagination – be it ruthless competing predator or majestic wild animal. As with *All the Grey Animals*, there are few visual cues to depict this wolf realistically, since we are provided only with an indication of the colour and size of this creature. As a result, viewers must resort to images and knowledge of this animal archived in their own minds, and the wolf-sized prism becomes a site on to which each individual can project his or her own perceptions of, and attitudes towards, wolves. This single rectangular prism unleashes a pack of imagined wolves in the various minds of those who view the work, demonstrating the subjective ways humanity views these creatures and the very personal way individuals go about conceiving them. In this way, the imagination is fundamental to the functioning of Coates's sculpture.

It is possible to read this work in the vein of wildlife conservation, or as a comment on the detrimental effects humans have had on the survival of certain species, since, apart from the grey wolf, the only other non-human animal that has been presented by Coates as a stand-alone sculpture in MDF cuboid form is *The Great Auk and Egg* (2010). This work comprises two rectangular prisms, one starkly painted along its diagonal axis so that half is black and half is white, and the other, smaller prism serving as the egg. The Great Auk became extinct during the nineteenth century, having been ruthlessly exploited by humans. The wolf might serve as a similar model for the threat humans pose to wildlife, but could also point to the ability of humans to intervene with measures that seek to restore populations – once listed on the IUCN Red List of Threatened Species as 'vulnerable', the grey wolf's status is now positioned as 'least concern'.[54] It is also possible to read Coates's sculpture in terms of metaphor, existing as it does as a lone wolf. Overall, the work demands that viewers use their imaginations – without which there is, in essence, no wolf, just an abstracted grey cuboid that shares the dimensions of the animal to which it refers.

185×49×26cm

It appears that *All the Grey Animals* and *Platonic Spirit: Running Grey Wolf* are preoccupied with interrogating human relations to other animals, be these manifested physically or imaginatively. However, how does this relate to Coates's concern with becoming-animal? Through the earlier becoming-animal performances, Coates attempted to see the world from the perspective of non-human animals, to 'become animal' in order to gain insight into what it means to be human.[55] In light of these concerns, another sculptural work that accompanied the exhibition of *All the Grey Animals* becomes particularly poignant – *Marcus Coates, White British, 185×49×26cm* (2012), a white rectangular prism with the exact dimensions of the artist himself.[56] Like the two works previously discussed, this sculpture lends itself to comparisons with the work of Robert Morris, specifically his *Column* (1960) and *Untitled (Box for Standing)* (1961). Both of these works were produced to the size of a human body, with *Untitled (Box for Standing)* made specifically to the artist's 'precise measurements' so that Morris himself could stand inside it.[57] *Column*, a six-foot tall, hollow, rectangular prism painted grey, was actually conceived by Morris to appear in a performance by the Living Theatre Company.[58] The idea was that the column would feature as a performer in the piece, and, after standing in the centre of the stage for three and a half minutes would fall over.[59] It has been suggested that, as a performer, the column assumed two different positions – standing and prone, imbuing this form with anthropomorphic qualities stemming from its role as a 'surrogate' for a dancer's body.[60] A similar anthropomorphic quality can be attributed to *Marcus Coates, White British, 185×49×26cm*, based as it is on the dimensions of the artist in order to serve as a stand-in for his body. However, additionally in this work, Marcus Coates is presented on the same reduced terms as the creatures in *All the Grey Animals*, depicted through a single, rectangular, monochrome prism.[61] As a result, Coates sculpturally blurs the boundary between humans and non-human animals, which become indistinguishable from one another but for their shade and size and identifiable only by the names provided.

It seems somewhat ironic that for all Coates's attempts to become animal over the years, and the great lengths he has gone to towards this end – twisted ankles and all – that it is through this reductive sculptural strategy that his aim becomes most visually realisable. However, this work is not about becoming-animal as Deleuze and Guattari conceive it. It is not even about imitation. The performative element that formed the basis of Coates's earlier work is absent from these installations, and exists instead in the 'theatricality' of the encounter between the viewer's body and the cuboids standing in for non-human animals in these works.[62] Having noted the debt these works appear to pay to minimalism, as unconventional as such a reading may have initially seemed in the context of Coates's practice, it is fitting to recall a comment made by Donald Judd about the work of Robert Morris. 'Morris' work', Judd claimed, 'implies that everything exists in the same way through existing in the most minimal way, but by clearly being art'.[63] This has some bearing, I think, on what Coates achieves with these sculptural works. When reduced to the size and proportions of his bare bones, and assuming the same simplified MDF form, Coates aligns the sculptural stand-in for his body with all the grey animals, in a way that proved difficult through his performance works. In doing so, Coates becomes one represented animal amongst many, albeit on these minimal, sculptural terms.

Notes

1 See Coates, *UR … A Practical Guide to Unconscious Reasoning*.
2 Ron Broglio has acknowledged that it has become common to read Coates's performances in terms of 'becoming-animal' as propounded by Deleuze and Guattari, and much criticism has made this link. See Broglio, *Surface Encounters*, p. 101. See additionally, Giovanni Aloi, *Art & Animals*, p. 60; Aloi, 'Different Becomings'; Max Andrews, 'Marcus Coates and Other Animals'; Sara Barnes and Andrew Patrizio, 'Darwin on the Threshold of the Visible', pp. 299–300; Broglio, pp. 101–25; Cull, *Theatres of Immanence*, pp. 105–44; Laura Cull, 'Affect in Deleuze, Hijikata, and Coates'; and Tracey Warr, 'Being Something'.

3   *In Profile: Marcus Coates* (DVD).
4   Warr, and Andrews (para. 2 of 15).
5   Cull, *Theatres*, p. 134. Further references to these particular 'becoming-animal' works can be found in: Aloi, 'Marcus Coates – Becoming Animal'; Andrews (paras 2 and 6 of 15); Barnes and Patrizio, pp. 297–300; Coates and Smith, 'Marcus Coates in Conversation with Valerie Smith', pp. 18–21; Cull, 'Affect', 197–99; Levy, 'Marcus Coates'; Mahoney, 'Marcus Coates'; Steiner, 'Animal Insertions and Human Projection', pp. 10, 15–16; and Warr.
6   Nagel, 'What Is It Like to Be a Bat?', p. 439.
7   Coates and Smith, p. 21.
8   Nagel, p. 439. See also Barnes and Patrizio, p. 299. Coates references Nagel in *Becoming a Bat*, an exercise included in Coates, *UR ...*, pp. 133–4.
9   Deleuze and Guattari, *A Thousand Plateaus*, p. 277. For more on the concept of *umwelt*, see von Uexküll, *A Foray into the Worlds of Animals and Humans*.
10 Baker, 'Sloughing the Human', p. 159. Baker quotes Deleuze and Guattari, p. 306. See Barnes and Patrizio, pp. 299–300, who also recognise the relevance of Baker's statement to Coates's work.
11 Cull, 'Affect', p. 194, and Cull, *Theatres*, p. 124. Cull quotes Deleuze and Guattari, pp. 277–8.
12 Cull, 'Affect', p. 195, and Cull, *Theatres*, p. 124.
13 Cull, 'Affect', pp. 192–3, 195, and Cull, *Theatres*, p. 125.
14 Deleuze and Guattari, p. 279.
15 *Ibid.*, p. 318.
16 *Ibid.*, p. 273.
17 Coates, *Journey to the Lower World*, [n. pag.].
18 *Ibid.*
19 Bergson, *Laughter*, pp. 3–4.
20 Berger, *Why Look at Animals?*, p. 13, and Derrida, 'The Animal That Therefore I Am', p. 11.
21 See, for instance, Eliade, *Shamanism*.
22 Coates, *Journey*.
23 See Aloi, 'Different Becomings', 10; Aloi, 'Marcus Coates – Becoming Animal', 18–20; Andrews (para. 9 of 15); Broglio, pp. 113–22; Coates, *Journey*; Levy (para. 2 of 5); Mahoney, p. 216; Steiner, pp. 7–8; and Walters, 'The Artist as Shaman'.
24 See for instance, Aloi, 'Different Becomings', 1–10; Andrews (para. 9 of 15); and Walters.
25 Walters, p. 37; Alec Finlay, in Coates, *Journey*; and Tisdall, *Joseph Beuys*, p. 16. On the debate surrounding Beuys's myth of origins, including his 1943 plane crash in Crimea and subsequent rescue by Tartars, see Buchloh, 'Twilight of an Idol'; and Kuspit, 'Joseph Beuys'.
26 Walters, p. 38.
27 Walters, quoting Joseph Beuys, p. 41.

28 Storr, 'The Idea of the Moral Imperative in Contemporary Art', p. 38.
29 Travis, 'Marcus Coates: 185x49x29cm' (para. 2 of 4).
30 Travis (para. 2 of 4).
31 The list of represented species and dimensions was provided by Workplace Gallery.
32 Coates, *Re-imagining Nature* (online video recording); and Coates and Smith, p. 21.
33 Coates, *Re-imagining*; and Coates and Smith, p. 21.
34 *Ibid.*
35 *Ibid.*
36 *Ibid.*
37 *Ibid.*
38 Michelson, 'Robert Morris', p. 21.
39 Morris, 'Notes on Sculpture, Part 1', p. 4.
40 *Ibid.*, pp. 6–7.
41 Michelson, pp. 22, 24.
42 Morris, 'Notes on Sculpture, Part 2', p. 20.
43 Judd, 'Specific Objects'.
44 *Ibid.*
45 Riley, 'Marcus Coates' (para. 5 of 7).
46 *Platonic Spirit* is a word play on the platonic solid form of Coates's grey wolf.
47 See Marvin, *Wolf*, for an account of human–wolf relations and a cultural history of the wolf.
48 See, for instance, Marvin, pp. 46–67, and Oates, 'Metamorphosis & Lycanthropy'.
49 See Van Horn, 'The Making of a Wilderness Icon', p. 206.
50 Baker, *Picturing the Beast*, p. 4.
51 Cronon, 'The Trouble with Wilderness', p. 7.
52 *Radical Nature*, ed. by Manacorda and Yedgar, p. 104.
53 Marvin, p. 8.
54 IUCN Red List of Threatened Species, 'Canis Lupus'.
55 *In Profile: Marcus Coates*.
56 These works were exhibited at Workplace Gallery, Gateshead, during 2012–13.
57 Paice, 'Box for Standing, 1961', p. 96.
58 Krauss, 'The Mind/Body Problem', pp. 8–9.
59 *Ibid.*, pp. 8–9.
60 Paice, 'Columns 1961', p. 90.
61 Travis (para. 2 of 4).
62 The critic Michael Fried used the term 'theatricality' to refer to the experience of encountering minimalist works, in which the viewer became conscious as a subject in relation to the objects he or she was spatially and temporally encountering; see Fried, 'Art and Objecthood', p. 153.
63 Judd, 'Black, White and Gray', p. 118.

13

'STINKING OF ME': TRANSFORMATIONS AND ANIMAL SELVES IN CONTEMPORARY WOMEN'S POETRY

Polly Atkin

In her poem 'What Comes After', Lorna Crozier's first-person speaker is her 'own big dog': 'a big sack of sleep / stinking of me' (ll. 1, 11–12).[1] The dog-speaker lives entirely in the dog-moment:

Walk, and I'm at the door,
eat, and I take what I offer.

(ll. 2–3)

The dog-speaker is not subject to the pressures of futurity a human speaker might be: she does 'not need anything but this' (l. 6). This twelve-line poem exemplifies a key trope in contemporary poetry: transformation from human to animal as evasion of self-awareness. It echoes tropes in much werewolf fiction, in which transformation symbolises the release of 'the beast within', overriding human self-consciousness. The self in Crozier's poem is split: Crozier's dog-speaker is simultaneously the higher-functioning creature ordering herself to '*lie down*' (l. 4; italics in original) and the unthinking creature taking the order. She claims not to 'think of what comes after' (l. 7) but the shortening of that phrase in the title suggests consequences are inescapable.

Gerry Turcotte notes that 'shapeshifters have always been with us, from earliest to postmodern times. They can be found in virtually every indigenous creation story; in fairy and Biblical tales; from medieval literature through to the present.'[2] Contemporary poetry draws on traditional shapeshifting narratives from various cultures, alongside Gothic and horror texts, and environmental and zoological literatures, shifting between high and low cultures and genres, creating poems which are hybrid and heterogeneous.

This chapter focuses on the British poets Liz Berry and Kim Moore, both because of the preponderance of metamorphoses in their poetry and because of what those transformations seem to be doing, and meaning. In these poems the speaker is, becomes, or imagines themselves becoming, an animal. Lori Gruen argues that 'much of the problem with the attitudes many people have toward animals stems from our removal from the animals themselves'.³ Berry's and Moore's poems trouble a sense of our bodies as autonomous, limited and more-than-animal.

The 'idea of congruence between the body and the body politic', as Alicia Ostriker puts it, is a key to much feminist poetry, as is the struggle to articulate and transcend 'the bondage of a female body'.⁴ This intersects compellingly with the ways in which shapeshifting has been used to explore the human condition. Ann-Sophie Lönngren recognises the 'literary continuum' of 'women becoming animals', arguing that

> the reoccurrence of the woman-animal transformation figure ... makes it appear to be what bell hooks calls a literary 'site of resistance', a space shared with other female characters where they can resist oppression, expectations and demands based on gender.⁵

This chapter examines how Berry's and Moore's poems enact sites of resistance, presenting transformation into the non-human as a necessary release from human social expectations for their female speakers.

This chapter also proposes a reading of Berry's and Moore's work as ecofeminist. Greta Gaard outlines how ecofeminism arises from

> a recognition that the position and treatment of women, animals, and nature are not separable [... connecting] not just sexism, speciesism, and the oppression of nature but also other forms of social injustice – racism, classism, heterosexism, ageism, ableism, and colonialism – as part of western culture's assault on nature.⁶

In so doing, ecofeminism positions 'dualistic separations of human/animal and nature/culture [as] as untenable as racial and sexual dualisms'.⁷ Equally, it seeks to denaturalise assumed associations between women and animals, recognising how 'the connection between woman and animal can be located in various strands of an elaborately constructed narrative'.⁸ An ecofeminist poetic does not reject the notion of synergy between women and animals, but questions the framing of that synergy and what it is used to justify.

Birds, pigs and little boys

The first poem, 'Bird', in Liz Berry's first collection, *Black Country* (2014), opens with the line 'When I became a bird, Lord, nothing could stop me' (l. 1).⁹ In depicting a girl drawing birds towards her from her open window, it owes something to Disney's Cinderella as well as older, darker tales. The speaker relates how she 'knelt / by [her] open window for the charm' (ll. 3–4): for the birds to come to her and make her one of them. 'Charm' is a Black Country dialect word denoting birdsong, but the echo of its meaning in standard English endows that song with transformative magic. This doubleness is ubiquitous in Berry's work. Stepping out of the window is leaving 'girlhood behind [her] like a blue egg' (l. 24), where girlhood implies both youth in general and the particular state of being a particular human girl.

In order to fly the coop she must first shed her clothes, those signifiers of human civilisation and socialisation: 'I shed my nightdress to the drowning arms of the dark, / my shoes to the sun's widening mouth' (ll. 11–12). It makes little sense that she is wearing shoes with her nightdress, apart from as anchors weighting her to the human world. The shedding of clothes is a key feature of shapeshifting iconography. The opposite – the donning of animal skins to become animal – is perhaps more in keeping with the function of clothing, especially shoes, in some of Berry's other poems, as I will discuss.[10] There is an implicit query here around whether the girl has put on the shoes specifically to take them off. Once 'bared', her transformation begins:

> I found my bones hollowing to slender pipes,
>   my shoulder blades tufting down.
>   I spread my flight-greedy arms
> to watch my fingers jewelling like ten hummingbirds,
> my feet callousing to knuckly claws.
>
> (ll. 13–17)

This imagery combines a traditionally feminised aesthetic ('slender', 'jewelling') with something which suggests both animalistic and less youthful human qualities ('callousing', 'knuckly'). The last act of transformation sees the speaker's 'lips calcified to a hooked kiss' (l. 19) followed by 'silence' (l. 20): her human voice is lost with her human lips. A new voice emerges through flight: 'no longer words but song' (l. 40). This process is not painless: before she sings, her body 'bawls' (l. 37), turned inside out. The overall suggestion is one of gain, however. The poem ends, 'I raised my throat to the wind / and this is what I sang ...' (ll. 41–2), with the implication that the poems that follow are the 'black upon black' (l. 40) singing of that girl-bird.

Of the forty-two poems in Berry's collection, there are only six ('5th Dudley Girl Guides', 'When I Was a Boy', 'My Mother's Wedding Shoes', 'The Way Home', 'The Assumption' and 'Irene') that do not feature animal imagery, and those feature other kinds of transformation. Metamorphoses weave through the collection, and many of the poems feature people who are not wholly human, or animals that are more than creatures. In 'Dog', for example, a lost loved one 'came back ... as dog' (l. 1); in 'Stone' the speaker's husband is compared to various gems and rocks, including 'agate ... sleek / and mottled as seal's skin' (ll. 10–12); a Fishwife has 'a plump trout' (l. 24) for a tongue and 'gasping gills raw beneath her blouse' (l. 28). 'The First Path' performs a reverse metamorphosis: feral 'mongrel' (l. 13) into human 'bride' (l. 59).

In the poems in which a first-person speaker transforms from human to animal, the metamorphosis always signals some kind of freedom: the animal offering a release from both the human body and human world. In an interview for *PracCrit* journal, Berry speaks of investigating the boundary between human and animal:

> I'm always conscious of and interested in the interplay between the human and the animal, the way that boundary can be pushed through at times. This is often in sensual moments, or intensely physical moments like sex, or when we're in pain, when we have children, when we feel afraid. I think we feel closer then to our animal selves. We forget our human or civilised ways.[11]

It is clear that Berry sees a distinction between the human and animal, but that that distinction is not definitive. Moreover, it is a learnt distinction, created through the performance of 'civilised ways', which can be circumvented or forgotten when we experience our bodies as animal.

Often, Berry's metamorphoses deal with what cannot be articulated, involving alteration of human speech into non-human vocalisation, as in 'Bird', or depicting words as independent creatures. The murdered Black Delph Bride describes herself as 'the tune / foxes yelped in the nettled banks' (ll. 13–14); in 'The Sea of Talk' the speaker's 'first vowels' (l. 11) were 'filmy and shape-shifting as jellyfish in the dark' (l. 12); in 'Woodkeeper' the speaker recalls 'your voice is a tawny owl, / mine a pipistrelle battering the dusk' (ll, 12–13). 'Echo' mirrors the transformation in 'Bird':

> I had a voice once
> until thirteen blew my speech
> like the yolk from an egg.
>
> (ll, 17–19)

This avian imagery comes from the same store, but where the hollowed bones in 'Bird' enable flight, and the finding of a new voice, here they only diminish. The speaker is left 'hollow, pining / in the cave of [her] bedroom' (ll. 20–1). If there is freedom, it is in disembodiment, like insubstantial Echo who sings *wherever girl's voices are lost* (l. 7; repeated as ll. 15, 23, 30; italics in original).

Berry links transitional moments – 'what happens to girls when they become women' – with myths and fairy tales, which are able to articulate those often uncanny shifts in symbolic terms.[12] These transitional female bodies are frequently abandoned entirely in Berry's poems, evidenced by 'Echo', or by Carmella the hairdresser, her customers 'ecstatic creatures, / capable still of being lifted from [their] bodies' ('Carmella', ll. 27–8). 'The Patron Saint of School Girls' similarly ends with a disavowal of the body as anchor or locus:

> I was ready for wings,
> to be lifted upwards like sun streaming
> through the top deck windows
> to wave goodbye to school and disappear
>
> (ll. 32–5)

Bird wings and angel wings are blurred here: does the girl want to '*tek flight [and] goo far fer the winter*' (l. 23), as in 'Bird', or does she want to leave behind her earthly existence, for ever? The two seem to be confused for many of Berry's speakers.

When the restraining body cannot be escaped, it is changed. In 'The Silver Birch', the young speaker is 'neither girl or boy' (l. 13) but rather 'a creature' (l. 3), furred, that 'came alive in dens and copses' (l. 9).[13] Being unfixed in her own self – not only a creature, but 'a sheaf / of unwritten-upon paper', her body 'a meadow' – allows her to explore her nascent sexuality unhindered by social mores. Similarly, in 'When I Was a Boy' the speaker can 'g[e]t straight / down to the real stuff' (ll. 10–11), and 'buil[d] remarkable things' (l. 16) when using one of her male aliases. Releasing the body from sexual and/or gendered overdetermination gives a sense of achievement as well as freedom. As a boy, the speaker tells us s/he

> swaggered down the street, ripe
> for danger or rode my bike
> with my blouse off, admiring my reflection
> in wing mirrors, legs kicked
> in a triumphant V, fist in the air.
>
> (ll. 21–5)

Performing 'boy' is used here as a way of avoiding the delicacy and decorum expected of a human girl, just as becoming an animal does in other poems.[14] Through reading this poem alongside the animal metamorphoses the function of transformation in this collection becomes clear.

Striking parallels to 'When I Was a Boy' can be seen in 'Sow', which, like 'The Silver Birch', examines gendered sexuality. 'Sow' opens with an epigraph from what Berry informs us is a Victorian etiquette guide, Eliza Sell's 'Etiquette for ladies': 'Dainty footwear turns a young lady into an altogether more beautiful creature.'[15] The speaker chooses 'new hooves' (l. 1) over beautifying dainty shoes, releasing the speaker's sow-self. The second stanza opens with the statement 'I've stopped denying meself' (l. 7), analogising appetite for food with sexual appetite: 'for I need a mon / wi a body like a trough of tumbly slop / to bury me snout in' (ll. 11–13). The third stanza recalls years of denial, and suffering:

'prancing like a pony for some sod to bridle / an shove down the pit, shying away / from 'is dirty fists' (ll. 15–17). Denial of one's natural appetites is presented as route to abuse, from within and without.

'Sow' is one of three poems in the collection in which shoes play a central role. The sow inside the speaker was 'squailin' an biting to gerrout' (l. 19) all the time, but her protests were not heard until the shoes catalysed her emergence. In 'The Red Shoes' and 'My Mother's Wedding Shoes' shoes similarly are transformative agents, that might either turn a girl into a wife, tying her to a 'mithering bed of marriage' ('My Mother's Wedding Shoes', l. 7), or allow her to run or dance away. Positioned amongst these poems, the shoes worn with the nightgown in 'Bird' take on more significance, and encourage the reader to question the direction of transformation: were those shoes hiding the speaker's true (bird) self all along? Like much of *Black Country*, 'Sow' is heavy in Black Country dialect words, and comes with a glossary. The dialect could be seen as indelicate footwear for metrical feet, but the language, like the Sow-speaker, has stopped denying itself, and instead revels in its expressive nature, linking to that sense of freedom in song in 'Bird'.

'Sow' ends with the same image as 'When I Was a Boy' recontextualised: the speaker with their legs inverted, 'trotters pointing to the heavens like chimdey pots' (l. 24), signing a 'V' to the sky, at the same time open, and in defiance. Directed to 'the heavens' and to the 'prissy an' crowing' weathercock on the church spire, the act suggests both an opposition between domestic and the public, and a rejection of religio-social control of the female body, embodied in the feminine sow versus the masculine cockerel (1 .26). Becoming a sow gives the speaker not only emotional strength but physical strength. Now she is her sow-self, she claims 'no mon dare scupper me' (l. 20). She knows who she is, what she wants and what she does not. This acts as a foil for a simplistic reading of 'When I Was a Boy', in which the speaker and/or poet believes that freedom and strength can be associated only with masculinity. 'Sow' shows strength is inside any one of us, should we dare to let it out. There is also a compelling contrast between the earthiness of the pig-self in 'Sow' and the ubiquity of ethereal bird images throughout the collection. Whilst the teenage girl-speakers seem to think they can only escape the confines of their female bodies by becoming unearthed or unbodied, the more mature speaker of 'Sow' realises that happiness lies in fully embracing her earthy physicality, 'riling on [her] back in the muck' (l. 22).

These are poems about identity and selfhood, but they are also poems about how we interact with the world, our relational position. The non-human in these poems could be seen merely as a foil for human expression or desire, but there is important deconstructive work being done in the slippage between genders, genres and species. Chantal Bourgault du Coudray positions shapeshifting narratives 'as part of a wider discourse that has circulated visions of a "dipsychic" way of being'; not only the 'dualistic notion of selfhood' but binarism in general. She also identifies efforts in postmodern feminist narratives to escape this trap of dualism.[16] In Berry's poems this attempt to deconstruct binary oppositions alongside her focus on place, myth and transitional moments places her work firmly within an ecofeminist discourse. Although, as Cate Sandilands discusses, ecofeminism is at times guilty of the kind of biological essentialism these poems work to deconstruct, it also allows inquiry into the cultural assumptions that continually reproduce those binaries, including the 'destructive beliefs that devalue the animal-like body in favour of the superior human mind'.[17]

In Berry's poetry, the animal body takes precedence. The speaker of 'Sow' may be 'out of [her] mind wi gruntin pleasure' (l. 23), but is fully inhabiting her body, revelling in its animal needs and enjoyments. Kate Rigby argues that 'the critique of dualism is a thread running through all forms of ecofeminist thought and connects it also with the poststructuralist project of the deconstruction of binary oppositions'.[18] In this sense Berry's transformation poems very much concur with an anti-speciesist ecofeminism, actively collapsing the boundaries between human woman and animal other, as they do between human female and human male.

In a feature for The Poetry School's online forum *Campus*, Berry writes of the process of drafting 'Sow', from first notes taken in 2010. The first few lines in the first draft, shown in photographs of Berry's notebooks, have clear elements in common with the final:

> In my new boots – like little hooves – I am an
> animal, proud, sexy, led by senses,
> I trot upright, head high, rhythmic feel my
> power propel me on.[19]

A following line acts as a note to herself about the embryonic poem: 'Where desire/sexuality/fantasy meets the animal'. A spider diagram lower down the page, in the same pen, links 'pro-dildo-feminism' to 'taking on the phallus', 'being a boy/man', 'Helen [of Troy?] but not', and 'female-masculinity'. In these brief notes, scribbled amongst reminders of meetings and other daily matter, the slippage in Berry's thought process between being an animal and 'being a boy/man' is traceable. Although it is clear that sex-positivity was central to the poem from the start, the sense of sexuality involved in those early notes is less self-focused than in the final version. The draft foregrounds sexiness, placing the speaker's 'power' in relation to her ability to command others, as suggested by the Helen of Troy reference. In the final version, the sow's power is that of self-determination and self-satisfaction.

What moved Berry from the draft to the poem was a decidedly (eco)feminist issue around animal language used to describe female bodies. She recalls:

> I was in the changing rooms at the swimming baths and I overheard a girl, who thought she was alone, stepping on to the scales and hissing at herself in a pained awful voice: 'You fat pig' ... I wanted to write a poem that could transform that moment and those words into something rebellious, defiant, unashamed; to take that idea of female animality and make it a source of pride and subversive sensuality.[20]

Berry explicitly links the frequently gendered slur 'fat pig' with the poem's project of inverting the insult, reclaiming it as a source of pride. A mid-stage draft includes lines that describe a reverse-metamorphosis, such as that in 'Dog':

> I am an animal ...
>   I have been lifted
> out of the muck and straw and slop
> and tremblingleg sniff of slaughter to
> be a girl, to be in the body of a
> girl, to be in disguise.
>
>   (ll. 3–8)

This suggests not the stripping back of the woman to reveal the sow, as the final draft implies, but that the woman or girl was always false, only ever a mask or performance. This same draft mentions a party game, in which choosing an animal 'reveal[s] your true self, or aptitude in the sack'. Sexuality and identity are closely knit in this elision. Berry notes she chose 'kitten', with its implications of softness, vulnerability and playfulness, but realises it was inaccurate. 'Sow', then, is a poem about self-knowledge, about recognising the truth of the animal we are, and not being ashamed of it. In its many drafts it was variously titled 'New Boots', 'Pig' and 'The Animal I Am', revealing a shift in focus as the poem developed from centring on the agent and/or moment of change ('New Boots') to the revelation of the already-present inner animal ('The Animal I Am'). The eventual title 'Sow' – a female pig – draws together both the animal and the female as focal points, underpinning the underlying meaning of transformation in the collection.

Speaking like wolves

There are clear parallels between Berry's work and Kim Moore's first collection *The Art of Falling* (2015).[21] Transformations and animal imagery abound in Moore's poems. In 'How the Stones Fell' the female speakers 'were born from stones' (l. 1); in 'That Summer' the addressee 'had a redwing in [their] chest instead of a heart' (l. 5); in 'Picnic on Stickle Pike' a woman performing oral sex on her partner becomes 'a long-necked bird, bending / its proud neck to feed' (ll. 18–19); in 'The Dead Tree' a tree's soul inhabits a human's body. It could be said that mutability is one of the abiding themes of this collection. The other is wolves.

The Art of Falling follows on from Moore's prize-winning pamphlet *If We Could Speak Like Wolves* (2012), many of the poems from which are included in *The Art of Falling*, including the title poem. This is one of several wolf poems Moore has written, which use the figure of the wolf in various ways. Often the wolf is a cipher for the self, or some element of the self, but wolves are also used to refer to female members of her family. Many traditional wolf-transformation narratives, and many recent screen incarnations, feature a 'sympathetic werewolf' lamenting their shift into a more brutal existence, and 'struggling to attain direct or indirect humanity … channel[ling] their energies into regaining or preserving their human form and dignity'. These unfortunates might appear in a 'wolf's form' but 'their inner character remains that of a human being'.[22] Moore's wolf-people could be said to be the opposite: women who appear to be human, and live as human, but are wolves on the inside. Moreover, they would never wish to not be wolves. In tracing the shifting depiction of female werewolves in twentieth- and twenty-first-century narratives, du Coudray notes how increasingly 'lycanthropy is presented as a condition uniquely conducive to exploring alternatives to patriarchal expectations of female behaviour'.[23] Moore's wolves fit within this paradigm.

Although the wolves in the poems are often symbolic, there is also a clear interest in real wolves, and in their habitats and behaviours. Du Coudray also identifies a tendency in recent werewolf fantasy narratives to draw on 'the work of environmentalists and particularly wolf biologists' to reconfigure the wolf as 'unfairly maligned in human culture', showing it instead to be 'loyal, family oriented, monogamous and affectionate'.[24] Many of Moore's poems celebrate this side of the wolf. 'If We Could Speak Like Wolves', for example, uses the mating behaviour of wolves to expose the ill-defined roles of human spouses. Wolf communication seems brutal – 'then each day hurt you in a dozen / different ways, bite heart-shaped chunks / of flesh from your thighs' (ll. 2–4) – but human communications seem worse by comparison. In the wolf relationship 'a mistake could be followed / by instant retribution' (ll. 7–8), and faithfulness and trust are proven physically. This clarity, knowing 'by smell / what we were born to' (ll. 15–16), enables the wolves to form a fully consensual and self-aware partnership, 'more complicated / than alpha, more simple than marriage' (ll. 19–20). Human relationships seem muddied, unfair and unequal by implication, with the concerned parties neither able to forget each other's mistakes nor able to easily 'tak[e] it in turns / to lead' (ll. 13–14). The relationship between wolves is not painless, but it is unambiguous that wolves are better.

The prose poem 'How Wolves Change Rivers' is more obviously environmentally focused. In the poem, wolves are shown to have a butterfly effect on their habitat, changing rivers:

> by killing the deer, by moving them on from the valleys, by the birds coming back to the trees, by singing to the water, with the return of the fish, with the great ambition of beavers, with the return of bears moving across the land like dry ships ... by the green coming back, by the green coming back. (ll. 3–7)

This is a poem not about the wild but about rewilding. The focus on the 'return' or 'coming back' of various flora and fauna in the poem emphasises the role wolves may play in reinvigorating an ecosystem once reintroduced. It ends with 'the river finding its spine once again' (l. 16) because of the wolves' influence on the rest of the system, pointing to their centrality. The poem is ekphrastic, inspired by a popular but controversial eponymous short film, narrated by George Monbiot, about the reintroduction of wolves to Yellowstone Park in the United States.[25] The controversy lies in debate about the theory that 'wolves are crucial for maintaining a healthy ecosystem'.[26] This theory credits the wolves with initiating a trophic cascade – the reinvigoration in the poem – undoing decades of harm. Some ecologists, such as Arthur Middleton, argue that this is an oversimplification; moreover, that 'by insisting that wolves fixed a broken Yellowstone, we distract attention from the area's many other important conservation challenges'.[27]

Interestingly, the collection does not acknowledge the source material, and does not allude to either specific geography or chronology, so the poem stands as its own record, relying on the reader to either know the context or not. Middleton posits that 'when we tell the wolf story, we get the Yellowstone story wrong'.[28] In her poem, Moore tells the wolf story divorced from the context of Yellowstone, and it takes on a different level of truth, but also tells a different kind of story. The disconnection from a specific geography problematises the ecological aspect of the poem. It could be about rewilding in Scotland, or indeed in Moore's home county of Cumbria, eliding some of the specific cultural meanings associated with the wolf in Yellowstone. It could equally well be a fantasy, located nowhere in particular.

Brian Johnson argues that in a North American context 'it is necessary to situate representations of popular animal species within a postcolonial framework of analysis that remains critical to settler-invader nationalism'.[29] Rewilding debates in the USA often revolve around notions of returning a cultured landscape to wilderness, ignoring or overwriting historical and contemporary indigenous land use. As David Stannard notes, 'the association of Indians with wolves was a common one' from the earliest colonial era in the Americas through the creation of the National Parks; the state-sanctioned culling of wolves in North America runs in parallel to the genocide of indigenous peoples.[30] Johnson describes the inverse of this in later aspirational 'wolf stories' which operate around an 'ecological rhetoric' but simultaneously 'evoke the indigenizing fantasies of settler-invader postcolonialism'.[31] The meaning of a wolf in Yellowstone is necessarily different from the meaning of a wolf in Cumbria, where the last wolf in England is often supposed to have been killed in the fourteenth century.[32] Equally different is the meaning of a wolf detached from a specific real-world setting, in which it might more easily take on some of the idealised meanings du Coudray sees in werewolf fantasy fiction.

If 'How Wolves Change Rivers' is telling a story, perhaps it is neither a Yellowstone nor a wolf story, as such, but a trophic cascade story: a narrative about the mutability of the environment, about landscape as shapeshifter. It is a poem about metamorphosis on a geological scale, about what produces the conditions for change and how change might be articulated. In this poem, the wolves change their landscape not by altering prey behaviour but by singing: they sing 'to the moon' (l. 1), 'to the wind' (l. 3), 'to the water' (l. 5). The wolves' singing is their communication with their ecosystem, suggesting they treat the moon, wind and water as fellow wolves to be spoken to. These wolves do not howl, but sing. Their singing may imply self-expression: that they are singing for the pleasure of it, and to express pleasure in their environment. Most importantly, the syntactical construction implies that their singing is an essential part of their effect on the environment: they change rivers '*by* singing' (l. 1), and it is this singing that the poem opens with, placing primacy on it as a catalysing action. This suggests a role for poetry in changing not only the self but the material world.

Many of Moore's metamorphoses and animal depictions are concerned with voice, and with the ability to communicate or to express oneself, echoing Berry's. They are also largely about knowing the self, like Berry's 'Sow', and voice and self-knowledge are continually intertwined. The first poem in Moore's collection, 'And the Soul', opens with a Platonic directive to find the animal within:

> And the soul, if she is to know herself
> must look into the soul and find
> what kind of beast is hiding.
>
> (ll. 1–3)

The speaker shapeshifts through the poem like Thetis or Tam Lin, eventually settling on the inevitable wolf. Importantly, the wolf must be given voice; its howl is the apotheosis of the soul-search:

> if it be a wolf,
> throw back your head
> and let it howl.
>
> (ll. 16–18)

As in Berry's poems, where song occurs only after flight, or power after transformation, or the laying off of false selves, this howl is released only once the wolf is acknowledged. This may stand as analogy for the function of the animal self in the whole collection: acknowledging the true self allows the true voice to manifest.

In the second poem in the collection, 'My People', the speaker declares 'the women / of my people are wolves and we talk to the moon in our sleep' (ll. 20–1). The speaker identifies with wolves, drawing a portrait of herself belonging to a long line of wolf-women painted in both positive and negative lights. It is unclear whether their failings are due to their wolfishness, or despite it. If they were less occupied being 'paid pence a minute to visit an old lady's house' (l. 3) or 'bring[ing] up children' (l. 9), they might listen more wakefully to the moon, or to their wolfish inclinations, letting their howl out. Although in 'If We Could Speak Like Wolves' communication and negotiation between wolves are presented as simultaneously simpler in their immediacy, more honourable, more instinctive and more complex in their expressiveness than human communication, in this poem wolf communication might be just as troubled.

Wolves appear elsewhere alongside other shapeshifting elements, often suggesting internal and external conflict. 'All my thoughts' recalls a failure in communication between the speaker and a loved one, in which she relates 'I couldn't look at you or speak' (l. 15). The lover asks her to vocalise 'the birds of [her] thoughts' (l. 18); they part, and 'all the wolves and all / the stars' (ll. 22–3) go with him. It is hard to know what these metaphorical wolves symbolise: perhaps a potential for self-knowledge, for wildness, for equal companionship. It is notable that, as in the Berry poems, the human speaker is unable to express herself until her thoughts take flight in other forms.

This links Moore's wolves to the sequence at the centre of her collection, 'How I Abandoned My Body to His Keeping', which depicts an abusive, violent relationship. In those poems, there are many transformations, but no wolves. Throughout the sequence the speaker moves between the inanimate and animate, landscape and animal, the forms often defined by their inability to express themselves. In 'When I Was a Thing with Feathers' the speaker's 'throat changed shape / and left [her] unable to articulate the edges of words' (ll. 2–3), recalling Berry's adolescent bird-girls. In 'Translation' the meaning of these shifts is filtered through Ovid, as the speaker asks 'Don't we all have a little Echo in us?' (l. 1). Here, as in Berry's 'Echo', transformation is configured as an escape, not from the body for its own sake but from the violence enacted upon the body, from the body's low cultural status that allows it to be abused:

> There was a time when I was translated by violence,
> there were times I prayed to be turned into a flower
> or a tree, something he wouldn't recognise as me.
>
> (l. 10–12)

The use of 'translation' rather than 'transformation' here is evocation again of self-expression and voice.

Moore ran a course for The Poetry School in spring 2016, 'The Act of Transformation', which she explained as addressing exactly these issues:

> Ovid's transformations are the loss of self and identity, and transformation of the self by another becomes the ultimate act of violence ... transformation of the body further becomes a way of exploring power, control and freedom.[33]

The course aimed to 'us[e] the body as [a] starting point' and 'encourage [participants] to think about (and with) the body in a different way'. The complete absence of wolves from 'How I Abandoned My Body to His Keeping' is particularly telling read through this. Wolves, in Moore's poetry, represent the chosen transformation rather than the forced one: a way of thinking with the body and with the wider world. In 'Body, Remember' the speaker pleads not only for self-knowledge but instinctive knowledge of others. Her wolves are fierce, but they are never meaninglessly violent: they have a sense of purposefulness and honour not always observed in her human and other non-human creatures. Moreover, their strength comes from living in harmony with their environment and their inner selves. Moore's wolves could never be 'changed / inside the flame' (ll. 5–6) of another's violent intent; would never find their moon-songs stuck between throat and teeth. Placed in this context, the wolves become not only symbols of freedom, strength, self-knowledge and harmony but a talisman pulling the poet towards actualising those ideals: the self the poet wishes to embody.

Conclusion

I have argued that animal transformations function in the work of Liz Berry and Kim Moore within an ecofeminist discourse. These poems, however, also trouble some of the common stances of ecofeminism. Both revel in their heterosexuality as part of critiquing patriarchal social practices, and could be seen to reinforce a heteronormativity that ecofeminism often rejects. Moreover, Moore's and Berry's animal selves are not neutral. Their relationship with animals as food or as equal citizens of the world is not benign. In these poems, reconnecting with one's animal nature means accepting all parts of that nature, including those that might seem problematic to humans, such as eating other animals, or being eaten. The animal selves they choose as counterparts – a much feared and admired predator long-eradicated from the poet's home country (Moore's wolf) and a domesticated animal raised for food and industry (Berry's sow) – point to the complexity of our own status as hunter or prey.

Both Berry and Moore use animal transformations and selves in their poems to enable their speakers to choose another way of being, outside the confines of human socialisation. Transformation is depicted as liberating because animals are depicted as unburdened by compulsion to hide their natures. Josephine

Donovan sees a 'new mode of relationship' between humans and other species emerging through art and critical theory which 'recognizes the varieties and differences among the species but does not quantify or rank them hierarchically'.[34] Whether these poems reject species hierarchy or invert it, reinforcing species relations as hierarchical, is debatable. In Moore's poems hierarchies of power are not denigrated in and of themselves, but injustice, inequality and manipulation are depicted as particularly human attributes. Berry's sow, meanwhile, gives no suggestion that she considers herself meat, or is considered such by others. She is as powerful as one of Moore's wolves.

The speakers of these poem shift in and out of different selves and modes of being: the choice is neither binary nor definitive. There is no wistful gazing back from the animal world to the human: the animal is always preferable. Moreover, they subvert increasingly unsupportable notions that animals have no inner lives, theory of mind, or social capacity. The poems place primacy on self-knowledge and self-identification, taking control of their own narratives, reflecting Caroline Walker Bynum's conclusion that

> if identity *is* shape carrying story – we need not decide between mind and body, inner and outer, biology and society, agency and essence. Rather we are living beings, shapes with stories, always changing but also always carrying traces of what we were before.[35]

These poems embrace the paradoxes implicit in their projects: for Berry and Moore, the animal world is a rich society of individuals equally as capable as human poets are of singing their own songs. In this context, the seemingly very human cultural act of writing a poem is no different from a wolf howling or bird singing. The wistfulness and wishfulness of taking this stance hover beneath the poems' surfaces: both poets know that as women they cannot speak as wolves or fly out of windows, but the uncertain ground of the poem enables a space where interspecies transformation and conversation is not only possible but normal. As poets, they can become anything within the arena of the poem. These poems represent a new generation of feminist poets who refuse to choose one state of being over the other, who see strength in hybridity and who draw strength from the non-human in all its complexity. Perhaps, like the rewilding of National Parks, or like the story of the wolves that sing those metamorphoses, such changes might initiate trophic cascades which transform landscapes far beyond the page.

Notes

1. Crozier, 'What Comes After', in *Whetstone*, p. 15.
2. Turcotte, 'Foreword', in *Werewolves and Other Shapeshifters*, ed. by McMahon-Coleman and Weaver, p. 1.

3 Gruen, 'Dismantling Oppression', p. 79.
4 Ostriker, 'The Nerves of a Midwife', p. 326.
5 Lönngren, *Following the Animal*, p. 88.
6 Gaard, 'Children's Environmental Literature', p. 323.
7 Kemmerer, 'Introduction', in *Sister Species*, ed. by Kemmerer, p. 12.
8 Gruen, p. 62.
9 Berry, *Black Country*, p. 1.
10 Sabine Baring-Gould gives a good account of transformation through the donning of animal skins in Norse and Icelandic sagas and myth, including transformation into birds. See *The Book of Were-wolves*, pp. 15–28. Ann-Sophie Lönngren gives an interesting reading of the donning of wolf-pelts to become a wolf in *Following the Animal*, pp. 113–15.
11 Berry, 'Interview'.
12 *Ibid.*
13 'The Silver Birch' and 'The First Path' are both ekphrastic poems from a series titled after paintings by George Shaw, and are intrinsically hybrid texts.
14 'When I Was a Boy' seems to draw on an eponymous Dar Williams song, with shared imagery and reference points, including shirtless cycling. See Dar Williams, 'When I Was a Boy'. This highlights the cultural hybridity and intertextuality of these transformative poems.
15 Berry, 'Sow', p. 26.
16 Coudray, *The Curse of the Werewolf*, p. 6.
17 Sandilands, *The Good-natured Feminist*, p. 17.
18 Rigby, 'The Goddess Returns', p. 47.
19 Berry, 'How I Did It'.
20 *Ibid.*
21 Moore, *The Art of Falling*.
22 Metzger, 'Battling Demons with Medical Authority', p. 344.
23 Coudray, 'The Cycle of the Werewolf', p. 65.
24 *Ibid.*, p. 59.
25 Chris and Steve Agnos, eds, 'How Wolves Change Rivers'.
26 GrrlScientist, 'How Wolves Change Rivers: Video'. The reintroduction of wolves to Yellowstone is treated in detail by Douglas W. Smith and Gary Ferguson in *Decade of the Wolf*.
27 Middleton, 'Is the Wolf a Real American Hero?'.
28 *Ibid.*
29 Johnson, 'National Species', p. 338.
30 Stannard quotes, amongst other compelling records, the Reverend Solomon Stoddard's assertion that 'Indians were wolves' and should 'be dealt with withal as wolves' (Stannard, 'Genocide', p. 432). See also Stannard, *American Holocaust*.
31 Johnson, p. 337.

32 For more on legend of the killing of the wolf at Humphrey Head, see Mrs Jerome Mercier, *The Last Wolf*, and Greer Chesher, 'A Testimony of Wolves', pp. 100–4. It is questionable whether this was really the last wolf in England.
33 Moore, 'The Act of Transformation'.
34 Donovan, 'Animal Rights and Feminist Theory', p. 183.
35 Bynum, 'Shape and Story'.

14

WEARING THE WOLF: FUR, FASHION AND SPECIES TRANSVESTISM

Catherine Spooner

The September 2015 issue of British *Elle* and several other fashion magazines carried a pull-out advertisement for Ralph Lauren's Autumn/Winter 2015 collection. Shot by the celebrated British photographer Jimmy Nelson on location in Finnish Lapland, the sequence of images featured a northern-European-looking blonde woman (the Dutch model Sanne Vloet) dressed in a variety of luxurious furry garments and ethnic-style jewellery, accompanied by Siberian huskies and juxtaposed with pictures of reindeer. In one particularly striking, wide-angle shot, Vloet gazes at the camera, dressed in a floor-length, high-collared white lace dress, a thigh-length, distinctively patterned pale fur gilet and a battered Stetson, holding two huskies on leashes. A snowy landscape stretches out behind her and to her right, leaving a vast white space to take up two-thirds of the left-hand side of the picture. The blankness of the snow draws attention to the complex textures of lace and fur in Vloet's ensemble and the dogs that accompany her; the dark accents of hat, hair, leashes and the dogs' patches bring definition to her figure and distinguish her from the landscape even as her whiteness suggests that she is part of it (see Figure 14.1).

The sequence of images featured in the advertisement brings together many of the signifiers that characterise female werewolf stories: wilderness, fur, whiteness, solitude and, of course, dogs. Although there is no werewolf depicted in these photographs, the images trade on a similar set of associations and mobilise a similar set of discourses. They provide a quintessential example of what happens when wolves, fur and fashion are brought together, and what it means to wear the wolf.

Werewolf mythology is intrinsically bound up with our cultural relationship with clothes. The first stories of werewolves, it is widely alleged, may have arisen from tales of men dressed in animal skins for hunting or ritual purposes.[1] Whilst it may be tempting to read the act of wearing a wolf-skin as demonstrating these early people's oneness with the wolf and closeness to nature, using animal skins as clothing is an act of culture, a means of mediating the natural world

14.1 Ralph Lauren Autumn/Winter 2015 campaign, Sanne Vloet with dogs

recalling Claude Lévi-Strauss's insistence that 'Mythic thought only accepts nature on condition that it is able to reproduce it'.² As such, it signals a binary opposition between nature and culture coming into place. One can only wear the wolf if one is not already a wolf. Subsequent werewolf narratives have continued to animate this binary opposition and, as Chantal Bourgault du Coudray suggests, to challenge and complicate it. Drawing on Žižek's analysis of the classic 'wild' child, Kaspar Hauser, which he uses to illuminate the position of the Enlightenment monster who is read as prelinguistic or 'natural' yet inserted into the symbolic order, she states that 'the werewolf also appears as a *bridge* between nature and culture, by exceeding both categories and representing slippages between them'.³

In this respect the werewolf can be read as what Marjorie Garber, in the context of transvestism, has called a 'third term'. For Garber, women dressed as men and vice versa are usually subsumed to one sex or the other by critical discourse, when in fact they operate as a third category in their own right. She explains:

> The 'third' is that which questions binary thinking and introduces crisis ... The 'third' is a mode of articulation, a way of describing a space of possibility. Three puts in question the idea of one: of identity, self-sufficiency, self-knowledge.⁴

In her conclusion, Garber insists that 'the wolf inscribes itself all over the text of transvestism', drawing attention to a number of apparently coincidental references to wolves in transvestite texts.⁵ Her examples include, most prominently, the wolf in Grandmother's clothes of the folk tale 'Little Red Riding Hood' and Nora Flood's comparison of Dr Matthew O'Connor's transvestism in Djuna Barnes's *Nightwood* (1936) to 'Red Riding Hood and the wolf in bed'.[6] She then goes on to explore in detail the fantasies of cross-dressed women entertained by Freud's Wolf-Man, which Freud famously interpreted as a means of repressing the 'primal scene' of viewing his parents having sex. Garber asserts that cross-dressing is in itself a primal scene repressed by critics who typically use it as a metaphor for other kinds of disturbance rather than as itself being the source of meaning. I propose, however, that, in relation to the wolf, Garber overlooks or represses another binary opposition which is at least equally significant to that of gender: the opposition between human and animal. The wolf in 'Little Red Riding Hood' may be cross-dressed as a woman, but he is also cross-dressed as a human. Similarly, in *Nightwood*, the perverse pleasure of human–animal transformation hinted at in Matthew O'Connor's hairy transvestism is realised in the deeply unsettling climax of the novel, when Nora's lover Robin drops down on all fours and communes with a dog, 'grinning and whimpering ... barking in a fit of laughter', in a Catholic church.[7] The werewolf does not have to cross gender boundaries in order to constitute a third term (although in some cases it does also invoke gender fluidity, as we shall see). To wear the wolf (or for the wolf to wear the woman) is a kind of species transvestism. The werewolf's erosion of species boundaries puts into question the 'identity, self-sufficiency, self-knowledge' not only of gender but of humanity itself.

This chapter resists, nevertheless, the idea that werewolves are privileged agents of transgression that invariably disrupt preconceptions about nature and culture, wilderness and civilisation, animal and human. As humans wearing wolves (or, occasionally, wolves wearing humans), werewolves are interpellated by a fashion system. Fur of all kinds is imbued with social and economic value by the fashion industry and its systems of representation. The kind of fur that werewolves 'wear' is determined by cultural expectations: just as the bodies of Western fine art analysed in Anne Hollander's *Seeing through Clothes* are shaped by the fashions of the day, the werewolf body is closely defined by the clothes it wears (or has taken off).[8] Individual representations of the werewolf therefore oscillate between confirming cultural expectations and disrupting them. Images of werewolves are, after all, part of culture and may reify the business of fashion even as they may simultaneously open a door to ways of seeing differently.

This chapter traces the heritage of the Ralph Lauren advertising campaign and explores its resonance as a set of images. In doing so it argues that the female werewolf in particular bridges the nature/culture dichotomy by refusing a clear distinction between fur and skin and thus between a clothed and naked state. This liminal status is profoundly ambivalent: it is based in potentially problematic cultural assumptions about the nature of femininity, indigenous peoples and indeed animals, but it also promises a fierce glamour, bodily freedom and intimacy with wilderness that remains seductive. The promise of transformation is the promise of fashion itself, and the female werewolf offers a model of metamorphosis that continues to inspire contemporary designers, stylists and photographers.

Clothes/fur/skin

The male werewolf has provided the dominant paradigm in cultural narratives from the Middle Ages to the present, from Marie de France's 'Bisclavret' in the twelfth century to Universal Pictures' *The Wolf Man* of 1941. Inevitably, then, many of our expectations regarding werewolves and clothes follow this paradigm. In male werewolf narratives, clothes are clearly marked as 'culture' and the removal of clothes often functions as a ritual of transition between the wild and the civilised, the animal and the human. As Hannah Priest comments of medieval werewolf narratives, 'the transformation from human to werewolf (and, more importantly, from werewolf back to human) is associated more with the removal and recovery of clothes than with shifts in bodily form'.[9] In 'Bisclavret', one of the earliest literary accounts of a werewolf, the titular werewolf is prevented from returning to his human form when his wife and her lover steal his clothes, and is restored once the clothes are returned to him. Similarly, Garry Marvin writes of a classical werewolf tale from Petronius's *Satyricon*: 'The shedding of clothes, markers of civilization, is essential for the movement towards the animal and their recovery equally essential for the return to human form'.[10] The loss of clothes in werewolf stories may be terrifying or liberating, but either way it marks an ontological boundary crossed.

This 'conceptualization of lycanthropic metamorphosis as a process of dressing and undressing', as Hannah Priest puts it in another article, persists into modern film.[11] In a classic werewolf movie such as John Landis's *An American Werewolf in London* (1981), the transition ritual enables the presentation of the male body as spectacle, transformation scenes conventionally beginning with a hyper-masculinised form of striptease as the werewolf violently tears off his garments to reveal a toned and muscular torso. Indeed, the star, David Naughton, consequently lost his advertising contract with Dr Pepper because it was felt that by putting his body on such overt display he had compromised his wholesome image. Neil Jordan's *The Company of Wolves*, released just three years later, accentuates the process of lycanthropic striptease so that, in the transformation sequences, the wolves are seen peeling back their human skin like one more piece of clothing. In contrast to the dandy vampire, forged in the tradition of Byron, the male werewolf in the English-language tradition typically shows scant regard for his appearance or indeed individual items of clothing, which are ripped or discarded in a display of rugged, 'natural' masculinity. (The 'natural' is often problematised in other ways in these narratives, as the remainder of this chapter will stress.) In the films of Stephenie Meyer's Twilight Saga, the werewolf pack's perpetual parade of semi-dress when in human form may be intentionally titillating for its presupposed female audience, but it also signals the Native American men's proximity to the wilderness, their 'wildness' as opposed to the hyper-civilised, buttoned-up vampires, who (with momentary exceptions when the romantic hero Edward exposes his scintillating body) always appear fully dressed. This positioning of indigenous peoples as approximate to the wolf is one that I will return to later on.

In contrast, narratives featuring female werewolves, while engaging with similar binary oppositions, are often more complex, a product of the closer cultural identification between the female body and the clothes it wears. In the nineteenth century, female werewolves were frequently portrayed as humans wearing fur, presenting a disconcerting continuity between their 'wild' and 'civilised' states. Notably, in nineteenth-century fashion women typically wore fur on the outside, while men's clothing used it as an interior lining.[12] There is something particularly suggestive about this in relation to the way that werewolves are conceptualised in the West, showing how fashion directly shapes cultural fantasy: if men have a beast within, hairy on the inside, women can be associated with animals more directly and particularly with their soft and seductive surfaces.

In nineteenth-century werewolf fiction, white fur is suggestively equivalent to white skin, neither fully distinguished from the other. In Clemence Housman's 'The Were-wolf' (1890), the werewolf in human form 'blanch[es] white as her furs' in the moment immediately before her discovery.[13] The shapeshifting Shetland cottager of George MacDonald's 'The Gray Wolf' (1871) does not possess the luxury of white fur, yet the narrator notes that 'Her face was very gray in complexion': if white fur stands in for skin, here grey skin stands in for fur.[14] In these female werewolf narratives, the distinctions between clothes, fur and skin are continually shifting and elusive, suggesting the fur-clothed woman is inherently wild and never fully transitions out of her wolf state.

Whiteness

The female werewolves of the nineteenth century are strikingly white: Frederick Marryat's 'The White Wolf of the Hartz Mountains' (1839), Gilbert Campbell's 'The White Wolf of Kostopchin' (1889) and White Fell of Clemence Housman's 'The Were-wolf' are key examples. Whilst the white Arctic wolf is a distinct sub-species in Canada, white wolves are rare in Europe, and the whiteness of these werewolves consequently marks them out as marvellous and to a degree unnatural.

In Marryat's story, an inset tale within his novel *The Phantom Ship*, the beautiful werewolf Christina appears 'dressed in a travelling dress, deeply bordered with white fur, and wore a cap of white ermine on her head'.[15] It is notable that the fur specified is fashionable ermine, not wolf fur, which at the time Marryat was writing was not particularly prized. In this apparently rustic tale there is therefore a hint of a system of commodities through which animals become objects of cultural and economic exchange. Later, Christina appears both as a 'large, white she-wolf' and in her human form, dressed 'in her white night-dress' as she digs up and cannibalises the corpse of her stepdaughter.[16] The white nightdress is a characteristic Gothic garment, used to clothe the heroine-victim and the female vampire alike.[17] Its presence in this story demonstrates the crossing of codes between other kinds of Gothic narrative, and particularly recalls Geraldine from Coleridge's Gothic poem 'Christabel', an ambiguous vampire or werewolf who removes her 'silken robe of white' to reveal, in one manuscript version, 'her bosom and half her side / … dark and rough as the Sea-Wolf's hide'.[18] The white robe in Gothic fiction is multiply overdetermined: it suggests purity and victimhood as well as the strategic deployment of those qualities for nefarious ends; it is patently a substitute for skin and offers itself up as a surface to be marked, a blank page on which the story of the heroine's body is written in blood and dirt. In 'The White Wolf of the Hartz Mountains', it provides a ground of femininity against which the act of cannibalism is set off: the presence of the white dress frames and accentuates the horror.

In Clemence Housman's 'The Were-wolf', the anti-heroine, White Fell, appears at the Scandinavian homestead wearing an elaborate costume that is described in some detail:

> The fashion of her dress was strange – half masculine, yet not unwomanly. A fine fur tunic, reaching but little below the knee, was all the skirt she wore; below were the cross-bound shoes and leggings that a hunter wears. A white fur cap was set low upon the brows, and from its edge strips of fur fell lappet-wise about her shoulders, two of which at her entrance had been drawn forward and crossed about her throat, but now, loosened and thrown back, left unhidden long plaits of fair hair that lay forward on shoulder and breast, down to the ivory-studded girdle where the axe gleamed.[19]

The illustrations by Everard Hopkins that accompanied the story's publication in the periodical *Atalanta* closely follow the description in the text, attempting to construct a plausibly authentic medieval Scandinavian costume.[20] White Fell's strangely androgynous clothes 'reveal the masculine in the feminine', as Hannah Priest (drawing on Karin Lesnik-Oberstein) suggests is a trait of female werewolves in general, again constructing the werewolf as the 'bridge' between binaries.[21] Interestingly, when White Fell wishes to appear more human, she 'cast[s] loose her robes till they trailed ample, and [speaks] as a mild woman'.[22] Her wolf nature, on the other hand, is revealed by the closeness of fit, the garments forming a kind of second skin: 'her arms were folded in her furs that were drawn tight about her body; the white lappets from her head were wrapped and knotted closely beneath her face'.[23] Crucially, this closeness of fit enables her freedom of movement: 'She had drawn her furs more closely to her, disposing them so, that instead of flying loose to her heels, no drapery hung lower than her knees, and this without a check to her wonderful speed, nor embarrassment by the cumbering of the folds'.[24] In the illustrations by Clemence's brother Laurence Housman to the book version of the text, White Fell's costume takes the form of a kind of white fur onesie.[25] In the illustration depicting her race with the hero Christian, the fur appears to merge with her skin, revealing disconcertingly wolflike haunches, and the cloak curls around her thighs like a tail (see Figure 14.2).[26] Clothing here is not a clear indicator of human or wolf identity, but demonstrates an unsettling ambiguity between the two.

14.2 'The Race'. Illustration by Laurence Housman to Clemence Housman's *The Were-wolf*

White Fell's ambiguous identity provides the clearest fictional example of the female werewolf as a version of Garber's 'third term', as a woman-dressed-as-wolf who is reducible to neither. If White Fell's androgyny makes her a cross-dresser in Garber's sense as well, this gender-disturbance is a sign or a symptom of her species transvestism. In all three of the white wolf stories I have mentioned, the white fur of the female werewolf remains unsoiled despite her depredations of human flesh. In the tales' refusal to tell the story of blood, sweat and dirt that characteristically marks the white garment in the Gothic text lies a lingering resistance to the incorporation of the female werewolf's body, through her death, into the materials of culture. In contrast to the male werewolves who return to their human body when killed, these three female werewolves return to wolf form, raising the question whether they are women wearing wolves, or wolves wearing women. Their whiteness is remarked on even in death. In Hopkins's illustration to 'The Were-wolf', the dead body of White Fell is surrounded by other wolves, an image unsupported by the story, in which the wolf pack initially pursue but then deliberately avoid White Fell, 'So abhorrent was that fell creature to beast as to man'.[27] In the engraving her white coat marks her difference from their grey ones; she is as other to them as she was to her human companions. The werewolf's whiteness, her snow camouflage, appears to indicate unity with the natural environment, but this is revealed as an illusion. Neither nature nor culture, the werewolf remains *super*natural, estranged from both.

Wolves/dogs/women

The whiteness of the nineteenth-century female werewolf is reproduced in the Ralph Lauren advertising campaign, although here its sense of otherness and difference translates into specialness, the pristine qualities of the white garment – and the snowy wilderness – equating to luxury and leisure. I now want to think more closely about the role of the animal in these images, and specifically the relationship between women, dogs and wolves. The white wolves in the stories I have discussed present an unsettling combination of femininity and animality. As Bram Dijkstra explains in his history of the femme fatale in *fin-de-siècle* art, *Idols of Perversity*, nineteenth-century discourse on degeneration often proposed that women were closer to animals, and in the sexological writing of Havelock Ellis and others documented the 'animal perversions' of women.[28]

In nineteenth-century art, this interest in women's supposedly animal nature resulted in a repeated motif of presenting women alongside animals, often domestic pets, in a way that either suggested their resemblance or imputed a bestial sexuality. As Dijkstra writes, 'In art these suggestions of a new outlet for feminine lubricity and disrespect for the male's reproductive responsibility certainly had something to do with the late nineteenth century's focus on the society woman and her dog. Not merely ordinary lapdogs, these creatures often took on formidable proportions.'[29] Wilhelm Trübner's 1873 painting of *Lovers with Dog* is a good example: in the human-animal erotic triangle Trübner depicts, the man is more interested in the woman; the woman is more interested in the dog. The Swiss artist Louise Breslau, who was the devoted owner of a borzoi or Russian wolfhound, made repeated images of intimacy between women and dogs, such as *The Pensive Life* (1908), *Young Girl on a Bed and Her Dog* (1912) and *Young Girl with a Borzoi* (1912). The poster for a German film of 1913, *Die Suffragette*, shows an elegantly attired, liberated woman with her borzoi – who needs a man when one has a dog? All of these associations are directly replicated in a shoot for the September 2014 issue of British *Vogue* by Mario Sorrenti, styled by Kate Moss, and featuring Lara Stone posing with a pair of wolflike dogs (British Lupines) in an intimate domestic environment.[30] Entitled 'The Wolf in Her', the sequence repeatedly shows Stone crouched on a bed or lying supine on a sofa with her arms draped around the dogs. In one shot, the dog is positioned suggestively between her splayed legs; the salacious connotations are inescapable. In another, the wolves are absent but a Dries Van Noten faux-fur stole falls between her open legs, suggesting pubic hair – or a tail. In a third image, Stone wears a Prada goat-skin dress, her nakedness beneath the fur evoking the classic werewolf juxtaposition of dress and undress, fur and skin, predator and prey, and implying her own incipient transformation.

Of the Victorian and Edwardian woman-with-dog paintings, Charles Wellington Furse's *Diana of the Uplands* (1903–4) is interesting in that it adds classical iconography: Diana, the Roman goddess of the hunt, was associated with wild animals and woodlands. This image bears a particular resemblance to the Ralph Lauren advertisement, which similarly positions its model as a lone huntress, a woman poised uneasily yet thrillingly between domestication and the call of the wild. Woman, all these images suggest, bears an affinity with dogs, and specifically with dogs that are hunters, dogs that evoke wolves.

In the Ralph Lauren advertisement, the association between domesticated dogs and wolves is reinforced by the fabrics used in the collection itself. Ralph Lauren has 'a long-standing commitment not to use fur products', a policy that was reiterated in the programme for the autumn 2015 show.[31] The garments that look like fur are actually made of dyed shearling, or sheepskin. While by no means vegetarian, shearling is a product of domesticated farm animals and therefore no more controversial than leather. Nevertheless, while this may be a deliberate ethical policy on behalf of the design house, it has a curious effect in these particular photographs. Sheep come to stand in for other, wilder creatures – wolves in sheep's clothing, if you like. This effect of substitution does not end with the clothes themselves. Similarly, the huskies stand in for their wilder counterparts, wolves, suggesting the exotic call of the wild while at the same time standing back from it. The model has the dogs on leads; she has the wilderness under control although she profits from its allure.

Woman/wilderness

What is at stake in positioning the woman in the wilderness in this way? The campaign, according to Lauren himself, was intended to convey 'a sensual, textural world, a warm cosy winter wonderland of strength and dimension'.[32] This rather meaningless statement of intent emphasises qualities that one might expect, and desire, the clothes to have: sensuality, texture, warmth, cosiness, strength, 'dimension' (whatever that means). They are more difficult to apply to the woman – 'sensuality' and 'strength' may be appropriate but 'warmth' does not fit this rather icy Nordic blonde, and texture, cosiness and dimension are meaningless as descriptors of a person. The designer's intent, moreover, is problematised by the associations brought by the oeuvre of the photographer, Jimmy Nelson, who is renowned not only for his fashion photography but also for his images of indigenous peoples.

Nelson's *magnum opus* is *Before They Pass Away*, published as a glossy coffee table collection in 2013 and reproduced in a slightly different format on his website. The result of three years spent travelling to remote parts of the globe in order to document the disappearing lifestyles of tribal peoples, the book received widespread attention in the media but proved controversial. Although the images were fêted by many for their beauty, and widely reproduced in magazines and colour supplements, they were also criticised for being staged to meet Western expectations and presenting a fetishised and nostalgic view of indigenous cultures. Stephen Corry, director of Survival International, pointed out that the peoples represented were struggling for survival in a complex global community rather than mutely 'passing away', and accused Nelson of 'echo[ing] a colonial vision which remains deeply destructive of peoples who try and reject its domination'.[33] More recently, the Maori actor Hinerauwhiri Paki has accused Nelson of exploiting her and her family by using her image without payment and in ways to which she had not consented. Paki's acting career was initiated when a Facebook video of her doing traditional *poi* dancing to Beyoncé went viral, a markedly different presentation of Maori culture from that of Nelson.[34]

The line between documentary photography and fashion shoot becomes blurred in Nelson's work: the photographs have appeared in fashion magazines where they do not look out of place, and have gone on to inspire a range of designers, stylists and photographers. His images of the Chukchi and Nenet peoples of Siberia bear closest comparison to the Ralph Lauren shoot. Snowy landscapes and huskies appear in all three sets of images, and one shot, of a herd of reindeer, is repeated identically in both the advertisement and the Chukchi narrative. Lit like a fashion shoot, with close attention to texture, colour and pattern, there are strong resemblances between the documentary images and the fashion campaign. The key difference, of course, is the ethnic origin of the model. Sanne Vloet conforms not only to Western beauty conventions but specifically to the WASP identity associated with Ralph Lauren as aspirational American brand. If both sets of images are, in their own way, performed, then Vloet's performance undermines the illusion of authenticity in all the images, revealing them as constructions.

Curiously, the decontextualised quotations from the Siberian people on Nelson's website emphasise the proximity of humans to animals. The Nenets page announces: 'If you don't drink warm blood and eat fresh meat, you are doomed to die on the tundra.'[35] On the Chukchi page, the quotation reads, 'The way you treat your dog in this life determines your place in heaven.'[36] The alignment of the 'native' with the animal world is problematic as it effectively positions them as part of the empty territory awaiting the coloniser – and Nelson's commemoration and mourning of the 'passing' of this empty territory both fails to contest this process and allows him to appropriate it for his artistic purposes. As David Punter argues, 'To assimilate the "native" to the animal is, as it were, to "clear the ground"; and thus we see one of the ways in which an imperial "logic" of extermination and genocide is preceded and accompanied at all points by a cultural logic ... that sequesters the notion of the "human".'[37] In Nelson's work the indigenous people are placed ambiguously between the human world and the animal one, between civilisation and wilderness. Within the narrative constructed by the images and their accompanying text, the Chukchi and Nenets act as a 'bridge' between binary oppositions of wild and civilised, human and animal, in a similar way to the werewolf. This liminality is then imported, through association, to the fashion shoot. If it is difficult to imagine the typical Ralph Lauren customer drinking warm blood on the tundra, they can nevertheless enjoy the thrill of the wild by proxy.

There is a further set of associations in the advertising campaign. Although the model and location are European, and the context brought by the photographer is Siberian, the association with Ralph Lauren, a stridently American brand, as well as details such as the Stetson hat and cowhide bag, inevitably bring the North American wilderness to mind. This was not lost on commentators on the catwalk show: on the *Vogue* website Nicole Phelps notes a 'Western' theme in the suede fringing, Victorian-styled cream lace dress and Navajo-style beading, while Alessandra Codinha considers, 'how could it be of any surprise that his collection came through just as dreamily American as he is?'[38] The 'ethnic' details of the jewellery and beading in the advertising campaign, however, problematise the term 'Western' and reveal its dual meaning, as cinematic genre and as an ethnocentric viewpoint. Western in the genre sense, the clothes nevertheless position the model as on the threshold between Western and indigenous culture, partially 'gone native'. The ethnically white model thus inevitably recalls one of the most prominent popular cultural representations of the white woman 'gone native': Mary McDonnell's performance as a white woman brought up by the Lakota people in the 1990 film *Dances with Wolves*.

In this film, a huge critical and commercial hit for the director and star Kevin Costner, the wolf Two Socks provides the conduit between white man and the wilderness. McDonnell's character, Stands With A Fist, performs much the same function. Stands With A Fist's story echoes that of the feral child – taken from her white settler family at the age of four, she has adapted to the ways of the plains tribe in order to survive. Dressed in animal skins, with ragged hair and only a rudimentary memory of the English language, she represents in a sanitised and acceptable way the woman who has crossed to the other side of the civilisation/wilderness divide. Indeed, the character drew widespread criticism as she appeared to have been inserted in the film so that the hero John Dunbar, played by Kevin Costner, could have a white-on-white romance. Fan blogs also return to the theme of her hair: as numerous viewers point out, despite having been brought up by the Lakota since an early age, Stands With A Fist wears her hair not in the waist-length braids of other female members of the tribe but in a layered cut fashionable in the early 1990s when the film was released. While of course this is a concession to contemporary ideas of female attractiveness, I would argue that it has further significance. McDonnell's ragged cut signifies wildness in a way that neat braids do not. It consciously recalls the shagginess of fur, aligning her with the wolf Two Socks. Both represent aspects of wilderness that the white man may attempt to tame, with varying degrees of success. This is underscored in the film by the way in which Dunbar's increasing intimacy with Two Socks is placed in deliberate counterpoint to his courtship of Stands With A Fist, the scene in which the wolf finally takes meat from his hand immediately preceding the consummation of his sexual relationship with the woman.

The association between fashion, wolves and indigenous peoples was made more explicitly still in another fashion shoot from a year prior to the Ralph Lauren campaign: 'Bad Girl Rihanna: The World's Wildest Style Icon' in the September 2014 issue of *W* magazine. This was, notably, the same date that 'The Wolf in Her' appeared in *Vogue*: the Autumn/Winter season of 2014 featured eccentric furs and folk- and fairy-tale-inspired fashion (with Red Riding Hood explicitly referenced in collections from Dolce and Gabbana, Fendi and Saint Laurent), lending itself to wolfish interpretations. The *W* shoot, photographed by Mert Alas and Marcus Piggott (Mert and Marcus) and styled by Edward Enninful, featured global R&B star Rihanna in a series of fur garments

14.3 'Bad Gal Rihanna: The World's Wildest Style Icon'. Rihanna photographed by Mert and Marcus, styled by Edward Enninful

and dramatic jewellery, head-dresses and make-up evoking both indigenous African designs and shamanic and voodoo ritual costumes. The strapline informed readers: 'Style icon, wild child, creature of the night. Bad gal RiRi comes alive after midnight.'[39] The image most resonant to the current discussion is one in which Rihanna appears crouched on a bed of leaves and bark, while two wolves lope in the background. She wears thigh-length, white leather boots by Marc Jacobs and a hooded grey fur cape by Alexander McQueen, accessorised with red face-paint, a septum ring, a 'tribal' necklace, Indian-style metal hand chains and long white fingernails (see Figure 14.3). The imagery clearly emulates Nelson's photographs in styling and composition while stripping out any documentary associations or the illusion of realism. The wolves are apparently added in after-production; the 'ethnic' references are self-consciously contradictory; the elaborate make-up and manicure contrast with the dirty 'natural' setting. The look is pure fantasy and the references to indigenous peoples, feral children and, indeed, werewolves are intentionally confrontational, designed to bolster the Rihanna brand, and underline her own transformation from sweet R&B singer to fierce diva.

The shoot lacks the subtlety of the Ralph Lauren campaign, and on the surface seems more overtly exploitative in its representation of indigenous peoples (and indeed, its use of real fur). Its very confrontationality, however, its self-conscious fakery, serves more clearly to expose the artificiality of Nelson's ethnographic images and demonstrate the machinery through which their claims to authenticity are constructed. Moreover, Rihanna's own ethnicity, as a black woman born in Barbados of African descent, further complicates the picture. On one level, the associations evoked by the shoot appear to confirm racist stereotypes of the 'wildness' and 'primitiveness' of black people. On another, however, its self-conscious performativity pokes fun at these stereotypes. Rihanna has no more claim to the imagery of traditional African communities, shamanism or voodoo than Sanne Vloet does to that of indigenous Siberian peoples or Native Americans. Here, however, the cultural appropriation is so knowing, so blatant, so camp that it is impossible to take at face value. Riri as 'creature of the night' makes intertextual reference to the howling wolves whose sweet music is appraised by Dracula as well as the thrilling object of desire fantasised by Janet in 'Touch-a Touch-a Touch Me' from *The Rocky Horror Picture Show*. Performing as werewolf, she 'introduces crisis' to the logical binaries of nature and culture, Western and Third World, 'exceeding both categories and representing slippages between them'.[40] The transformational ability of fashion is alluded to both in the editorial (she 'comes alive after midnight') and in the context of Rihanna's own career, in which self-reinvention has been a constant theme. For Rihanna, Enninful, and Mert and Marcus, wearing the wolf becomes a playful and deliberately provocative gesture that evokes this wider metamorphic potential.

It would be very easy to conclude, particularly in relation to the edgier images of Rihanna, that the Ralph Lauren advertising campaign is simply trading on a set of cultural associations for commercial profit, and in doing so diluting them. This is the clichéd interpretation of the fashion industry, as a parasite feeding on more 'authentic' representations for the gain of individuals who are mysteriously outside and above the process of representation. Such a reading is, of course, over-simplified. As I have demonstrated in the course of this chapter, fashion has always played a part in how werewolf narratives are constructed – they are always already shaped by our cultural relationship with clothes. The echo of *Dances with Wolves* in the Ralph Lauren shoot calls attention to the way in which woman, wilderness and wolf are made proximate in werewolf discourses, and that underscoring these discourses is a range of debates about the disappearance of indigenous cultures and the natural environment. The advertising campaign participates in the production of these debates and contributes to the construction of the ongoing mythology of the werewolf. The seductive glamour with which it proposes its vision of woman's intimacy with the wilderness is representative of a wider set of presumptions and desires that circulate around the relationship between woman and wolf.

To wear the wolf, or indeed for the wolf to wear the woman, is to engage with the multiple ways in which the dualisms of western culture are bridged or challenged in our responses to the natural world. However, as I stressed at the beginning of this chapter, you can wear the wolf only if you are not already a wolf. Species transvestites may, through their furry transformation, become a 'third term', but they do not become a wolf. (This is not to deny that other transformations, such as across gender, are indeed possible.) Even those female werewolves who, like Housman's White Fell, return to wolf form after death are rejected by the animal pack. Just as the extraordinary whiteness of the nineteenth-century female werewolves signals their difference, not only from the human but also from the natural world, so too do contemporary fashion photographs expose our dream of oneness with the wolf as anthropomorphic and colonialist fantasy. Despite trading on the glamour of the wolf, the Ralph Lauren advertisement reminds us of the disappointingly prosaic truth that women who run with the wolves are not, actually, wolves.

Notes

1 See, for example, Coudray, *The Curse of the Werewolf*, p. 2. Matthew Beresford provides an extended account of sources for this idea in *The White Devil*, pp. 20–4.
2 Lévi-Strauss, *The Raw and the Cooked*, p. 341.
3 Coudray, p. 3. Coudray is referring to Slavoj Žižek, *Enjoy Your Symptom!*, p. 136.
4 Garber, *Vested Interests*, p. 11.
5 Ibid., p. 375.
6 Barnes, *Nightwood*, p. 117.
7 Ibid., p. 238.
8 Hollander, *Seeing through Clothes*.
9 Priest, Introduction, in *She-wolf*, ed. by Priest, p. 6.
10 Marvin, *Wolf*, p. 52.
11 Priest, '"Bogeysliche as a boye"', in *Sexual Culture*, p. 97.
12 James Laver notes how, during the vogue for furs in the 1890s, 'women wore furs in the form not only of trimmings, but of whole fur coats, whereas men's fur coats had the fur on the inside, the fur being visible only in the collar and cuffs'. Women wore fur boas, muffs and tippets throughout the century. Laver, *Costume and Fashion*, pp. 210–11.
13 Clemence Housman, 'The Were-wolf', p. 231.
14 George MacDonald, 'The Gray Wolf', p. 115.
15 Frederick Marryat, 'The White Wolf of the Hartz Mountains', pp. 23–41 (p. 31).
16 Ibid., pp. 40, 39.

17 For more on the significance of the white dress in Gothic texts, see Spooner, *Fashioning Gothic Bodies*; Spooner, 'Costuming Vampires'.
18 Coleridge, *Poems*, ed. by Beer, p. 266, n. 1. The *Oxford English Dictionary* lists 'sea-wolf' as an obsolete term for seal or sea lion, suggesting a link to another legendary shapeshifter, the selkie.
19 Clemence Housman, p. 214.
20 Both sets of illustrations to *The Were-wolf* are reproduced in Easley and Scott's anthology. Hopkins's illustrations accompany Clemence Housman's text and are referenced as such. Laurence Housman's illustrations appear in an appendix and are referenced separately.
21 Priest, *She-wolf*, p. 18.
22 Clemence Housman, p. 237.
23 *Ibid.*, p. 237.
24 *Ibid.*, p. 239.
25 Laurence Housman, 'Illustrations for Clemence Housman's The Were-wolf', in *Terrifying Transformations*, ed. by Easley and Scott, pp. 333–9 (p. 336).
26 *Ibid.*, p. 337.
27 Clemence Housman, pp. 249, 239.
28 Havelock Ellis, cited in Dijkstra, *Idols of Perversity*, p. 297.
29 Dijkstra, p. 299.
30 Amusingly, the dogs are given their own contributor profile in the magazine, replaying the dissolution of human/animal boundaries in a comic register: 'Modelling beside Lara Stone are Mr Wolf and Summer Sunbeam, a pair of British Lupines – a breed of dog which bears an uncanny resemblance to a wolf. Proper professionals, they recently starred in the television drama *Penny Dreadful*, their diet is raw and they keep fit by swimming wherever they can find water' ('Vogue Notices: Wolf Hall', p. 94).
31 'About Our Products', *Ralph Lauren*; Phelps, 'Fall 2015'. While Ralph Lauren may have committed to not using fur, its record on other environmental policies is shaky. The company has been targeted by a variety of environmental action campaigns and was ranked in the bottom 50 per cent of companies rated by GoodGuide for environmental policies, practices and performance. See 'Brand: Ralph Lauren'.
32 Drain, 'Ralph Lauren Launches Fall 2015 Ad Campaign'.
33 Corry, 'Turning a Blind Eye to Pure Old Vibrations'.
34 'Taupo Teen Angry Over Misused Photo'.
35 'Nenets'.
36 'Chukchi'.
37 Punter, *Postcolonial Imaginings*, p. 146.
38 Phelps; Codhinha, 'Ralph Lauren Fall 2015 RTW'.
39 'Bad Gal Rihanna'.
40 Coudray, p. 3; Garber, p. 11.

Bibliography

Printed and internet sources

Aarsleff, Hans, *From Locke to Saussure: Essays on the Study of Language and Intellectual History*, 2nd edn (Minneapolis: University of Minnesota Press, 1983)

Abbott, Stacey, *Celluloid Vampires: Life after Death in the Modern World* (Austin: University of Texas Press, 2007)

—— 'Dracula on Film and Television, 1960–Present', in *A Cambridge Companion to Dracula*, ed. by Roger Luckhurst (Cambridge: Cambridge University Press, 2018)

Abel, Richard, and Rick Altman, *The Sounds of Early Cinema* (Bloomington and Indianapolis: Indiana University Press, 2001)

'About Our Products', *Ralph Lauren* <www.ralphlauren.com/helpdesk/index.jsp?display=shopping&subdisplay=product> [accessed 11 July 2016]

Aesop, *Fables of Aesop*, trans. by S.A. Handsford (Harmondsworth: Penguin, 1979)

Afanas'ev, Aleksandr, *Russian Fairy Tales*, trans. and ed. by Norbert Guterman (New York: Pantheon, 1945)

—— *Baba Yaga: The Wild Witch of the East in Russian Fairy Tale*, trans. and ed. by Sibelan Forrester (Jackson: Mississippi University Press, 2013)

Ager, Rob, 'Rob Ager's Take on the Room 237 Controversy', *Ager on Film*, 17 October 2013 <www.collativelearning.com/ageronfilm/?p=156> [accessed 2 December 2016]

Ahlberg, Jeremiah L., 'Rousseau and the Original Sin', *Revista Portuguesa de Filosofia*, 57 (2001), 773–90

Aldana Reyes, Xavier, *Body Gothic: Corporeal Transgression in Contemporary Literature and Horror Film* (Cardiff: University of Wales Press, 2014)

—— *Horror Film and Affect: Towards a Corporeal Model of Viewership* (New York and London: Routledge, 2016)

Allderidge, Patricia, *Richard Dadd* (London: Academy Editions, 1974)

Aloi, Giovanni, 'Marcus Coates – Becoming Animal', *Antennae*, 4 (2007), 18–20

—— 'Different Becomings', *Art & Research*, 4.1 (2011), 1–10

—— *Art & Animals* (London: I.B. Tauris, 2012)

Altman, Rick, *Silent Film Sound* (New York: Columbia University Press, 2004)

Andermahr, Sonya, and Lawrence Phillips, *Angela Carter: New Critical Readings* (London and New York: Bloomsbury, 2014)

Anderson, Steve, '*True Blood* Title Sequence', *Critical Commons* (2010) <http://criticalcommons.org/Members/ironman28/clips/trueBloodTitleSequence.mo/view> [accessed 10 June 2011]

Andrews, Max, 'Marcus Coates and Other Animals', *Picture This* (2009) <www.picture-this.org.uk/library/essays1/2007/marcus-coates-and-other-animals> [accessed 1 February 2016]

Anghelides, Peter, *Kursaal* (London: BBC Books, 1998)

[Arbuthnot, John,] *It Cannot Rain But it Pours* (London: J. Roberts, 1726)

Armitt, Lucie, 'The Fragile Frames of *The Bloody Chamber*', in *The Infernal Desires of Angela Carter: Fiction, Femininity, Feminism*, ed. by Joseph Bristow and Trev Lynn Broughton (London and New York: Longman, 1997), pp. 88–99

–––– 'Twentieth-century Gothic', in *Terror and Wonder: The Gothic Imagination*, ed. by Dale Townshend (London: British Library, 2014), pp. 170–1

Armstrong, Kelley, *Bitten*, Women of the Underworld, 1 (London: Time Warner, 2001)

Arnds, Peter, *Lycanthropy in German Literature* (Basingstoke: Palgrave Macmillan, 2015)

Aroles, Serge, *Marie-Angélique (Haut-Mississippi, 1712–Paris, 1775): Survie et résurrection d'une enfant perdue dix années en forêt* (Bonneuil-sur-Marne: Terre Editions, 2004)

––– *L'Enigme des Enfants-Loups: Une certitude biologique mais un déni des archives, 1304–1954* (Paris: Publibook, 2007)

––– 'L'énigme des enfants-Loups', *Loup.org*, 8 January 2008 <www.loup.org/spip/L-enigme-des-enfants-Loups,850.html> [accessed 3 December 2016]

Atwood, Margaret, *The Blind Assassin* (Toronto: McClelland and Stewart, 2000)

Auerbach, Nina, *Our Vampires, Ourselves* (Chicago: University of Chicago Press, 1997)

Bacchilega, Cristina, *Postmodern Fairy Tales: Gender and Narrative Strategies* (Philadelphia: University of Pennsylvania Press, 1997)

'Bad Gal Rihanna: The World's Wildest Style Icon', photographed by Mert Alas and Marcus Piggott, styled by Edward Enninful, *W*, September 2014, <www.wmagazine.com/people/celebrities/2014/08/rihanna-wild-style-icon/photos/slide/1> [accessed 27 July 2016]

Baker, Steve, *Picturing the Beast*, 2nd edn (Urbana and Chicago: University of Illinois Press, 2001)

––– 'Sloughing the Human', in *Zoontologies: The Question of the Animal*, ed. by Cary Wolfe (Minneapolis and London: University of Minnesota Press, 2003), pp. 147–64

Baring-Gould, Sabine, *The Book of Were-wolves: Being an Account of a Terrible Superstition* (London: Smith, Elder and Co., 1865)

Barnes, Djuna, *Nightwood* (1936; London: Faber and Faber, 1985)

Barnes, Jennifer Lynn, *Raised by Wolves* (London: Quercus, 2010)

Barnes, Sara, and Andrew Patrizio, 'Darwin on the Threshold of the Visible: Contemporary Art and Evolution', in *The Art of Evolution: Darwin, Darwinisms, and Visual Culture*, ed. by Barbara Larson and Fae Brauer (Hanover, NH, and London: University Press of New England, 2009), pp. 288–312

Batty, Holly, 'Harry Potter and the (Post)human Animal Body', *Bookbird: A Journal of International Children's Literature*, 53.1 (2015), 24–37

Beer, Gillian, *Darwin's Plots: Evolutionary Narrative in Darwin, George Elliot and Nineteenth-entury Fiction*, 3rd edn (Cambridge: Cambridge University Press, 2009)

Bentham, Jeremy, 'Interview with John Nathan-Turner', *Doctor Who Monthly*, no. 51, April 1981, pp. 29–33

Benzaquén, Adriana S., *Encounters with Wild Children: Temptation and Disappointment in the Study of Human Nature* (Montreal: McGill-Queen's University Press, 2006)

Beresford, Matthew, *The White Devil: The Werewolf in European Culture* (London: Reaktion, 2013)

Berger, John, 'Why Look at Animals', in *About Looking* (London: Bloomsbury Publishing, 1980), pp. 3–28

—— *Why Look at Animals?* (London: Penguin Books, 2009)

Bergson, Henri, *Laughter: An Essay on the Meaning of the Comic*, trans. by Cloudesley Brereton and Fred Rothwell (New York: Macmillan Company, 1914)

Berry, Liz, *Black Country* (London: Chatto and Windus, 2014)

—— 'How I Did It: "Sow"', *Poetry School: Campus* <http://campus.poetryschool.com/sow/> [accessed 1 September 2015]

—— 'Interview by Lily Blacksell', *PracCrit*, 4 (August 2015) <www.praccrit.com/interviews/pig-wood-interview-by-lily-blacksell/> [accessed 2 September 2015]

Bettelheim, Bruno, *The Uses of Enchantment: The Meaning and Importance of Fairy Tales* (London: Penguin Books, 1991)

Bewell, Alan J., 'Wordsworth's Primal Scene: Retrospective Tales of Idiots, Wild Children, and Savages', *ELH*, 50.2 (1983), 321–46

Bhattacharjee, Yudhijit, 'A Pack of …?', *Science*, 319.5869 (14 March 2008), 1467, DOI: <http://dx.doi.org/10.1126/science.319.5869.1467b> [accessed 1 November 2018]

Black, Max, *Models and Metaphors: Studies in Language and Philosophy* (Ithaca, NY: Cornell University Press, 1962)

Blake, Michael, *Dances with Wolves* (New York: Fawcett Gold Medal, 1988)

Blécourt, Willem de, *Werewolf Histories*, Palgrave Historical Studies in Witchcraft and Magic (Basingstoke: Palgrave Macmillan, 2015)

Bodart, Joni Richards, *They Suck, They Bite, They Eat, They Kill: The Psychological Meaning of Supernatural Monsters in Young Adult Fiction* (Lanham, MD: Scarecrow, 2012)

Boddice, Rob, 'Introduction', in *Anthropocentrism: Humans, Animals, Environments*, ed. by Rob Boddice (Leiden: Koninklijke Brill NV, 2011), pp. 1–18

Booy, Miles, *Love and Monsters: The Doctor Who Experience, 1979 to the Present* (London: I.B. Tauris, 2012)

Boss, Pete, 'Vile Bodies and Bad Medicine', *Screen*, 27.1 (1986), 14–24

Botting, Fred, *Limits of Horror: Technology, Bodies, Gothic* (Manchester: Manchester University Press, 2011)

Bouchard, Serge, *Quinze lieux communs les armes* (Montreal: Boréal, 1993)

Boyle, T.C., *Wild Child and Other Stories* (London: Bloomsbury, 2011)

'Brand: Ralph Lauren', *Project Just*, 7 April 2016 <http://projectjust.com/brand_ralphlauren/> [accessed 27 July 2017]

Bremmer, J.N., 'Romulus and Remus and the Foundation of Rome', Roman Myth and Mythography special issue, *Institute of Classical Studies Bulletin*, 52 (July 1987), 45–98

Bristow, Joseph, and Trev Lynn Broughton, eds., *The Infernal Desires of Angela Carter: Fiction, Femininity, Feminism* (London and New York: Longman, 1997)

Brodski, Michael, 'The Cinematic Representation of the Wild Child: Considering Truffaut's *L'Enfant Sauvage*', *Gothic Studies*, 21.1 (May 2019)

Broglio, Ron, *Surface Encounters: Thinking with Animals and Art* (Minneapolis: University of Minnesota Press, 2011)

Brontë, Charlotte, *Jane Eyre*, ed. by Sally Minogue (1847; Ware: Wordsworth, 1999)

Brophy, Philip, 'Horrality – The Textuality of Contemporary Horror Films', *Screen*, 27.1 (1986), 2–13

Brown, G.J., 'A Historian Looks at 1 Timothy 2:11–14', *Priscilla Papers*, 26.3 (2012), 7–11

Browning, Robert, *The Ring and the Book*, ed. by Richard Altick (Harmondsworth: Penguin, 1971)

Buchloh, Benjamin, 'Twilight of an Idol', in *Joseph Beuys: The Reader*, ed. by Claudia Mesch and Viola Michely (London and New York: I.B. Tauris, 2007), pp. 109–26

Buffon, Georges-Louis, Leclerc, Comte de, *Barr's Buffon. Buffon's Natural History*, trans. by James Smith Barr, 10 vols (1749–88; London: H. D. Symonds, 1797)

—— *Natural History, General and Particular*, trans. by William Smellie, 20 vols (London: T. Cadell and W. Davies, 1812)

Buller, Henry, 'Safe from the Wolf: Biosecurity, Biodiversity, and Competing Philosophies of Nature', *Environment and Planning*, 40 (2008), 1583–97

Burgess, Melvin, *The Cry of the Wolf* (London: Andersen Press, 1990)

Burningham, Kate, and Geoff Cooper, 'Being Constructive: Social Constructionism and the Environment', *Sociology*, 33.2 (1999), 297–316

Butler, David, ed., *Time and Relative Dissertations in Space: Critical Perspectives on Doctor Who* (Manchester: Manchester University Press, 2007)

Buxton, Richard, 'Wolves and Werewolves in Greek Thought', in *Interpretations of Greek Mythology*, ed. by Jan Bremmer (London: Routledge, 1987), pp. 6–79

Bynum, Caroline Walker, 'Shape and Story: Metamorphosis in the Western Tradition' (1999 Jefferson Lecture), transcript of lecture, *National Endowment for the Humanities*, <www.neh.gov/news/press-release/1999-03-22> [accessed 2 September 2015]

Campbell, Gilbert, 'The White Wolf of Kostopchin', in *Terrifying Transformations: An Anthology of Victorian Werewolf Fiction*, ed. by Alexis Easley and Shannon Scott (Kansas City, MO: Valancourt Books, 2013), pp. 135–68

Campbell, SueEllen, Gregory McNamee and Gary Wockner, eds, *Comeback Wolves: Western Writers Welcome the Wolf Home* (Boulder, CO: Johnson Books, 2005)

Candland, Douglas Keith, *Feral Children and Clever Animals: Reflections on Human Nature* (Oxford: Oxford University Press, 1993)

Carter, Angela, *The Bloody Chamber and Other Stories*, new edn (1979; London: Vintage, 1995)

—— *The Sadeian Woman: An Exercise in Cultural History* (1979; London: Virago, 2000)

—— *Shaking a Leg: Collected Journalism and Writings* (London: Vintage, 2013)

—— 'Peter and the Wolf', in *Black Venus* (1985; London: Vintage, 2015), pp. 81–92

Chandler, Robert, ed., *Russian Magic Tales: From Pushkin to Platonov* (London and New York: Penguin, 2012)

Chapman, James, *Inside the TARDIS* (London: I.B. Tauris, 2013)

Charles, Alec, 'The Ideology of Anachronism: Television, History and the Nature of Time', in David Butler, ed., *Time and Relative Dissertations in Space: Critical Perspectives on Doctor Who* (Manchester: Manchester University Press, 2007), pp. 108–22

Charnas, Suzy McKee, 'Boobs', in *Children of the Night: Stories of Ghosts, Vampires, and 'Lost Children'*, ed. by Martin H. Greenberg (Nashville: Cumberland House, 1999), pp. 11–35

Chesher, Greer, 'A Testimony of Wolves', in *Comeback Wolves: Western Writers Welcome the Wolf Home*, ed. by SueEllen Campbell, Gregory McNamee and Gary Wockner (Boulder, CO: Johnson Books, 2005), pp. 100–4

'Chukchi', Jimmy Nelson <www.beforethey.com/tribe/chukchi> [accessed 11 July 2016]

Clayton, George Wickham, 'Bearing Witness to a Whole Bunch of Murders: The Aesthetics of Perspective in the *Friday the 13th* Films', unpublished thesis (2013). Roehampton University. Available at: <http://roehampton.openrepository.com/roehampton/handle/10142/302655>

Clover, Carol J., *Men Women and Chainsaws: Gender in the Modern Horror Film* (London: BFI Publishing, 1992)

Coates, Marcus, *Journey to the Lower World* (Newcastle-upon-Tyne: Platform Projects and Morning Star, 2005)

—— *UR ... A Practical Guide to Unconscious Reasoning* (London: Book Works and Create London, 2014)

Coates, Marcus, and Valerie Smith, 'Marcus Coates in Conversation with Valerie Smith', in *Marcus Coates*, ed. by Marcus Coates, Anthony Spira and Rosalind Horne (London: Koenig Books, 2016), pp. 17–26

Coates, Peter, *Nature: Western Attitudes since Ancient Times* (Berkeley: University of California Press, 1998)

Cocks, Geoffrey, *The Wolf at the Door* (New York: Peter Lang, 2004)

Codinha, Alessandra, 'Ralph Lauren Fall 2015 RTW', *Vogue*, 19 February 2015 <www.vogue.com/fashion-week-review/10540687/ralph-lauren-fall-2015-rtw/> [accessed 11 July 2016]

Cohen, Jeffrey Jerome, ed., *Monster Theory: Reading Culture* (Minneapolis and London: University of Minnesota Press, 1996)

Cohen, Jeffrey J., 'The Werewolf's Indifference', *Studies in the Age of Chaucer*, 34 (2012), 351–6

Coleridge, Samuel Taylor, *The Notebooks of Samuel Taylor Coleridge, 1804–1818*, vol. 3, ed. by Kathleen Coburn (London: Routledge, 1973)

—— *Poems*, ed. by John Beer (London: Everyman, 1993)

Condillac, Étienne, Bonnot, Abbé de, *Essay on the Origin of Human Knowledge*, ed. and trans. by Hans Aarsleff, Cambridge Texts in the History of Philosophy (1746; Cambridge: Cambridge University Press, 2001)

Connor, Bernard, *History of Poland* (London, 1698)
Corry, Stephen, 'Turning a Blind Eye to Pure Old Vibrations', *Truthout*, 1 June 2014 <www.truth-out.org/opinion/item/23986-turning-a-blind-eye-to-pure-old-vibrations> [accessed 10 July 2016]
Coudray, Chantal Bourgault du, 'The Cycle of the Werewolf: Romantic Ecologies of Selfhood in Popular Fantasy', *Australian Feminist Studies*, 18.40 (2003), 57–72
—— *The Curse of the Werewolf: Fantasy, Horror and the Beast Within* (London and New York: I.B. Tauris, 2006)
Crawford, Joseph, *The Twilight of the Gothic: Vampire Fiction and the Rise of the Paranormal Romance*, Gothic Literary Studies (Cardiff: University of Wales Press, 2014)
Creed, Barbara, '*Ginger Snaps*: The Monstrous Feminine as *femme animale*', in *She-wolf: A Cultural History of Female Werewolves*, ed. by Hannah Priest (Manchester: Manchester University Press, 2015), pp. 180–95
Cremer, Andrea, *Nightshade* (London: Atom, 2010)
Cronon, William, 'The Trouble with Wilderness or, Getting Back to the Wrong Nature', *Environmental History*, 1.1 (1996), 7–28
Crozier, Lorna, *Whetstone* (Toronto: McLelland and Stewart, 2005)
Cull, Laura, 'Affect in Deleuze, Hijikata, and Coates: The Politics of Becoming-Animal in Performance', *Journal of Dramatic Theory and Criticism*, 26.2 (2012), 189–203
—— *Theatres of Immanence: Deleuze and the Ethics of Performance* (Basingstoke: Palgrave Macmillan, 2012)
Curran, Stuart, 'Mary Robinson's *Lyrical Tales* in context', in *Revisioning Romanticism: British Women Writers, 1776-1837*, ed. by Carol Shiner Wilson and Joel Haefner (Philadelphia: University of Pennsylvania Press, 1994), pp. 17–35
Darlington, David, 'You're Killing My Lesbian Subtext …!!', interview with Rona Munro, *DeejSaint*, 25 November 2007 <http://web.archive.org/web/20110604155734/http://www.btinternet.com/~david.darlington/rona2007.html> [accessed 30 June 2017]
Darwin, Charles, *The Origin of Species* (London: John Murray, 1859)
Le Dauphiné Libéré, 'Franck Michel explique pourquoi il a tué le loup', *Loup.org*, 18 February 2009 <www.loup.org/spip/Franck-Michel-explique-pourquoi-il,955.html> [accessed 3 December 2016]
Dawson, Jill, *Wild Boy* (London: Sceptre, 2003)
Day, Aidan, *Angela Carter: The Rational Glass* (Manchester and New York: Manchester University Press, 1998)
Dearborn, Kerry, 'Bridge over the River Why: The Imagination as a Way to Meaning', *North Wind: A Journal of George MacDonald Studies*, 16 (1997), 29–40; 45–6
'Definitions of SF', in *The Encyclopedia of Science Fiction*, ed by Brian Stableford, Peter Nicholls and John Clute (London: Orbit, 1999), 311–14
Defoe, Daniel, *Mere Nature Delineated, or a body without a soul* (London: T. Warner, 1726)
Defonseca, Misha, *Misha: A Mémoire of the Holocaust Years* (Boston: Mt Ivy Press, 1997)
Deleuze, Gilles, and Félix Guattari, *A Thousand Plateaus*, trans. by Brian Massumi (1980; London and New York: Bloomsbury, 2013)

Derrida, Jacques, 'The Animal That Therefore I Am (More to Follow)', in *The Animal That Therefore I Am*, trans. by David Willis (New York: Fordham University Press, 2008), pp. 1–51

Devlin-Glass, Frances, and Lyn McCredden, eds, *Feminist Poetics of the Sacred: Creative Suspicions* (New York: Oxford University Press, 2001)

Dicks, Terrance, *Doctor Who – Inferno* (London: Target, 1984)

Dijkstra, Bram, *Idols of Perversity: Fantasies of Feminine Evil in Fin-de-Siècle Culture* (Oxford: Oxford University Press, 1986)

Dimovitz, Scott A., *Angela Carter: Surrealist, Psychologist, Moral Pornographer* (Abingdon: Routledge, 2016)

Donovan, Josephine, 'Animal Rights and Feminist Theory', in *Ecofeminism: Women, Animals, Nature*, ed. by Greta Gaard (Philadelphia: Temple University Press, 1993), pp. 167–94

Douglas, Adam, *The Beast Within: A History of the Werewolf* (London: Chapmans, 1992)

Douthwaite, Julia V., *The Wild Girl, Natural Man, and the Monster: Dangerous Experiments in the Age of Enlightenment* (Chicago, IL, and London: University of Chicago Press, 2002)

Drain, Kelsey, 'Ralph Lauren Launches Fall 2015 Ad Campaign', *Fashion Times*, 13 July 2015 <www.fashiontimes.com/articles/22415/20150713/ralph-lauren-launches-fall-2015-ad-campaign.htm> [accessed 11 July 2016]

Duncan, Glen, *The Last Werewolf* (Edinburgh: Canongate, 2012)

Dundes, Alan, ed., *Red Riding Hood: A Casebook* (Madison: University of Wisconsin Press, 1989)

Eagleton, Terry, 'Culture and Nature', in *The Idea of Culture*, Blackwell Manifestos (Oxford: Blackwell, 2000), pp. 87–111

Easley, Alexis, and Shannon Scott, eds, *Terrifying Transformations: An Anthology of Victorian Werewolf Fiction* (Kansas City, MO: Valancourt Books, 2013)

Edgeworth, Maria, and Richard Lovell Edgeworth, *Practical Education*, 2 vols (London: J. Johnson, 1798)

Eigen, Joel, 'James Hadfield', *ODNB Online*, <www.oxforddnb.com/view/article/41013> [accessed 23 November 2015]

Elferen, Isabella van, *Gothic Music: The Sounds of the Uncanny* (Cardiff: University of Wales Press, 2012)

Eliade, Mircea, *Shamanism: Archaic Techniques of Ecstasy*, trans. by Willard R. Trask (London: Routledge & Kegan Paul, 1964)

Ellis-Etchison, John W., '"But not every question has a good answer": Baba Yaga as Embodied Wisdom in Slavic Folk and Fairy Tales', in *Turning Points and Transformations: Essays on Language, Literature and Culture*, ed. by Christine DeVine and Marie Hendry (Cambridge: Cambridge University Press, 2011), pp. 75–92

An Enquiry How The Wild Youth Lately Taken in the Woods Near Hanover (and now brought over to England) Could Be Left, and By What Creature He Could Be Suckled (London: H. Parker, 1726)

The Epic of Gilgamesh, trans. by Maureen Gallery Kovacs (Stanford, CA: Stanford University Press, 1989)

European Commission, *Status, Management and Distribution of Large Carnivores – Bear, Lynx, Wolf and Wolverine* (2013) <http://ec.europa.eu/environment/nature/conservation/species/carnivores/pdf/task_1_part2_species_country_reports.pdf> [accessed 21 August 2017]

European Union Directive, *Habitats Directive: 92/r43 EEC of 21 May* (1992) <http://eur-lex.europa.eu/legal-content/en/TXT/?uri=CELEX%3A31992L0043> [accessed 6 September 2017]

Evernden, Neil, *The Social Creation of Nature* (Baltimore: The Johns Hopkins University Press, 1992)

Ferguson, Gary, and Douglas W. Smith, *Decade of the Wolf: Returning the Wild to Yellowstone* (Guilford, CT: Lyons Press, 2005)

Feuerbach, Anselm von, *Casper Hause. An Account of an individual kept in a dungeon, separated from all communication with the world, from early childhood to about the age of seventeen* (London: Simpkin and Marshall, 1833)

Fiamengo, Janice Anne, ed., *Other Selves: Animals in the Canadian Literary Imagination* (Ottawa: University of Ottawa Press, 2007)

Fisher, Nora, 'The Last Irish Wolf', *The Irish Naturalist's Journal*, 5.2 (March 1934), 41

Forrester, Sibelan, 'The Wild Witch of the East', in *Russian Magic Tales from Pushkin to Platonov*, ed. by Robert Chandler (New York: Penguin, 2012), pp. 419–33

France, Marie de, 'Bisclavret', in *The Lais of Marie de France*, trans. by Glyn S. Burgess and Keith Busby (London: Penguin, 1999)

Franck, Kaja, '"Something that is either werewolf or vampire": Interrogating the Lupine Nature of Bram Stoker's *Dracula*', in *Werewolves, Wolves and the Gothic*, ed. by Robert McKay and John Millar, Gothic Literary Studies (Cardiff: University of Wales Press, 2017), pp. 135–52

Franck, Kaja, and Sam George, 'Contemporary Werewolves', in *Twenty-first-Century Gothic: An Edinburgh Companion*, ed. by Maisha Wester and Xavier Aldana Reyes (Edinburgh: Edinburgh University Press, 2019), pp. 144–57

Franklin, Adrian, *Nature and Social Theory* (London: Sage, 1992)

Frayling, Christopher, *Inside the Bloody Chamber: On Angela Carter, the Gothic, and Other Weird Tales* (London: Oberon, 2015)

Freud, Sigmund, *Civilisation and Its Discontents*, trans. by James Strachey (1930; New York: Norton, 1961)

—— 'From the History of an Infantile Neurosis' [1918], in *The 'Wolfman' and Other Cases*, trans. by Louise Adey Huish (London: Penguin, 2002), pp. 205–320

Fried, Michael, 'Art and Objecthood', in *Art and Objecthood* (Chicago: University of Chicago Press, 1998), pp. 148–68

Frost, Brian, *The Essential Guide to Werewolf Literature* (Madison: The University of Wisconsin Press, 2003)

Fudge, Erica, 'Book Review of Dorothee Brantz, *Beastly Natures: Animals and Humans and the Study of History*', *The American Historical Review*, 116.4 (2011), 1074–5
Gaard, Greta, 'Children's Environmental Literature: From Ecocriticism to Ecopedagogy', *Neohelicon*, 36 (2009), 321–34
Gaard, Greta, ed., *Ecofeminism: Women, Animals, Nature* (Philadelphia: Temple University Press, 1993)
Gabler, Neal, *Walt Disney: The Triumph of the American Imagination* (New York: Alfred Knopf, 2006)
Garber, Marjorie, *Vested Interests: Cross-dressing and Cultural Anxiety* (London: Penguin, 1993)
Gelder, Ken, *Reading the Vampire* (London: Routledge, 1994)
George, Sam, 'How Long Have We Believed in Vampires?', *The Conversation*, 27 October 2017 <https://theconversation.com/how-long-have-we-believed-in-vampires-85639> [accessed 3 July 2018]
George, Sam, and Bill Hughes, eds, *Open Graves, Open Minds: Representations of the Undead from the Enlightenment to the Present Day* (Manchester: Manchester University Press, 2013)
—— *Gothic Studies*, Special Issue: Werewolves and Wildness, 21.1 (May 2019)
Gerstein, Mordicai, *Victor: A Novel Based on the Life of the Savage of Aveyron* (New York: Farrar, Straus & Giroux, 1998)
Gesell, Arnold, *Wolf Child and Human Child* (1940; London: Scientific Book Club, 1942)
Giaimo, Cara, 'The ATU Fable Index: Like the Dewey Decimal System, But with More Ogres', *Atlas Obscura*, 14 June 2017 <www.atlasobscura.com/articles/aarne-thompson-uther-tale-type-index-fables-fairy-tales> [accessed 19 April 2019]
Gifford, Terry, *Pastoral*, New Critical Idiom (London and New York: Routledge, 1999)
Godwin, William, 'On Choice of Reading', in *The Enquirer: Reflections on Education, Manners and Literature* (London: G.G. and J. Johnson, 1797), pp. 134–5
Goldenberg, Suzanne, 'Montana and Idaho Plan Open-season Public Wolf Hunt', *Guardian*, 9 July 2009 <www.theguardian.com/environment/2009/jul/09/wolf-hunting> [accessed 9 December 2016]
Goldsmith, Oliver, *A History of the Earth and Animated Nature*, 6 vols (London: F. Wingrave; J. Johnson, 1805)
Goscilo, Helena, 'Introduction', in *Politicizing Magic: An Anthology of Russian and Soviet Fairy Tales*, ed. by Marina Balin, Helena Groscilo and Mark Lipovetsky (Evanston, IL: Northwestern University Press, 2005), pp. 5–21
Gottschall, Jonathan, *The Storytelling Animal* (New York: Houghton Mifflin, 2013)
Gradinaru, Olga, 'Myth and Rationality in Russian Popular Fairy Tales', *Echinox Journal*, 17 (2009), 315–22
Graves, Will N., *Wolves in Russia: Anxiety through the Ages* (Calgary, Alberta: Detselig Enterprises, 2007)

Gray, Scott, Martin Geraghty and David A. Roach, 'Bad Blood', Part 1, *Doctor Who Magazine*, no. 338, 7 January 2004, pp. 36–42

—— 'Bad Blood', Part 2, *Doctor Who Magazine*, no. 339, 4 February 2004, pp. 36–42

—— 'Bad Blood', Part 3, *Doctor Who Magazine*, no. 340, 3 March 2004, pp. 34–40

—— 'Bad Blood', Part 4, *Doctor Who Magazine*, no. 341, 31 March 2004, pp. 19–25

—— 'Bad Blood', Part 5, *Doctor Who Magazine*, no. 342, 28 April 2004, pp. 29–36

Greysmith, David, *Richard Dadd* (London: Studio Vista, 1973)

Grimm, Jacob and Wilhelm, *Kinder- und Hausmächen* (Berlin: Realschulbuchhandlung, 1812)

—— *Grimm's Complete Fairy Tales* (Garden City: International Collectors Library, 1900)

—— *Selected Tales*, trans. by Joyce Crick (Oxford: Oxford University Press, World's Classics, 2005)

Groom, Nick, *The Gothic: A Very Short Introduction* (Oxford: Oxford University Press, 2012)

GrrlScientist, 'How Wolves Change Rivers: Video', *Guardian*, 3 March 2014 <www.theguardian.com/science/grrlscientist/2014/mar/03/how-wolves-change-rivers> [accessed 18 September 2015]

Gruen, Lori, 'Dismantling Oppression: An Analysis of the Connection between Women and Animals', in *Ecofeminism: Women, Animals, Nature*, ed. by Greta Gaard (Philadelphia: Temple University Press, 1993), pp. 60–91

Guerrini, Anita, 'Animal Experiments and Antivivisection Debate in the 1820s', in *Frankenstein's Science: Experimentation and Discovery in Romantic Culture, 1780–1830*, ed. by Christa Knellwold and Jane Goodall (Aldershot: Ashgate, 2008), pp. 71–86

Gutenberg, Andrea, 'Shape-shifters from the Wilderness: Werewolves Roaming the Twentieth Century', in *The Abject of Desire: The Aestheticization of the Unaesthetic in Contemporary Literature and Culture*, ed. by Konstanze Kutzbach and Monika Mueller (Amsterdam and New York: Rodopi, 2007), pp. 149–80

Habermas, Jürgen, 'What Is Universal Pragmatics?', in *On the Pragmatics of Communication*, ed. by Maeve Cooke (Oxford: Polity, 1999), pp. 21–103

Halberstam, Judith, *Skin Shows: Gothic Horror and the Technology of Monsters* (Durham, NC, and London: Duke University Press, 1995)

Halfyard, Janet K., 'Love, Death, Curses, and Reverses (in E Minor): Music, Gender, and Identity in *Buffy the Vampire Slayer* and *Angel*', in *Music, Sound, and Silence in Buffy the Vampire Slayer*, ed. by Paul Attinello, Janet K. Halfyard, and Vanessa Knights (Farnham: Ashgate, 2010), pp. 15–32

Hall, Donald, ed., *Claims for Poetry* (Ann Arbor: University of Michigan Press, 1982)

Haney, Jack, ed., *An Anthology of Russian Folktales*, trans. and ed. by Jack Haney (Armonk, NY: M.E. Sharpe, 2009)

Hansen, Elaine Tuttle, *Mother without Child: Contemporary Fiction and the Crisis of Motherhood* (Berkeley: University of California Press, 1997)

BIBLIOGRAPHY

Haraway, Donna, 'A Manifesto for Cyborgs: Science, Technology, and Social Feminism in the 1980s', in *Feminism/postmodernism*, ed. by Linda J. Nicholson (New York: Routledge, 1990)

Hardyng, John, *The Chronicle of John Hardyng*, ed. by Henry Ellis (1437–64; London: F.C. and J. Rivington, 1812)

Harris, Charlaine, *Club Dead*, The Southern Vampire Mysteries, 3 (London: Orion, 2003)

Harrison, Robert Pogue, *Forests: The Shadow of Civilization* (Chicago: University of Chicago Press, 1992)

Hayward, Philip, ed., *Terror Tracks: Music, Sound and Horror Cinema* (London and Oakville: Equinox, 2009)

Hearne, Betsy Gould, *Beauty and the Beast: Visions and Revisions of an Old Tale*, new edn (Chicago: University of Chicago Press, 1991)

Heinlein, Robert A. [as Anson MacDonald], 'By His Bootstraps', *Astounding Science Fiction*, October 1941, pp. 9–47

—— *The Menace from Earth* (Riverdale, NY: Baen Books, 1987)

Heller, Agnes, *The Theory of Need in Marx*, intro. by Stephen Bodington and Ken Coates, Radical Thinkers, 16 (London: Verso, 1976)

Hills, Matt, *Triumph of a Time Lord: Regenerating Doctor Who in the Twenty-first Century* (London: I.B. Tauris, 2010)

An Historical Account of the Discovery and Education of a Savage Man: Or, the First Developments, Physical and Moral, of the Young Savage Caught in the Woods Near Aveyron in the Year 1798 (London: Richard Phillips, 1802)

Hitchcock, Susan Tyler, *Mad Mary Lamb* (New York: W.W. Norton, 2005)

Hollander, Anne, *Seeing through Clothes* (1975; Berkeley and Los Angeles: University of California Press, 1993)

Horn, Gavin Van, 'The Making of a Wilderness Icon: Green Fire, Charismatic Species, and the Changing Status of Wolves in the United States', in *Animals and the Human Imagination: A Companion to Animal Studies*, ed. by Aaron Gross and Anne Vallely (New York: Columbia University Press, 2012), pp. 203–37

Hornaday, William, *The American Natural History* (New York: Charles Scribner's Sons, 1904)

—— *The Minds and Manners of Wild Animals* (New York: Charles Scribner's Sons, 1922)

Housman, Clemence, 'The Were-wolf', in *Terrifying Transformations: An Anthology of Victorian Werewolf Fiction*, ed. by Alexis Easley and Shannon Scott (Kansas City, MO: Valancourt Books, 2013), pp. 205–51

Housman, Laurence, 'Illustrations for Clemence Housman's The Were-wolf', in *Terrifying Transformations: An Anthology of Victorian Werewolf Fiction*, ed. by Alexis Easley and Shannon Scott (Kansas City, MO: Valancourt Books, 2013), pp. 333–49

Howell, Maggie, 'Wolves Do Not Kill for Sport. That Is a Fact', *Wolf Conservation Center*, 28 March 2016 <http://nywolf.org/wolves-do-not-kill-for-sport-that-is-a-fact/> [accessed 1 December 2016]

Howkins, Alun, 'The Commons, Enclosure, and Radical Histories', in *Structures and Transformations in Modern British History*, ed. by David Feldman and Jon Lawrence (Cambridge: Cambridge University Press, 2011), pp. 118–41

Hudson, Dale, 'Of Course There Are Werewolves and Vampires: True Blood and the Right to Rights for Other Species', *American Quarterly*, 65.3 (September 2013), 661–87

Hudson, Nicholas, 'Dialogue and the Origins of Language: Linguistic and Social Evolution in Mandeville, Condillac, and Rousseau', in *Compendious Conversations: The Method of Dialogue in the Early Enlightenment*, ed. by Kevin L. Cope (Frankfurt: Peter Lang, 1992), pp. 3–14

Hughes, Bill, '"But by Blood no Wolf Am I": Language and Agency, Instinct and Essence – Transcending Antinomies in Maggie Steifvater's *Shiver* Series', in *Werewolves, Wolves and the Gothic*, ed. by Robert McKay and John Miller (Cardiff: University of Wales Press, 2017), pp. 227–50

Hughes, Ted, *Birthday Letters* (London: Faber & Faber, 1998)

Hurley, Kelly, *The Gothic Body: Sexuality, Materialism, and Degeneration at the Fin de Siècle* (Cambridge: Cambridge University Press, 1996)

Ingram, Allan, *The Madhouse of Language* (London: Routledge, 1991)

'IUCN Red List of Threatened Species' <www.iucnredlist.org/details/3746/0> [accessed 11 February 2016]

Jacobs, Francis G., *Criminal Responsibility* (London: Weidenfeld and Nicolson, 1971)

Jacobs, Joseph, *English Fairy Tales* (London: David Nutt, 1890)

Jaggar, Alison M., *Feminist Politics and Human Nature* (Lanham, MD: Rowman and Littlefield, 1983)

Jameson, Fredric, *The Political Unconscious: Narrative as a Socially Symbolic Act* (London: Routledge, 1989)

Jarrar, Osama, 'Language, Ideology, and Fairy Tales: George MacDonald's Fairy Tales as a Social Critique of Victorian Norms of Sexuality and Sex Roles', *North Wind: A Journal of George MacDonald Studies*, 28 (2009), 33–49

Jenks, Andrew W., *Russia in a Box: Art and Identity in an Age of Revolution* (DeKalb: Northern Illinois University Press, 2005)

Jennings, Hope, 'Genesis and Gender: The Word, the Flesh and the Fortunate Fall in "Peter and the Wolf" and "Penetrating to the Heart of the Forest"', in *Angela Carter: New Critical Readings*, ed. by Sonya Andermahr and Lawrence Phillips (London and New York: Bloomsbury, 2014), pp. 165–75

Johns, Andreas, *Baba Yaga: The Ambiguous Mother and Witch of the Russian Folktale* (New York: Peter Lang, 2010)

Johnson, Brian, 'National Species: Ecology, Allegory, and Indigeneity in the Wolf Stories of Roberts, Seton, and Mowat', in *Other Selves: Animals in the Canadian Literary Imagination*, ed. by Janice Anne Fiamengo (Ottawa: University of Ottawa Press, 2007), pp. 333–52

Jones, Karen R., *Wolf Mountains: A History of Wolves along the Great Divide* (Calgary: University of Calgary Press, 2002)

—— 'Writing the Wolf: Canine Tales and North American Environmental-Literary Tradition', in *A Fairytale in Question: Historical Interactions between Humans and Wolves*, ed. by Patrick Masius and Jana Sprenger (Cambridge: The White Horse Press, 2015), pp. 175–202

Judd, Donald, 'Black, White and Gray', in *Donald Judd: Complete Writings: 1959–1975* (Nova Scotia and New York: The Press of the Nova Scotia College of Art and Design and New York University Press, 1975), pp. 117–19

—— 'Specific Objects', in *Donald Judd: Complete Writings 1959–1975* (Nova Scotia and New York: The Press of the Nova Scotia College of Art and Design and New York University Press, 1975), pp. 181–9

Kalof, Linda, 'The Shifting Iconography of Wolves over the Twentieth Century', in *A Fairytale in Question: Historical Interactions between Humans and Wolves*, ed. by Patrick Masius and Jana Sprenger (Cambridge: The White Horse Press, 2015), pp. 203–28

Karlin, Daniel, 'The Jungle Books: Introduction', *The Kipling Society* <www.kiplingsociety.co.uk/rg_jungle_intro.htm> [accessed 10 November 2018]

Kehr, Dave, review of *The Wolf Man* (1941), *The Chicago Reader*, 8 October 2008 <www.chicagoreader.com/chicago/the-wolf-man/Film?oid=1056197> [accessed 22 February 2016]

Kemmerer, Lisa, ed., *Sister Species: Women, Animals, and Social Justice* (Chicago: University of Illinois Press, 2011)

Kipling, Rudyard, *The Jungle Books*, ed. by W.W. Robson (1894, 1895; Oxford: Oxford University Press, 2008)

—— *The Two Jungle Books*, illus. by J. Lockwood Kipling, C.I.E., and W.H. Drake (London: Macmillan, 1926)

Klause, Annette Curtis, *Blood and Chocolate* (New York: Random House Children's Book, 1997)

Kliuchevskii, Vasili, and Marshall Shatz, *A Course of Russian History: The Time of Catherine the Great* (Armonk, New York: M.E. Sharpe, 1997)

Koetsier, Julius, and Charles Forceville, 'Embodied Identity in Werewolf Films of the 1980s', *Image & Narrative*, 15.1 (2014), 44–55

Kosinski, Jerzy, *The Painted Bird* (Boston: Houghton Mifflin, 1965)

Krasner, James, *The Entangled Eye: Visual Perception and the Representation of Nature in Post-Darwinian Narrative* (Oxford: Oxford University Press, 1992)

Krasniewicz, Louise, *Walt Disney: A Biography* (Santa Barbara: Greenwood, 2010)

Krauss, Rosalind, 'The Mind/Body Problem: Robert Morris in Series', in *Robert Morris: The Mind Body Problem*, ed. by Rosalind Krauss, Thomas Krens, David Anti and Maurice Berger (New York: Guggenheim Museum Publications, 1994), pp. 2–16

Kristeva, Julia, 'Revolution in Poetic Language', in *The Kristeva Reader*, ed. by Toril Moi (Oxford: Blackwell, 1986), pp. 89–136

Kuspit, Donald, 'Joseph Beuys: Between Showman and Shaman', in *Joseph Beuys: Diverging Critiques*, ed. by David Thistlewood (Liverpool: Liverpool University Press and Tate Gallery Liverpool, 1995), pp. 27–50

Lane, Harlan, *The Wild Boy of Aveyron* (Cambridge, MA: Harvard University Press, 1976)

Lane, Meghan, 'Who Was Peter the Wild Boy', *BBC News Magazine*, 8 August, 2011 <www.bbc.co.uk/news/magazine-14215171> [accessed 1 August 2015]

Lankester, Edwin Ray, *Degeneration: A Chapter in Darwinism* (London: Macmillan and Company, 1880)

Lau, Kimberly J., *Erotic Infidelities: Love and Enchantment in Angela Carter's The Bloody Chamber* (Detroit, MI: Wayne State University Press, 2014).

Laver, James, *Costume and Fashion: A Concise History* (London: Thames and Hudson, 1982)

Lawrence, Elizabeth A., 'Werewolves in Psyche and Cinema: Man-beast Transformation and Paradox', *Journal of American Culture*, 19.3 (fall 1996), 103–13

Leach, Edmund, *A Dictionary of Social Sciences* (London: Tavistock, 1964)

Leggatt, Judith, and Kristin Burnett, 'Biting Bella: Treaty Negotiation, Quileute History, and Why "Team Jacob" Is Doomed to Lose', in *Twilight & History*, ed. by Nancy R. Reagan (Hoboken, NJ: John Wiley & Sons, 2010), pp. 26–46

Lerner, Neil, ed., *Music in the Horror Film* (New York and London: Routledge, 2010)

Levine, George, *Darwin and the Novelists: Patterns of Science in Victorian Fiction* (Cambridge, MA: Harvard University Press, 1988)

Lévi-Strauss, Claude, *The Raw and the Cooked: Introduction to a Science of Mythology: 1*, trans. by John and Doreen Weightman (London: Jonathan Cape, 1970)

Levy, Alastair J., 'Marcus Coates', *Artvehicle 20* (2007) <www.artvehicle.com/events/94> [accessed 10 February 2016]

Lindow, John, *Norse Mythology: A Guide to the Gods, Heroes, Rituals, and Beliefs* (Oxford: Oxford University Press, 2001)

Linkin, Harriet Kramer, 'Isn't It Romantic? Carter's Bloody Revision of the Romantic Aesthetic in "The Erl-King"', *Contemporary Literature*, 35 (1994), 305–23

Linné, Carl von [Linnaeus], *Systema Naturae*, 10th edn (Stockholm, 1758)

Locke, John, *Some Thoughts Concerning Education*, ed. by the Rev. R.H. Quick (1693; Cambridge: Cambridge University Press, 1889)

—— *An Essay Concerning Human Understanding*, ed. by Roger Woolhouse (1689; Harmondsworth: Penguin, 1997)

London, Jack, *White Fang* (New York: Macmillan, 1906)

Lönngren, Ann-Sophie, *Following the Animal: Power, Agency, and Human–animal Transformations in Modern, Northern-European Literature* (Newcastle upon Tyne: Cambridge Scholars, 2015)

Lopez, Barry, *Of Wolves and Men* (London: Simon and Schuster, 1978)

Losure, Mary, *Wild Boy: The Real Life of the Savage of Aveyron* (Somerville, MA: Candlewick Press, 2013)

McCarthy, Cormac, *The Crossing* (New York: Alfred Knopf, 1994)

McCrum, Robert, 'To Hell and Back', *The Guardian*, 27 October 2018, pp. 32–4

MacDonald, George, *A Dish of Orts: Chiefly Papers on the Imagination and on Shakspere* (London: Sampson Low, Marston & Company, 1895)

—— *The Complete Fairy Tales*, ed. by U.C. Knoepflmacher (London: Penguin, 1999)
—— 'The History of Photogen and Nycteris: A Day and Night Märchen', in *The Complete Fairy Tales*, ed. by U.C. Knoepflmacher (London: Penguin, 1999), pp. 304-41
—— 'The Gray Wolf', in *Terrifying Transformations: An Anthology of Victorian Werewolf Fiction*, ed. by Alexis Easley and Shannon Scott (Kansas City, MO: Valancourt Books, 2013), pp. 112-21
McKay, Robert, and John Miller, eds, *Werewolves, Wolves and the Gothic* (Cardiff: University of Wales Press, 2017)
McLuhan, Eric, and Frank Zingrone, eds, *Essential McLuhan* (London: Taylor and Francis, 1997)
McLuhan, Marshall, *Understanding Media: The Extensions of Man* (Corte Madeira: Gingko Press, 2013)
McMahon-Coleman, Kimberley, and Roslyn Weaver, eds, *Werewolves and Other Shapeshifters in Popular Culture: A Thematic Analysis* (Jefferson, NC: McFarland, 2012)
McMahon-Coleman, Kimberley, and Roslyn Weaver, 'The Alpha Race: Racial and Social Politics of Shapeshifting', in *Werewolves and Other Shapeshifters in Popular Culture: A Thematic Analysis* (Jefferson, NC: McFarland, 2012), pp. 92-116
Macnaghten, Phil, and John Urry, *Contested Natures* (London: Sage, 1998)
Mahoney, Emma, 'Marcus Coates', in *British Art Show 6*, ed. by Alex Farquharson and Andrea Schlieker (London: Hayward Gallery Publishing, 2006), p. 216
Makinen, Merja, 'Angela Carter's "The Bloody Chamber" and the Decolonization of Feminine Sexuality', *Feminist Review*, 42 (autumn 1992, 2-15
Malson, Lucien, *Wolf Children and the Problem of Human Nature: With the Complete Text of the Wild Boy of Aveyron* (New York: Monthly Review Press, 1972)
Maltby, Richard, *Hollywood Cinema, Second Edition* (Oxford: Blackwell Publishing, 2003)
Manacorda, Francesco, and Ariella Yedgar, eds, *Radical Nature: Art and Architecture for a Changing Planet 1969-2009* (London: Koenig Books, 2009)
Mandeville, Bernard, *The Fable of the Bees; or, Private Vices, Publick Benefits*, ed. by F.B. Kaye, 2 vols (1705-34; Oxford: Clarendon Press, 1924; repr. Indianapolis: Liberty Fund, 1988)
Marcuse, Herbert, *Eros and Civilization: A Philosophical Inquiry into Freud*, new edn (London: Routledge, 1998)
Marryat, Frederick, 'The White Wolf of the Hartz Mountains', in *Terrifying Transformations: An Anthology of Victorian Werewolf Fiction*, ed. by Alexis Easley and Shannon Scott (Kansas City, MO: Valancourt Books, 2013), pp. 23-41
Martin, Philip, *Doctor Who - Mindwarp* (London: Target, 1989)
Marvin, Garry, 'Wolves in Sheep's (and Other's) Clothing', in *Beastly Natures: Animals, Humans, and the Study of History*, ed. by Dorothee Brantz (Charlottesville: University of Virginia Press, 2010), pp. 59-80
—— *Wolf* (London: Reaktion, 2012)
Marx, Karl, *Capital*, vol. 1, trans. by Ben Fowkes, intro. by Ernest Mandel (Harmondsworth: Penguin, 1976)

Marx, Karl, and Friedrich Engels, *The Communist Manifesto*, ed. by Gareth Stedman Jones (London: Penguin, 2002)

Mech, David, *The Wolf: The Ecology and Behavior of an Endangered Species* (Garden City, NY: The American Museum of Natural History, 1970; repr. Minneapolis: University of Minnesota Press, 2003)

—— 'Is Science in Danger of Sanctifying the Wolf?', *Biological Conservation*, 150 (2012), 143–9

Mech, L. David, and Luigi Boitani, eds, *Wolves: Behavior, Ecology, and Conservation* (Chicago: University of Chicago Press, 2003)

Mech, L. David, Douglas W. Smith, and Daniel R. McNulty, *Wolves on the Hunt: The Behavior of Wolves Hunting Wild Prey* (Chicago: University of Chicago Press, 2015)

Medoff, Rafael, 'Was Walt Disney Antisemitic?', *The David S. Wyman Institute for Holocaust Studies*, January 2014 <http://new.wymaninstitute.org/2014/01/was-walt-disney-antisemitic/> [accessed 30 November 2016]

Menzies, Sutherland, 'Hughes, the Wer-Wolf', etext at <http://gaslight.mtroyal.ab.ca/hugues.htm> [accessed 20 August 2015]. Originally published in *The Court Magazine and Monthly Critic, and the Lady's Magazine and Museum*, August 1838 (London: Dobbs and Co.), pp. 264–74

Mercier, Mrs Jerome, *The Last Wolf: A Story of England in the Fourteenth Century* (Grange: H.T. Mason, 1920)

Merrill, Jamie, 'Rewilding: Reintroduction Extinct Species Back to Britain Will Be "Enormous" Challenge, Study Finds', *The Independent*, 30 August 2015 <www.independent.co.uk/news/uk/home-news/rewilding-reintroduction-extinct-species-back-to-britain-will-be-enormous-challenge-study-finds-10478370.html> [accessed 30 August 2015]

Messenger, Jean Goodwin, *Hannah: From Dachau to the Olympics and Beyond* (Windsor, CO: White Pelican Press, 2005)

Metzger, Nadine, 'Battling Demons with Medical Authority: Werewolves, Physicians and Rationalization', *History of Psychiatry*, 24.3 (September 2013), 341–55

Meyer, Stephenie, *Twilight* (London: Atom, 2005)

—— *New Moon* (London: Atom, 2006)

—— *Eclipse* (London: Atom, 2007)

—— *Breaking Dawn* (London: Atom, 2008)

Michelson, Annette, 'Robert Morris – An Aesthetics of Transgression', in *Robert Morris*, ed. by Julia Bryan-Wilson (Cambridge, MA, and London: The MIT Press, 2013), pp. 7–50

Middleton, Arthur, 'Is the Wolf a Real American Hero?', *New York Times*, 9 March 2014 <www.nytimes.com/2014/03/10/opinion/is-the-wolf-a-real-american-hero.html?_r=1> [accessed 8 January 2016]

Midgley, Mary, *Animals and Why They Matter* (Athens: The University of Georgia Press, 1983)

Mills, Pat, John Wagner and Alan Gibbons, 'The Dogs of Doom', Part 1, *Doctor Who Weekly*, no. 27, 16 April 1980, pp. 3–7
—— 'The Dogs of Doom', Part 2, *Doctor Who Weekly*, no. 28, 23 April–5 June 1980, pp. 3–6
—— 'The Dogs of Doom', Part 3, *Doctor Who Weekly*, no. 29, 30 April 1980, pp. 3–6
—— 'The Dogs of Doom', Part 4, *Doctor Who Weekly*, no. 30, 7 May 1980, pp. 3–6
—— 'The Dogs of Doom', Part 5, *Doctor Who Weekly*, no. 31, 14 May 1980, pp. 3–7
—— 'The Dogs of Doom', Part 6, *Doctor Who Weekly*, no. 32, 21 May 1980, pp. 3–6
—— 'The Dogs of Doom', Part 7, *Doctor Who Weekly*, no. 33, 28 May 1980, pp. 3–6
—— 'The Dogs of Doom', Part 8, *Doctor Who Weekly*, no. 34, 5 June 1980, pp. 4–7
Milne, Anne, 'At The Precipice of Community: Feral Openness and the Work of Mary Robinson', *ABO: Interactive Journal for Women in the Arts, 1640–1830*, 2.1 (March 2012), DOI: <http://dx.doi.org/10.5038/2157-7129.2.1.2> [accessed 1 December 2018]
'Misha Defonseca: tricher avec les loups', *L'Express*, 29 February 2008 <www.lexpress.fr/culture/misha-defonseca-tricher-avec-les-loups_470661.html> [accessed 3 December 2016]
Mitts-Smith, Debra, *Picturing the Wolf in Children's Literature* (New York: Routledge, 2012)
Moi, Toril, 'Introduction', in *The Kristeva Reader*, ed. by Toril Moi (Oxford: Blackwell, 1986), pp. 1–22
Montesquieu, Charles-Louis de, Secondat, Baron de La Brède et de, *The Spirit of Laws*, 4 vols (1748; London: T. Evans, 1777)
Mooney, Darren, 'Non-review Review: *The Wolf Man* (1941)', *the movie blog*, 31 October 2012 <http://themovieblog.com/2012/10/31/non-review-review-the-wolf-man-1941/> [accessed 22 February 2016]
Moore, Kim, 'The Act of Transformation', *Poetry School: Campus* <www.poetryschool.com/courses-workshops/online/the-act-of-transformation.php> [accessed 2 September 2015]
—— *If We Could Speak Like Wolves* (Sheffield: Smith/Doorstop Books, 2012)
—— *The Art of Falling* (Bridgend: Seren, 2015)
Moran, Richard, 'Daniel M'Naughtan', *ODNB Online* (Oxford: Oxford University Press, 2008) <www.oxforddnb.com/view/article/39433> [accessed 23 November 2015]
Morris, Robert, 'Notes on Sculpture, Part 1', in *Continuous Project Altered Daily: The Writings of Robert Morris* (Cambridge, MA, and London: The MIT Press, 1993), pp. 1–10
—— 'Notes on Sculpture, Part 2', in *Continuous Project Altered Daily: The Writings of Robert Morris* (Cambridge, MA, and London: The MIT Press, 1993), pp. 11–21
Moss, Betty, 'Desire and the Female Grotesque in Angela Carter's "Peter and the Wolf"', in *Angela Carter and the Fairy Tale*, ed. by Danielle M. Roemer and Cristina Bacchilega (Detroit, MI: Wayne State University Press, 2001), pp. 187–203
Murie, Adolph, *The Wolves of Mount McKinley* (Seattle: University of Washington Press, 2001)
Mutch, David, 'A Russian Lacquer Revival: Artists Freed from State Interference Are Returning to Religious Themes', *Christian Science Monitor*, 30 November 1992, p. 10

Nagel, Thomas, 'What Is It Like to Be a Bat?', *Philosophical Review*, 83.4 (October 1974), 435–50

Neary, Lynn, '"Dog Boy": The Complicated Humanity of a Wild Child', *NPR Books*, 10 April 2010 <www.npr.org/templates/story/story.php?storyId=125781157> [accessed 3 December 2016]

Nelson, Jimmy, *Before They Pass Away* (Kempen: teNeues, 2013)

'Nenets', Jimmy Nelson <www.beforethey.com/tribe/nenets> [accessed 11 July 2016]

Newton, Michael, *Savage Girls and Wild Boys: A History of Feral Children* (London: Faber & Faber, 2003)

Novak, Maximillian E., 'The Wild Child Comes to Tea', in *The Wild Man Within: An Image in Western Thought from the Renaissance to Romanticism*, ed. by Edward Dudley and Maximillian E. Novak (Pittsburgh: University of Pittsburgh Press, 1972), pp. 183–221

Nykvist, Karin, 'The Body Project', in *Interdisciplinary Approaches to Twilight*, ed. by Mariah Larsson and Ann Steiner (Lund: Nordic Academic Press, 2011), pp. 29–46

Oates, Caroline, 'Metamorphosis & Lycanthropy in Franche-Compté, 1521–1643', in *Fragments for a History of the Human Body, Part 1*, ed. by Michel Feher, Ramona Naddaff and Nadia Tazi (New York: Zone Books, 1989), pp. 305–63

O'Connor, Flannery, 'Revelation', in *Literature*, ed. by X.J. Kennedy and Dana Gioia, 7th edn (Boston: Pearson, 2013), pp. 319–32

O'Connor, Ralph, *The Earth on Show: Fossils and the Poetics of Popular Science, 1802–1856* (Chicago and London: University of Chicago Press, 2007)

O'Donnell, Elliot, *Werewolves* (London: Methuen, 1912)

Ong, Walter J., *Orality and Literacy: The Technologizing of the Word* (London and New York: Routledge, 1982)

Osborn, Andrew, 'Siberian Boy, 7, Raised by Dogs after Parents Abandoned Him', *Independent*, 3 August 2004 <www.independent.co.uk/news/world/europe/siberian-boy-7-raised-by-dogs-after-parents-abandoned-him-555343.html> [accessed 3 December 2016]

Ostriker, Alicia, 'The Nerves of a Midwife: Contemporary American Women's Poetry, 1977', in *Claims for Poetry*, ed. by Donald Hall (Ann Arbor: University of Michigan Press, 1982), pp. 309–27

Otten, Charlotte, ed., *A Lycanthropy Reader: Werewolves in Western Culture* (New York: Syracuse University Press, 1986)

Otter, Chris, *The Victorian Eye: A Political History of Light and Vision in Britain 1800–1910* (London: University of Chicago Press, 2008)

Oxford Living Dictionaries <https://en.oxforddictionaries.com/definition/integument> [accessed 24 November 2018]

Paice, Kimberly, 'Box for Standing, 1961', in *Robert Morris: The Mind Body Problem*, ed. by Rosalind Krauss, Thomas Krens, David Anti and Maurice Berger (New York: Guggenheim Museum Publications, 1994), pp. 96–7

—— 'Columns 1961', in *Robert Morris: The Mind Body Problem*, ed. by Rosalind Krauss, Thomas Krens, David Anti and Maurice Berger (New York: Guggenheim Museum Publications, 1994), pp. 90–1

'A Particular Account of Peter the Wild Boy Extracted from the Parish Register at North Church, in the County of Hertford', *The Annual Register … 1784 and 1785* (London: J. Dodsley, 1787), pp. 43–5

Pascoe, Judith, Introduction, Mary Robison, *Selected Poems*, ed. by Judith Pascoe (Peterborough, Canada: Broadview Press, 2000), pp. 19–61

Peirse, Alison, *After Dracula: The 1930s Horror Film* (London: I.B. Tauris, 2013)

—— 'Dracula on Film, 1932–1959', in *A Cambridge Companion to Dracula*, ed. by Roger Luckhurst (Cambridge: Cambridge University Press, 2018), pp. 179–91

Perrault, Charles, *Histoires ou Contes du temps passé. Avec Moralitiés* (Paris: Barbin, 1697)

—— *Little Red Riding Hood, Cinderella, and Other Classic Fairy Tales of Charles Perrault*, ed. by Jack Zipes, trans. by Angela Carter (1977; London: Penguin Books, 2008)

—— 'Little Red Riding-Hood', in *The Complete Fairy Tales*, trans. by Christopher Betts (1697; Oxford: Oxford University Press, World's Classics, 2009)

Perry, Ben Edwin, *Studies in the Text History of the Life and Fables of Aesop* (Chicago: Scholars Press, 1981)

Perryman, Neil, 'Doctor Who and the Convergence of Media: A Case Study in "Transmedia Storytelling"', *Convergence: The International Journal of Research into New Media Technologies*, 14 (2008), 21–39

Peter the Wild Boy (Northchurch: St Mary's, 2012)

Phelps, Nicole, 'Fall 2015 Ready to Wear: Ralph Lauren', *Vogue*, 19 February 2015 <www.vogue.com/fashion-shows/fall-2015-ready-to-wear/ralph-lauren> [accessed 11 July 2016]

Platt, Marc, and Paul Vyse, 'Loop the Loup', *Doctor Who Yearbook 1994* (London: Marvel Comics, 1994), pp. 16–20

Plautus, *Asinaria: The One about the Asses*, trans. by John Henderson (Madison: University of Wisconsin Press, 2006)

Pluskowski, Aleksander, *Wolves and the Wilderness in the Middle Ages* (Woodbridge: The Boydell Press, 2006)

Pogue Harrison, Robert, *Forests: The Shadow of Civilization* (Chicago: University of Chicago Press, 1992)

'Posts Tagged "John Pertwee"', *The Doctor Who Interviews* <https://drwhointerviews.wordpress.com/tag/jon-pertwee/> [accessed 30 January 2016]

Priest, Hannah, '"Bogeysliche as a boye": Performing Sexuality in William of Palerne', in *Sexual Culture in the Literature of Medieval Britain*, ed. by Amanda Hopkins, Robert Allen Rouse and Cory James Rushton (Cambridge: D.S. Brewer, 2014)

—— 'I Was a Teenage She-wolf: Boobs, Blood and Sacrifice', in *She-wolf: A Cultural History of Female Werewolves*, ed. by Hannah Priest (Manchester: Manchester University Press, 2015), pp. 129–47

Priest, Hannah, ed., *She-wolf: A Cultural History of Female Werewolves* (Manchester: Manchester University Press, 2015)

Prichard, James Cowles, *A Treatise on Insanity and Other Disorders Affecting the Mind* (Philadelphia: Haswell, Barrington, and Haswell, 1837)

Prins, Herschel, *Offenders, Deviants or Patients?*, 2nd edn (London: Routledge, 1995)

Propp, Vladimir, *Morphology of the Folktale*, trans. by Laurence Scott, ed. by Louis A. Wagner (1928; Austin: University of Texas Press, 1968)

Punter, David, *Gothic Pathologies: The Text, the Body and the Law* (London: Macmillan Press, 1998)

—— *Postcolonial Imaginings: Fictions of a New World Order* (Edinburgh: Edinburgh University Press, 2000)

Punter, David, ed., *A New Companion to the Gothic* (Chichester: Wiley-Blackwell, 2012)

Rayner, Jacqueline, *Wolfsbane* (London: BBC Books, 2003)

Reece, Gregory L., 'Oh Grandmother, What Big Teeth You Have!', in *Creatures of the Night: In Search of Ghosts, Vampires, Werewolves and Demons* (London: I.B. Taurus, 2012), pp. 97–125

Reinhardt, Ilka, 'Current Situation of the Wolf in Europe – From a Scientific Perspective', *LUPUS: German Institute for Wolf Management and Research* (n. d.) <http://ec.europa.eu/environment/nature/conservation/species/carnivores/pdf/3_Reinhardt.pdf> [accessed 21 August 2018]

Reynolds, George W.M., *Wagner the Werewolf*, ed. by Dick Collins (Ware: Wordsworth, 2006)

Rhodes, Gary D., *Dracula* (Sheffield: Tomahawk Press, 2014)

Rice, Anne, *The Wolf Gift*, The Wolf Gift Chronicles, 1 (London: Arrow Books, 2010)

Richards, Justin, *Time Lord Fairy Tales* (London: BBC Books, 2015)

Richards Bodart, Joni, *They Suck, They Bite, They Eat, They Kill: The Psychological Meaning of Supernatural Monsters in Young Adult Fiction* (Plymouth: The Scarecrow Press, 2012)

Rigby, Kate, 'The Goddess Returns: Ecofeminist Reconfigurations of Gender, Nature and the Sacred', in *Feminist Poetics of the Sacred: Creative Suspicions*, ed. by Frances Devlin-Glass and Lyn McCredden (New York: Oxford University Press, 2001), pp. 23–54

Riley, Travis, 'Marcus Coates: Proxy Kate MacGarry Gallery, London', *Aesthetica*, 9 (2012) <www.aestheticamagazine.com/marcus-coates-proxy-kate-macgarry-gallery-london/> [accessed 16 November 2016]

Riordan, James, 'Russian Fairy Tales and Their Collectors', in *A Companion to the Fairy Tale*, ed. by Hilda Ellis Davidson and Anna Chaudri (Rochester, NY: D.S. Brewer, 2003), pp. 217–25

Robinson, Mary, *Selected Poems*, ed. by Judith Pascoe (Peterborough, Ontario: Broadview Press, 2000)

Robson, W.W., Introduction, Rudyard Kipling, *The Jungle Books*, ed. by W.W. Robson (Oxford: Oxford University Press, 1987), pp. xii–xxxiv

Rochère, Martine Hennard Dutheil de la, *Reading, Translating, Rewriting: Angela Carter's Translational Poetics* (Detroit: Wayne State University Press, 2013)

Roemer, Danielle M., and Cristina Bacchilega, eds, *Angela Carter and the Fairy Tale* (Detroit, MI: Wayne State University Press, 2001)

Romero, Simon, 'Native Americans Score Historic Wins in Midterms after Years of Efforts', *The New York Times*, 7 November 2018, paras 1–2 <www.nytimes.com/2018/11/07/us/elections/native-americans-congress-haaland-davids.html> [accessed 11 April 2019]

'Room 237', *IMDb* <www.imdb.com/title/tt2085910/> [accessed 30 November 2016]

Roosevelt, Theodore, *The Wilderness Hunter* (New York: G.P. Putnam's Sons, 1893)

Rosenblat, Herman, *Angel at the Fence: The True Story of a Love that Survived* (New York: Harper Collins, 2009)

Rossello, Diego Hernán, 'Hobbes and the Wolf-man: Melancholy and Animality in Modern Sovereignty', *New Literary History*, 43.2 (September 2012), pp. 255–79.

Rousseau, Jean-Jacques, *Emile: Or, On Education*, ed. by Allan Bloom (1763; New York: Basic Books, 1979)

—— *Essay on the Origin of Languages*, in *On the Origin of Language: Two Essays*, trans. by John H. Moran and Alexander Gode (Chicago: University of Chicago Press, 1986), pp. 5–74

—— *Discourse on the Origin of Inequality*, trans. by Franklin Phillip, ed. by Patrick Coleman (1755; Oxford: Oxford University Press, 1994)

—— 'Jean-Jacques Rousseau, Citizen of Geneva, to Christophe de Beaumont, Archbishop of Paris', 1762, in *Rousseau on Philosophy, Morality, and Religion*, ed. by Christopher Kelly (Hanover and London: Dartmouth College Press, 2007), pp. 162–226

Ruddell, Caroline, and Brigid Cherry, 'More than Cold and Heartless: The Southern Gothic Milieu of *True Blood*', in *True Blood: Investigating Vampires and Southern Gothic*, ed. by Brigid Cherry (London: I.B. Taurus, 2012), pp. 39–58

Ruddick, Sara, *Maternal Thinking: Toward a Politics of Peace* (New York: Ballantine Books, 1990)

Russell, W.M.S., and Clare Russell, 'The Social Biology of Werewolves', in *Animals in Folkore*, ed. by J.R. Porter and W.M.S. Russell (Ipswich and Cambridge: D.S. Brewer and Rowman & Littlefield for The Folklore Society), pp. 143–82

Ruwe, Donnelle, 'Guarding the British Bible for Rousseau: Sarah Trimmer, William Godwin, and the Pedagogical Periodical', *Children's Literature*, 29 (2001), 1–17

Samber, Robert, *Histories, or Tales of Past Times. By M. Perrault* (London: J. Pote, 1729)

Sandilands, Catriona, *The Good-natured Feminist: Ecofeminism and the Quest for Democracy* (Minneapolis: University of Minnesota Press, 1999)

'Save Western Wildlife' Facebook group <www.facebook.com/SaveWesternWildlife> [accessed 2 December 2016]

'Save Western Wildlife Is a Terrorist Organization' Facebook group <www.facebook.com/Save-Western-Wildlife-is-a-Terrorist-Organization-257292857733483/> [accessed 2 December 2016]

Schaeffer, Denise, 'Reconsidering the Role of Sophie in Rousseau's "Emile"', *Polity*, 30.4 (1998), 607–26

Sconduto, Leslie A., *Metamorphoses of the Werewolf: A Literary Study from Antiquity through the Renaissance* (Jefferson, NC and London: McFarland, 2008)

Scull, Andrew, ed., *The Asylum as Utopia* (London: Routledge, 1991)

Sedgwick, Marcus, *The Dark Horse* (London: Orion Books, 2002)

Segal, David, 'It's Back. But What Does It Mean? Aide to Kubrick on "Shining" Scoffs at "Room 237" Theories', New York Times, 27 March 2013 <www.nytimes.com/2013/03/31/movies/aide-to-kubrick-on-shining-scoffs-at-room-237-theories.html> [accessed 2 December 2016]

Sendak, Maurice, *Where the Wild Things Are* (New York: Harper & Row, 1963)

Shakespeare, William, *The Winter's Tale*, ed. by Ernest Schanzer (1609; London: Penguin, 1986)

Shattuck, Roger, *The Forbidden Experiment: The Story of the Wild Boy of Aveyron* (London: Quartet Books, 1980)

Shields, Rachel, 'Adopted by Wolves? Bestselling Memoir Was a Pack of Lies', Independent <www.independent.co.uk/news/world/europe/adopted-by-wolves-bestselling-memoir-was-a-pack-of-lies-790000.html> [accessed 2 December 2016]

Shields, Stephanie A., 'Passionate Men, Emotional Women: Psychology Constructs Gender Difference in the Late 19th Century', *History of Psychology*, 10.2 (2007), 92–110

Sibielski, Rosalind, 'Gendering the Monster Within: Biological Essentialism, Sexual Difference, and Changing the Symbolic Functions of the Monster in Popular Werewolf Texts', in *Monster Culture in the 21st Century: A Reader*, ed. by Marina Levina and Diem-My T. Bui (London and New York: Bloomsbury, 2013), pp. 115–29

Siegemund-Broka, Austin, '"True Blood" Star on Shocker: "It's a Pivotal Moment" for Sookie (Q&A)', *The Hollywood Reporter*, 6 July 2014 <www.hollywoodreporter.com/live-feed/true-blood-joe-manganiello-alcide-716838> [accessed 30 August 2015]

Silva, Sara Graça da, and Jamshid J. Tehrani, 'Comparative Phylogenetic Analyses Uncover the Ancient Roots of Indo-European Folktales', *Royal Society Open Science*, 20 January 2016 <http://rsos.royalsocietypublishing.org/content/3/1/150645> [accessed 1 January 2017]

Singh, J.A.L., 'The Diary of the Wolf Children of Midnapore (India)', in J.A.L. Singh and Robert M. Zingg, *Wolf-children and Feral Man* (1942; Hamden, CT: Archon Books, 1966), pp. 3–126

Singh, J.A.L., and Robert M. Zingg, *Wolf-children and Feral Man* (1942; Hamden, CT: Archon Books, 1966)

Skea, Ann, 'Wolf-Masks: From *Hawk* to *Wolfwatching*' <http://ann.skea.com/Wolves.htm> [accessed 2 December 2018]

Skogen, Ketil, Olve Krange and Helene Figari, *Wolf Conflicts: A Sociological Study* (New York and Oxford: Berghahn Books, 2017)

Sleeman, W.H., 'An Account of Wolves Nurturing Children in Their Dens' (Plymouth, 1852); repr. *Zoologist*, 12, 3rd series (1888), 87–98

Sleeping Beauty and Other Favourite Fairy Tales, trans. by Angela Carter, ill. by Michael Foreman (London: Gollancz, 1982)

Sleight, Graham, *The Doctor's Monsters: Meanings of the Monstrous in Doctor Who* (London: I.B. Tauris, 2012)

Smith, Douglas, and Gary Ferguson, *Decade of the Wolf: Returning the Wild to Yellowstone* (Guilford, CT: Lyons Press, 2005)

Spooner, Catherine, *Fashioning Gothic Bodies* (Manchester: Manchester University Press, 2004)

—— *Contemporary Gothic* (London: Reaktion, 2006)

——'Costuming Vampires', in *Gothic: The Dark Heart of Film*, ed. by James Bell (London: BFI, 2013), pp. 20–1

Stannard, David, *American Holocaust: Columbus and the Conquest of the New World* (New York: Oxford University Press, 1992)

—— 'Genocide in the Americas', *The Nation*, 19 October 1992, pp. 430–4

Steiner, Shepherd, 'Animal Insertions and Human Projection: The Politics of Marcus Coates', in *Marcus Coates*, ed. by Marcus Coates, Anthony Spira and Rosalind Horne (London: Koenig Books, 2016), pp. 7–16

Sterndale, R.A., *Natural History of the Mammalia of India and Ceylon* (Calcutta: Thacker Spink, 1884)

Stevenson, Robert Louis, *Dr Jekyll and Mr Hyde* (London: Penguin, 2012)

Stiefvater, Maggie, *Shiver* (London: Scholastic Children's Books, 2009)

—— *Linger* (London: Scholastic Children's Books, 2010)

—— *Forever* (London: Scholastic Children's Books, 2011)

Stoker, Bram, *Dracula*, ed. by Nina Auerbach and David J. Skal (1897; New York: Norton, 1997)

———— *Dracula*, ed. by Roger Luckhurst (1897; Oxford: Oxford University Press, 2011)

Storr, Robert, 'The Idea of the Moral Imperative in Contemporary Art', in *Art Criticism*, 7, ed. by Donald Kuspit (New York: [n. pub.], 1991), pp. 36–41

Stypczynski, Brent A., *The Modern Literary Werewolf: A Critical Study of the Mutable Motif* (Jefferson, NC: McFarland, 2013)

Summers, Montague, *The Werewolf in Lore and Legend* (1933; New York: Dover, 2003)

Sundmark, Björn, '"Traveling Beastward": An Ecocritical Reading of George MacDonald's Fairy Tales', *North Wind: A Journal of George MacDonald Studies*, 27 (2008), 1–15

Swan, Susan Z., 'Gothic Drama in Disney's *Beauty and the Beast*: Subverting Traditional Romance by Transcending the Animal–Human Paradox', *Critical Studies in Mass Communication*, 16.3 (1999), 350–69

[Swift, Jonathan], *The Most Wonderful Wonder that ever appeared to the Wonder of the British Nation* (London: printed for A. More, 1726)

Szarycz, Ireneusz, 'Morsels on the Tongue: Evidence of a Pre-Christian Matriarchy in Russian Fairy Tales', *Studia Slavica*, 46 (2001), 63–72

Tankel, Jonathan D., 'The Impact of *The Jazz Singer* on the Conversion to Sound', *Journal of University Film Association*, 30.1 (winter 1978), 21–5

Tatar, Maria, ed., *Beauty and the Beast: Classic Tales about Animal Brides and Grooms from around the World* (New York: Penguin, 2017)

'Taupo Teen Angry over Misused Photo', *Newshub*, 2 July 2016 <www.newshub.co.nz/nznews/taupo-teen-angry-over-misused-photo-2016070208#axzz4E2LTOVWI> [accessed 10 July 2016]

Teffi, Nadezhda, 'Baba Yaga', in *Russian Magic Tales from Pushkin to Platonov*, ed. by Robert Chandler (New York: Penguin, 2012), pp. 419–33

Tehrani, Jamshid J., 'The Phylogeny of Little Red Riding Hood', *PLOS One*, 13 November 2013 <http://dx.doi.org/10.1371/journal.pone.0078871> [accessed 1 January 2017]

Tennant, C.M., *Peter the Wild Boy* (London: James Clarke & Co, 1939)

'This Is Uncanny: Number-play in Stanley Kubrick's "The Shining"', *Theibtaurisblog*, 14 May 2012 <https://theibtaurisblog.com/2012/05/14/the-uncanny-number-play-in-stanley-kubricks-the-shining/> [accessed 2 December 2016]

Thomson, Richard, *Tales of an Antiquary*, 3 vols (London: Henry Colburn, 1828)

Thorpe, Nick, *The Danube* (New Haven: Yale University Press, 2013)

Tiffin, Jessica, 'The Bloodied Text: Angela Carter', in *Marvelous Geometry: Narrative and Metafiction in Modern Fairy Tale* (Detroit, MI: Wayne State University Press, 2009), pp. 65–100

Tisdall, Caroline, *Joseph Beuys* (London: Thames & Hudson, 1979)

Tomasello, Michael, *Origins of Human Communication* (Cambridge, MA: MIT Press, 2008)

Townshend, Dale, ed. *Terror and Wonder: The Gothic Imagination* (London: British Library, 2014)

Travis, Rebecca, 'Marcus Coates: 185x49x29cm, Workplace Gallery, Gateshead', *This Is Tomorrow* (2012) <http://thisistomorrow.info/articles/marcus-coates-185x49x29cm> [accessed 16 November 2016]

Turner, Bryan S., *The Body and Society: Explorations of Social Theory*, 2nd edn (London: Sage Publications, 1996)

Twitchell, James B., *The Living Dead: A Study of the Vampire in Romantic Literature* (Durham, NC: Duke University Press, 1981)

Van Horn, Gavin, 'The Making of a Wilderness Icon: Green Fire, Charismatic Species, and the Changing Status of Wolves in the United States', in *Animals and the Human Imagination*, ed. by Aaron Gross and Anne Vallely (New York: Columbia University Press, 2012), pp. 203–37

Vickery, Amanda, 'Golden Age to Separate Spheres? A Review of the Categories and Chronology of English Women's History', *The Historical Journal*, 36.1 (1993), 383–414

Vieira, Mark A., *Hollywood Horror: From Gothic to Cosmic* (New York: Harry N. Abrams, 2003)

Vincent, Rachel, *Stray*, Shifters, 1 (London: Mira, 2009)

'Vogue Notices: Wolf Hall', *British Vogue*, September 2014, p. 94

Von Uexküll, Jakob, *A Foray into the Worlds of Animals and Humans: With a Theory of Meaning*, trans. by Joseph D. O'Neil (Minneapolis and London: University of Minnesota Press, 2010)

Waite, R.G.L., *Hitler, the Psychopathic God* (New York: Da Capo Press, 1993)

Waller, Alison, *Constructing Adolescence in Fantastic Realism*, Children's Literature and Culture (New York and London: Routledge, 2011)

Waller, Gregory, 'Introduction', in *American Horrors: Essays on the Modern American Horror Film*, ed. by Gregory Waller (Urbana and Chicago: University of Illinois Press, 1987), pp. 1–13

Walsh, Jill Paton, *Knowledge of Angels* (Cambridge: Colt Books, 1994)

Walters, Victoria, 'The Artist as Shaman: The Work of Joseph Beuys and Marcus Coates', in *Between Art and Anthropology: Contemporary Ethnographic Practice*, ed. by Arnd Schneider and Christopher Wright (Oxford and New York: Berg, 2010), pp. 35–48

Warner, Marina, *From the Beast to the Blonde: On Fairy Tales and Their Tellers*, new edn (London: Vintage, 1995)

Warr, Tracey, 'Being Something', in *Marcus Coates* (Ambleside: Grizedale Books, 2001), [n.pag.]

Weinstock, Jeffrey Andrew, *The Ashgate Encyclopaedia of Literary and Cinematic Monsters* (Aldershot: Ashgate, 2014)

Whitlock, F.A., *Criminal Responsibility and Mental Illness* (London: Butterworths, 1963)

'Why Don't Wolves Eat All That They Kill?', *Wolves and Moose of Isle Royale* <http://isleroyalewolf.org/node/42> [accessed 1 December 2016]

Wiesel, Elie, *Night*, trans. by Marion Wiesel (New York: Hill and Wang, 1960)

—— *Legends of Our Time* (New York: Knopf Doubleday Publishing Group, 2011)

Wilkomirski, Binjamin, *Fragments: Memories of a Childhood, 1939–1948* (London: Picador, 1997)

Williams, Raymond, *Keywords: A Vocabulary of Culture and Society*, rev. edn (London: Fontana, 1983)

—— 'Culture', in *Keywords: A Vocabulary of Culture and Society*, rev. edn. (London: Flamingo, 1983), pp. 87–93

—— 'Ideas of Nature', in *Culture and Materialism*, rev. ed., Radical Thinkers (London: Verso, 2005), pp. 67–85

Wilson, Laura, '*Dans ma peau*: Shape-shifting and Subjectivity', in *She-wolf: A Cultural History of Female Werewolves*, ed. by Hannah Priest (Manchester: Manchester University Press, 2015), pp. 196–209

Wilson, Natalie, 'It's a Wolf Thing: The Quileute Werewolf/Shape-Shifter Hybrid as Noble Savage', in *Theorizing Twilight: Critical Essays on What's at Stake in a Post-vampire World*, ed. by Maggie Parke and Natalie Wilson (Jefferson, NC, and London: McFarland), pp. 194–208

'The Wolf in Her', photographed by Mario Sorrenti, styled by Kate Moss, *British Vogue*, September 2014, pp. 346–57

Wollert, Edwin, 'Wolves in Native American Culture', *Wolf Song of Alaska* <www.wolfsongalaska.org/chorus/node/179> [accessed 30 November 2016]

Wood, Robin, *Hollywood from Vietnam to Reagan* (New York: Columbia University Press, 1986)

Wordsworth, William, and Samuel Taylor Coleridge, *Lyrical Ballads*, ed. by Fiona Stafford (1798; Oxford: Oxford University Press, 2013)
Wright, David, *Mental Disability in Victorian England* (Oxford: Clarendon, 2001)
Wyatt, Jean, 'The Violence of Gendering: Castration Images in Angela Carter's *The Magic Toyshop*, *The Passion of New Eve*, and "Peter and the Wolf"', *Women's Studies*, 25.6 (1996), 549–70
Yolen, Jane, *Children of the Wolf* (New York: Viking, 1984)
Young, Erin S., 'Flexible Heroines, Flexible Narratives: The Werewolf Romances of Kelley Armstrong and Carrie Vaughn', *Extrapolation*, 52 (2011), 204–26
Young, Robert J.C., *Colonial Desire: Hybridity in Theory, Culture and Race* (London: Routledge, 1995)
Zingg, Robert M., 'Feral Man and Cases of Extreme Isolation of Individuals', in J.A.L. Singh and Robert M. Zingg, *Wolf-children and Feral Man* (1942; Hamden, CT, Archon Books, 1966), pp. 131–365
Zipes, Jack, *The Trials and Tribulations of Little Red Riding Hood*, 2nd edn (New York: Routledge, 1993)
—— *Breaking the Magic Spell: Radical Theories of Folk and Fairy Tales* (Lexington: University of Kentucky, 2002)
Žižek, Slavoj, *Enjoy Your Symptom! Jacques Lacan in Hollywood and Out* (London and New York: Routledge, 2001)

Audio and video

Coates, Marcus, *In Profile: Marcus Coates* (UK: Picture This, 2007) [DVD]
—— *Re-imagining Nature*, Synchronicity Earth, 29 April 2015, online video recording <www.synchronicityearth.org/events/disappearing-nature> [accessed 13 February 2016]
How Wolves Change Rivers, ed. by Chris Agnos and Dawn Agnos, narr. by George Monbiot, online video recording, YouTube, 13 February 2014 <www.youtube.com/watch?v=ysa5OBhXz-Q> [accessed 18 January 2016]
'Legend of the Cybermen', writ. by Mike Maddox, *Doctor Who* [CD/download] (London: Big Finish, 2010)
'Loup-Garoux', writ. by Marc Platt, *Doctor Who* [CD/download] (London: Big Finish, 2001)
Power, Cat, 'Werewolf', *You Are Free* (Matador, 2003) [on CD]
Whedon, Joss, 'Welcome to the Hellmouth' audio commentary, *Buffy the Vampire Slayer: Season One*, 2000
Williams, Dar, *The Honesty Room* (Burning Field Music, PCD 003D, 1993)

Television

Being Human, created by Toby Whithouse (UK: BBC, 2008–13)
Broadchurch, created by Chris Chibnall (UK: Kudos Film and Television / Shine Group, 2013–17)

BIBLIOGRAPHY

Buffy the Vampire Slayer, created by Joss Whedon (The WB, 1997–2001 and UPN, 2001–3)
---- 'New Moon Rising', writ. by Marti Noxon, dir. by James A. Contnor, 4.19
---- 'Phases', writ. by Rob Des Hotel and Dean Batali, dir. by Bruce Seth Green, 2.15
---- 'Wild at Heart', writ. by Marti Noxon, dir. by David Grossman, 4.6

Doctor Who, created by Sydney Newman, C.E. Webber, Donald Wilson et al. (UK: BBC, 1963–89, 1996 (with Universal/20th Century Fox), 2005–)
---- '42', dir. by Graeme Harper, writ. by Chris Chibnall (first broadcast 19 May 2007 by BBC; DVD box set *Doctor Who: The Complete Third Series*, 2 Entertain, 2007)
---- 'The Ark in Space', dir. by Rodney Bennett, writ. by Robert Holmes and John Lucarotti [uncredited] (first broadcast 25 January–15 February 1975 by BBC; DVD Special Edition: 2 Entertain, 2013)
---- 'The Greatest Show in the Galaxy', dir. by Alan Wareing, writ. by Stephen Wyatt (first broadcast 14 December 1988–4 January 1989 by BBC; DVD: 2 Entertain, 2012)
---- 'Inferno', dir. by Douglas Camfield, writ. by Don Houghton (first broadcast 9 May–20 June 1970 by BBC; DVD: 2006)
---- 'In the Forest of the Night', dir. by Sheree Folkson, writ. by Frank Cottrell Boyce (first broadcast 25 October 2014 by BBC; DVD box set *Doctor Who: The Complete Eighth Series*, 2 Entertain, 2014)
---- 'Mindwarp', dir. by Ron Jones, writ. by Philip Martin (first broadcast as 'The Trial of a Time Lord', episodes 5–8, 4 October–25 October 1986 by BBC; DVD box set *Doctor Who: The Trial of a Time Lord,* 2 Entertain, 2008)
---- 'The Next Doctor', dir. by Andy Goddard, writ. by Russell T. Davies (first broadcast 25 December 2008 by BBC; DVD box set *Doctor Who: The Complete Specials*, 2 Entertain, 2010)
---- 'Planet of Evil', dir. by David Maloney, writ. by Louis Marks (first broadcast 27 September–18 October 1975 by BBC; DVD: 2 Entertain, 2007)
---- 'The Seeds of Doom', dir. by Douglas Camfield, writ. by Robert Banks Stewart (first broadcast 31 January–6 March 1976 by BBC; DVD: 2 Entertain, 2010)
---- 'State of Decay', dir. Peter Moffat, writ. Terrance Dicks (first broadcast 22 November–13 December 1980 by BBC; DVD box set *Doctor Who: The E-Space Trilogy*, 2 Entertain, 2009)
---- 'Survival', dir. by Alan Wareing, writ. by Rona Munro (first broadcast 22 November–6 December 1989 by BBC; DVD: 2 Entertain, 2007)
---- 'Tooth and Claw', dir. by Euros Lyn, writ. by Russell T. Davies (first broadcast 22 April 2006 by BBC; DVD box set: *Doctor Who: The Complete Second Series*, 2 Entertain, 2006)
---- 'Warriors' Gate', dir. by Paul Joyce, writ. by Stephen Gallagher (first broadcast 3 January–24 January 1981 by BBC; DVD box set *Doctor Who: The E-Space Trilogy*, 2 Entertain, 2009)

Doomwatch, created by Kit Pedler and Gerry Davis, writ. by Kit Pedler, Gerry Davis et al. (UK: BBC, 1970–72)

Teen Wolf, developed by Jeff Davis (USA: MTV, 2011–)
True Blood, created by Alan Ball, based on the novels by Charlaine Harris (HBO, 2008–14)
---- 'Fire in the Hole', writ. by Brain Buckner, dir. by Lee Rose, 7.3 (HBO, 2014)
---- 'I Don't Wanna Know', writ. by Chris Offitt, dir. by Scott Winant, 1.10 (HBO, 2008)
---- 'It Hurts Me Too', writ. by Alexander Woo, dir. by Michael Lehmann, 3.3 (HBO, 2010)

Film

An American Werewolf in London, dir. by John Landis (USA: Universal, 1981)
La Belle et la Bête, dir. by Jean Cocteau (France: DisCina, 1946)
Blitz Wolf, dir. by Tex Avery (USA: MGM, 1942)
Bram Stoker's Dracula, dir. by Francis Ford Coppola (USA: American Zoetrope, 1992)
Bride of Frankenstein, dir. by James Whale (USA: Universal, 1935)
The Company of Wolves, dir. by Neil Jordan (UK: Palace Pictures, 1984)
Dances with Wolves, dir. by Kevin Costner (USA: Tig Productions, 1990)
Deliverance, dir. by John Boorman (USA: Warner Bros, 1972)
Dr. Jekyll and Mr. Hyde, dir. by John S. Robertson (USA: Famous Players-Lasky Corporation, 1920)
Dr. Jekyll and Mr. Hyde, dir. by Rouben Mamoulian (USA: Paramount, 1931)
Dracula, dir. by Tod Browning (USA: Universal, 1931)
L'Enfant Sauvage, dir. by François Truffaut (France: Les Films du Carrosse, 1969)
Forbidden Planet, dir. by Fred M. Wilcox (USA: MGM, 1956)
Frankenstein, dir. by James Whale (USA: Universal, 1931)
Frozen, dir. by Adam Green (USA: A Bigger Boat, 2010)
Frozen, dir. by Chris Buck and Jennifer Lee (USA: Walt Disney, 2013)
Ginger Snaps, dir. John Fawcett (Canada: Telefilm, 2000)
Monster by Moonlight: The Immortal Saga of the Wolf Man, dir. by David J. Skal (USA: Universal Studios, 1999)
Red Riding Hood, dir. by Catherine Hardwicke (USA: Warner Bros, 2011)
She-wolf of London, dir. by Jean Yarbrough (USA: Universal Pictures, 1946)
The Shining, dir. by Stanley Kubrick (USA: Warner Bros, 1980)
Son of Frankenstein, dir. by Rowland V. Lee (USA: Universal, 1939)
Teen Wolf, dir. by Rod Daniel (USA: Atlantic Releasing Corporation, 1985)
The Three Little Pigs, dir. by Burt Gillett (USA: Walt Disney Productions, 1933)
Twilight, dir. by Catherine Hardwicke (USA: Summit Entertainment, 2008)
The Twilight Saga (USA: Summit Entertainment, 2015) [DVD]
Underworld series, dir. by Len Wiseman, *et al.* (USA: Lakeshore Entertainment, 2003–)
The Undying Monster, dir. by John Brahm (USA: Universal Productions, 1942)
Universal Horror, dir. by Kevin Brownlow (USA: Photoplay Productions, 1998) [DVD]
Vampires Suck, dir. by Jason Friedberg and Aaron Seltzer (USA: Regency, 2010)
Van Helsing, dir. by Stephen Sommers (USA: Sommers Company, 2004)

The Werewolf, dir. by Henry MacRae (USA: Bison Film Company, 1913)
Werewolf of London, dir. by Stuart Walker (USA: Universal, 1935)
What We Do in the Shadows, dir. by Jemaine Clement and Waika Taititi (New Zealand: Madman Entertainment, 2014)
Wolf, dir. by Mike Nichols (USA: Columbia, 1994)
Wolf Children, dir. by Mamoru Hosoda (Japan: Studio Chizu, 2012)
The Wolf Man, dir. by George Waggner (USA: Universal, 1941)
The Wolfman, dir. by Joe Johnston (USA: Universal, 2010)
Young Frankenstein, dir. by Mel Brooks (USA: 20th Century Fox, 1974)

Index

Note: literary works can be found under author's names. Page numbers in *italic* refer to illustrations.

abjection; the abject 169–70, 173
　see also Kristeva, Julia
adolescence; puberty 12, 155, 163–4, 165–7, 168, 169, 175, 214–15, 222
　see also teenagers; Young Adult fiction
advertisements *see* fashion
Aesop 8, 22–3, 32n.3, 39, *40*, 41–2, 46n.20
　see also fables
Afanas'ev, Alexander Nikolayevich *see* fairy tales
agency; autonomy 4, 6, 7, 12, 17n.25, 45, 130, 150, 151, 153–4, 155, 159, 160n.14, 224
　see also subjectivity
Alas, Mert 238–9, *239*
alienation 61, 149, 154, 157, 167
　see also commodification; reification
Amala and Kamala *see* wolf-children
An American Werewolf in London (1981 film) 10, 71, 80–3, 185, 188–9n.9, 230
Andersen, Hans Christian *see* fairy tales
androgyny 232, 234
　see also femininity; gender; masculinity; transvestism
animal(s) 1, 7–8, 9, 31, 43, 95–6, 113, 147, 162n.38, 163, 164, 168, 171, 173, 195–201, 203, 213–14, 217–18, 223–4, 232
　bat(s) 76, 83n.6, 195–6, 209n.8
　bear(s) 3, 38, 49, *50*, 51, 56, 65n.5, 90, 96, *97*, 203, 220

bird(s) 59, 96, 151, 152, 153–4, 157, 194–5, 196, 207, 212–13, 214–15, 216, 219, 220, 222, 224, 225n.10
cat(s) 22, 36, 43, 82, 96, 121, 179
dog(s) 13, 22, 24, 29, 30, 39–41, 54, 76, 102, 139, 141, 171–2, 179, 183, 211, 213–14, 218, 227, 228, 229, 234–6, 237, 242n.30
domestic 2, 34, 38–9, 41, 43, 91, 156, 223, 234–5
fish 214, 203, 220
fox(es) 22, 38, 43, 109, 193, 196, 203, 214
humans as 1, 4, 11, 53–5, 61, 63, 101–8, 116, 147, 153, 166, 168, 169–70, 173, 176n.20, 212, 231, 234, 237
　see also becoming–animal
in literature 22, 163
inner *see* 'beast within'
pig(s) 25, 26, 54, 56, 87, 96, 215–16, 217–18
raising humans 4, 8, 49, 65n.5, 65n.8
　see also wolf-children
reindeer 227, 237
relations with humans 2, 5, 203, 207, 214, 223–4, 237
rights 171, 173
seal(s) 213–14, 242n.18
　see also selkie
sheep 2, 22, 38–9, 41–3, *42*, 46n.20, 87, 235
　see also pastoral; pastoralism
stoat 193–4, 196, *197*
wild 10, 24, 34, 36, 38, 43, 101–2, 103–4, 105, 200, 235

animal–human boundary 6, 8, 10, 11,
    12–13, 71, 77, 82, 83, 95, 113, 114,
    131, 147, 157, 158–9, 169–70, 172,
    173, 175, 197, 208, 214, 229, 237,
    242n.30
  see also human–animal
animality 2, 5, 6, 10–11, 12, 14, 43, 48, 55,
    71, 131, 132, 138, 147, 149, 150, 153,
    157, 158, 159, 160n.14, 163, 165,
    166, 167, 169, 176n.20, 218,
    234
anthropocentrism 174–5
anthropology 8, 16n.18, 45–6n.2, 56,
    64–5n.5, 204–5
anthropomorphism 25, 165, 208, 241
anti-Semitism 8, 21, 25–6
  see also Holocaust, the; Nazis; 'race'
Arbuthnot, John 58
  It Cannot Rain But it Pours (1726)
    15n.13, 66n.32
Armstrong, Kelly, *Bitten* (2003) 7, 17n.25
Aroles, Serge 29
art 3, 14, 73, 93, 152, 153, 154, 158, 204, 208,
    224, 229, 234–5
  painting 13, 93, 104, 170, 234–5
  photography 193–5, *194, 195*, 227, 228,
    229–30, 235–41, 239
  sculpture and installations 13, 170, 193,
    199–203, *200, 201, 204*, 205–8, *206*
  video 193, 194–5, 198–9, 205, 236
Atwood, Margaret 21
Auerbach, Nina 75, 130
D'Aulnoy, Marie-Catherine Le Jumel de
    Barneville, Baroness *see* fairy tales
autonomy *see* agency

Baring-Gould, Sabine, *The Book of
    Were-Wolves* (1865) 105, 109, 110,
    111, 112, 131, 225n.10
Barnes, Djuna, *Nightwood* (1936) 229
bat(s) *see* animals
Bear-boy of Lithuania *see* wild children
bear(s) *see* animals
'beast within' 10–11, 12, 14, 16n.19, 79–80,
    82, 128n.19, 164–6, 168, 175, 211, 218,
    221, 231
beauty 72, 96, 98, 129, 138, 236, 237
'Beauty and the Beast' *see* fairy tales

becoming-animal 13, 153, 193–7, 198, 207,
    208n.2, 211, 212
  see also Deleuze, Gilles; transformation
Being Human (2008–13 TV series) 82, 130,
    185
Berger, John 173, 175, 197
Bergson, Henri 197
Berry, Liz 13, 211–18, 221, 222, 223–4
  'Bird' 212–13
  Black Country (2014) 212
  'Carmella' 214–15
  'Dog' 213, 218
  'Echo' 214, 222
  'The First Path' 214
  'My Mother's Wedding Shoes' 216
  'The Patron Saint of Schoolgirls' 215
  'The Red Shoes' 216
  'The Sea of Talk' 214
  'The Silver Birch' 215
  'Sow' 215–16, 217–18, 221, 223–4
  'Stone' 213–14
  'When I Was a Boy' 215
  'Woodkeeper' 214
Bettelheim, Bruno 128n28, 163, 164–5
Beuys, Joseph 199, 209n.25
Bible, The 22, 37, 41, 93, 148, 149, 211
  see also Christianity; religion
Big Bad Wolf *see* Wolf, Big Bad
Bilibin, Ivan 91, 97, *98*
binary oppositions 117, 120, 126, 163, 217,
    224, 228, 229, 231, 237
birds *see* animals
'Bisclavret' *see* Marie de France
blood 6, 14n.8, 74, 109, 111, 116, 159, 167,
    183, 188, 232, 234, 237
'Bluebeard' *see* fairy tales
body, the 49, 53, 60, 63, 80, 81–2, 94, 131,
    138, 148, 157, 159n.4, 164, 165, 166,
    172, 196, 200, 201, 208, 212, 213,
    214, 215, 222–3, 224, 229, 230, 231,
    234
  female 138, 148, 212, 215, 216, 217, 218,
    231, 232, 234
  representation of 148, 207–8, 229,
    230
  transformation of 80–2, 83n.6, 94, 138,
    165, 166, 212, 213, 215, 222, 230, 234
  see also flesh; skin

Index

body horror *see* horror, body
Boy Who Cried Werewolf, The (1973 film) 80
Bram Stoker's Dracula (1992 film) 83n.6
  see also Stoker, Bram
Brontë, Charlotte, *Jane Eyre* (1847) 107
Browning, Robert, *The Ring and the Book* (1868) 109
Buffon, Georges-Louis Leclers, Comte de 36, 50
  see also species
Buffy the Vampire Slayer (1997–2003 TV series) 9, 70, 71, 176n.1
Burgess, Melvin, *The Cry of the Wolf* (1990) 24
Byron, George, Lord 230

Campbell, Gilbert, 'The White Wolf of Kostopchin' (1889) 231
cannibalism 88, 95, 109, 232
Cantor, Mircea 205
capitalism 12, 148, 150, 152, 154, 158, 159, 160n.17
  see also commodification; Marx, Karl
Carter, Angela 4, 12, 13, 147–62, 165, 185, 188, 189n.28
  'The Bloody Chamber' 152–3
  The Bloody Chamber and Other Stories (1979) 12, 147, 150–9
  'The Company of Wolves' 154–6, 165
  'The Erl-King' 151–2, 153–4
  'The Lady of the House of Love' 153–4
  'Peter and the Wolf' (1985) 15n.14, 148–50
  The Sadeian Woman (1979) 148, 152, 153, 160n.14
  'The Tiger's Bride' 153
  'Wolf-Alice' 15n.14, 148, 156–8
  see also The Company of Wolves (1984 film); fairy tales
Chaney, Jr, Lon *see The Wolf Man* (1941 film)
Charnas, Suzy McKee, 'Boobs' (1999) 165
child-rearing 62, 113–14, 116, 117, 120, 121, 123
  see also maternity; wolf-children
children's literature 24, 69n.63, 163
  see also education; fables; fairy tales; Young Adult fiction
Christianity 2, 41, 48, 56, 95, 136, 148
city, the 11, 23, 30, 48, 90, 110, 132, 140, 150
  see also country, the
civilisation 2, 3, 4, 15n.13, 31, 49, 56, 76, 77, 79, 80, 87, 90, 91, 131, 132, 134, 137, 150, 163, 170, 171, 178, 188, 213, 214, 229, 230, 231, 237, 238
  see also culture; nature; wilderness; wildness
class 11, 77, 119, 129–43, 160n.14, 212
clothes 42, 43, 56–7, 108, 151, 153, 213, 227–42
  see also fashion; fur; skin; transvestism
Coates, Marcus 13, 193–210
Coleridge, Samuel Taylor 61, 67n.44, 232
colonialism 124, 212, 241
  see also postcolonialism
commodification; commodities 12, 148, 149, 150, 151, 152–4, 155, 156, 157, 159, 160n.20, 232
  see also alienation; capitalism; Marx, Karl; reification
The Company of Wolves (1984 film) 5, 80, 162n.46, 230
  see also Carter, Angela
Condillac, Étienne Bonnot de 3, 68n.53, 157
  see also language, acquisition of
conservation 37, 45, 45n.2, 47n.27, 206, 207, 220
  see also ecology; rewilding
Coudray, Chantal Bourgault du 6–7, 16, 180, 216–17, 219, 221, 228
country, the; countryside 132, 138, 140, 193
  see also city, the; forests; pastoralism; wilderness
crime; criminal 1, 9, 11, 37, 38, 42, 42, 74, 87, 90, 101–12, 131, 134
Crozier, Lorna, 'What Comes After' 211
culture 1, 3, 4, 5, 6, 8, 9, 12, 13, 24, 34, 44, 45n.2, 62, 96, 147, 149, 150, 153, 155, 156, 164, 198, 203, 211, 212, 219, 227–8, 229–30, 234, 236, 238, 240, 241
  folk 149
  popular 80, 81, 133, 163, 211

youth 70
see also civilisation, nature, society
The Curse of the Werewolf (1961 film) 80

Dadd, Richard 102, 103–4
Dances with Wolves (1990 film) 238, 240
Darwinism 113, 118, 119, 126, 127, 127n.16
Defoe, Daniel, *Mere Nature Delineated* (1776) 58, 59, 67n.41
Defonseca, Misha 28–9
degeneration theory 11, 113, 119–20, 124, 126, 234
see also Darwinism
Deleuze, Gilles 13, 16n.19, 196–7, 208, 208n.2
see also becoming-animal
Depression, the 8, 25
Derrida, Jacques 197
desire 106, 107, 109, 114, 115, 117, 118, 147, 149, 153, 155, 159, 170, 216, 217, 236, 240, 241
desublimation 148, 150
see also sublimation
Dijkstra, Bram 234–5
Dion, Mark 206, *206*
disease 104, 129, 132, 167, 169, 173, 183
Disney, Walt 8, 25–6, 27, 73, 163, 212
see also fairy tales
Doctor Who (TV series) 12–13, 178–89
dog(s) see animals
domestication see animals, domestic
domestic sphere; domesticity 91, 123, 162n.42, 168, 169, 172, 216, 234–5
Doré, Gustave, *frontispiece 40*
Dracula (1931 film) 73–4, 75–6
see also see Stoker, Bram
Dracula, Count see Stoker, Bram
Dr. Jekyll and Mr. Hyde (1920 film) 74
see also Stephenson, Robert Louis
Dr. Jekyll and Mr. Hyde (1931 film) 70, 73, 79
see also Stephenson, Robert Louis
dualism 148, 212, 217, 241

ecofeminism 212, 217, 223
see also ecology; feminism

ecology; environmentalism 5, 7, 9, 13, 34, 35, 36, 44, 181, 183, 187, 205, 211, 219, 220, 221, 242n.31
Edgeworth, Maria and Richard 3, 59
see also Peter the Wild Boy
education 11, 56, 58–9, 114, 120–4, 125, 126
see also child-rearing; language, acquisition of
L'Enfant Sauvage (*The Wild Child*) (1970 film) 68n.53
see also Itard, Jean-Marc-Gaspard; wild children
Engels, Friedrich 150
see also Marx, Karl
Enlightenment, the 1, 2–4, 5, 6, 7, 12, 14, 16n.20, 55–6, 149–50, 157, 180, 228
see also modernity
Enninful, Edward 238–9, *239*, 240
environmentalism see ecology
eroticism 6, 147, 157, 162n.38, 185, 188, 235
see also desire; sexuality
essentialism 7, 148, 153, 217, 224
evolution see Darwinism
Expressionism 74

fables 8, 22–3, 39, 41, 65n.10, 189n.28
see also Aesop; fairy tales; genre
fairy tales; folktales 10, 11, 12, 22, 27, 32, 32n.7, 49, 65n.10, 87–100, 99n.5, 128n.25, 131, 204, 211, 214, 238
Afanas'ev, Alexander Nikolayevich 88, 90, 94
Andersen, Hans Christian 115
D'Aulnoy, Marie-Catherine Le Jumel de Barneville, Baroness 22
'Beauty and the Beast' 22, 154, 161n.33, 163
'Bluebeard' (Perrault) 152, 154, 156
Grimms brothers 22, 65n.10, 88, 89, 128n.25
'Little Redcap' (Grimm brothers) 65n.10, 89, 90
'Little Red Riding Hood' (Perrault) *frontispiece* 2, 5, 8, 12, 14n.6, 22, 65n.10, 94, 150, 151, 155, 164–5, 167–9, 172, 186, 228–9, 238

INDEX

Perrault, Charles 2, 22, 65n.10, 88, 94, 99n.1, 128n.25, 161–2n.36, 164
  Russian 10, 87–100
  'Sleeping Beauty' 154
  see also fables; folklore; genre; myth
fantasy; the fantastic 4, 74, 90, 114, 115, 116, 117–19, 124–7, 139, 217, 219, 220, 221, 229, 231, 239, 240
  see also genre; Gothic
fashion 13–14, 227–42
  see also clothes
femininity; feminine, the 6, 95, 115, 123, 128n.27, 154, 158, 165, 216, 229, 232, 234
  see also gender; masculinity; women
feminism 6, 7, 12, 153, 154, 160n.9, 161n.26, 165, 212, 217, 218, 224
  see also ecofeminism; gender; patriarchy; sexuality; women
Fenrir see myth, Norse
feral children see wild children
fiction 1, 2, 4–7, 8, 10–11, 12, 13, 14, 21, 24, 28, 49, 50, 55, 56, 62, 64, 69n.63, 79, 105, 107, 109, 124, 130, 147, 166, 170, 172, 204, 211, 231, 234
  see also genre; lies; realism; storytelling
flesh 7, 12, 36, 109, 147–62, 219, 234
  see also meat; skin
folklore 16n.24, 64–5n.4, 71, 88, 95
  werewolves in 2, 15n.17, 16n.18, 71, 110, 131, 183
  wolves in 39, 87–100
folktales see fairy tales; folktales
forests 3, 10, 38, 49, 56, 59, 60, 62, 87–91, 92, 93, 95–6, 97, 98, 99, 105–6, 110, 111, 154, 155, 167, 186–7, 188, 195
fox(es) see animals
Frankenstein see Shelley, Mary
Frankenstein (1931 film) 73, 74, 77, 80, 188n.9
Freud, Sigmund 31, 149
  Wolf-Man, the 16n.19, 27, 229
  see also psychoanalysis
Frozen (2010 film) 73
Frozen (2013 film) 73
fur 13, 83n.6, 89, 91, 94, 108, 141, 153, 156, 178, 182, 206, 215, 227–42
  see also hunting; skin

furiosus 102, 103, 107, 108, 110
  see also mental illness

Galanin, Nicholas 205
Gelder, Ken 179
gender 7, 13, 14, 113, 115, 116, 120–1, 122, 123–4, 125, 128n.27, 131, 148, 165, 166, 168, 212, 215, 216, 218, 229, 234
  see also femininity; masculinity; sexuality; women
genre 4, 5–6, 10, 11–12, 14, 15n.13, 70, 71, 73, 74, 80–1, 83, 115, 124, 125–6
Gilgamesh, Epic of 8, 23
Ginger Snaps (2000 film) 82, 185
Godwin, William 11, 122–3, 126
Gothic 1, 5, 6, 9, 12, 13, 14, 15n.17, 16n.20, 70, 74–5, 76, 147, 158, 179, 180, 181, 211, 232, 234
  genre 5, 6, 12, 70, 130
  horror 4, 5
    see also horror
  language 105
  literature 4, 5, 6, 12, 16n.20, 73, 74–5, 110, 163, 211, 232, 234
  mode 1, 5, 6, 158, 179, 180, 181
  Southern 140
    see also Harris, Charlaine; *True Blood* (2008–14 TV series)
  see also eco-Gothic; fantasy; genre; horror
Grey Wolf 10, 88, 89, 91, 92, 93–5, 96, 99
Grimm brothers see fairy tales
Guattari, Pierre-Félix see Deleuze, Gilles
gypsies 133, 135

Harraway, Donna 131
Harris, Charlaine, Sookie Stackhouse novels 139
  see also *True Blood* (2008–14 TV series)
Hauser, Kaspar see wild children
heteronormativity 223
  see also heterosexuality; homosexuality; sexuality
heterosexuality 138, 212
  see also heteronormativity; homosexuality; sexuality
Hobbes, Thomas 131

Holocaust, the 8, 21, 26–7, 28–9
    fake accounts of 28–9
    see also anti-Semitism; Nazis
homosexuality; lesbianism 129, 185, 188
    see also heteronormativity;
        heterosexuality; sexuality
horror 4, 5, 6, 70, 71, 79, 83, 162n.46, 182,
        211, 232
    body 74, 80, 180, 181
    film 4, 9, 70, 71, 73–5, 76, 80–1, 130,
        133, 136, 162n.46, 171, 172,
        180
    stories 4, 32
Housman, Clemence, 'The Were-wolf'
    (1890) 231, 232–4, 241
Housman. Laurence 233, 233, 242n.20
howl(ing) see wolf/wolves, howl
The Howling (1981 film) 80, 81
Hughes, Ted
    'The Howling of Wolves' 64n.2
    'Life After Death' 9, 48–9, 64
    Lupercal (1960) 64n.2
    Wolfwatching (1989) 64n.2
human–animal 12, 60, 113, 158, 163, 175, 197,
        212, 229, 235, 242n.30
    relations 5, 96, 197, 199, 203, 208
    see also animal–human boundary;
        binary oppositions; transformation
humanism 7, 12, 147, 150, 153, 159, 161n.26,
        161n.30
    see also anthropocentrism
hunters; hunting 8, 10, 24, 30, 34, 38, 39,
        45, 51, 50, 87, 90, 111, 121, 171, 188,
        205, 223, 227, 232, 235
    see also fur; skin; wolves, as hunters 10,
        34, 35, 36, 38, 89, 90
hybridity 5, 12, 147, 156, 158, 163, 166, 170,
        179, 180, 181, 182, 183, 184, 187, 211,
        224

identity 5, 7, 10, 13, 16, 163, 164, 166, 167,
        170, 171, 173–5, 181, 197, 216–18, 223,
        224, 228–9, 233–4, 237
    see also agency; subjectivity
illustration 42, 91, 124, 232–4
imitation 26, 57, 58, 59, 196, 208
    of animals 57, 58, 60, 193, 196
    see also becoming-animal

immigration 9, 131
    see also migration; postcolonialism;
        'race'
indigenous peoples 13–14, 137, 142, 211,
        220–1, 229, 231, 236–41
insanity see mental illness
instinct 4, 7, 25, 30, 38, 54, 147, 149, 153–4,
        157, 160n.8, 160n.9, 164, 174, 180,
        222, 223
intertextuality 5, 12, 70, 81, 157, 179, 225n.14,
        240
Itard, Jean-Marc-Gaspard 15n.9, 55, 61,
        68n.53
    see also *L'Enfant Sauvage (The Wild
        Child)* (1969 film); wild children
I Was a Teenage Werewolf (1957 film) 80

Kipling, Rudyard 4, 24, 31, 51
    Mowgli 24, 30, 51, 52, 55
    see also colonialism; wolf-children
Kristeva, Julia 16n.19, 149, 160n.8, 160n.14,
        170
    see also abjection; language
Kubrick, Stanley 8, 26–8

Lacan, Jacques 157
    see also language
Lamb, Mary 102–3, 104, 109
language 3, 5, 7, 8, 13, 62, 64, 106, 148,
        149, 150, 153–4, 156, 157, 158, 163,
        166, 170–3, 174–5, 183, 216, 218,
        238
    acquisition of 31, 48, 56, 59–60, 61, 64, 156
    see also education
    non-verbal 59–60, 62–3, 148, 156, 157,
        170, 171–2
    origins of 2, 3, 8, 157
Lauren, Ralph 13, 227, 228, 229, 234–8, 240–1
Laurence, H., 'Norman of the Strong Arm'
    (1827) 195
Leblanc, Marie-Angélique see wild
    children
Lévi-Strauss, Claude 228
Lewis, C.S. 24
lies 8, 21, 22, 26, 27, 28–9, 30, 32
    see also wolves, as deceivers
liminality 88, 95, 131–3, 164, 169, 175, 229,
        237

INDEX

'Little Red Riding Hood' *see* fairy tales
'Little Redcap' *see* fairy tales
Locke, John 9, 11, 48, 56, 59, 68n.53, 120, 121, 122, 126
   see also education
Lon Chaney, Jr *see The Wolf Man* (1941 film)
London, Jack, *White Fang* (1906) 24
loup-garou 133, 167, 178
   see also werewolf
lunacy *see* mental illness
lupicide 50, 204
   see also wolves, extinction of
lupophilia 204, 205
lupophobia 2, 8, 34, 43, 50, 72–3, 175, 204, 205
lycanthropy 5, 6, 12, 13, 105, 106, 129, 131, 132, 151, 156, 165, 166, 167, 168, 171, 174, 175, 178, 179, 180, 182–6 *passim*, 219, 230
   as psychological disorder 10, 102, 105, 106, 111, 131, 132, 166
   see also werewolf
Lycaon 4, 184
   see also Ovid

McCarthy, Cormac, *The Crossing* (1994) 24
MacDonald, George
   'The Gray Wolf' (1871) 231
   'The History of Photogen and Nycteris' (1879) 11, 113–28
   see also fairy tales
McNaghten, Daniel 101, 103, 104, 107, 108, 109
McNaghten Rules 104–5, 108–9, 110
madness *see* mental illness
magic 11, 88, 89, 94, 108, 115, 116, 117–19
   see also fairy tales; supernatural
Marcuse, Herbert 16n.19, 149, 159, 159n.5, 160n.9, 161n.22, 162n.38, 162n.47
   see also Marx, Karl
Marryat, Captain Frederick, 'The White Wolf of the Hartz Mountains' (1839) 231–2
Marvin, Garry 8, 50, 72, 73, 204–5, 230
Marx, Karl 150, 152, 157, 159
   see also capitalism; commodification; Engels, Friedrich

masculinity 95, 156, 158, 165, 216, 217, 230–1, 232
   see also femininity; gender; sex; sexuality
materialism 12, 153, 159, 161n.26, 161n.33
maternity; motherhood 4, 30, 48, 51, 53, 63, 97, 113–14, 116, 123, 138
   see also child-rearing; women
meat 12, 54, 87, 96, 106, 109, 147, 148, 151, 152–3, 154, 155–6, 158, 162n.39, 165, 224, 237, 238
   see also animals; body, the; flesh; skin
melancholy 9, 62, 64, 71, 72, 131, 182
menstruation 157, 165
mental illness 11, 69n.61, 101–12
   and animality 104, 110–11
   and the law
   see also moral insanity
Menzies, Sutherland, 'Hughes, The Wer-Wolf' (1838) 105, 106
metafiction 13, 182
metamorphosis *see* transformation
metaphor *see* werewolf, as metaphor; wolf, as metaphor
Meyer, Stephenie, Twilight series (books) 11, 129–30, 133, 136–9, 166, 173–4, 176n.20
   see also Twilight Saga (films)
Midgley, Mary 173
Milton, John 127.8
mimesis *see* imitation
minimalism 13, 199, 202–3, 208, 210n.62
   see also art
M'Naughton *see* McNaghten
modernity 2, 6, 8, 11, 14, 15n.13, 24, 30, 148, 149, 180, 181
   see also Enlightenment, the
Monboddo, James Burnett, Lord 3, 157
monsters; monstrosity 2, 5, 6, 10, 12, 13, 23, 34, 43, 53, 71, 76–80 *passim*, 82, 83, 97, 120, 129, 130–3 *passim*, 136, 139, 141, 142, 147, 151, 154, 158, 163, 166, 168, 169, 171, 172–3, 178–82 *passim*, 185, 187, 228
Montesquieu, Charles-Louis de Secondat, Baron de La Brède et de 58
moon *see* wolves, and the moon; werewolves, lunar influence on

Moore, Kim 13, 211–12, 218–24
   'And the Soul' 221–2
   The Art of Falling (2015) 218, 219
   'Body, Remember' 223
   'How I Abandoned My Body to His Keeping' 222, 223
   'How the Stones Fell' 218
   'How Wolves Change Rivers' 220–1
   If We Could Speak Like Wolves (2012) 219
   'If We Could Speak Like Wolves' 219
   'My People' 222
   'Picnic on Stickle Pike' 218–19
   'That Summer' 218
   'Translation' 222
   'When I Was a Thing with Feathers' 222
moral insanity 11, 108–9, 110
   see also mental illness
Morris, Robert 199, *201*, 202–3, 207, 208
Moss, Kate 235
Mowgli *see* Kipling, Rudyard
music 9–10, 57, 61, 62, 70–1, 72, 73, 75, 78, 79, 81–2, 122, 157, 240
myth 4, 8, 23, 43, 48, 49, 55, 64, 64–5n.4, 141, 170, 178–9, 181–2, 184, 185, 187–8, 204, 214, 217, 225n.10, 227, 228, 240
   Germanic 24
   Greek 4, 8, 23
   Hebrew 149
   Native American 23–4
   Norse 8, 23, 225n.10
   Roman 4, 8, 23, 49
   see also folklore; religion

Nagel, Thomas 195–6
Native Americans 11, 23–4, 137–8, 176n.20, 231, 238, 240
   see also indigenous peoples
nature 1–9 *passim*, 12, 13–14, 34, 35–6, 43, 44, 45, 46n.4, 48, 56, 58, 59–60, 62–4, 89, 95, 118, 125, 132, 138, 147–51 *passim*, 153, 154–7, 158, 162n.38, 163, 164, 167, 169, 171, 178, 187, 197, 203–4, 212, 223, 227–8, 229, 230, 234, 239, 240, 241
   human 1, 3, 10, 44, 58, 66n.28, 68n.49, 95, 103, 108, 148
   state of 9, 48, 56, 59, 60, 63, 64
   of wolf *see* wolf, nature of
   see also culture; wilderness; wildness
nature-culture 1, 4, 12, 56, 212, 229
   see also binary oppositions
Nazis 8, 25–8
   see also anti-Semitism; Holocaust, the
Nelson, Jimmy 13, 227, 236–8, 240
noble savage 31, 63
   see also indigenous peoples; nature; Rousseau, Jean-Jacques; wild man; wildness
non-human 45, 91, 120, 159, 163, 170, 171, 196, 197, 199, 207, 208, 212, 214, 216, 223, 224
   see also animal(s); nature
Nosferatu (1922 film) 74

Original Sin 48, 56, 60, 66n.28
   see also Christianity; noble savage
Otherness; Other, the 5, 8, 13, 15n.13, 60, 76, 83, 108, 130–3 *passim*, 136, 139, 142, 150, 154, 163, 164, 166–73 *passim*, 175, 180, 196, 197, 217, 234
Ovid 4, 65n.7, 184, 223

painting *see* art
paranormal romance 1, 4, 5–6, 7, 12, 147, 151, 154, 158, 159n.1, 162n.46, 164
   see also desire; genre; romantic fiction; Young Adult fiction
pastoral (genre) 1–5 *passim*, 7, 8, 14, 15n.13, 149
   see also genre
pastoralism; pastoral societies 2, 3, 5, 8, 10, 34, 39, 41, 87, 149
patriarchy 10, 12, 13, 132, 149, 151, 152, 159, 160n.17, 219, 223
   see also feminism; women
performance 13, 75, 77, 133, 134, 182, 183, 193, 196–9, 200, 207–8, 214, 215, 218, 237, 238, 240
principle 162n.47
Perrault, Charles *see* fairy tales
Peter the Wild Boy (Peter of Hanover) *see* wild children
Petronius, *Satyricon* 230
The Phantom of the Opera (1925 film) 70, 74
photography *see* art

pig(s) *see* animal(s)
Piggott, Marcus 238
Plath, Sylvia 48
poetry 9, 14, 48, 56, 59–60, 61–4, 172, 211–26
postcolonialism 220–1
  see also colonialism
postmodernism 7, 15n.20, 81, 217
postmodernity 184, 211
poststructuralism 217
Priest, Hannah 16, 230, 232
Propp, Vladimir 97
  see also fairy tales; folk tales
puberty *see* adolescence

'race'; racism 119, 124, 125, 131, 141, 176n.20, 212, 240
  see also anti-Semitism; postcolonialism
rationalism 16n.20, 180
rationality 10, 16n.20, 56, 58, 63, 101–2, 109, 110, 116, 119, 126, 149, 158, 164, 180, 187
realism 21, 25, 119, 158, 162n.44, 206, 239
  magical 89
reification 12, 147, 151, 154, 160n.17, 161n.26, 162n.39, 229
  see also alienation; commodification
reindeer *see* animal(s)
religion 93, 94, 95, 115, 216
  see also Christianity; myth
repression 148, 149, 150, 153, 159, 185, 229
  see also sublimation
rewilding *see* wolves, rewilding
Reynolds, G.M.W., *Wagner the Wehr-wolf* 4, 11, 106–8
Rice, Anne, *The Wolf Gift* (2010) 7
Rihanna 238–40, *239*
Rilke, Rainer Maria 1, 170, 171, 172
Ritchie, Leitch, 'The Man-Wolf' (1830) 105
ritual 198–9, 227, 230, 239
Robinson, Mary, 'The Savage of Aveyron' 9, 61–4
romance (genre) 1, 4
  see also genre; paranormal romance
romance (love) 6, 12, 27, 91, 93, 138, 139, 141, 151, 154, 158, 163, 167, 238
romantic fiction 5, 6, 12, 158, 162n.46, 164
  see also genre; paranormal romance

Romanticism 1, 7, 9, 48, 60, 61–4
Romulus and Remus *see* wolf-children
Rousseau, Jean-Jacques 3, 9, 11, 31, 48, 56, 58, 59, 63, 113, 120–2, 123, 126, 157
Rowling, J.K., Harry Potter (novels and films) 134

Sade, Donatien Alphonse François, Marquis de 152, 159
science 4, 9, 11, 16n.20, 35–6, 37, 45, 76, 77, 113–28, 129, 168, 171, 179, 180, 187
  see also technology
science fiction 180, 181, 184
  see also fantasy; genre
Sconduto, Leslie 16, 181
sculpture *see* art
seal(s) *see* animal(s)
Sedgwick, Marcus, *The Dark Horse* (2002) 8, 24, 30, 69n.63
self-consciousness 158, 211, 239, 240
  see also subjectivity
selkie 96, 242n.18
  see also seal(s); shapeshifters
sex 27, 93, 94, 122, 141, 151, 152, 154, 158, 159, 169, 185, 212, 214, 215, 217, 219, 228, 229, 238
sexuality 4, 5, 12, 13, 116, 132, 140, 147, 148, 162n.47, 163, 164–5, 167–8, 169, 212, 215, 217, 218, 234
Shakespeare, William
  The Tempest 179
  The Winter's Tale 49, 62
shamanism 13, 95, 193, 197–9, *198*, 239, 240
shapeshifters 4–5, 6, 10, 12, 17n.25, 72, 83n.6, 88, 89, 96–7, 131, 137, 139, 164, 166, 178, 181, 188, 204, 211–12, 213, 217, 221, 222, 231, 242n.18
  see also loup-garou; selkie; werecat; werewolf
sheep *see* animal(s)
Shelley, Mary, *Frankenstein* (1818) 113
shepherds 2, 22, 23, 39, 40, 41, 42, 42, 45–6n.2, 46n.20, 49
  see also animals, sheep; pastoral; pastoralism
she-wolf *see* wolf; wolves
She-wolf of London (1946 film) 132

The Shining (1989 film) *see* Kubrick, Stanley
silence 73, 75, 213
  see also music; sound (in film)
Silver Bullet (1985 film) 80
silver bullets 172
Sirius Black (see Rowling, J.K.)
skin 1, 42, 45, 46n.20, 81, 82, 96–7, 106, 107, 108, 124, 151, 152–3, 156, 158, 166, 178, 198, 199, 205, 213, 214, 225n.10, 227, 229–33 *passim*, 235, 238
  see also flesh; fur; hunting; meat
'Sleeping Beauty' *see* fairy tales
snow 73, 168, 227, 234, 236–7
socialism 12, 161n.26
  see also capitalism; Marx, Karl
sociality 2, 3, 14, 150
sociobiology 7
song *see* wolf, song; music
Sorrenti, Mario 235
sound 9, 10, 48, 55, 61, 70–84, 157, 180
  effects 71, 73, 75, 78, 79, 82
  see also film; music; silence; transformation, sound of
special effects (in film) 80, 81
  see also sound, effects
species 1, 6, 23, 37, 38, 57, 106, 138, 139, 163, 173, 181, 197, 200, 203, 207, 212, 217, 220, 224, 229, 231, 234, 241
speech *see* language
Stevenson, Robert Louis, *Dr Jekyll and Mr Hyde* (1886) 132, 179
  see also Dr. Jekyll and Mr. Hyde (1920 film); *Dr. Jekyll and Mr. Hyde* (1931 film)
stoat *see* animals
Stoker, Bram, *Dracula* (1897) 10, 16–17n.24, 71–2, 83n.6, 132, 133, 135–6, 240
Stone, Lara 235
storytelling 4, 5, 8, 9, 21, 23, 25, 28, 32, 48, 51, 55, 62, 64, 187, 204, 224, 227
  see also folk tales
Stubbe, Peter (also Stube, Stump, Stumpf) 1, 46–7n.23
subjectivity 7, 147, 149, 153, 164, 170–1, 174, 175
  see also agency; identity; self-consciousness

sublimation 148, 153, 155, 159, 159n.5
  see also desublimation; psychoanalysis
supernatural 2, 6, 53, 88, 89, 99, 108, 114, 133, 136, 137, 139, 141, 158, 171, 180, 187, 234
  see also magic
Suvin, Darko 124
Sweeney Todd 109, 110
Swift, Jonathan, *The Most Wonderful Wonder that ever appeared to the Wonder of the British Nation* (1726) 15n.13, 66n.32
symbolic order 157, 228
  see also Kristeva, Julia; Lacan, Jacques; language
sympathy 10, 50, 62, 64, 82, 126

tabula rasa see Locke, John
technology 73, 101, 180, 181, 182, 183
  see also science
teenagers 114, 138, 163–77, 185, 216
  see also adolescence; Young Adult fiction
Teen Wolf (1985 film) 80, 133, 165
Teen Wolf (2011– TV series) 165, 184
Teffi, Nadezhda 98–9
Thomson, Richard, 'The Wehr-Wolf' (1828) 105–6
The Three Little Pigs (1933 film) 8, 25–7
Tolkien, J.R.R. 24
transformation 14, 43, 88, 89, 103, 148, 150, 153, 155, 159, 164, 180, 181, 182, 183, 187, 188, 213, 223, 224, 230, 239, 240, 241
  of genres 2, 12, 55, 56, 147, 157, 160n.17, 162n.46, 183
  human/animal 12, 83n.6, 96, 150, 152–3, 157, 178, 179, 188, 211–24, 225n.10, 229
  human/(were)wolf 13, 43–4, 78, 79–82, 106–8, 109, 110, 113, 117, 119–20, 129, 130, 133, 134, 135, 138, 156, 157, 158, 164–7 *passim*, 169, 170, 171–5, 219, 221, 230, 235, 241
  sound of 10, 71, 77, 81–2
transvestism 13, 228–9, 234, 241
  see also clothes; skin

INDEX

True Blood (2008-14 TV series) 11, 130, 133, 139-41
  see also Harris, Charlaine
Twilight (2008 film) 11, 138
Twilight Saga (films) 11, 137, 231
Twilight series (books) *see* Meyer, Stephenie

Underworld (film series) 133, 184
The Undying Monster (1942 film) 132
Universal Studios 71, 73, 74, 76-7, 80, 81, 129, 133, 134, 179, 188n.9, 230
  see also horror, film
urban life *see* city, the
utopianism 1, 4, 7, 14, 63, 149, 153, 157, 158, 159, 160n.13

vampires 2, 5, 6, 10, 11, 16-17n.24, 71, 74, 111, 130-4 *passim*, 136, 138, 139-40, 141-2, 147, 166, 178, 180, 184-5, 230, 231, 232
Vampires Suck (2010 film) 138
Van Helsing (2004 film) 133
Vasnetsov, Victor 91, 92
Victor of Aveyron *see* wild children
video *see* art, video
Vincent, Rachel, *Stray* (2009) 17n.25
Vloet, Sanne 227, 228, 237, 240

Walsh, Jill Paton, *Knowledge of Angels* (1994) 4, 30-1
werecat 17n.25, 188
weres *see* shapeshifters
The Werewolf (1913 film) 184
Werewolf of London (1935 film) 4, 10, 71, 76, 77-80, 129, 133, 134, 179, 185
werewolves
  in art 13
  Classical 4, 9, 34, 230
  contemporary 2, 4, 5-7, 44, 211, 219
  female 5, 6-7, 13-14, 96, 113-28, 132, 140-1, 147, 159n.1, 165, 166, 167-8, 171-4, 175, 219, 222, 227, 229-34, 240, 241
  in film 4, 9-10, 11, 70-84, 129-43, 179, 188n.9, 230
  in folklore 10, 12, 71, 119, 131, 164-5, 179, 211, 227

  and Gothic 5, 14, 147, 211
  involuntary 107
  in literature 12, 13
  lunar influence on 72, 77, 81, 107, 133
  and madness 10-11, 102-12
  medieval 9, 34, 43, 110, 166, 211, 230
  as metaphor 5, 10, 12, 106, 131, 136, 142, 163, 167, 168-70, 175, 182
  and nature 1, 2, 5-8 *passim*, 12, 13-14, 111-12, 147, 164, 169, 187, 227, 229, 230, 234, 237, 240
  sympathetic 5-6, 77, 79, 82-3, 130, 147, 159n.1, 163-77, 219
  transformation into, *see* transformation
  in TV 11, 12-13, 129-43, 178-89
  as victims *see* werewolves, sympathetic
  victims of 77, 78
  Victorian 10, 11, 105-8, 110, 231-4
  voluntary 96, 107
  and wolves 1, 4, 8, 34, 38, 39, 43-4, 46-7n.23, 188, 204, 221
  working-class 11, 129-43
  see also loup garou; shapeshifters
What We Do in the Shadows (2014 film) 141
Whedon, Joss *see Buffy the Vampire Slayer*
wild children 1, 3, 9, 14, 15n.9, 48-69, 228
  Bear-boys of Lithuania 49, 50, 65n.5
  Blanc, Marie-Angélique, Le (The Wild Girl of Champagne) 3, 29, 156
  feral children 3, 8, 13, 28-9, 30, 49, 55-6, 63, 188, 238, 239
  Hauser, Kasper 55-6, 228
  and language 3, 8, 156, 157, 228, 238
  in literature 4, 8, 9, 48-69, 148
  Peter the Wild Boy (Peter of Hanover) 3, 4, 9, 15n.13, 55-9, 60, 63, 64, 65n.5, 67n.33, 67n.35, 67n.44, 69n.63
  raised by animals 3, 4, 5, 8, 56, 148, 156
  see also wolf-children
  Victor of Aveyron 4, 9, 55, 56, 60-2, 63, 64, 57n.44, 68n.53, 69n.61, 69n.63
wilderness 8-11 *passim*, 13, 14, 30, 35, 36, 44, 73, 88, 130, 156, 163, 168, 180, 187, 204, 205-6, 220, 227, 229, 231, 234, 236-8, 240, 241
  see also nature

Wild Girl of Champagne, The (Marie-Angélique Le Blanc) *see* wild children
wild man 15n.13, 57, 179
  see also noble savage; wild children
wildness 4, 8, 9, 29–32, 41, 44, 57, 59, 71, 96, 97, 102, 150, 153, 154, 156, 222, 231, 238, 240
witches 10, 11, 24, 87, 89, 90, 95, 96, 97, 99, 113–28
  Baba Yaga 88, 89, 91, 94–9
Wolf (1994 film) 133
wolf; wolves
  'at the door' 27
  behaviour 9, 36
  'boy who cried' 21
  children raised by
    see wolf-children
  communication 38, 156, 170, 171–2, 219, 222
  as deceiver 8, 21–33, 39, 41–2, 43, 169
  extinction of 1, 24, 50, 111, 203–4, 226n.32
  fear of *see* lupophobia
  as helper 3, 4, 10, 23, 28, 49, 64, 87–100, 187
  howling 9, 10, 48–9, 70–1, 73, 76, 77, 78, 82, 154, 156, 157, 221, 224
  inner *see* 'beast within'
  'in sheep's clothing' 21, 111
  as metaphor 10, 24, 27, 87, 165, 169, 219
  and the moon 72
  nature of 9, 21, 23, 24, 25, 34, 35–6, 38, 39, 41–2, 44, 50, 89, 117, 167, 169, 232
  as noble 8, 24, 27, 53
  as outlaw 105
  pack 2, 6, 7, 17n.25, 24, 29, 30, 31, 35, 36, 38, 51, 71, 73, 130, 139, 140, 148, 168, 175, 186, 196, 206, 234, 241
    see also wolf, as social
  as predator 2, 3, 10, 23, 24, 25, 34, 36–7, 37, 43, 87, 103, 147, 154, 172

  rewilding 2, 9, 44–5, 130, 142, 204–5, 220, 224
  as sexual predator 2, 27, 93, 155, 165, 168, 169
  she-wolf 49, 58, 67n.41, 132, 222, 232
  skin 1, 106, 107, 108, 205, 225n.10, 227–42
    see also fur; skin
  as social 2, 6, 35, 37–8
  teeth 36, 37, 72, 91, 93, 167, 181, 182, 223
  whistle 2
  see also animal(s)
Wolf, Big Bad 2, 25, 27, 39, 65n.10, 141, 165, 186
wolf-children 8, 9, 10, 12, 29, 30, 48–69
  Amala and Kamala 4, 15n.14, 29, 48, 53–5, 54, 60, 61, 64, 69n.63
  Mowgli *see* Kipling, Rudyard
  Romulus and Remus 3, 23, 28, 49, 51, 51, 64n.2, 67n.41
  see also wild children
Wolfen (1981 film) 80
The Wolfman (2010 film) 133
The Wolf Man (1941 film) 4, 10, 11, 76, 77, 79, 80, 83, 129, 133–6, 185, 188n.9, 230
Wolf-Man, the *see* Freud, Sigmund
wolf-skin *see* fur; wolf/wolves, skin
women 5, 6–7, 12, 13–14, 90, 96–7, 114, 115–16, 140–1, 154, 165, 212, 214, 219, 222, 224, 228, 229, 231, 234–5, 241
  see also feminism; gender; sex
Wordsworth, William 9, 61, 62, 67n.44, 67–8n.46, 68n.57
  'The Idiot Boy' (1798) 59–60, 61

Young Adult fiction 1, 4, 12, 163–77
  see also adolescence; children's literature; paranormal romance; teenagers

Zipes, Jack 115, 164
Žižek, Slavoj 180, 228
zoanthropy 53
  see also lycanthropy
Zvorykin, Boris Vasilyevich 91

EU authorised representative for GPSR:
Easy Access System Europe, Mustamäe tee 50,
10621 Tallinn, Estonia
gpsr.requests@easproject.com

www.ingramcontent.com/pod-product-compliance
Lightning Source LLC
Chambersburg PA
CBHW050208240426
43671CB00013B/2254